RANDOM HOUSE
WEBSTER'S

WIT & HUMOR
QUOTATIONARY

Leonard Roy Frank

Editor

Random House
New York

Random House Webster's Wit & Humor Quotationary
Copyright © 2000 Leonard Roy Frank

This book is available for special purchases in bulk by organizations and institutions, not for resale, at special discounts. Please direct your inquiries to the Random House Special Sales Department, toll-free 888-591-1200 or fax 212-572-4961.

Please address inquiries about electronic licensing of reference products, for use on a network or in software or on CD-ROM, to the Subsidiary Rights Department, Random House Reference, fax 212-940-7370.

Visit the Random House Reference Web site at www.randomwords.com

Typeset and printed in the United States of America.

Library of Congress Cataloging-in-Publication Data

Random House Webster's wit and humor quotationary / Leonard Roy Frank, editor.— 1st ed.
    p. cm.
Includes bibliographical references and index.
ISBN 0-375-70931-2
1. Quotations, English. 2. Wit and humor. I. Title: Wit & humor quotationary. II. Title: Wit and humor quotationary. III. Title: Quotationary. IV. Frank, Leonard Roy.
PN6084.H8 R365 2000   082′.02′07—dc21   00-059170

First Edition
0 9 8 7 6 5 4 3 2 1
November 2000

ISBN:0-375-70931-2

New York   Toronto   London   Sydney   Auckland

☞ CONTENTS ☜

Acknowledgments

I am happy to express my appreciation to a number of people who helped me while editing this book. First and foremost is my friend Wade Hudson who was always available with fresh ideas and support when I got bogged down for one reason or another or just needed a break from the editing routine. I have been very fortunate in having Elizabeth Pomada and Michael Larsen as my literary agents; they have not only counseled me wisely in publishing matters but have also become, in the four years of our association, my good friends. Another friend, Robert Arbegast, has come up with timely solutions to my computer-programming problems. Special thanks are due Cecil White for the research assistance he generously provided.

I am also deeply grateful to the Random House editors who worked closely with me over the last year: Charles Levine, for the initial thrust in getting this project off the ground; my principal editor, Wendalyn Nichols, who made many valuable suggestions in shaping the book's format and content; and Beth Levy, who handled production smoothly and with dispatch.

⌒ *INTRODUCTION* ⌒

Soon after publication, in late 1998, of *Random House Webster's Quotationary*, I began thinking about another editing project to undertake. The *Quotationary's* 20,000 entries (arranged by category) had been distilled from double that number in my database, which in turn was the digitized essence of 35 years of reading, study, and observation. Having this large store of ready-to-use quotations broadened my range of options.

I decided to compile *Random House Webster's Wit & Humor Quotationary* upon realizing, after visits to the reference and humor sections of many bookstores and libraries, that missing from their shelves was a first-rate, up-to-date, wide-ranging collection of witticisms arranged by author. The many available humor quotation books arranged by category are useful as resources, but to me they do not offer the sheer reading pleasure derived from perusing choice quips, bons mots, and clever comments grouped together in sections by author. (I use the word *author* in the sense of "originator of the quotation.") What shines through many sections in this book is the personality of the authors, giving added humor and resonance to each entry and, synergistically, to each section as a whole.

It is my hope that this book will fill a gap in the field of humor collections, and provide people with an amusing, even delightful, reading experience—that it will serve as a history of humor through the ages, a reference tool for writers and speakers, and an inspiration for those who will be creating the humor of the twenty-first century.

A NOTE
⟮ ABOUT THE TEXT ⟯

It will be helpful for readers to know some of the principles that guided me as I assembled this collection. The book is not fundamentally a scholarly work: not every entry is exactly as it appeared in the source from which it was taken. I took liberties in polishing a small number of the entries, particularly with translated quotations. I also modified punctuation where it seemed necessary, Americanized the spelling of some words, and compressed certain quotations without using ellipsis points, which I thought would be distracting.

The great majority of entries stand on their own, independent of context. I tried to provide more context to the remaining entries by placing in appended brackets relevant information such as: the name of the person, book, film, etc. referred to in the entry; the quotation's literary, social, or historical context; the year in which the line was first spoken or published; and, in some very few instances, the source from which the entry was taken. Where authorship could not be verified, I added the word "Attributed" in brackets.

Most of the material gathered here was intentionally humorous, but this was not always the case, as with Ulysses S. Grant's famous observation, "Venice would be a fine city if it were only drained." I deemed effect more important than intent—humor is in the ear of the listener. In selecting individual entries, I used the following criteria: wittiness or funniness (either funny ha-ha or funny a-ha); brevity (most entries are a single sentence); clarity (the point of most entries is easily grasped); and universality (the appeal is broad-based and multicultural). My tendency was to favor better-known rather than lesser-known authors because author recognition enhances the reader's appreciation of a humorous remark and also makes it easier to remember. (That is why people attribute so many quotations of unknown authorship to writers like Mark Twain, Oscar Wilde, and George Bernard Shaw.)

For misquotations, mistaken authors and other errors in the text, I take full responsibility. Anyone with corrections and suggestions or new material which might be suitable for a revised edition of this work are invited to contact me at my e-mail address: lfrank@igc.org.

Leonard Roy Frank
San Francisco
July 2000

HOW TO
⪜ USE THIS BOOK ⪝

The editors and I have endeavored to make this book as easy to read and use as possible. The more than 6,000 entries are organized in sections alphabetically by author. The Anonymous section, while in proper alphabetical sequence, is the only one not headed by a named individual. To assist readers in identifying authors, I have supplied key biographical facts following their names in the section headings. To aid readers in finding specific quotations as quickly as possible, all entries in a section are numbered and arranged alphabetically according to each entry's first word. Quite a few entries are cross-referenced to other individual entries, to which they are related either in substance or form.

Readers will note plagiarism, or something close to it, among the authors in certain instances. For example, George Orwell's "cuttlefish" aphorism (entry number 23 in his section) closely parallels John Ray's observation on the same subject originally published in the 17th century. More frequently, authors borrow old ideas and use them for their own purposes. Particular formats lend themselves to various usages. For example, Ted Turner adapted the format in the proverb "Early to bed, early to rise, makes a man healthy, wealthy and wise" for his own saying "Early to bed, early to rise, work like hell, and advertise." Evan Esar and James Thurber had their own versions of the earlier proverb.

Although the book's comprehensive Index is primarily organized by category, there are many headings for key words and phrases. The Index also includes headings for individuals (e.g., Abraham Lincoln and Winston Churchill) and places (e.g., San Francisco and New York) named or referred to in specific quotations. Names of the section authors in the text do not appear in the Index. Individuals listed as an Index heading do not necessarily have their own sections.

Arranged alphabetically under each Index heading are the names of each author whose quotations qualify for a particular subject. To facilitate locating quotations in the text, there appears in the Index next to each author's name the entry number of the quotation in question. For authors with multiple entries on a given subject, two or more entry numbers follow their names.

EDWARD ABBEY (1927–1989). *American writer*

1 England has never enjoyed a genuine social revolution. Maybe that's what's wrong with that dear, tepid, vapid, insipid, stuffy, little country.

2 His style is mistaken for fantastic, drug-crazed exaggeration, but that was to be expected. As always in America, they only laugh at you when you tell the truth. [On Hunter S. Thompson.]

3 What's the difference between a whore and a congressman? A congressman makes more money.

GOODMAN ACE (1899–1982). *American radio personality and humorist*

1 I keep reading between the lies.

2 TV—a clever contraction derived from the words Terrible Vaudeville. We call it a medium because nothing's well done.

JANE ACE (1905–1974). *American radio personality and humorist*

1 He was just about to get a job when he got intentional flu.

2 I'm a ragged individualist. [Attributed.]

3 I'm completely uninhabited.

4 Time wounds all heels. [Also attributed to Groucho Marx and others.]

MARCEL ACHARD (1899–1974). *French playwright and screenwriter*

The career of a writer is comparable to that of a woman of easy virtue. You write first for pleasure, later for the pleasure of others, and finally for money.

DEAN ACHESON (1893–1971). *American secretary of state*

1 A memorandum is written not to inform the reader but to protect the writer.

2 A real Centaur—part man, part horse's ass. A rough appraisal, but curiously true. [On Lyndon B. Johnson.]

3 How do I know what I think until I hear what I say?

4 I try to be as philosophical as the old lady who said that the best thing about the future is that it only comes one day at a time.

5 The first requirement of a statesman is that he be dull.

6 Trust him as much as you would a rattlesnake with a silencer on its rattle! [Advice to Harry S. Truman on J. Edgar Hoover.]

LORD ACTON (John Emerich Acton, 1834–1902). *English historian*

1 Advice to persons about to Write History—Don't.

2 Power tends to corrupt, and absolute power corrupts absolutely. —See also Ross Perot 3; Anthony Price 1; George Bernard Shaw 89; Adlai E. Stevenson 15

BROOKS ADAMS (1848–1927). *American historian*

Philosophers are hired by the comfortable class to prove that everything is all right. [As paraphrased by Oliver Wendell Holmes, Jr.]

FRANKLIN P. ADAMS (F.P.A., 1881–1960). *American journalist and humorist*

1 A first edition of his work is a rarity, but a second is rarer still.

2 Middle age occurs when you are too young to take up golf and too old to rush up to the net.

3 Nothing is more responsible for the good old days than a bad memory.

4 The trouble with this country is that there are too many politicians who believe, with a conviction based on experience, that you can fool all of the people all of the time. —See also Abraham Lincoln 52

5 There are plenty of good five-cent cigars. The trouble is they cost a quarter. What this country really needs is a good five-cent nickel. —See also Thomas R. Marshall 3

6 There is no accounting for tastes, as the woman said when somebody told her her son was wanted by the police.

7 To Herbert Bayard Swope without whose friendly aid and counsel every line in this book was written. [Book dedication.]

8 When the political columnists say "every thinking man," they mean themselves; and when candidates appeal to "every intelligent voter," they mean everybody who is going to vote for them.

HENRY ADAMS (1838–1918). *American historian*

1 It's impossible to underrate human intelligence—beginning with one's own.

2 No man should be in politics unless he would honestly rather not be there.

3 Nothing in education is so astonishing as the amount of ignorance it accumulates in the form of inert facts.

4 Philosophy: unintelligible answers to insoluble problems.

5 Politics, as a practice, whatever its professions, has always been the systematic organization of hatreds.

6 Practical politics consists in ignoring facts.

7 The chief wonder of education is that it does not ruin everybody concerned in it, teachers and taught.

8 We combat obstacles in order to get repose, and, when got, the repose is insupportable.

JOHN ADAMS (1735–1826). *American president*

What a poor, ignorant, malicious, short-sighted, crapulous mass is Tom Paine's *Common Sense.*

JOSEPH ADDISON (1672–1719). *English essayist and playwright*

1 Sir Roger heard them both and after having paused some time told them, with the air of a man who would not give his judgment rashly, that much might be said on both sides.

2 There is no defense against reproach but obscurity.

GEORGE ADE (1866–1944). *American playwright and humorist*

1 A friend who is very near and dear may in time become as useless as a relative.

2 After being turned down by many publishers, he decided to write for posterity. —See also Charles Lamb 11

3 For parlor use, the vague generality is a lifesaver.

4 He had been kicked in the head by a mule when young, and believed everything he read in the Sunday papers.

5 R-E-M-O-R-S-E! / Those dry Martinis did the work for me; / Last night at twelve I felt immense, / Today I feel like thirty cents.

6 She told him it was terrible to hear such things as he told her, and to please go ahead.

7 The music teacher came twice a week to bridge the awful gap between Dorothy and Chopin.

8 "Whom are you?" said he, for he had been to night school.

HERBERT AGAR (1897–1980). *American historian*

1 Snobs talk as if they had begotten their own ancestors.

2 The truth which makes men free is for the most part the truth which men prefer not to hear. —See also Aldous Huxley 12

LOUIS AGASSIZ (1807–1873). *Swiss-born American naturalist*
I can't afford to waste my time making money.

JAMES AGATE (1877–1947). *English drama critic*

1 Long experience has taught me that in England nobody goes to the theater unless he or she has bronchitis.

2 The English instinctively admire any man who has no talent and is modest about it.

3 To force myself to earn more money, I determined to spend more.

JAMES AGEE (1909–1955). *American writer and film critic*

1 I would like to recommend this film to those who can stay interested in Ronald Colman's amnesia for two hours, and who could with pleasure eat a bowl of Yardley's shaving soap for breakfast. [On the 1942 film *Random Harvest*.]

2 Several tons of dynamite are set off in this picture—none of it under the right people. [On the 1947 film *Tycoon*.]

SPIRO T. AGNEW (1918–1996). *Maryland governor and U.S. vice president*

1 A spirit of national masochism prevails, encouraged by an effete corps of impudent snobs who characterize themselves as intellectuals. [Referring to Vietnam War protesters, 1969.]

2 In the United States today we have more than our fair share of the nattering nabobs of negativism. They have formed their own Four H Club: the hopeless, hysterical hypochondriacs of history.

3 To some extent, if you've seen one city slum, you've seen them all.

EDWARD ALBEE (1928–). *American playwright*

1 Musical beds is the faculty sport around here. [In the 1962 film *Who's Afraid of Virginia Woolf?*]

2 Sometimes a person has to go a very long distance out of his way to come back a short distance correctly.

LOUISA MAY ALCOTT (1832–1888). *American writer*
People want to be amused, not preached at, you know. Morals don't sell nowadays.

ALEXANDER (356–323 B.C.). *Greek king and general*

I die with the help of too many physicians. [Attributed.]

NELSON ALGREN (1909–1981). *American journalist and novelist*

1 "If God made anything better than a girl," Dover thought, "He sure kept it to Himself."

2 Never play cards with a man called Doc. Never eat at a place called Mom's. Never sleep with a woman whose troubles are worse than your own.

3 Money can't buy everything; for example, poverty.

FRED ALLEN (1894–1956). *American comedian and radio personality*

1 A celebrity is a person who works hard all his life to become well known, and then wears dark glasses to avoid being recognized.

2 A gentleman is any man who wouldn't hit a woman with his hat on. —See also H. L. Mencken 5

3 A molehill man is a pseudo-busy executive who comes to work at 9 A.M. and finds a molehill on his desk. He has until 5 P.M. to make this molehill into a mountain.

4 An advertising agency is 85 percent confusion and 15 percent commission.

5 An associate producer is the only guy in Hollywood who will associate with a producer.

6 California is a great place—if you happen to be an orange.

7 Committee: a group of men who individually can do nothing but as a group decide that nothing can be done. —See also John Kenneth Galbraith 12

8 Hanging is too good for a man who makes puns; he should be drawn and quoted.

9 He dreamed he was eating shredded wheat and woke up to find the mattress half gone.

10 He is so narrow-minded that if he fell on a pin, it would blind him in both eyes.

11 Her hat is a creation that will never go out of style; it will just look ridiculous year after year.

12 Hollywood is a place where people from Iowa mistake each other for movie stars.

13 I have just returned from Boston. It is the only thing to do if you find yourself up there.

14 I like long walks, especially when they are taken by people who annoy me.

15 I play a musical instrument some, but only for my own amazement.

16 Imitation is the sincerest form of television. —See also C. C. Colton 3; Elbert Hubbard 19

17 It was so quiet here, I was jolted by the sound of a caterpillar backing into a globule of dew.

18 Jack Benny couldn't ad-lib a belch after a Hungarian dinner.

19 More chorus girls are kept than promises.

20 Most of us spend the first six days of each week sowing wild oats, then we go to church on Sunday and pray for a crop failure.

21 "Mr. Allen, do you wear a toupee?" The hair is real—it's the head that's a fake.

22 Mr. Allen Is Quite Deaf. If You Care to Applaud, Please Do So Loudly. [Placard Allen used in his vaudeville act.]

23 My agent gets 10 percent of everything I get, except my blinding headaches.

24 On ships they call them barnacles; in radio they attach themselves to desks and are called vice presidents.

25 Once you leave New York, you're out of town.

26 Population explosion: when people take leave of their census.

27 Television is a device that permits people who haven't anything to do to watch people who can't do anything.

28 The last time I saw him he was walking down Lover's Lane holding his own hand.

29 The minds that control television are so small that you could put them in the navel of a flea and still have room for a network vice president's heart.

30 What's on your mind?—if you'll forgive the overstatement.

GRACIE ALLEN (1905–1964). *American comedienne and radio personality*

1 I was so surprised at being born that I didn't speak for a year and a half.

2 I'm the candidate who forgot to take off her hat before she threw it in the ring.

3 "Say goodnight, Gracie." [George Burns] Goodnight, Gracie. [Signature closing lines for their radio and television broadcasts.]

4 "What is it that sings and has four legs?" [George Burns] Two canaries.

WOODY ALLEN (1935–). *American writer, actor, film maker, and humorist*

1 A fast word about oral contraception. I asked a girl to go to bed with me and she said "no."

2 A relationship is like a shark. You know, it has to constantly move forward or it dies. And I think what we've got here is a dead shark.

3 A wife lasts only for the length of the marriage, but an ex-wife is there for the rest of your life.

4 All literature is a footnote to *Faust*. I have no idea what I mean by that.

5 At the time of Needleman's death, he was halfway through a new study of semantics, proving (as he so violently insisted) that sentence structure is innate but that whining is acquired.

6 Basically my wife was immature. I'd be at home in the bath and she'd come in and sink my boats.

7 Bisexuality immediately doubles your chances for a date on Saturday night.

8 Blanche told her new husband that although he made a reasonable living as a human guinea pig, she wanted to keep her job in the shoe department of Entwhistle's. Too proud to be supported, Leon reluctantly agreed, but insisted that when she reached the age of ninety-five she must retire.

9 Can we actually "know" the universe? My God, it's hard enough finding your way around in Chinatown.

10 "Do you know anything about penis envy?" [Annie] "Me? I'm one of the few males who suffers from that." [Alvy, in the 1977 film *Annie Hall,* coscripted with Marshall Brickman.]

11 Eighty percent of success is showing up.

12 Electroshock therapy at the Veterans Hospital helped, although wires got crossed with a behavioral psychology lab and I along with several chimpanzees all performed *The Cherry Orchard* together in perfect English.

13 Following are excerpts from the soon-to-be-published memoirs of Virgil Ives, who is currently serving the first of four consecutive ninety-nine-year sentences for various felonies. Mr. Ives plans on working with children when he gets out.

14 He was a professional bank robber, but sixty-five was the mandatory retirement age, so he had to get out. Spent his last few years in mail fraud, but the postal rates went up and he lost everything. [Referring to the fictional character Virgil Ives.]

15 Hey, don't knock masturbation! It's sex with someone I love.

16 "His girl friend's mother he's marrying?" Aunt Tillie yelped as she slid to the floor unconscious. "Fifty-five and a *shiksa*," my mother screamed, searching now for a cyanide capsule she had reserved for just such occasions.

17 His one regret in life is that he is not someone else. [Closing sentence, "About the Author," *Side Effects,* 1981.]

18 How can I believe in God when just last week I got my tongue caught in the roller of an electric typewriter?

19 I do not believe in God. For if there is a God, then tell me, Uncle, why is there poverty and baldness?

20 I don't believe in an afterlife, although I am bringing along a change of underwear.

21 I don't know the question, but sex is definitely the answer.

22 I don't think being funny is anyone's first choice.

23 I don't want to achieve immortality through my work. I want to achieve it through not dying.

24 I don't want to live in a city where the only cultural advantage is that you can make a right turn on a red light. [On Los Angeles.]

25 I took a speed-reading course where you run your finger down the middle of the page and was able to read *War and Peace* in twenty minutes. It's about Russia.

26 I was dropped by New York University because of bad marks. I was a film major.

27 I was suicidal and would have killed myself, but I was in analysis with a strict Freudian. If you kill yourself, they make you pay for the sessions you miss.

28 I'd call him a sadistic, hippophilic necrophile, but that would be beating a dead horse.

29 If I come back in another life, I want to be Warren Beatty's fingertips.

30 If it turns out that there is a God, I don't think he's evil. But the worst thing that you can say about him is that basically he's an underachiever. —See also Anonymous 31; Oscar Wilde 49

31 If only God would give me some clear sign! Like making a large deposit in my name at a Swiss bank.

32 In comparison to my own folks, who had been married inexplicably for forty years (out of spite it seemed), Emily and John seemed like the Lunts. My folks, naturally, could not discuss even the weather without accusations and recriminations just short of gunfire.

33 Is sex dirty? Only if it's done right.

34 It has been four weeks and it is still hard for me to believe Sandor Needleman is dead. I was present at the cremation and at his son's request, brought the marshmallows, but few of us could think of anything but our pain. [Opening paragraph, "Remembering Needleman," *Side Effects*, 1981.]

35 It seemed the world was divided into good and bad people. The good ones slept better, while the bad ones seemed to enjoy the waking hours much more.

36 It's impossible to experience one's own death objectively and still carry a tune.

37 It's not that I'm afraid to die. I just don't want to be there when it happens. —See also Francis Bacon 2

38 Life is divided into the horrible and the miserable.

39 Money is better than poverty, if only for financial reasons.

40 More than any other time in history, mankind faces a crossroads. One path leads to despair and utter hopelessness. The other, to total extinction. Let us pray we have the wisdom to choose correctly.

41 Most of the time I don't have much fun; the rest of the time I don't have any fun at all.

42 My grandfather had a wonderful funeral. My grandfather was a very insignificant man, actually. At his funeral his hearse *followed* the other cars. It was a nice funeral, though, you would have liked it—it was a catered funeral. It was held in a big hall with accordion players. On the buffet table there was a replica of the deceased in potato salad.

43 My second favorite organ! [Referring to his brain.]

44 My wife, inviting me to sample her very first soufflé, accidentally dropped a spoonful of it on my foot, fracturing several small bones. ["My Philosophy," *Getting Even*, 1971.]

45 Not only is there no God, but try getting a plumber on weekends.

46 Of all the famous men who ever lived, the one I would most like to have been was Socrates. Not just because he was a great thinker, because I have been known to have some reasonably profound insights myself, although mine invariably revolve around a Swedish airline stewardess and some handcuffs.

47 "Oh, you see an analyst?" [Annie] "Y-y-yeah, just for fifteen years." [Alvy] "Fifteen years?" [Annie] "Yeah, uh, I'm going to give him one more year and then I'm going to Lourdes." [Alvy]

48 On the plus side, death is one of the few things that can be done as easily lying down. —See also Kingsley Amis 1

49 Sex without love is an empty experience, but, as empty experiences go, it's one of the best.

50 Suddenly he and Juliet were making love—or was it merely sex? He knew there was a difference between sex and love, but felt that either act was wonderful unless one of the partners happened to be wearing a lobster bib.

51 That was the most fun I've ever had without laughing. [Referring to sex.]

52 The lion and the calf shall lie down together, but the calf won't get much sleep.

53 The message is, God is love, and you should lay off fatty foods.

54 The universe is merely a fleeting idea in God's mind—a pretty uncomfortable thought, particularly if you've just made a down payment on a house.

55 These modern analysts! They charge so much. In my day, for five marks Freud himself would treat you. For ten marks, he would treat you and press your pants. For fifteen marks, Freud would let you treat him, and that included a choice of any two vegetables.

56 This trial is a travesty; it's a travesty of a mockery of a sham of a mockery of a travesty of two mockeries of a sham. I move for a mistrial.

57 To you I'm an atheist; to God, I'm the Loyal Opposition.

58 When I was kidnapped, my parents snapped into action: they rented my room.

59 When you have dinner with Howard Cosell, he broadcasts the meal.

60 Who am I to demand perfection? I, with my myriad faults. I made a list of my faults, but could not get past: 1) Sometimes forgets his hat.

61 You can live to be a hundred if you give up all the things that make you want to live to a hundred.

62 "You know I just like to smoke a little something before sex; it helps me relax." [Annie] "How 'bout if I give you some sodium pentothal and then you can sleep through the whole thing." [Alvy]

63 You're the opposite of a paranoid: you go around with the insane delusion that people like you.

GREG ALLMAN (1947–). *American rock musician*
Before I got into rock 'n' roll, I was going to be a dentist.

HENRI AMIEL (1821–1881). *Swiss poet, philosopher, and diarist*
Charm: the quality in others that makes us more satisfied with ourselves.

KINGSLEY AMIS (1922–1995). *English novelist and poet*

1 Death has got something to be said for it: / There's no need to get out of bed for it. / Wherever you may be, / They bring it to you, free. —See also Woody Allen 48

2 He was of the faith chiefly in the sense that the church he currently did not attend was Catholic.

3 If you can't annoy somebody with what you write, I think there's little point in writing.

4 Outside every fat man there is an even fatter man trying to close in. [1963] —See also Cyril Connolly 5; George Orwell 26

ANACHARSIS (6th century B.C.). *Scythian prince and philosopher*
Laws are like cobwebs that entangle the weak but are broken by the strong.

WALTER TRUETT ANDERSON (1923–). *American psychologist and writer*
Reality Isn't What It Used to Be. [Book title, 1990.] —See also Anonymous 118;
   Bernard Levin 2; Paul Valéry 7

MAYA ANGELOU (1928–). *American writer and poet*
1 The need for change bulldozed a road down the center of my mind.
2 You may not get what you paid for, but you will pay for what you get.

ANONYMOUS
1 A fool and his money are soon partying. —See also Evan Esar 1; Kin Hubbard 1; Helen Rowland 2; William Shenstone 1
2 A joint a day keeps reality away. [Graffiti.]
3 A little coitus / Never hoitus. [Graffiti.]
4 A taxpayer is someone who doesn't have to take a civil service examination to work for the government.
5 A true gentleman is a man who knows how to play the bagpipes—but doesn't.
6 A woman without a man is like a fish without a bicycle. [Often attributed to Gloria Steinem.] —See also Patsi Dunn
7 Abstinence is a good thing, but it should always be practiced in moderation.
8 Adolescence is a stage between infancy and adultery.
9 Age is mostly a matter of mind; if you don't mind, it doesn't matter.
10 An apple a day keeps the doctor away; an onion a day keeps everyone away. [American proverb.]
11 And here is the weather forecast. Tomorrow will be muggy. Followed by Toogy, Weggy, Thurgy and Frigy.
12 Better dead wrong than dead.
13 Bigamy is having one husband too many. Monogamy is the same.
14 Blessed are they who can laugh at themselves, for they shall never cease to be amused.
15 Breathes there a man with soul so dead, / Who never to his wife hath said, / Breakfast be damned, come back to bed!
16 Californians are not without their faults.
17 Chaste makes waste. [Graffiti.]
18 Chipped dishes never break. [French proverb.]
19 Creditors have better memories than debtors. [English proverb.]
20 Crime doesn't pay—as well as politics.
21 "Daddy, why is Mommy so pale?" Shut up and keep digging.
22 Dear Lord, Help me to be the kind of person my dog thinks I am. —See also Holbrook Jackson 1
23 Dear Lord, Please let me prove that winning the lottery won't spoil me.
24 Death is nature's way of telling you to slow down.
25 Do not adjust your mind—the fault is in reality. [Graffiti.]
26 Don't look at me, Sir, with—ah—in that tone of voice. [British humor magazine *Punch,* 1884.]
27 Due to a lack of interest tomorrow has been canceled. [Graffiti.]

28 Eschew obfuscation!

29 Every country has its own constitution; ours is absolutism tempered by assassination. [Russian, 1700s.]

30 God help the man who won't marry until he finds the perfect woman, and God help the woman if he finds her!

31 God is alive and well and working on a much less ambitious project. [Graffiti.] —See also Woody Allen 30; Oscar Wilde 49

32 God is alive and well—at Pilgrim State Hospital. [Graffiti.]

33 God is alive and well. He just doesn't want to get involved. [Graffiti.]

34 God is an atheist. [Graffiti.]

35 God is coming back and She's really pissed. [Graffiti.]

36 "God is dead"—Nietzsche. [Below.] "Nietzsche is dead"—God. [Graffiti.]

37 God is not dead. He's alive and autographing Bibles at your local independent bookstore. [Graffiti.]

38 Gratitude is for favors to come.

39 Growing old is mandatory; growing up is optional.

40 "Have I told you about my grandchildren?" No, and I appreciate it.

41 He laughs best who laughs last. —See also Laurence J. Peter 13; Mary Pettibone Poole 3

42 He that is his own doctor has a fool for a patient. [English proverb.]

43 He that makes an ass of himself must not take it ill if men ride him. [English proverb.]

44 He's a Marxist-Lennonist—Groucho and John.

45 "Here's a nickel, my good man. But tell me, how did you ever become so destitute?" I was like you, sir, always giving vast sums to the poor.

46 Hypochondria is the only disease I haven't got. [Graffiti.]

47 I always wanted to be a procrastinator but never got around to it.

48 I believe we should all pay our tax bill with a smile. I tried—but they wanted cash.

49 "I hear your husband tried to get a government job. What's he doing now?" Nothing—he got the job.

50 I hope life isn't a big joke, because if it is, I don't get it.

51 I plan on living forever. So far, so good.

52 I'd rather have a bottle in front of me than a frontal lobotomy.

53 Ideas are like children: there are none so wonderful as our own.

54 If all you've got is a hammer, nearly everything looks like a nail.

55 If anything can go wrong, it will. [The original "Murphy's Law," 1949] —See also George Orwell 9

56 If at first you don't succeed, punt. [Larry King's motto.] —See also Evan Esar 8; W. C. Fields 24

57 If I dealt in candles, the sun would never set; if I peddled umbrellas, it would never rain; if I made coffins, no one would ever die; if I sold hats, people would be born without heads. [Composite Yiddish proverb.]

58 If it runs, leave it alone. [Instruction that came with the early Model T Ford at a time when mechanics were scarce and motorists were mostly on their own.]

59 If it sounds too good to be true, it probably is. [American proverb.]

60 If it weren't for the last minute, nothing would get done.

61 If it works, it's obsolete.

62 If it's stupid but works, it ain't stupid.

63 If people didn't pick on me, I wouldn't be paranoid. [Graffiti.]

64 If the phone doesn't ring, you'll know it's me.

65 If there's ever a price on your head, take it.

66 If voting changed anything, they'd make it illegal. [Graffiti.]

67 If you can keep your head when all about you are losing theirs, perhaps you have misunderstood the situation. —See also Edward R. Murrow 1

68 If you don't like the way I drive, get off the sidewalk!

69 If you have to ask who "they" are, you're one of them. [Graffiti.]

70 If you resolve to give up smoking, drinking and loving, you don't actually live longer, it just seems longer.

71 If you're not part of the steamroller, you're part of the road.

72 In any given set of circumstances, the proper course of action is determined by subsequent events. ["McDonald's Corollary to Murphy's Law."]

73 In Texas they really raise hell about the new, more open sexual morality. This one old geezer said he was against it for three reasons. "First, it's against the law of nature. Second, it's destructive of family living. And third, I ain't getting none of it."

74 In the U.S. government's fight with Bill Gates, I'm for the government—I always like to root for the little guy. [1999]

75 Is there life before death? [Graffiti.]

76 "Is this ship really unsinkable?" [Passenger about to depart on the *Titanic*] "God himself couldn't sink this ship." [Deckhand]

77 It's a sign of age if you feel like the morning after the night before and you haven't been anywhere.

78 Just because you're paranoid doesn't mean they're not out to get you.

79 Just when you finally figure out where it's at, somebody moves it.

80 Lean, thin hair, can't be photographed very well, not much personality, and so forth. Also dances. [Film studio executive commenting on Fred Astaire after a 1928 screen test.] —See also Jack Warner 2

81 Life's a bitch, and then you die. [Graffiti.]

82 Many a man owes his success to his first wife and his second wife to his success.

83 May the best day of your past be the worst day of your future. [Chinese proverb.]

84 Modesty is the art of encouraging people to find out for themselves how wonderful you are.

85 Mom and Dad never spoke to each other: how could they know they had any problems?

86 My friend stopped smoking yesterday. He is survived by his wife and two children.

87 "My, what a beautiful baby." [Passerby] "Oh, that's nothing—you should see her photograph!" [Mother]

88 Never judge a book by its movie.

89 Never pick a fight with anyone who buys ink by the barrel and paper by the ton. [Referring to newspaper publishers.]

90 Never put off till tomorrow what you can get someone else to do for you today. —See also Ed Howe 5; Aldous Huxley 8; Mark Twain 87

91 Never seeing you again would be too soon.

92 No call alligator long mouth till you pass him. [Jamaican proverb.]

93 (1) Nothing is as easy as it looks. (2) Everything takes longer than you think. (3) If there is a possibility of several things going wrong, the one that will cause the most damage will be the one to go wrong. ["Murphy's Law: Corollaries."]

94 Nothing sucks like success. [Graffiti.] —See also Alexandre Dumas 2; Bob Dylan 11

95 O god, if there is a god, save my soul, if I have a soul. [English soldier, 1704.]

96 Old thieves never die; they just steal away.

97 Please visit again when you can't stay so long.

98 Politics makes strange bedfellows—rich. —See also Groucho Marx 17; William Shakespeare 19; Charles Dudley Warner 2

99 Professional football is getting very rough. You have to wear shoulder pads, a face mask, and a hard helmet—and that's just to sit in the stands.

100 Quick believers need broad shoulders. [English proverb.]

101 Real problems have no solutions.

102 Retired California policeman Steven Radford has spent $20,000 on seven cosmetic surgery procedures to make himself look like Tom Arnold. [*The New Republic,* 18 September 1995.]

103 Sages learn from the mistakes of others; fools, not even from their own.

104 Save water—shower with a friend. [Graffiti.]

105 She looked, / He didn't. / She is, / He isn't. [Highway sign.]

106 Show me a man who thinks he understands women, and I'll show you a man who is in for a big surprise.

107 Skinny cooks can't be trusted.

108 Some television programs are so much chewing gum for the eyes. [Often attributed to John Mason Brown.]

109 Taxes on wealth is capital punishment. —See also Sydney J. Harris 7

110 The bigger they come, the harder they hit. ["Perkins' Postulate."] —See also Bob Fitzsimmons; James Thurber 15

111 The dictionary is the only place where success comes before work.

112 The difference between God and Santa Claus is that there is a Santa Claus. [Graffiti.]

113 The easiest way to change history is to become a historian.

114 The fairest silk is the soonest stained. [English proverb, 1732.]

115 The Golden Rule: whoever has the gold makes the rules.

116 The less you bet, the more you lose when you win.

117 The neurotic builds castles in the air, the psychotic lives in them, and the psychiatrist collects the rent.

[118] The past ain't what it used to be—it never was. —See also Walter Truett Anderson; Bernard Levin 2; Paul Valéry 7

[119] The poor have little; / Beggars none; / The rich too much; / Enough, not one.

[120] The squeaky wheel doesn't always get greased; sometimes it gets replaced.

[121] The way of the transgressor is hard—on everyone.

[122] There are no traffic jams when you go the extra mile.

[123] There are none so empty as those who are full of themselves. [English proverb.]

[124] There are two kinds of adhesive tape: that which won't stay on and that which won't come off. ["Telesco's Law of Nursing."]

[125] There are three stages of life: youth, middle age and "you're looking good."

[126] There are two sides to every question, as long as it doesn't concern us personally.

[127] They that buy an office must sell something.

[128] Those in the free seats are the first to hiss.

[129] Though I yield to no one in my admiration for President Coolidge, I do wish he did not look as if he had been weaned on a pickle. [Often attributed Alice Roosevelt Longworth.]

[130] To err is human, but to really foul things up requires a computer.

[131] Train up a child in the way he should go—and walk there yourself once in a while.

[132] 'Twixt optimist and pessimist / The difference is droll: / The optimist the doughnut sees, / The pessimist, the hole.

[133] Two can live as cheaply as one—if one doesn't eat.

[134] V.D. is nothing to clap about. [Graffiti.]

[135] "What is the significance of the French Revolution?" It is too early to say. [20th-century Chinese philosopher.]

[136] "What would have made combining a family and career easier for you?" [Doctor to a mother of four children] Being born a man.

[137] "What's the difference between ignorance and apathy?" I don't know and I don't care.

[138] When in Rome, do as the Romeos do.

[139] Where does the light go when it goes out?

[140] Where there's marriage without love, there will be love without marriage.

[141] Where there's too much, something is missing. [Yiddish proverb.]

[142] Who marries for money earns it. [English proverb.]

[143] Who tells the truth must have one foot in the stirrup. [Turkish proverb.]

[144] "Why don't sharks attack lawyers?" Professional courtesy.

[145] Why is it that after dialing a wrong number you never get a busy signal? —See also James Thurber 20

[146] With money in your pocket, you are wise and handsome, and you sing well too. [Yiddish proverb.]

[147] Women's faults are many / Men have only two: / Everything they say / And everything they do.

148 "How do you know a politician is lying?" When you see his lips move.

149 "You're going to live to be eighty." [Doctor] "But I am eighty!" [Patient] "See, what did I tell you?"

150 Your main fault is, you are good for nothing.

JEAN ANOUILH (1910–1987). *French playwright*

1 Every man thinks God is on his side. The rich and powerful know he is.

2 Inspiration is a farce poets have invented to give themselves importance.

3 Saintliness is also a temptation.

4 What you get free costs too much.

5 "Why, that chicken has no beak," the man pronounced impeccably.

6 You can't get to the top by sitting on your bottom.

7 You can't win: if you succeed, you'll be envied; if you fail, you'll be pitied.

8 You can't win: if you tell lies, you'll be distrusted; if you tell the truth, you'll be disliked.

9 You can't win: if you're right, no one remembers; if you're wrong, no one forgets.

JOHN ARBUTHNOT (1667–1735). *Scottish physician and writer*

1 All political parties die at last of swallowing their own lies.

2 Biography, one of the new terrors of death.

ARISTOPHANES (450?–388? B.C.). *Greek playwright*

These impossible women! How they get around us! The poet was right: we can't live with them, or without them!

ARISTOTLE (384–322 B.C.). *Greek philosopher*

"Have I bored you to death with my chatter?" Not really; I was paying no attention to you.

MICHAEL ARLEN (1895–1956). *British novelist and playwright*

1 It is amazing how nice people are to you when they know you are going away.

2 She not only expects the worst but makes the worst of it when it happens.

LOUIS "SATCHMO" ARMSTRONG (1900–1971). *American jazz musician*

1 "How would you define jazz?" Man, if you gotta ask, you'll never know.

2 Music is my mistress, and she plays second fiddle to no one.

NEIL A. ARMSTRONG (1930–). *American astronaut*

Nine summers ago, I went for a visit, / To see if the moon was green cheese. / When we arrived, people on earth asked: "Is it?" / We answered: "No cheese, no bees, no trees." [1978]

ISAAC ASIMOV (1920–1992). *Russian-born American writer*

Violence is the last refuge of the incompetent. —See also Samuel Johnson 64

HERBERT ASQUITH (1852–1928). *British prime minister*

1 The War Office kept three sets of figures: one to mislead the public, another to mislead the Cabinet, and the third to mislead itself. [Referring to World War I.]

2 Youth would be an ideal state if it came a little later in life.

MARGOT ASQUITH (1864–1945). *British society figure and wit*
1 He couldn't see a belt without hitting below it. [On David Lloyd George.]
2 He's very clever, but sometimes his brains go to his head. [On F. E. Smith.]
3 My sort of looks are of the kind that bore me when I see them on other people.
4 No, no, Jean. The *t* is silent, as in *Harlow*. [Remark to Jean Harlow, who had repeatedly mispronounced Margot.]
5 She tells enough white lies to ice a wedding cake. [On Lady Desborough.]

LADY ASTOR (Nancy Astor, 1879–1964). *American-born English member of Parliament*
1 I don't drink because I want to know when I am having a good time.
2 I married beneath me—all women do.
3 What would we say if men changed the length of their trousers every year?

BROOKS ATKINSON (1894–1984). *American drama critic*
1 I have no objection to churches so long as they do not interfere with God's work.
2 Those who rule us are like you and me. It is a frightening situation.

CLEMENT ATTLEE (1883–1967). *British prime minister*
Russian communism is the illegitimate child of Karl Marx and Catherine the Great.

W. H. AUDEN (1907–1973). *English-born American poet*
1 Almost all of our relationships begin and most of them continue as forms of mutual exploitation, a mental or physical barter, to be terminated when one or both parties run out of goods.
2 My face looks like a wedding cake left out in the rain.
3 Some books are undeservedly forgotten; none are undeservedly remembered.

ST. AUGUSTINE (A.D. 354–430). *Christian theologian*
1 As a youth I had been woefully at fault, particularly in early adolescence. I had prayed to you for chastity and said, "Give me chastity and continence, but not yet."
2 The playthings of our elders are called business.
3 To abstain from sin when a man cannot sin is to be forsaken by sin, not to forsake it.

JANE AUSTEN (1775–1817). *English novelist*
1 I have been a selfish being all my life in practice, though not in principle.
2 Lady Middleton exerted herself to ask Mr. Palmer if there was any news in the paper. "No, none at all," he replied, and read on.
3 Oh! do not attack me with your watch. A watch is always too fast or too slow. I cannot be dictated to by a watch.
4 You have delighted us long enough. [Mr. Bennet to his daughter Mary who had been singing, *Pride and Prejudice*, 1813.]

ALAN AYCKBOURN (1939–). *English playwright*

1 I think Patrick plans to wean our child straight on to calculators.

2 My mother used to say, Delia, if S-E-X ever rears its ugly head, close your eyes before you see the rest of it.

3 She has her high days and low days, a bit like the church. It depends what miracle drug the doctor's currently got her on.

4 Some women enjoy tremendously being told they look a mess—and they actually thrill to the threat of physical violence. I've never met one that does, mind you, but they probably do exist. In books. By men.

FRANCIS BACON (1561–1626). *English philosopher*

1 Fame is like a river, that bears up things light and swollen, and drowns things weighty and solid.

2 I do not believe that any man fears to be dead, but only the stroke of death.
—See also Woody Allen 37

3 It is impossible to love and be wise.

ARTHUR "BUGS" BAER (1886–1969). *American journalist*

1 Alimony is like buying oats for a dead horse.

2 He had insomnia so bad that he couldn't sleep when he was working.

3 It was as helpful as throwing a drowning man both ends of a rope.

4 It was so quiet that you could hear a pun drop.

5 She was a brunette by birth but a blonde by habit.

WALTER BAGEHOT (1826–1877). *English economist and journalist*

1 A constitutional statesman is in general a man of common opinions and uncommon abilities.

2 It is good to be without vices, but it is not good to be without temptations.

3 People dread to be thought unsafe in proportion as they get their living by being thought to be safe.

4 Poverty is anomaly to rich people; it is very difficult to make out why people who want dinner do not ring the bell.

5 Stupidity is nature's favorite resource for preserving steadiness of conduct and consistency of opinion.

6 The most melancholy of human reflections, perhaps, is that on the whole it is a question whether the benevolence of mankind does most good or harm.

7 The reason why so few good books are written is that so few people who can write know anything.

F. LEE BAILEY (1933–). *American lawyer*

I get paid for seeing that my clients have every break the law allows. I have knowingly defended a number of guilty men. But the guilty never escape unscathed. My fees are sufficient punishment for anyone.

HOWARD BAKER (1925–). *Tennessee senator*

If you don't like the question that's asked, answer some other question. [Referring to news conferences.]

RUSSELL BAKER (1925–). *American journalist and humorist*

1 A winner is somebody you mess with only if you don't mind getting your block knocked off.

2 Caution: These verses may be hazardous to your solemnity. [Introduction to an anthology of poetry.]

3 Frozen food is not progress.

4 He's a Democrat, whatever that means, besides brain-dead. [On Bill Clinton, 1995.]

5 He's perhaps the greatest unread poet the English language has produced. [On John Milton.]

6 How come it's a subsidy when Pan American Airlines asks the Government for a hundred million dollars to keep flying, but when people ask for considerably less to keep going it is a Federal handout?

7 In America, it is sport that is the opiate of the masses. —See also Karl Marx 5

8 Inanimate objects are classified scientifically into three major categories—those that don't work, those that break down and those that get lost.

9 It seems to be a law in American life that whatever enriches us anywhere except in the wallet inevitably becomes uneconomic.

10 People seem to enjoy things more when they know a lot of other people have been left out of the pleasure.

11 People who have the power to make things happen don't do the things that people do, so they don't know what needs to happen.

12 So there he is at last. Man on the moon. The poor magnificent bungler! He can't even get to the office without undergoing the agonies of the damned, but give him a little metal, a few chemicals, some wire and twenty or thirty billion dollars, and, vroom!, there he is, up on a rock a quarter of a million miles up in the sky. [1969]

13 The only thing I was fit for was to be a writer, and this notion rested solely on my suspicion that I would never be fit for real work, and that writing didn't require any.

14 The true biker exults in laying down an onslaught of noise that loosens the wisdom teeth of passers-by and blows soup right out the bowl along the road.

15 There are good reasons why everybody should heed politicians' advice not to believe the media. One of the best is that the media report what politicians say.

16 There are no liberals behind steering wheels.

17 There is no business like show business—except sports business.

18 What successful advertising men, not to mention most politicians, understand clearly is that people will in fact do what is bad for them in the long run if offered a reward that can be collected in the short run.

19 What sweeter words can fall on the human ear? It's going to be May all week long.

20 Why do we expect our presidents to control destiny when they cannot even control the House of Representatives?

MIKHAIL BAKUNIN (1814–1876). *Russian anarchist and writer*
If God really existed, it would be necessary to abolish him.

JAMES BALDWIN (1924–1987). *American writer*

1 Anyone who has ever struggled with poverty knows how extremely expensive it is to be poor.

2 Children have never been very good at listening to their elders, but they have never failed to imitate them. —See also Joseph Joubert 1

3 It comes as a great shock to see Gary Cooper killing off the Indians and, although you are rooting for Gary Cooper, that the Indians are you. [Referring to his experience as a child.]

4 Money, it turned out, was exactly like sex, you thought of nothing else if you didn't have it and thought of other things if you did.

5 To act is to be committed, and to be committed is to be in danger.

6 You don't realize that you're intelligent until it gets you into trouble.

ARTHUR JAMES BALFOUR (1848–1930). *British prime minister*

1 I thought he was a young man of promise, but it appears he is a young man of promises. [On Winston Churchill.]

2 Nothing matters very much, and few things matter at all. [Attributed.]

HONORÉ de BALZAC (1799–1850). *French novelist*

1 Friendships last when each friend thinks he has a slight superiority over the other.

2 I do not regard a broker as a member of the human race.

3 Insignificant folk cannot be crushed, they lie too flat beneath the foot.

4 Silence, sir! I will hear no more: you make me doubt myself.

5 "Temptations can be got rid of." "How?" "By yielding to them." —See also Oscar Wilde 99

6 The majority of husbands remind me of an orangutan trying to play a violin. [*The Physiology of Marriage,* 1828.]

7 When in Turkey, do as the turkeys do.

JOHN KENDRICK BANGS (1862–1922). *American writer and humorist*

1 Being an Episcopalian interferes neither with my business nor my religion.

2 I can't tell a lie—not even when I hear one.

3 Pandemonium did not reign; it poured.

TALLULAH BANKHEAD (1903–1965). *American actress*

1 Cocaine isn't habit-forming. I should know—I've been using it for years. [1952]

2 I don't know what I am, darling. I've tried several varieties of sex. The conventional position makes me claustrophobic. And the others give me either stiff neck or lockjaw.

3 I'll come and make love to you at five o'clock. If I'm late, start without me.

4 I'm as pure as the driven slush.

5 If I had to live my life again, I'd make the same mistakes, only sooner.

6 Only good girls keep diaries. Bad girls don't have the time.

7 There is less in this than meets the eye. [On revival of Maurice Maeterlinck's play *Aglavaine and Selysette.*]

MAURICE BARING (1874–1945). *English journalist*

If you would know what the Lord God thinks of money, you have only to look at those to whom he gives it.

CLIVE BARNES (1927–). *English drama critic*

1 Television is the first truly democratic culture—the first culture available to everyone and entirely governed by what the people want. The most terrifying thing is what people do want.

2 This is the kind of show to give pornography a dirty name. [On the 1969 musical *Oh, Calcutta!*]

PETER BARNES (1931–). *English playwright and screenwriter*
"How do you know you're God?" [Claire] "Simple. When I pray to Him, I find I'm talking to myself." [Earl of Gurney, in the 1969 play *The Ruling Class.*]

RICHARD J. BARNET (1929–). *American political scientist*
International politics has always been treated by diplomats as something of a game. Winners get to be called statesmen.

J. M. BARRIE (1860–1937). *English novelist and playwright*
1 A man who is high up loves to think that he has done it all himself; and the wife smiles, and lets it go at that.
2 Ambition is the last infirmity of noble minds.
3 I am not young enough to know everything.
4 If it's heaven for climate, it's hell for company. [1891] —See also Mark Twain 41
5 If you have charm, you don't need to have anything else; and if you don't have it, it doesn't much matter what else you have.
6 It is not real work unless you would rather be doing something else.
7 Life is a long lesson in humility.
8 Never ascribe to an opponent motives meaner than your own.
9 She was a large woman who seemed not so much dressed as upholstered.
10 The printing press is either the greatest blessing or the greatest curse of modern times, one sometimes forgets which.
11 The tragedy of a man who has found himself out.

ETHEL BARRYMORE (1879–1959). *American actress*
1 For an actress to be a success, she must have the face of a Venus, the brains of a Minerva, the grace of Terpsichore, the memory of a Macaulay, the figure of Juno, and the hide of a rhinoceros.
2 I don't see why Walter Winchell is allowed to live.
3 I never let them laugh. They wouldn't dare. [On her audiences.] —See also Ralph Richardson
4 You grow up the day you have the first real laugh—at yourself.

JOHN BARRYMORE (1882–1942). *American actor*
1 A man is not old until regrets take the place of dreams.
2 America is the country where you buy a lifetime supply of aspirin for one dollar, and use it up in two weeks.
3 My only regret in the theater is that I could never sit out front and watch me.
4 The good die young, because they see it's no use living if you've got to be good.
5 You never realize how short a month is until you pay alimony.

BRUCE BARTON (1886–1967). *American businessman and writer*
1 Christ would be a national advertiser today. I am sure, as He was a great advertiser in His own day. He thought of His life as business. [*The Man Nobody Knows,* 1925.]
2 Conceit is God's gift to little men.

BERNARD M. BARUCH (1870–1965). *American financier*

1 An elder statesman is somebody old enough to know his own mind and to keep quiet about it.

2 As I grow old, I find myself less and less inclined to take the stairs two at a time. [At age 85.]

3 To me, old age is always fifteen years older than I am. [At age 85.]

4 Vote for the man who promises least; he'll be the least disappointing.

5 When beggars and shoeshine boys, barbers and beauticians can tell you how to get rich, it is time to remind yourself that there is no more dangerous illusion than the belief that one can get something for nothing. [Referring to the stock market.]

MIKHAIL BARYSHNIKOV (1948–). *Latvian ballet dancer*

No dancer can watch Fred Astaire and not know that we all should have been in another business.

ROY BEAN (1825?-1903). *American jurist*

Bring in the guilty bastard. We'll give him a fair trial, and then we'll hang him.
   —See also Molière 3

PIERRE de BEAUMARCHAIS (1732–1799). *French playwright*

1 If you are mediocre and you grovel, you shall succeed.

2 We drink without being thirsty and make love at any time; that is all that distinguishes us from other animals.

3 Youth is unhappy because it is faced with this terrible choice: love without peace, or peace without love.

LORD BEAVERBROOK (William Maxwell Aitken, 1879–1964). *Canadian-born British publisher, financier, and cabinet minister*

1 Buy old masters. They fetch a better price than old mistresses.

2 Churchill? He's a busted flush! [Explaining his refusal to hire Winston Churchill to write for one of his newspapers, 1932.]

3 He did not seem to care which way he traveled providing he was in the driver's seat. [On David Lloyd George.]

4 Never has anyone gone so far with so little. [On Averell Harriman.]

5 With the publication of his private papers in 1952, he committed suicide 25 years after his death. [On Field Marshal Douglas Haig, inept commander of the British Expeditionary Force in France during World War I.]

SAMUEL BECKETT (1906–1989). *Irish playwright*

1 "Charming spot. Inspiring prospects. Let's go." [Estragon] "We can't." [Vladimir] "Why not?" [Estragon] "We're waiting for Godot." [Vladimir, in the 1955 play *Waiting for Godot*.]

2 "Do you believe in a life to come?" [Clov] "Mine was always that." [Hamm, in the 1957 play *Endgame*.]

3 We are all born crazy. Some remain that way.

THOMAS BEECHAM (1879–1961). *British conductor and impresario*

1 Movie music is noise even more painful than my sciatica.

2 No operatic star has yet died soon enough for me.

3 There are two golden rules for an orchestra: start together and finish together. The public doesn't give a damn what goes on in between.

HENRY WARD BEECHER (1813–1887). *American clergyman*
Selfishness is that detestable vice which no one will forgive in others, and no
  one is without in himself.

MAX BEERBOHM (1872–1956). *English drama critic and writer*
1 Beauty and the lust for learning have yet to be allied.
2 I was a modest, good-humored boy. It is Oxford that has made me
  insufferable.
3 Most women are not as young as they're painted.
4 Only mediocrity can be trusted to be always at its best.
5 The dullard's envy of brilliant men is always assuaged by the suspicion that
  they will come to a bad end.
6 To give an accurate and exhaustive account of that period would need a
  far less brilliant pen than mine.

BRENDAN BEHAN (1923–1964). *Irish playwright*
1 A general and a bit of shooting makes you forget your troubles; it takes
  your mind off the cost of living.
2 Ah, bless you, Sister, may all your sons be bishops. [Last words.]
3 Critics are like eunuchs in a harem: they know how it's done, they've seen
  it done every day, but they're unable to do it themselves.
4 I was court-martialed in my absence, and sentenced to death in my absence, so I said they could shoot me in my absence.
5 There's no such thing as bad publicity except your own obituary.
6 We're all the kids our mothers warned us against. [1958] —See also Robin
  Morgan 2; Nicholas Von Hoffman
7 "What is the message of your play?" [A theater-goer who had just seen *The
  Hostage*] Message? Message? What the hell do you think I am, a bloody
  postman? [1958] —See also Samuel Goldwyn 22

S. N. BEHRMAN (1893–1973). *American playwright*
There are two kinds of people in one's life: people whom one keeps waiting and the people for whom one waits.

HILAIRE BELLOC (1870–1953). *French-born English writer and poet*
1 Whatever happens, we have got / The Maxim Gun, and they have not. [On
  British imperialism in Africa, 1898.]
2 When I am dead, I hope it may be said: / His sins were scarlet, but his
  books were read.

ROBERT BENCHLEY (1889–1945). *American writer, actor, and humorist*
1 A dog teaches a boy fidelity, perseverance, and to turn around three times
  before lying down.
2 Benchley came out of a night club one evening and, tapping a uniformed
  figure on the shoulder, said, "Get me a cab." The uniformed figure turned
  around furiously and informed him that he was not a doorman but a rear
  admiral. "O.K.," said Benchley, "Get me a battleship."

3 "Don't you know drinking is a slow death?" [F. Scott Fitzgerald] So who's in a hurry?

4 Drawing on my fine command of language, I said nothing.

5 Drinking makes such fools of people, and people are such fools to begin with, that it's compounding a felony.

6 Except for an occasional heart attack, I feel as young as I ever did.

7 Freelance writer: one who gets paid per word, per piece, or perhaps.

8 I do most of my work sitting down. That's where I shine.

9 I have tried to know absolutely nothing about a great many things, and I have succeeded fairly well.

10 In America there are two classes of travel: first class and with children.

11 It took me fifteen years to discover that I had no talent for writing, but I couldn't give it up because by that time I was too famous.

12 My only solution for the problem of habitual accidents is for everybody to stay in bed all day. Even then, there is always the chance that you will fall out.

13 Often Daddy sat up very late working—on a case of Scotch.

14 She sleeps alone at last. [Proposed epitaph for an actress.]

15 Streets flooded. Please advise! [Telegram to *The New Yorker* on arriving in Venice.]

16 Tell us your phobias, and we will tell you what you're afraid of.

17 The biggest obstacle to professional writing is the necessity for changing a typewriter ribbon.

18 There are two classes of people in the world: those who constantly divide people into two classes, and those who do not.

DAVID BEN-GURION (1886–1973). *Israeli prime minister*
In Israel, in order to be a realist you must believe in miracles.

TONY BENN (1925–). *British member of Parliament*
1 Britain today is suffering from galloping obsolescence. [1963]

2 It is the same each time with progress. First they ignore you, then they say you are mad, then dangerous, then there's a pause, and then you can't find anyone who disagrees.

3 The House of Lords is the British Outer Mongolia for retired politicians.

ALAN BENNETT (1934–). *English writer and actor*
1 All modesty is false, otherwise it's not modesty.

2 All women dress like their mothers, that is their tragedy. No man ever does. That is his. —See also Oscar Wilde 8

3 Everywhere one looks, decadence. I saw a bishop with a mustache the other day.

4 "Have you ever thought, Headmaster, that your standards might perhaps be a little out of date?" [Franklin] "Of course they're out of date. Standards are always out of date. That is what makes them standards." [Headmaster, in the 1969 play *Forty Years On*.]

5 I want a future that will live up to my past.

6 I wonder whether Jesus did odd carpentry jobs around people's houses? "I'm sorry, Mrs. Cohen, I shan't be in for the next forty days. No. Not really a holiday. Just coming to terms with myself, really!"

7 I'm in favor of free expression provided it's kept rigidly under control.

8 I've never understood this liking for war. It panders to instincts already catered for within the scope of any respectable domestic establishment.

9 If you think squash is a competitive activity, try flower-arranging.

10 Mark my words, when a society has to resort to the lavatory for its humor, the writing is on the wall.

11 Mr. Craven's always been on the side of progress: he had false teeth when he was twenty-seven.

12 My degree was a kind of inoculation. I got just enough education to make me immune from it for the rest of my life.

13 One of the few lessons I have learned in life is that there is invariably something odd about women who wear ankle socks.

14 "Suffer the little children to come unto me." You might know that Jesus wasn't married.

15 They're going to sit up and take notice. They're going to have to be made to realize who we are. My father had a chain of dry cleaners.

16 We started off trying to set up a small anarchist community, but people wouldn't obey the rules.

17 We were put to Dickens as children, but it never took. That unremitting humanity soon had me cheesed off.

18 When one is on one's best behavior, one isn't always at one's best.

ARNOLD BENNETT (1867–1931). *English journalist and novelist*

1. Good taste is better than bad taste, but bad taste is better than no taste at all.

2 It is only people of small moral stature who have to stand on their dignity.

3 Journalists say a thing that they know isn't true, in the hope that if they keep on saying it long enough it will be true.

4 Pessimism, when you get used to it, is just as agreeable as optimism.

5 The price of justice is eternal publicity.

JACK BENNY (1894–1974). *American comedian and radio personality*

1 I don't deserve this, but then I have arthritis, and I don't deserve that either. [In accepting an award.]

2 I don't want to tell you how much insurance I carry with Prudential Life. All I can say is that when I go, *they* go. [Attributed.]

3 "Your money or your life? Come on, hurry up!" [Holdup man] I'm thinking it over! [The public Benny was notorious for his miserly ways.] —See also George Burns 8

JEREMY BENTHAM (1748–1832). *English political philosopher*
Lawyers are the only persons in whom ignorance of the law is not punished.

LLOYD BENTSEN (1921–). *Texas senator and U.S. secretary of the treasury*
"I have as much experience in the Congress as Jack Kennedy did when he sought the presidency." [Dan Quayle] Senator, I served with Jack Kennedy.

I knew Jack Kennedy. Jack Kennedy was a friend of mine. Senator, you're no Jack Kennedy. [Televised vice presidential candidates debate, 1988.] — See also Ronald Reagan 27

BERNARD BERENSON (1865–1959). *American art historian*
1. Consistency requires you to be as ignorant today as you were a year ago.
2 Genius is the capacity for productive reaction against one's training.
3 Governments last as long as the under-taxed can defend themselves against the over-taxed.

EDGAR BERGEN (1903–1978). *American comedian, ventriloquist, and radio personality*
Hard work never killed anybody, but why take a chance? [As spoken by his puppet Charlie McCarthy.]

MILTON BERLE (1908–). *American comedian and television personality*
1 He's the kind of guy who can brighten a room by leaving it.
2 I can't tell you his age, but when he was born the wonder drug was mercurochrome.
3 I never stole a joke; I just find them before they're lost.
4 Sex at eighty-four is terrific, especially the one in the winter.
5 The other night I asked my wife Ruth, "Do you feel that the sex and excitement has gone out of our marriage?" She answered, "I'll discuss it with you during the next commercial."
6 This is over my head. [Self-epitaph.]
7 We owe a lot to Thomas Edison. Were it not for him, we'd all be watching television by candlelight. [Attributed.]

IRVING BERLIN (1888–1889). *Russian-born American songwriter*
1 The world would not be in such a snarl / If Marx had been Groucho instead of Karl. [Birthday message to Groucho Marx, 1966.]
2 "They Were All Out of Step But Jim." [Song title, 1918.]

ISAIAH BERLIN (1909–1997). *Russian-born British philosopher*
When a man speaks of the need for realism, one may be sure that this is the prelude to some bloody deed.

SARAH BERNHARDT (1844–1923). *French actress*
"Do you mind if I smoke?" [Oscar Wilde] I don't care if you burn.

YOGI BERRA (1925–). *American baseball player and manager*
1 "Good afternoon, Mr. Berra. My, you look mighty cool today." [Grandmotherly woman, on a very warm day] Thank you, ma'am. You don't look so hot yourself.
2 I don't know if it's good for baseball, but it sure beats the hell out of rooming with Phil Rizzuto. [On the marriage of Joe DiMaggio and Marilyn Monroe.]
3 I guess the first thing I ought to say is that I thank everybody for making this day necessary. [On being inducted into the Baseball Hall of Fame, 1972.]
4 I really didn't say everything I said.
5 If Casey Stengel were alive today, he'd be turning over in his grave.

6 If the people don't want to come out to the park, nobody's gonna stop 'em.
—See also Samuel Goldwyn 14

7 If you don't know where you're going, when you get there you'll be lost.
—See also Laurence J. Peter 16

8 It ain't over till it's over.

9 It's déjà vu all over again. [Attributed.]

10 Ninety percent of baseball is half mental.

11 Nobody goes to that restaurant anymore—it's too crowded.

12 Slump? I ain't in no slump. I just ain't hitting.

13 This is the earliest I've ever arrived late. [Attributed.]

14 When you come to a fork in the road, take it.

15 You can observe a lot by watchin'.

ANEURIN BEVAN (1897–1960). *British member of Parliament and cabinet minister*

1 He is a man suffering from petrified adolescence. [On Winston Churchill.]

2 A man walking backward with his face to the future. [On Walter Elliot.]

3 I read the newspapers avidly. It is my one form of continuous fiction.

4 League of Nations society at Geneva introduced him to a whole range of ideas strange to a Tory. There he acquired a progressive vocabulary, and this, allied to the amiability that flows from weakness of character, deceives many people into thinking that his political intentions are honorable. Actually there is nothing in his conduct to justify such a conclusion. [On Anthony Eden, 1943.]

5 Listening to a speech by Chamberlain is like paying a visit to Woolworth's: everything in its place and nothing above sixpence. [On Neville Chamberlain.]

6 Righteous people terrify me; virtue is its own punishment.

7 This island is made mainly of coal and surrounded by fish. Only an organizing genius could produce a shortage of coal and a shortage of fish at the same time. [On Great Britain.]

8 We know what happens to people who stay in the middle of the road: they get run over.

LORD BEVERIDGE (William Henry Beveridge, 1879–1963). *British economist*
Scratch a pessimist, and you often find a defender of privilege.

AMBROSE BIERCE (1842–1914?). *American journalist and writer*

1 Abnormal, *adj.* Not conforming to standard. In matters of thought and conduct, to be independent is to be abnormal, to be abnormal is to be detested. [*The Devil's Dictionary,* 1911.]

2 Abstainer, *n.* A weak person who yields to the temptation of denying himself a pleasure.

3 Acquaintance, *n.* A person we know well enough to borrow from, but not well enough to lend to.

4 Admiration, *n.* Our polite recognition of another's resemblance to ourselves.

5 All are lunatics, but he who can analyze his delusion is a philosopher.

[6] Alliance, *n.* In international politics, the union of two thieves who have their hands so deeply inserted in each other's pockets that they cannot separately plunder a third.

[7] Alone, *adj.* In bad company.

[8] Apothecary, *n.* The physician's accomplice, undertaker's benefactor and grave worm's provider.

[9] Beggar, *n.* One who has relied on the assistance of his friends.

[10] Bigot, *n.* One who is obstinately and zealously attached to an opinion that you do not entertain.

[11] Bore, *n.* A person who talks when you wish him to listen.

[12] Brain, *n.* An apparatus with which we think that we think.

[13] Bride, *n.* A woman with a fine prospect of happiness behind her.

[14] Calamity, *n.* A more than commonly plain and unmistakable reminder that the affairs of this life are not of our own ordering. Calamities are of two kinds: misfortune to ourselves, and good fortune to others.

[15] Cannon, *n.* An instrument employed in the rectification of national boundaries.

[16] Christian, *n.* One who believes that the New Testament is a divinely inspired book admirably suited to the spiritual needs of his neighbor. One who follows the teachings of Christ in so far as they are not inconsistent with a life of sin.

[17] Consolation, *n.* The knowledge that a better man is more unfortunate than yourself.

[18] Consult, *v.t.* To seek another's approval of a course already decided on. — See also Josh Billings 50

[19] Congratulation, *n.* The civility of envy.

[20] Conservative, *n.* A statesman who is enamored of existing evils, as distinguished from the Liberal, who wishes to replace them with others.

[21] Corporation, *n.* An ingenious device for obtaining individual profit without individual responsibility.

[22] Coward, *n.* One who in a perilous emergency thinks with his legs.

[23] Deliberation, *n.* The act of examining one's bread to determine which side it is buttered on.

[24] Destiny, *n.* A tyrant's excuse for crime and a fool's excuse for failure.

[25] Dice, *n.* Small polka-dotted cubes of ivory, constructed like a lawyer to lie on any side, but commonly on the wrong one.

[26] Diplomacy, *n.* The patriotic art of lying for one's country.

[27] Distance, *n.* The only thing that the rich are willing for the poor to call theirs and keep.

[28] Duty, *n.* That which sternly impels us in the direction of profit, along the line of desire.

[29] Eccentricity, *n.* A method of distinction so cheap that fools employ it to accentuate their incapacity.

[30] Education, *n.* That which discloses to the wise and disguises from the foolish their lack of understanding.

[31] Egotist, *n.* A person of low taste, more interested in himself than in me.

32 Famous, *adj.* Conspicuously miserable.

33 Fashion, *n.* A despot whom the wise ridicule and obey.

34 Fidelity, *n.* A virtue peculiar to those who are about to be betrayed.

35 Freedom, *n.* A political condition that every nation supposes itself to enjoy in virtual monopoly.

36 Friendless, *adj.* Having no favors to bestow. Destitute of fortune. Addicted to utterance of truth and common sense.

37 Friendship, *n.* A ship big enough to carry two in fair weather, but only one in foul.

38 Future, *n.* That period of time in which our affairs prosper, our friends are true and our happiness is assured.

39 Good to eat and wholesome to digest, as a worm to a toad, a toad to a snake, a snake to a pig, a pig to a man, and a man to a worm. [On the cycle of digestion.]

40 Happiness, *n.* An agreeable sensation arising from contemplating the misery of another.

41 Hatred, *n.* A sentiment appropriate to the occasion of another's superiority.

42 History, *n.* An account mostly false, of events mostly unimportant, which are brought about by rulers mostly knaves, and soldiers mostly fools.

43 Hypocrisy—prejudice with a halo.

44 I think I think; therefore, I think I am. —See also Friedrich Nietzsche 3

45 Impiety, *n.* Your irreverence toward my deity.

46 Impostor, *n.* A rival aspirant to public honors.

47 Impunity, *n.* Wealth.

48 In Dr. Johnson's famous dictionary patriotism is defined as the last resort [sic] of a scoundrel. With all due respect to an enlightened but inferior lexicographer I beg to submit that it is the first. —See also Samuel Johnson 64

49 Income, *n.* The natural and rational gauge and measure of respectability.

50 Insurrection, *n.* An unsuccessful revolution. Disaffection's failure to substitute misrule for bad government.

51 Irreligion, *n.* The principal one of the great faiths of the world.

52 Kleptomaniac, *n.* A rich thief.

53 Lawful, *adj.* Compatible with the will of a judge having jurisdiction.

54 Lawyer, *n.* One skilled in circumvention of the law.

55 Liberty, *n.* One of Imagination's most precious possessions.

56 Litigation, *n.* A machine which you go into as a pig and come out of as a sausage.

57 Love, *n.* A temporary insanity cured by marriage.

58 Mammon, *n.* The god of the world's leading religion.

59 Moral, *adj.* Conforming to a local and mutable standard of right. Having the quality of general expediency.

60 Noise, *n.* A stench in the ear.

61 Patience, *n.* A minor form of despair disguised as a virtue.

62 Patriot, *n.* One to whom the interests of a part seem superior to those of the whole. The dupe of statesmen and the tool of conquerors.

63 Peace, *n.* In international affairs, a period of cheating between two periods of fighting.

[64] Philosophy, *n.* A route of many roads leading from nowhere to nothing.

[65] Please, *v.* To lay the foundation for a superstructure of imposition.

[66] Politeness, *n.* The most acceptable hypocrisy.

[67] Politics, *n.* A strife of interests masquerading as a contest of principles. The conduct of public affairs for private advantage.

[68] Positive, *adj.* Mistaken at the top of one's voice.

[69] Pray, *v.* To ask that the laws of the universe be annulled in behalf of a single petitioner confessedly unworthy.

[70] Predicament, *n.* The wage of consistency.

[71] Pun, *n.* A form of wit to which wise men stoop and fools aspire.

[72] Radicalism, *n.* The conservatism of tomorrow injected into the affairs of today.

[73] Rebel, *n.* A proponent of a new misrule who has failed to establish it.

[74] Religion, *n.* A daughter of Hope and Fear, explaining to Ignorance the nature of the Unknowable.

[75] Religious tolerance is a kind of infidelity.

[76] Revolution, *n.* In politics, an abrupt change in the form of misgovernment.

[77] Saint, *n.* A dead sinner revised and edited.

[78] Scribbler, *n.* A professional writer whose views are antagonistic to one's own.

[79] Self-esteem, *n.* An erroneous appraisement.

[80] Self-evident, *adj.* Evident to one's self and nobody else.

[81] Success, *n.* The one unpardonable sin against one's fellows.

[82] The covers of this book are too far apart. [Attributed.] —See also Christopher Lehmann-Haupt 1

[83] There could only be two worse writers than Stephen Crane, namely two Stephen Cranes.

[84] To the small part of ignorance that we arrange and classify we give the name knowledge.

[85] Urbanity, *n.* The kind of civility that urban observers ascribe to dwellers in all cities but New York.

[86] Where there's a will, there's a won't.

JOSH BILLINGS (1818–1885). *American writer and humorist*

[1] A cheerful old man or old woman is like the sunny side of a woodshed in the last of winter.

[2] A dog is the only thing on this earth that loves you more than he loves himself.

[3] Adam invented love at first sight, one of the greatest labor-saving machines the world ever saw.

[4] Advice is like a doctor's pills: it is often advisable to receive them without taking them.

[5] As a general thing, if you want to get at the truth of a particular argument, hear both sides and believe neither.

[6] As long as we are lucky we attribute it to our smartness; our bad luck we give the gods credit for.

[7] As scarce as truth is, the supply has always been in excess of the demand.

[8] Be sure you are right then go ahead; but in case of doubt, go ahead anyway.

9 Chastity is like an icicle. If it once melts, that's the last of it.

10 Consider the postage stamp: its usefulness consists in the ability to stick to one thing till it gets there.

11 Deference is silent flattery.

12 Don't ever prophesy; for if you prophesy wrong, nobody will forget it; and if you prophesy right, nobody will remember it.

13 Envy is the pain we feel at the excellencies of others.

14 Every man has a perfect right to his opinion, provided it agrees with ours.

15 Everybody in this world wants watching, but none more than ourselves.

16 Flattery is like cologne water, to be smelt of, not swallowed. —See also Adlai E. Stevenson 8

17 God save the fools! And don't let them run out, for if it wasn't for them, wise men couldn't get a living. —See also Mark Twain 81

18 He is a man of small caliber but a good deal of bore.

19 I don't care how much a man talks, if he will only say it in a few words.

20 I have come to the conclusion that what everybody praises wants close watching.

21 I haven't much doubt that man sprang from the monkey, but where did the cussed monkey spring from?

22 I never knew an auctioneer to lie, unless it was absolutely necessary.

23 I often hear affectionate husbands call their wives "My Duck." I wonder if this ain't a sly allusion to their big bills.

24 I think the fools do more hurt in this world than the rascals.

25 If a man is right, he can't be too radical; if he is wrong, he can't be too conservative.

26 If a man was completely virtuous, I doubt whether he would be happy, he would be so lonesome. —See also Mark Twain 17

27 If I was asked which was the best way in these days of temptation to bring up a boy, I should say: bring him up the back way.

28 If I was going to civilize a parcel of heathen on some distant isle, I should debate some time in my mind which to send, dancing masters or missionaries.

29 If you can't get half a loaf, take a whole one—a whole loaf is better than no bread.

30 If you don't know how to lie, cheat and steal, turn your attention to politics and learn.

31 If you would make yourself agreeable wherever you go, listen to the grievances of others but never relate your own.

32 In repenting of sins, men are apt to repent of those they ain't got and overlook those they have.

33 In youth we run into difficulties; in old age, difficulties run into us. [*Everybody's Friend, or: Josh Billings' Encyclopedia and Proverbial Philosophy of Wit and Humor,* 1874.]

34 It ain't because lovers are so sensitive that they quarrel so often; it is because there is so much fun in making up.

35 It ain't often that a man's reputation outlasts his money.

36 It don't require much talent to give good advice, but to follow it does.

37 It is a great deal easier to look upon those who are below us with pity than to look upon those who are above us without envy.

38 It isn't so astonishing, the number of things that I can remember, as the number of things I can remember that aren't so. [As paraphrased by Mark Twain.]

39 It takes a smart man to conceal from others what he don't know.

40 Laziness is a good deal like money; the more a man has of it, the more he seems to want.

41 Man was created a little lower than the angels, and has been getting a little lower ever since.

42 Men judge each other by their success, not by their undertakings; but the Lord judges by the undertakings, not by the success.

43 Misfortune and twins hardly ever come singly.

44 Money is like promises, easier made than kept.

45 Money never made a man disgraceful yet, but men have often made money disgraceful.

46 Money will buy a pretty good dog, but it won't buy the wag of his tail.

47 Most men are like eggs, too full of themselves to hold anything else.

48 Most of the happiness in this world consists in possessing what others can't get.

49 Most people repent of their sins by thanking God they ain't so wicked as their neighbors.

50 Most people when they come to you for advice come to have their own opinions strengthened, not corrected. —See also Ambrose Bierce 18

51 Nature never makes any blunders; when she makes a fool, she means it.

52 "Necessity is the mother of invention," and patent right is the father.

53 Never run into debt, not if you can find anything else to run into.

54 Never work before breakfast; if you have to work before breakfast, get your breakfast first.

55 One half the troubles of this life can be traced to saying "yes" too quick, and not saying "no" soon enough.

56 One half the wisdom of this world consists in not saying anything.

57 Our honesty is as much the effect of interest as principle.

58 People who haven't got anything to say can always find the most to talk about.

59 Pity costs nothing, and ain't worth nothing.

60 Pyrotechnically considered, laughing is the fireworks of the soul.

61 Religion is too often cut as the clothes are, according to the prevailing fashion.

62 Remember the poor—it costs nothing.

63 Rise early, work hard and late, live on what you can't sell, give nothing away, and if you don't die rich and go to the devil, you may sue me for damages.

64 Self-made men are most always apt to be a little too proud of the job. [1874] —See also John Bright

65 Solitude—a good place to visit, but a poor place to stay. —See also Laurence J. Peter 41

66 The best medicine I know for rheumatism is to thank the Lord it ain't the gout.

67 The best reformers the world has ever seen are those who commence on themselves. —See also George Bernard Shaw 42

68 The chains of slavery are none the less galling for being made of gold.

69 The good things that men do can oftener be traced to their vanity than to their virtue.

70 The great art in writing well is to know when to stop.

71 The happiest time in any man's life is when he is in red-hot pursuit of a dollar with a reasonable prospect of overtaking it.

72 "The law of nations": ironclad gunboats.

73 The man who never makes any blunders seldom makes any good hits.

74 The miser and the glutton, two facetious buzzards: one hides his store and the other stores his hide.

75 The more humble a man is before God, the more he will be exalted; the more humble he is before man, the more he will get rode roughshod.

76 The most bitter sarcasm sleeps in silent words.

77 The most that learning can do for us is to teach us how little we know.

78 The mule is half horse and half jackass, and then comes to a full stop, nature discovering her mistake.

79 The only way to please everybody is to make everybody think you are a bigger fool than they are.

80 The quickest way to take the starch out of a man who is always blaming himself is to agree with him.

81 The trouble with most folks ain't so much their ignorance, as knowing so many things that ain't so.

82 The wicked work harder to reach hell than the righteous do to get to heaven. —See also C. C. Colton 14

83 There ain't much fun in physic, but there is a good deal of physic in fun.

84 There are people so addicted to exaggeration that they can't tell the truth without lying.

85 There are two kinds of fools: those who can't change their opinions and those who won't.

86 There is one advantage in being poor: there ain't no danger of mistaking flattery for praise.

87 Time is like money; the less we have of it to spare the further we make it go.

88 To enjoy a good reputation, give publicly, and steal privately.

89 "Vote early and vote often" is the politician's golden rule.

90 We mingle in society not so much to meet others as to escape ourselves.

91 When a fellow gets to going downhill, it does seem as though everything has been greased for the occasion.

92 When a man comes to me for advice, I find out the kind of advice he wants, and I give it to him. —See also Harry S. Truman 8

93 When learning and wisdom hitch up together, they are a bully team.

94 Wisdom that don't make us happier ain't worth plowing for.

95 Young man, sit down and keep still; you will have plenty of chances yet to make a fool of yourself before you die.

LARRY BIRD (1956–). *American basketball player and coach*

1 I hate to lose more than I like to win. —See also Samuel Johnson 33

2 That was God disguised as Michael Jordan. [On the Chicago Bulls' star, soon after he had scored 63 points in a double-overtime playoff loss to Bird's Boston Celtics, 1986.]

LORD BIRKETT (1883–1962). *British lawyer*

I do not object to people looking at their watches when I am speaking. But I strongly object when they start shaking them to make certain they are still going.

OTTO von BISMARCK (1815–1898). *German chancellor*

1 A statesman who attempts to conduct his foreign policies on firm principles is like a man who attempts to walk through a dense forest with a long pole clamped horizontally between his teeth.

2 Every courtesy to an opponent, even to the gallows.

3 Politics is the art of the possible, the attainable—the art of the next best.

4 Universal suffrage is the government of a house by its nursery.

5 When you say you agree to a thing on principle, you mean that you have not the slightest intention of carrying it out in practice.

6 When you want to fool the world, tell the truth.

EUBIE BLAKE (1883–1983). *American jazz musician and composer*

1 "At what age does the sex drive end?" You'll have to ask somebody older than me. [At age 97.]

2 If I'd known I was gonna live this long, I'd have taken better care of myself. [On his 100th birthday.]

WILLIAM BLAKE (1757–1827). *English poet and artist*

1 A petty sneaking knave I knew— / O! Mr. Cr—, how do ye do?

2 He has observed the Golden Rule, / Till he's become the Golden Fool.

3 If the sun and moon should doubt, / They'd immediately go out.

4 Priests in black gowns were walking their rounds, / And binding with briars my joys and desires.

5 Prisons are built with stones of law, brothels with bricks of religion.

6 Prudence is a rich, ugly old maid courted by incapacity.

7 The man who never alters his opinion is like standing water and breeds reptiles of the mind.

8 The road of excess leads to the palace of wisdom.

9 Why of the sheep do you not learn peace? / Because I don't want you to shear my fleece.

LADY BLESSINGTON (Marguerite Gardiner, 1789–1847). *Irish writer*

1 Despotism subjects a nation to one tyrant; democracy, to many.

2 Love and enthusiasm are always ridiculous, when not reciprocated by their objects.

3 People are always willing to follow advice when it accords with their own wishes.

4 Society punishes not the vices of its members, but their detection.

5 The most certain mode of making people content with us is to make them content with themselves. —See also Lord Chesterfield 15; Samuel Johnson 58

6 The vices of the rich and great are mistaken for errors; and those of the poor and lowly, for crimes.

7 Virtue has more admirers than followers.

ALAN S. BLINDER (1945–). *American economist*

I have a general rule: Whenever something becomes worth more than the whole state of California, sell it. [On the soaring prices of Internet stocks, 1999.]

HERBERT "HERBLOCK" BLOCK (1909–). *American cartoonist*

1 If it's good, they'll stop making it.

2 So much for the international news—the facts will be along later. [Television broadcaster, cartoon caption, 1986.]

HUMPHREY BOGART (1899–1957). *American actor*

1 Money has only one use—to give one independence from his enemies.

2 They'll nail anyone who ever scratched his ass during the National Anthem. [Referring to members of the House Committee on Un-American Activities, 1947.]

3 "What in heaven's name brought you to Casablanca?" [Claude Rains] "My health. I came to Casablanca for the waters." [Bogart] "What waters? We're in the desert." [Rains] "I was misinformed." [Bogart, in the 1942 film *Casablanca*.]

4 "You despise me, don't you?" [Peter Lorre] Well, if I gave it any thought, I would. [In *Casablanca*.]

JOHN B. BOGART (1848–1921). *American journalist*

When a dog bites a man, that is not news because it happens so often. But if a man bites a dog, that is news.

NIELS BOHR (1885–1962). *Danish nuclear physicist*

1 An expert is a man who has made all the mistakes, which can be made, in a very narrow field.

2 Prediction is very difficult, especially about the future. [Attributed.]

DEREK BOK (1930–). *American educator and university president*

If you think education is expensive—try ignorance.

ERMA BOMBECK (1927–1996). *American writer and humorist*

1 Guilt: the gift that keeps on giving.

2 Housekeeping makes you about as exciting as your food blender. The kids come in, look you in the eye, and ask if anybody's home.

3 I had no intention of giving her my vital statistics. "Let me put it this way, according to my girth, I should be a ninety-foot redwood."

4   I was too old for a paper route, too young for Social Security and too tired
    for an affair. [Explaining why she started a humor column.]
5   I've been on a constant diet for the last two decades. I've lost a total of 789
    pounds. By all accounts, I should be hanging from a charm bracelet.
6   I've seen kids ride bicycles, run, play ball, set up a camp, swing, fight a war,
    swim and race for eight hours—yet have to be driven to the garbage can.
7   If a man watches three football games in a row, he should be declared
    legally dead.
8   *If Life Is a Bowl of Cherries, What Am I Doing in the Pits?* [Book title, 1971.]
9   In general, my children refused to eat anything that hadn't danced on TV.
10 Know the difference between success and fame. Success is Mother Teresa.
    Fame is Madonna.
11 My mother phones daily to ask, "Did you just try to reach me?" When I
    reply, "No," she adds, "So, if you're not too busy, call me while I'm still
    alive," and hangs up.
12 Never go to a doctor whose office plants have died.
13 Never lend your car to anyone to whom you have given birth.
14 The bad times I can handle. It's the good times that drive me crazy. When
    is the other shoe going to drop?
15 The only reason I would take up jogging is so that I could hear heavy
    breathing again.
16 There is nothing sadder in this world than to awake Christmas morning and
    not be a child.
17 Those magazine dieting stories always have the testimonial of a woman
    who wore a dress that could slipcover New Jersey in one photo and thirty
    days later looked like a well-dressed thermometer.

DANIEL J. BOORSTIN (1914–). *American historian*

1   A sign of celebrity is often that his name is worth more than his services.
2   Education is learning what you didn't even know you didn't know.
3   God is the Celebrity-Author of the World's Best Seller. We have made God
    into the biggest celebrity of all, to contain our own emptiness.
4   Nothing is real unless it happens on television.
5   The celebrity is a person who is known for his well-knownness.
6   The great obstacle to knowledge is the illusion of knowledge.
7   "Truth" has been displaced by "believability" as the test of the statements
    which dominate our lives. Almost anything can be made to seem true —
    especially if we wish to believe it.
8   Two centuries ago when a great man appeared, people looked for God's
    purpose in him. Today we look for his press agent.
9   When the gods wish to punish us, they make us believe our own
    advertising.

JAMES H. BOREN (1925–). *American business executive*

1   Einstein's theory of relativity, as practiced by congressmen, simply means
    getting members of your family on the payroll.

2 I got the bill for my surgery. Now I know what those doctors were wearing masks for.

3 Nothing is impossible until it is sent to a committee.

4 (1) When in charge, ponder. (2) When in trouble, delegate. (3) When in doubt, mumble. ["Boren's Guidelines" for bureaucrats.]

JOHN COLLINS BOSSIDY (1860–1928). *American physician*
This good old Boston / The home of the bean and the cod, / Where the Lowells talk to the Cabots / And the Cabots talk only to God.

DAVID BOWIE (1947–). *English rock singer*
You must understand that this is not a woman's dress I'm wearing. It's a man's dress. [Bowie is well-known for his sensational stage costumes.]

BEN BRADLEE (1921–). *American newspaper editor*
1 I'm lucky, but I knew what to do with luck when it hit me.

2 Oh, Kay, I'd give my left one for that. [Responding to publisher Katharine Graham's offer of the editorship of *The Washington Post*.]

RICHARD BRANSON (1950–). *English entrepreneur*
I believe in benevolent dictatorships, provided I am the dictator.

WERNHER von BRAUN (1912–1977). *German-born American rocket scientist*
1 Basic research is what I'm doing when I don't know what I'm doing.

2 There is just one thing I can promise you about the outer space program: your tax dollar will go farther.

BERTOLT BRECHT (1898–1956). *German playwright*
1 Eats first, morals after.

2 The man who laughs simply has not heard the terrible news.

3 The wickedness of the world is so great you have to run your legs off to avoid having them stolen from under you.

4 What is robbing a bank compared with founding a bank?

5 Whenever there are tremendous virtues, it's a sure sign something's wrong.

GERALD BRENAN (1894–1987). *British writer*
1 A bad memory is the mother of invention.

2 Everyone is a bore to someone. That is unimportant. The thing to avoid is being a bore to oneself.

3 O death, where is thy jolly old sting? As Bertie Wooster said when his Aunt Agatha died leaving him a cool fifty thousand. —See also Jerome K. Jerome 2

4 Old age takes away from us what we have inherited and gives us what we have earned.

5 The more we feel sorry for ourselves, the less sorry others will feel for us. People don't waste their small store of sympathy on those who can provide it so richly for themselves.

6 Those who have some means think that the most important thing in the world is love. The poor know that it is money.

JIMMY BRESLIN (1931–). *American journalist*
1 As a reporter I like to keep in the middle and be disliked by both sides.
2 The office of president is such a bastardized thing, half royalty and half democracy, that nobody knows whether to genuflect or spit.
3 When you stop drinking, you have to deal with this marvelous personality that started you drinking in the first place.
4 Yesterday makes me tired.

RAYMOND BRET-KOCH (20th century). *French artist*
It's a beautiful, well-constructed façade, but without central heating. [On Clare Boothe Luce.]

FANNY BRICE (1891–1951). *American comedienne*
1 Having a baby is like pushing a piano through a transom.
2 He just wanted to get that knife into me. He'd cut you if you had dandruff. [Referring to a surgeon.]
3 I never liked the men I loved, and never loved the men I liked.

JOHN BRIGHT (1811–1889). *English member of Parliament*
He is a self-made man, and worships his creator. [On Benjamin Disraeli, 1868.] —See also Josh Billings 64

DAVID BRINKLEY (1920–). *American broadcast journalist*
1 *Everyone Is Entitled to My Opinion.* [Book title his daughter's friend suggested, 1996.]
2 If you turn on your set and see nothing is happening, do not call a serviceman: you have tuned in the U.S. Senate.

VERA BRITTAIN (1893–1970). *English writer*
I know one husband and wife who, whatever the official reasons given to the court for the breakup of their marriage, were really divorced because the husband believed that nobody ought to read while he was talking and the wife believed that nobody ought to talk while she was reading.

DAVID S. BRODER (1929–). *American journalist*
1 Anybody that wants the presidency so much that he'll spend two years organizing and campaigning for it is not to be trusted with the office.
2 Indignation is something skillful politicians can switch on and off like a light bulb—a useful tool in debates and negotiations.

JOSEPH BRODSKY (1940–1996). *Russian-born American poet*
1 A big step for me, and small step for mankind. [Comment on hearing that he had been awarded the Nobel Prize for Literature in 1987.]
2 Bad literature is a form of treason.
3 Life is a battle not between bad and good, but between bad and worse.
4 Snobbery? It's only a form of despair.

MEL BROOKS (1926–). *American writer, actor, and film director*
1 That's it, baby! When you got it, flaunt it! [*The Producers,* 1968.] —See also Malcolm S. Forbes 11
2 Humor is just another defense against the universe.

3 Tragedy is if I cut my finger. Comedy is if you walk into an open sewer and die.

4 "You've been accused of vulgarity." Bullshit! [1975 *Playboy* interview.]

RICHARD BROTHERS (1757–1824). *British religious leader*

I and the world happened to have a slight difference of opinion; the world said I was mad, and I said the world was mad. I was outvoted, and here I am. [When asked to explain his imprisonment in Bedlam, London's insane asylum.]

LORD BROUGHAM (Henry Peter Brougham, 1778–1868). *British jurist and member of Parliament*

A lawyer is a learned gentleman who rescues your estate from your enemies and keeps it for himself.

HEYWOOD BROUN (1888–1939). *American journalist and humorist*

1 A liberal is a man who leaves the room when the fight starts.

2 Everybody favors free speech in the slack moments when no axes are being ground.

3 If anyone corrects your pronunciation of a word in a public place, you have every right to punch him in the nose.

4 Repartee is what you wish you'd said.

5 They told me that the fish were cold-blooded and felt no pain. But they were not fish who told me.

CHARLES H. BROWER (1901–1984). *American advertising executive*

There is no such thing as "soft sell" and "hard sell." There is only "smart sell" and "stupid sell."

JOHN MASON BROWN (1900–1969). *American drama critic*

1 Charm is a glow within a woman that casts a most becoming light on others.

2 Tallulah Bankhead barged down the Nile last night as Cleopatra—and sank. [Referring to her performance in a play.]

RITA MAE BROWN (1944–). *American writer and poet*

1 Familiarity breeds consent.

2 If the world were a logical place, men would ride side-saddle.

3 In America, the word revolution is used to sell pantyhose.

4 Love is the wild card of existence.

5 The reward for conformity is that everyone likes you except yourself.

6 Where there is no faith, devils are a necessity.

LENNY BRUCE (1925–1966). *American comedian*

1 Comedy = Tragedy + Distance.

2 Every day people are straying away from the church and going back to God.

3 In the Halls of Justice the only justice is in the halls.

4 My mother-in-law broke up my marriage. One day my wife came home early and found us in bed together.

5 Now the problem I had in understanding the law was because of the language of the law. Instead of taking each word and finding out the case that the word related to, once in a while I got lazy and I would apply common sense. And then I got really screwed up.

6 People should be taught what is, not what should be. All my humor is based on destruction and despair. If the whole world were tranquil, without disease and violence, I'd be standing in the bread line—right back of J. Edgar Hoover.

7 The whole motivation for any performer: "Look at me, Ma!"

8 We're all hustlers; we're all as honest as we can afford to be.

JOHN BUCHAN (1875–1940). *Scottish writer*

1 An atheist is a man who has no invisible means of support.

2 "Back to Glasgow to do some work for the cause," I said lightly. "Just so," he said, with a grin. "It's a great life if you don't weaken." [1919]

3 Modern life is the silent compact of comfortable folk to keep up pretenses.

JAMES BUCHANAN (1791–1868). *American president*

1 If you are as happy, my dear sir, on entering this house as I am in leaving it and returning home, you are the happiest man in this country. [Remark to his successor, Abraham Lincoln, 1861.]

2 We have met the enemy and we are theirs. [Letter to his wife, after his party had been defeated in an election.]

PAT BUCHANAN (1938–). *American presidential assistant, broadcast journalist, and presidential candidate*

1 Bill Clinton's foreign policy experience stems mainly from having breakfast at the International House of Pancakes.

2 "If you were elected president in 2000, what would your first official act be?" [Reporter] Probably turn to Bill Clinton and read him his Miranda rights. [Buchanan had just thrown his hat into the presidential ring.]

ART BUCHWALD (1925–). *American journalist and humorist*

1 As the economy gets better, everything else gets worse.

2 Have you ever seen a candidate talking to a rich person on television?

3 I always wanted to get into politics, but I was never light enough to make the team. [Referring to his portliness.]

4 I worship the quicksand he walks in. [On Richard M. Nixon.]

5 In this country, when you attack the Establishment, they don't put you in jail or a mental institution. They do something worse. They make you a member of the Establishment.

6 This is not an easy time for humorists because the government is far funnier than we are. —See also Will Rogers 41

WILLIAM F. BUCKLEY, JR. (1925–). *American writer and publisher*

1 Following Mrs. Roosevelt in search of irrationality is like following a burning fuse in search of an explosive; one never has to wait very long. [On Eleanor Roosevelt, 1959.]

2 He is a man of his most recent word. [On Lyndon B. Johnson.]

3 History selects its heroes and its villains, and few of us resist participation either at the parade or at the guillotine.

4 I'd rather entrust the government of the United States to the first four hundred people listed in the Boston telephone directory than to the faculty of Harvard University.

5 Idealism is fine, but as it approaches reality the cost becomes prohibitive.
   —See also John Galsworthy

6 Note to all writers, everywhere: one cannot be a Communist and a philosopher, if you will permit an ipsedixitism.

7 One way to cut down on the number of favorite sons would be to decree that the one with the fewest votes at the end of the first ballot would be publicly executed. [On national political conventions.]

8 Professor Galbraith is horrified by the number of Americans who have bought cars with tail fins on them, and I am horrified by the number of Americans who take seriously the proposals of Mr. Galbraith. [*Up from Liberalism,* 1959.]

9 The Beatles are not merely awful. They are so unbelievably horrible, so appallingly unmusical, so dogmatically insensitive to the magic of the art, that they qualify as crowned heads of antimusic. [1964]

10 The editors of *National Review* regretfully announce that their patience with President Lyndon B. Johnson is exhausted. [Two weeks into Johnson's presidency, 1963.]

11 The mistake is often made of assuming that the audience of Jack Paar is as loose-minded as he is.

12 We are all for principles, and the more deep-seated the better; though to be sure there are those who believe that any politician who is about to come down with an incipient case of principle should lie down until he gets over it.

WARREN BUFFETT (1930–). *American investment manager*
Rule No. 1: Never lose money. Rule No. 2: Never forget Rule No. 1.

CHARLES BUKOWSKI (1920–1994). *German-born American writer and poet*

1 Almost everybody is born a genius and buried an idiot.

2 An intellectual is a man who says a simple thing in a difficult way; an artist is a man who says a difficult thing in a simple way.

3 Of course, it's possible to love a human being—if you don't know them too well.

4 *Play the Piano Drunk Like a Percussion Instrument Until the Fingers Begin to Bleed a Bit.* [Book title, 1979.]

5 Sexual intercourse is kicking death in the ass while singing.

6 Show me a man who lives alone and has a perpetually clean kitchen, and 8 times out of 9 I'll show you a man with detestable spiritual qualities.

7 The difference between a Democracy and a Dictatorship is that in a Democracy you vote first and take orders later; in a Dictatorship you don't have to waste your time voting.

8 There's always somebody about to ruin your day, if not your life.

9 What's the difference between a guy in the big house and the average guy you pass in the street? The guy in the big house is a Loser who tried.

EDWARD GEORGE BULWER-LYTTON (1803–1873). *English writer and member of Parliament*

1 If you wish to be loved, show more of your faults than your virtues.

2 In other countries poverty is a misfortune—with us it is a crime.

3 It is difficult to say who cause the most mischief: enemies with the worst intentions or friends with the best.

4 Men never forgive those in whom there is nothing to pardon.

LUIS BUÑUEL (1900–1983). *French film director*
Thanks to God, I'm still an atheist.

JACOB BURCKHARDT (1818–1897). *Swiss historian*
Alongside all swindlers, the state now stands as swindler-in-chief.

ANTHONY BURGESS (1917–1994). *English writer*
He said it was artificial respiration, but now I find I am to have his child.

GEORGE BURNS (1896–1996). *American comedian and radio personality*

1 Do you know what it means to come home at night to a woman who'll give you a little love, a little affection, a little tenderness? It means you're in the wrong house, that's what it means.

2 Happiness is having a large, loving, caring, close-knit family in another city.

3 It's nice to be here. When you're ninety-nine years old, it's nice to be anyplace. [Remark to a nightclub audience.]

4 Nobody ever dominated a theater like Al Jolson. And nobody was ever as quick to admit it as he was, either.

5 Old-timers don't have to come in first. They get credit for just showing up. [1991]

6 The most important thing in acting is honesty: if you can fake that, you've got it made. [Attributed.]

7 Too bad that all the people who know how to run the country are busy driving taxicabs and cutting hair. [Attributed.] —See also Kin Hubbard 32

8 When Jack Benny has a party, you not only bring your own scotch, you bring your own rocks. —See also Jack Benny 3

WILLIAM S. BURROUGHS (1914–1997). *American writer*

1 A paranoid is a man who knows a little of what's going on.

2 In my writing I am acting as a map-maker, an explorer of psychic areas—a cosmonaut of inner space.

3 1. Never give anything away for nothing. 2. Never give more than you have to (always catch the buyer hungry and always make him wait). 3. Always take back everything if you possibly can. [On drug pushing.]

RICHARD BURTON (1925–1984). *Welsh actor*
Be as vicious about me as you please. You will only do me justice. [Remark to a magazine interviewer.]

ROBERT BURTON (1577–1640). *English clergyman and writer*

1 One was never married, and that's his hell; another is, and that's his plague.

2 They are proud in humility; proud in that they are not proud.

BARBARA BUSH (1925–). *American first lady*

Who knows, somewhere out there in the audience may even be someone who will one day follow in my footsteps and preside over the White House as the president's spouse. I wish him well. [Commencement address, 1990.]

GEORGE BUSH (1924–). *American president*

1 I do not like broccoli, and I haven't liked it since I was a little kid. I am President of the United States, and I am not going to eat it anymore.

2 Now is no time to speculate or hypothecate, but rather a time for action, or at least not a time to rule it out, though not necessarily a time to rule it in, either. [Remark during the Iraq-Kuwait crisis, 1990.]

3 People say I'm indecisive, but I don't know about that.

4 What's wrong with being a boring kind of guy?

5 Why don't you just roll me under the table and let me sleep it off? [Remark to the Japanese prime minister after fainting at a state dinner in Tokyo, 1992.]

SAMUEL BUTLER (1835–1902). *English writer*

1 All philosophies, if you ride them home, are nonsense; but some are greater nonsense than others.

2 All progress is based upon a universal innate desire on the part of every organism to live beyond its income.

3 An honest God's the noblest work of man.

4 Any fool can tell the truth, but it requires a man of some sense to know how to lie well.

5 Conscience is thoroughly well-bred and soon leaves off talking to those who do not wish to hear it.

6 Genius is a supreme capacity for saving other people from having to take pains.

7 God cannot alter the past, but historians can.

8 Greater luck hath no man than this, that he lay down his wife at the right moment.

9 He is considered the most graceful speaker who can say nothing in the most words. —See also Abraham Lincoln 8

10 I do not mind lying, but I hate inaccuracy.

11 I read once of a man who was cured of a dangerous illness by eating his doctor's prescription which he understood was the medicine itself.

12 In law, nothing is certain but the expense.

13 Invention is not infrequently the mother of necessity.

14 It has been said that the love of money is the root of all evil. The want of money is so quite as truly.

15 It is the function of vice to keep virtue within reasonable bounds.

16 It was very good of God to let Thomas Carlyle and Mrs. Carlyle marry one another and so make only two people miserable instead of four.

17 Life is like playing a violin solo in public and learning the instrument as one goes on.

¹⁸ Life is the art of drawing sufficient conclusions from insufficient premises.

¹⁹ Man is God's highest present development. He is the latest thing in God.

²⁰ Morality is the custom of one's country and the current feeling of one's peers. Cannibalism is moral in a cannibal country.

²¹ Nothing is potent against love save only impotence.

²² O Lord, keep us this day from being found out!

²³ People in general are equally horrified at hearing the Christian religion doubted, and at seeing it practiced.

²⁴ The advantage of doing one's praising for oneself is that one can lay it on so thick and exactly in the right places.

²⁵ The best liar is he who makes the smallest amount of lying go the longest way.

²⁶ The healthy stomach is nothing if not conservative. Few radicals have good digestions.

²⁷ The oldest books are only just out to those who have not read them.

²⁸ The tendency of modern science is to reduce proof to absurdity by continually reducing absurdity to proof.

²⁹ The three most important things a man has are, briefly, his private parts, his money, and his religious opinions.

³⁰ There are two great rules of life, the one general and the other particular. The first is that everyone can, in the end, get what he wants if he only tries. This is the general rule. The particular rule is that every individual is more or less an exception to the general rule.

³¹ There should be some schools called deformatories to which people are sent if they are too good to be practical.

³² There's many a good tune played on an old fiddle.

³³ This age will serve to make a pretty good farce for the next.

³⁴ 'Tis better to have loved and lost than never to have lost at all.

³⁵ To live is like to love—all reason is against it, and all healthy instinct for it.

³⁶ We pay a person the compliment of acknowledging his superiority whenever we lie to him.

³⁷ When people get it into their heads that they are being specially favored by the Almighty, they had better as a general rule mind their p's and q's.

LORD BYRON (George Gordon Byron, 1788–1824). *English poet*

¹ A little still she strove, and much repented, / And whispering "I will ne'er consent"—consented.

² After all, what is a lie? 'Tis but the truth in masquerade.

³ As he knew not what to say, he swore.

⁴ Christians have burnt each other, quite persuaded / That all the Apostles would have done as they did.

⁵ He was the mildest mannered man / That ever scuttled ship or cut a throat.

⁶ I am always more religious upon a sunshiny day.

⁷ I deny nothing but doubt everything.

⁸ I have been more ravished myself than anybody since the Trojan war. [Letter, 1819.]

9 I have no consistency, except in politics; and that probably arises from my indifference on the subject altogether.

10 I love wisdom more than wisdom loves me.

11 I think people can never have *enough* of religion, if they are to have any.

12 In general I do not draw well with literary men—not that I dislike them but—I never know what to say to them after I have praised their last publication.

13 Let us have wine and women, mirth and laughter, / Sermons and soda water the day after.

14 "Mr. Southey is indeed a wonderful poet. He will be read when Homer and Virgil are forgotten." [Richard Porson] But not till then.

15 One of the pleasures of reading old letters is the knowledge that they need no answer.

16 Ready money *is* Aladdin's lamp.

17 Society is now one polished horde, / Formed of two mighty tribes, the Bores and Bored.

18 The cardinal is at his wit's end—it is true that he had not far to go.

19 The English winter—ending in July, / To recommence in August.

20 The "good old times"—all times when old are good.

21 The poem will please if it is lively—if it is stupid it will fail—but I will have none of your damned cutting and slashing. [Letter to his publisher, John Murray, 1819.]

22 There is a tide in the affairs of women, / Which, taken at the flood, leads— God knows where.

23 There is, in fact, no law or government at all in Italy; and it is wonderful how well things go on without them.

24 There's nought, no doubt, so much the spirit calms / As rum and true religion.

25 'Tis strange—but true; for truth is always strange; / Stranger than fiction: if it could be told. —See also Mark Twain 132, 133

JAMES CAAN (1939–). *American actor*
Sometimes it seems like that is the choice—either kick ass or kiss ass.

JAMES BRANCH CABELL (1878–1959). *American writer*
1 People marry for a variety of reasons, and with varying results; but to marry for love is to invite inevitable tragedy.
2 The optimist proclaims we live in the best of all possible worlds; and the pessimist fears this is true.

HERB CAEN (1916–1997). *American journalist*
1 A strange and touching scene at Cypress Lawn Monday. A young man killed in a motorcycle accident was buried along with the Harley-Davidson he was riding at the time of the crash. "It was his whole life," sobs his mother.
2 Gossip? It's the mother's milk of journalism. —See also Jim Hightower 3; Jesse Unruh
3 I regret that I have but one life to live in San Francisco. [Where his column had appeared regularly between 1938 and 1996.]
4 In answer to queries, I'm pleased to report that historic John's Grill on Ellis, reopened after a disastrous fire, is unchanged from the original. The food is no worse than it ever was.
5 Isn't it nice that people who prefer Los Angeles to San Francisco live there?
6 Never trust a man who parts his name on the side. [Referring to J. Edgar Hoover.]
7 One day if I do go to heaven, I'm going to do what every San Franciscan does who goes to heaven: he looks around and says, "It ain't bad, but it ain't San Francisco." [Remarks at the celebration of Herb Caen Day in San Francisco, 14 June 1996.]
8 The trouble with Oakland is that when you get there it's there! —See also Gertrude Stein 7
9 There must be another way, if only because there has to be.

VICTOR L. CAHN (1948–). *American writer and humorist*
1 Admire, *v.* Resent.
2 Bore, *n.* One who fails to regard us as interesting.
3 Earth, *n.* A piece of lint in the navel of the universe.
4 Egotist, *n.* A man who believes a woman virtuous because she refuses to go to bed with him.
5 Frankly speaking, *adv.* Not frankly speaking.
6 Genuine, *adj.* Not totally fraudulent.
7 Have, *v.* To no longer desire.
8 Innocent, *adj.* Undiscovered.
9 Laissez-faire, *n.* An economic doctrine which states that no act can be evil if it earns a profit.
10 Mercy, *n.* Kindness offered to those who pose no immediate threat.
11 Never, *adv.* Not yet, anyway.

12 Nominate, *v.* To expose to public ridicule.

13 Paper-shredder, *n.* The ultimate weapon for ensuring that secret government documents will not fall into the right hands.

14 Radical, *n.* A fascist out of power.

15 Trust, *v.* To lay oneself open to deception.

16 Unafraid, *adj.* Unaware.

17 Virtuous, *adj.* Lacking opportunity to be otherwise.

MICHAEL CAINE (1933–). *English actor*

1 Never be cheerful on a job if you're doing a fiddle. [Bill Naughton's line spoken by Caine in the 1966 film *Alfie*.]

2 The poor speak very fast, with quick movements, to attract attention. The rich move slowly and they speak slowly; they don't need to get your attention because they've already got it.

JOHN C. CALHOUN (1782–1850). *South Carolina senator and U.S. vice president*

We see slavery now in its true light, and regard it as the most safe and stable basis for free institutions in the world. [1838]

JOSEPH A. CALIFANO, JR. (1931–). *American lawyer, presidential assistant, and secretary of health, education and welfare*

Were Moses to go up Mt. Sinai today, the two tablets he'd bring down with him would be aspirin and Prozac. [1995]

SIMON CAMERON (1799–1889). *Pennsylvania senator and secretary of war*

An honest politician is one who when he is bought will stay bought.

MRS. PATRICK CAMPBELL (1865–1940). *English actress*

1 It doesn't matter what you do in the bedroom as long as you don't do it in the street and frighten the horses. [When told of a homosexual affair between two actors.]

2 Laugh and the world laughs with you, snore and you sleep alone.

ALBERT CAMUS (1913–1960). *French writer*

1 An intellectual is someone whose mind watches itself.

2 As I usually do when I want to get rid of someone whose conversation bores me, I pretended to agree.

3 My sensuality was so real that even for a ten-minute adventure I'd have disowned father and mother. I had principles, to be sure, such as that the wife of a friend is sacred. But I simply ceased quite sincerely, a few days before, to feel any friendship for the husband.

4 Some people talk in their sleep. Lecturers talk while other people sleep.

ELIAS CANETTI (1905–1995). *Bulgarian-born Austrian philosopher*

1 A miscalculation? The world?

2 All the pessimists in world history together are nothing against reality.

3 At the wishes of many people, he decided to write the same thing yet again.

4 Horror at the sight of death turns into satisfaction that it is someone else who is dead.

5 In love, assurances are practically an announcement of their opposite.

6 Newspapers help you forget the previous day.

7 The hopeful things in every system: whatever is left out of it.

8 The paranoiac is the exact image of the ruler. The only difference between them lies is their position in the world.

EDDIE CANTOR (1892–1964). *American comedian and radio personality*
It took me twenty years to become an overnight success. [Attributed.]

AL CAPONE (1899–1947). *American gangster*

1 Anyone who sleeps in the trunk of a car deserves to be shot.

2 Everybody calls me a racketeer. I call myself a businessman.

3 When I sell liquor, it's called bootlegging; when my patrons serve it on silver trays on Lake Shore Drive, it's called hospitality.

4 You can get a lot more done with a kind word and a gun, than with a kind word alone. [Attributed.]

TRUMAN CAPOTE (1924–1984). *American writer*

1 Failure is the condiment that gives success its flavor.

2 I don't care what anybody says about me as long as it isn't true.

3 I remember things the way they should have been.

4 It's a scientific fact that if you stay in California, you lose one point of IQ every year.

5 Mrs. P had only one fault; she was perfect. Otherwise, she was perfect.

6 None of the Beat writers have anything interesting to say, and none of them can write, not even Mr. Kerouac. What they do isn't writing at all—it's typing. [1959]

7 Venice is like eating an entire box of chocolate liqueurs at one go.

AL CAPP (1909–1979). *American cartoonist*
A product of the untalented, sold by the unprincipled to the utterly bewildered. [On abstract art.]

GEORGE CARLIN (1937–). *American comedian*

1 A house is a place where you keep your stuff while you go out to get more stuff.

2 Do infants enjoy infancy as much as adults enjoy adultery?

3 Every day I beat my own previous record for number of consecutive days I've stayed alive.

4 Everyone driving slower than you is an idiot. Everyone driving faster than you is a maniac.

5 How is it possible to have a civil war?

6 I got a lot of ideas. Trouble is, most of them suck.

7 I went to a bookstore and asked the saleswoman, "Where's the self-help section?" She said if she told me, it would defeat the purpose.

8 If God dropped acid, would he see people?

9 If you try to fail and succeed, which have you done?

10 In labor news, longshoremen walked off the piers today; rescue operations are continuing.

11 Most people work just hard enough not to get fired and get paid just enough money not to quit. [*Brain Droppings*, 1997.]

12 Tonight's forecast: dark. Continuing dark throughout the night and turning widely scattered light in the morning.

13 When you open a bag of cotton balls, is the top one meant to be thrown away?

JANE CARLYLE (1801–1866). *Scottish poet*

1 I am not at all the sort of person you and I took me for. [Letter to her husband, Thomas, 1822.]

2 Not a hundredth part of the thoughts in my head have ever been or ever will be spoken or written—as long as I keep my senses, at least.

THOMAS CARLYLE (1795–1881). *English historian*

1 Charles Lamb I sincerely believe to be in some considerable degree insane. A more pitiful, rickety, gasping, staggering, stammering Tomfool I do not know. Poor Lamb! Poor England, when such a despicable abortion is named genius!

2 France was long a despotism tempered by epigrams.

3 I have no patience whatever with these gorilla damnifications of humanity. [Referring to Charles Darwin's evolutionary theories.]

4 If Jesus Christ were to come today, people would not even crucify him. They would ask him to dinner, and hear what he had to say, and make fun of it.

5 Man has set man against man, washed against unwashed.

6 The difference between Orthodoxy or My-doxy and Heterodoxy or Thy-doxy.

7 The idea of a pigheaded soldier who will obey orders, and fire on his own father at the command of his officer, is a great comfort to the aristocratic mind.

8 There is a great discovery still to be made in literature, that of paying literary men by the quantity they do not write.

DALE CARNEGIE (1888–1955). *American writer and speaker*

Any fool can criticize, condemn, and complain—and most fools do.

"UNCLE DON" CARNEY (20th century). *American radio personality*

There, I guess that will hold the little bastards for another night! [Carney's career hosting a nationally broadcast children's radio program in the 1930s ended abruptly with those words when, thinking the microphone was dead, he signed off to his engineer.]

JON CARROLL (1943–). *American journalist*

1 Marriage is a lot like life, only with more fun parts. The only secret is showing up every day with an open heart. [1999]

2 The difference between constructive criticism and destructive criticism is simple: any criticism you give is constructive; any criticism you get is destructive.

LEWIS CARROLL (Charles Lutwidge Dodgson, 1832–1898). *English writer*

1 "Be what you would seem to be"—or, if you'd like it put more simply—"Never imagine yourself not to be otherwise than what it might appear to others that what you were or might have been was not otherwise than

what you had been would have appeared to them to be otherwise." [*Alice in Wonderland,* 1865.]

2   "Contrariwise," continued Tweedledee, "if it was so, it might be; and if it were so, it would be: but as it isn't, it ain't. That's logic."

3   "If everybody minded their own business," the Duchess said, in a hoarse growl, "the world would go round a great deal faster than it does."

4   It's a poor sort of memory that only works backwards.

5   "Let the jury consider their verdict," the King said, for about the twentieth time that day. "No, no!" said the Queen. "Sentence first—verdict afterwards."

6   Now, here, it takes all the running you can do, to keep in the same place. If you want to get somewhere else, you must run at least twice as fast as that!

7   "One can't believe impossible things." "I daresay you haven't had much practice," said the Queen. "When I was your age, I always did it for half an hour a day. Why, sometimes I've believed as many as six impossible things before breakfast."

8   "Reeling and Writhing, of course, to begin with," the Mock Turtle replied to the question of what was taught in school, "and then the different branches of Arithmetic—Ambition, Distraction, Uglification, and Derision."

9   Take care of the sense, and the sounds will take care of themselves.

10 "That's the reason they're called lessons," the Gryphon remarked: "because they lessen from day to day."

11 The rule is, jam tomorrow and jam yesterday—but never jam today.

12 'Twas brillig, and the slithy toves / Did gyre and gimble in the wabe; / All mimsy were the borogoves, / And the mome raths outgrabe. [An example of Carroll's "jabberwocky," or invented nonsense words.] —See also William Shakespeare 9

13 What I tell you three times is true.

14 What's the French for fiddle-de-dee?

15 "When *I* use a word," Humpty Dumpty said, in rather a scornful tone, "it means just what I choose it to mean—neither more nor less." "The question is," said Alice, "whether you *can* make words mean so many different things." "The question is," said Humpty Dumpty, "which is to be master—that's all."

16 "Where shall I begin, please your Majesty?" he asked. "Begin at the beginning," the King said, gravely, "and go till you come to the end; then stop."

EDWARD CARSON (1854–1935). *Anglo-Irish jurist and First Lord of the Admiralty*

My only great qualification for being put at the head of the Navy is that I am very much at sea.

JACK CARSON (1910–1963). *American actor*

A fan club is a group of people who tell an actor he is not alone in the way he feels about himself.

JOHNNY CARSON (1925–). *American television talk-show host*
1 He couldn't ad-lib a fart after a baked-bean dinner. [Attributed.]
2 I know a man who gave up smoking, drinking, sex, and rich food. He was healthy right up to the time he killed himself.
3 I told my wife that there was a chance that radiation might hurt my reproductive organs, but she said in her opinion it's a small price to pay.

JIMMY CARTER (1924–). *American president*
1 God answers all our prayers. Sometimes the answer is yes. Sometimes the answer is no. Sometimes the answer is, you've to got to be kidding!
2 I've looked on a lot of women with lust. I've committed adultery in my heart many times. This is something that God recognizes I will do—and I have done it—and God forgives me for it. [1976 *Playboy* interview.]
3 If I'm elected, at the end of four years or eight years I hope people will say, "You know, Jimmy Carter made a lot of mistakes, but he never told me a lie." [1976]
4 Iran under the great leadership of the shah is an island of stability in one of the most troubled areas of the world. This is a great tribute to you, your majesty, and to your leadership and to the respect, admiration, and love which your people give to you. [Toasting the shah a year before he was deposed, Tehran, 1977.]
5 I've never won an argument with her; and the only times I thought I had I found out the argument wasn't over yet. [Referring to his wife, Rosalynn.]
6 The tobacco industry, the tobacco farmers, the federal government, all citizens ought to have an accurate and enlightened education program and research program to make the smoking of tobacco even more safe than it is today. [Speech in North Carolina, 1978.]

JAMES CARVILLE (1944–). *American political consultant*
1 He's about a half a quart low. [On Ross Perot.]
2 I used to think that if there was reincarnation, I wanted to come back as the President or the Pope or as a .400 baseball hitter. But now I would like to come back as the bond market. You can intimidate everybody.
3 If I did anything that stupid, I'd lie about it, too. [Referring to Bill Clinton's relationship with Monica Lewinsky.]

CASANOVA (1725–1798). *Italian adventurer*
Life is like a beautiful flirt, whom we love and to whom, finally, we grant every condition she imposes as long as she doesn't leave us.

CONTE CAMILLO BENSO di CAVOUR (1810–1861). *Italian prime minister*
1 I have found out the art of deceiving diplomats: I speak the truth, and they never believe me.
2 What rascals we should be if we did for ourselves what we do for our country.

MIGUEL de CERVANTES SAAVEDRA (1547–1616). *Spanish writer*
1 Everyone is as God made him, and often a great deal worse.
2 Thank you for nothing!
3 The rich widow cries with one eye and rejoices with the other.

4 Whether the pitcher hits the stone, or the stone the pitcher, 'tis bad for the pitcher.

NICOLAS CHAMFORT (1741–1794). *French writer*

1 A little boy asked his mother for jam. "Give me too much."

2 A man must swallow a toad every morning if he wishes to be sure of finding nothing still more disgusting before the day is over.

3 A woman of ninety said to M. de Fontenelle, then ninety-five, "Death has forgotten us." "Shh," said M. de Fontenelle, putting his finger to his lips.

4 Bachelors' wives and old maids' children are always perfect.

5 Celebrity: being known by those who do not know you.

6 France: a country in which it is often useful to display one's vices, and always dangerous to show one's virtues.

7 In France they ignore those who set fires and punish those who give the alarm.

8 Love as it exists in society is merely the mingling of two fantasies and the contact of two skins.

9 M. —— said, , "I heard something to the discredit of M. de ——; I would have believed it six months ago, but we have been reconciled."

10 "Man," said M. ——, "is a foolish animal, judging from myself."

11 Men of reason have endured: men of passion have lived.

12 Most collectors of verses and sayings proceed as though they were eating cherries; they choose the best first, and wind up eating them all.

13 Nature intended illusions for the wise as well as for fools lest the former should be rendered too miserable by their wisdom.

14 Society is made up of two great classes: those who have more dinners than appetite, and those who have more appetite than dinners. —See also Holbrook Jackson 3

15 The relations between men and women are like those between Europe and the Indies: at once commerce and war.

16 There are more fools than wise men, and even in the wise there is more folly than wisdom.

17 Tyrants allow the crimes of their predecessors to be transmitted to posterity to divert attention from the horror that they themselves inspire.

RAYMOND CHANDLER (1888–1959). *American writer*

1 A big hard-boiled city with no more personality than a paper cup. [On Los Angeles.]

2 If my books had been any worse, I should not have been invited to Hollywood; and if they had been any better, I should not have come. [On becoming a screenwriter.]

3 It was a blonde. A blonde to make a bishop kick a hole in a stained-glass window.

4 She gave me a smile I could feel in my hip pocket.

5 You were dead, you were sleeping the big sleep.

CHER (1946–). *American singer and actress*

The trouble with some women is they get all excited about nothing—and marry him.

LORD CHESTERFIELD (Philip Dormer Stanhope, 1694–1773). *English statesman*

1 Advice is seldom welcome; and those who need it the most always like it the least.
2 An injury is much sooner forgotten than an insult.
3 Be wiser than other people if you can, but do not tell them so.
4 I am neither well nor ill, but unwell.
5 I wish to God that you had as much pleasure in following my advice, as I have in giving it to you.
6 If the multitude ever deviate into the right, it is always for the wrong reason.
7 In my mind, there is nothing so illiberal and so ill-bred, as audible laughter. I am sure that since I have had the full use of my reason, no human being has ever heard me laugh.
8 Men are much more unwilling to have their weaknesses and their imperfections known than their crimes.
9 Most people enjoy the inferiority of their best friends.
10 The Duke of Newcastle loses an hour in the morning, and is looking for it all the rest of the day.
11 The greatest favors may be done so awkwardly and bunglingly as to offend; and disagreeable things may be done so agreeably as almost to oblige.
12 The less one has to do, the less time one finds to do it in.
13 The only solid and lasting peace, between a man and his wife, is, doubtless, a separation.
14 Those who suppose that men in general act rationally because they are called rational creatures know very little of the world.
15 Those whom you can make like themselves will, I promise you, like you very well. —See also Lady Blessington 5; Samuel Johnson 58
16 To govern mankind one must not overrate them. —See also H. L. Mencken 62

G. K. CHESTERTON (1874–1936). *English writer*

1 Angels can fly because they take themselves lightly.
2 Art, like morality, consists in drawing the line somewhere.
3 Blessed is he that expecteth nothing, for he shall be gloriously surprised. —See also Alexander Pope 6
4 Democracy means government by the uneducated, while aristocracy means government by the badly educated.
5 If a thing is worth doing, it is worth doing badly. —See also Gypsy Rose Lee 3
6 If there were no God, there would be no atheists.
7 Journalism largely consists in saying "Lord Jones Dead" to people who never knew that Lord Jones was alive.
8 "My country, right or wrong" is a thing that no patriot would think of saying, except in a desperate case. It is like saying "My mother, drunk or sober."

9 People who make history know nothing about history. You can see that in the sort of history they make.

10 Psychoanalysis is confession without absolution.

11 Reason is itself a matter of faith. It is an act of faith to assert that our thoughts have any relation to reality at all.

12 Silence is the unbearable repartee.

13 The Bible tells us to love our neighbors, and also to love our enemies; probably because they are generally the same people.

14 The Christian ideal has not been tried and found wanting. It has been found difficult; and left untried.

15 The human race, to which so many of my readers belong, has been playing at children's games from the beginning, and will probably do it till the end, which is a nuisance for the few people who grow up.

16 The man who cannot believe his senses, and the man who cannot believe anything else, are both insane.

17 The only way of catching a train I ever discovered is to miss the train before.

18 The test of a good religion is whether you can joke about it.

19 There are only two ways of succeeding. One is by doing very good work; the other is by cheating.

20 There is nothing that fails like success. —See also Alexandre Dumas 2; George Bernard Shaw 79

21 To be clever enough to get all that money one must be stupid enough to want it.

22 Tolerance is the virtue of the man without convictions.

23 Tradition means giving votes to the most obscure of all classes, our ancestors. It is the democracy of the dead.

24 We don't need a censorship of the press. We have a censorship by the press.

25 Yawn: a silent shout.

26 You will hear everlastingly, in all discussions about newspapers, companies, aristocracies, or party politics, this argument that the rich man cannot be bribed. The fact is, of course, that the rich man is bribed; he has been bribed already. That is why he is a rich man.

MAURICE CHEVALIER (1888–1972). *French entertainer*
"How do you feel about being elderly?" Considering the alternative, it's not too bad at all. [At age 72.]

JULIA CHILD (1912–). *American chef and television personality*
1 Noodles are not only amusing but delicious.

2 Red meat and gin. [When asked, at age 84, to what she credited her longevity.]

3 These scareheads, they're going to kill gastronomy! [On "the food police's" emphasis on dieting.]

SHIRLEY CHISHOLM (1924–). *New York congresswoman and educator*
Any time things appear to be going better, you have overlooked something. ["Chisholm's Law of Inevitability."]

CHOU EN-LAI (1898–1976). *Chinese foreign minister*
All diplomacy is a continuation of war by other means.

WINSTON CHURCHILL (1874–1965). *British prime minister*
1 A fanatic is one who can't change his mind and won't change the subject.
2 A sheep in sheep's clothing. [On his political opponent Clement Attlee.]
3 A terminological inexactitude. [Campaign speech, 1905.]
4 "Am reserving two tickets for you for my premiere, come and bring a friend—if you have one." [Telegram from George Bernard Shaw] Impossible to be present for the first performance. Will attend the second—if there is one. [Return telegram.]
5 An appeaser is one who feeds a crocodile—hoping it will eat him last.
6 An empty taxi arrived at 10 Downing Street, and when the door was opened Clement Attlee got out. [Attributed, but Churchill denied having said it.]
7 Be on your guard! I am going to speak in French—a formidable undertaking and one which will put great demands upon your friendship for Great Britain. [Speech in Paris after the liberation of France in 1945.]
8 "Bevan is indisposed." Nothing trivial, I hope. [On his political opponent Aneurin Bevan.]
9 Clement Attlee is a modest man who has a good deal to be modest about. [Attributed.]
10 Democracy, it has been said, is the worst form of government except all those other forms that have been tried from time to time. [1938] —See also William Ralph Inge 2
11 Dictators ride to and fro upon tigers from which they dare not dismount. And the tigers are getting hungry.
12 Don't talk to me about naval tradition. It's nothing but rum, sodomy and the lash.
13 Dull, duller, Dulles. [On American secretary of state John Foster Dulles.]
14 Everyone has his day and some days last longer than others.
15 Everyone threw the blame on me. I suppose it is because they think I shall be able to bear it best.
16 Government of the duds, by the duds, and for the duds. [Describing a socialist government.]
17 He can best be described as one of those orators who, before they get up, do not know what they are going to say; when they are speaking, do not know what they are saying; and, when they have sat down, do not know what they have said. [On Charles Beresford.]
18 He has all of the virtues I dislike and none of the vices I admire. [On Stafford Cripps.]
19 He occasionally stumbled over the truth, but hastily picked himself up and hurried on as if nothing had happened. [On Stanley Baldwin; attributed.]
20 He would not stoop; he did not conquer.
21 History will bear me out, particularly as I shall write that history myself.
22 I am always ready to learn, although I do not always like being taught.

23 I am fond of pigs. Dogs look up to us. Cats look down on us. Pigs treat us as equal. [Attributed.]

24 I am prepared to meet my Maker. Whether my Maker is prepared for the great ordeal of meeting me is another matter. [When asked on his 75th birthday if he feared death.]

25 I go by tummy time, and I want my dinner.

26 I have always been a bit shy of the really extemporary speech ever since I heard it said that an extemporary speech was not worth the paper it was written on. [Campaign speech, 1955.]

27 I like things to happen; and if they don't happen, I like to make them happen.

28 I never followed the advice of my military staff unless I happened to agree with it.

29 I remember, when I was a child, being taken to the celebrated Barnum's Circus, which contained an exhibition of freaks and monstrosities, but the exhibit on the program which I most desired to see was the one described as "The Boneless Wonder." My parents judged that that spectacle would be too revolting and demoralizing for my youthful eyes, and I have waited fifty years to see the Boneless Wonder sitting on the Treasury Bench. [On Ramsay MacDonald in a House of Commons speech, 1933.]

30 "I'm in favor of kissing Roosevelt on both cheeks." [Edward Marsh] Yes, but not on all four. [Referring to Franklin D. Roosevelt, whose friendship was vital to British survival during World War II.] —See also Napoleon 23; Margaret Thatcher 1

31 If he trips, he must be sustained; if he makes mistakes, they must be covered; if he sleeps, he must not be wantonly disturbed; if he is no good, he must be pole-axed. [On the prime minister.]

32 If Hitler invaded hell, I would make at least a favorable reference to the devil in the House of Commons. [Following the German invasion of Russia in 1941.]

33 If you're not a liberal at 20, you have no heart, and if you're not a conservative at 40, you have no head. —See also David Lloyd George 3

34 In those days Mr. Baldwin was wiser than he is now; he used frequently to take my advice.

35 It is a socialist idea that making profits is a vice; I consider the real vice is making losses.

36 It is the ability to foretell what is going to happen tomorrow, next week, next month, and next year. And to have the ability afterwards to explain why it didn't happen. [On what it takes to succeed in politics.]

37 It is very easy for rich people to preach the virtues of self-reliance to the poor.

38 It was one of those events which are incredible until they happen.

39 Kites rise highest against the wind—not with it.

40 Magnificent in defeat and insufferable in victory. [On the sometimes difficult but almost always successful Field Marshal Bernard Law Montgomery.]

41 My foul-weather friend. [On newspaper publisher Lord Beaverbrook.]

42 Narzies. [Churchill's mocking pronunciation of *Nazis*.]

43 Never in the field of human conflict was so much owed by so many to so few. [Referring to Royal Air Force pilots during the Battle of Britain in 1940.]

44 No lover ever studied every whim of his mistress as I did those of President Roosevelt. [Remark to John Colville as recorded in his diary, 1948.]

45 Nothing in life is so exhilarating as to be shot at without result. [Referring to his experience during the Boer War, 1898.]

46 Now this is not the end. It is not even the beginning of the end. But it is, perhaps, the end of the beginning. [Following the British victory at El Alamein in 1942.]

47 Russia is a riddle wrapped in a mystery inside an enigma.

48 Scientists should be on tap but not on top.

49 Socialism is the philosophy of failure, the creed of ignorance and the gospel of envy.

50 The British Government is a strange paradox, decided only to be undecided, resolved to be irresolute, adamant for drift, solid for fluidity, all-powerful to be impotent. [1936]

51 The honorable gentleman should not generate more indignation than he can conveniently contain. [In a House of Commons debate.]

52 The inherent vice of capitalism is the unequal sharing of blessings. The inherent virtue of socialism is the equal sharing of miseries.

53 The nation had the lion's heart. I had the luck to give the roar. [On his role as Britain's prime minister during World War II.]

54 The prime minister has nothing to hide from the president of the United States. [On stepping from his bath, during a White House visit, in the presence of his startled host, Franklin D. Roosevelt.]

55 The trouble with socialism is socialism; the trouble with capitalism is capitalists.

56 There, but for the grace of God, goes God. [On Stafford Cripps; also attributed to Herman J. Mankiewicz, who was referring to Orson Welles.]

57 They say that "familiarity breeds contempt." I would like to remind you that without a degree of familiarity we could not breed anything.

58 They told me how Mr. Gladstone read Homer for fun, which I thought served him right.

59 This is the sort of English up with which I will not put. [Marginal note on a state document.]

60 To jaw-jaw is always better than to war-war.

61 Too often the strong, silent man is silent only because he does not know what to say, and is reputed strong only because he has remained silent.

62 We are all worms. But I do believe that I am a glowworm.

63 We must be very careful not to assign to this deliverance attributes of a victory. Wars are not won by evacuations. [On the forced evacuation at Dunkirk, 1940.]

64 When I warned the French Government that Britain would fight on alone whatever they did, their generals told their prime minister and his divided

Cabinet, "In three weeks England will have her neck wrung like a chicken." Some chicken! Some neck! [Referring to England's dire situation after the fall of France in 1940, Canadian Parliament speech, 1941.]

65 "Winston, if I were married to you, I'd put poison in your coffee." [Lady Astor] If I were your husband, I'd drink it.

66 Writing a book is an adventure. To begin with, it is a toy and an amusement; then it becomes a mistress, and then it becomes a master, and then a tyrant. The last phase is that just as you are about to be reconciled to your servitude, you kill the monster, and fling him out to the public.

67 "You're drunk." [Bessie Braddock] And you, madam, are ugly, but I shall be sober in the morning.

CICERO (106–43 B.C.). *Roman statesman and orator*

1 How large an income is thrift!

2 I only wish I could discover the truth as easily as I can expose falsehood.

3 There is nothing so absurd that some philosopher has not said it.

4 When your argument has little or no substance, abuse your opponent.

E. M. CIORAN (1911–1995). *Romanian-born French writer*

1 A statesman who shows no signs of senility is the one I'm afraid of.

2 Beware of the thinkers whose minds function only when fueled by a quotation.

3 Each day is a Rubicon in which I aspire to be drowned.

4 Each generation raises monuments to the executioners of the one which preceded it.

5 Events—tumors of time.

6 Friendship has meaning and appeal only when one is young. In old age what we dread more, obviously, is that our friends should outlive us.

7 Happy in love, Adam would have spared us History.

8 I anticipated witnessing in my lifetime the disappearance of our species. But the gods have been against me.

9 It is characteristic of pain not to be ashamed of repeating itself.

10 Life is possible only by the deficiencies of our imagination and our memory.

11 Melancholy: an appetite no misery satisfies.

12 My doubts about Providence never last long: Who, except for Providence, would be in a position to distribute so punctually our ration of daily defeats?

13 No one recovers from the disease of being born, a deadly wound if ever there was one.

14 One can imagine everything, predict everything, save how low one can sink.

15 Refinement is the sign of deficient vitality, in art, in love, and in everything.

16 So long as there is a single god *standing,* man's task is not done.

17 The more one hates Man, the riper one is for God, for a dialogue with nobody.

18 This earth—sin of the Creator!

19 This morning I *thought,* hence lost my bearings, for a good quarter of an hour.

20 To be called a deicide is the most flattering insult that can be addressed to an individual or to a people.

21 *To be or not to be.* Neither one nor the other.

22 To have accomplished nothing and to die of the strain.

23 To love one's neighbor is inconceivable. Does one ask a virus to love another virus?

24 Truths begin by a conflict with the police and end by calling them in.

25 When the mob espouses a myth, expect a massacre or, worse still, a new religion.

26 When we must make a crucial decision, it is extremely dangerous to consult anyone else, since no one, with the exception of a few misguided souls, sincerely wishes us well.

JAMES FREEMAN CLARKE (1810–1888). *American clergyman*
The difference between a politician and statesman is: A politician thinks of the next election and a statesman thinks of the next generation.

KARL von CLAUSEWITZ (1780–1831). *Prussian general and military theorist*
The day after tomorrow there will be a great battle, for which the entire Army is longing. I myself look forward to this day with joy as I would to my own wedding day. [Letter, 1806.]

HENRY CLAY (1777–1852). *Kentucky senator and U.S secretary of state*
"You, sir, speak for the present generation; but I speak for posterity." [Alexander Smyth, a windbag congressman.] Yes, and you seem resolved to speak until the arrival of your audience.

GEORGES CLEMENCEAU (1841–1929). *French premier*
1 America is the only nation in history which miraculously has gone directly from barbarism to degeneration without the usual interval of civilization. [Attributed.]

2 How can I talk to a fellow who thinks himself the first man in two thousand years to know anything about peace on earth? [On Woodrow Wilson.]

3 Mr. Wilson bores me with his Fourteen Points; why God Almighty has only ten. [At the Versailles Peace Conference in 1919; attributed.]

4 War is much too serious a business to be left to the generals. [Attributed.]
  —See also Charles de Gaulle 10; Robert B. Reich 2

BILL CLINTON (1946–). *American president*
1 Being president is like running a cemetery; you've got a lot of people under you and nobody's listening.

2 But I want to say one thing to the American people. I want you to listen to me. I'm going to say this again: I did not have sexual relations with that woman, Miss Lewinsky. I never told anybody to lie, not a single time. Never. These allegations are false. And I need to go back to work for the American people.

3 "Do you believe in life after death?" [David Mariness] I have to; I need a second chance.

4 I do not regard this impeachment vote as some great badge of shame. I do not. [1999 television interview.]

5 I thought to myself, "That's a pretty good speech, but not good enough to give twice." [Referring to the wrong speech coming up on a TelePrompTer.]

6 It depends on what the meaning of the word "is" is. [Testimony in the Monica Lewinsky scandal.]

7 The crown jewel of the federal prison system. [On the White House.] —See also Harry S. Truman 24

8 There's a poll saying that 40 percent of the American people think Hillary's smarter than I am. What I don't understand is how the other 60 percent missed it.

9 When I was in England, I experimented with marijuana a time or two, and I didn't like it, and I didn't inhale, and I never tried it again. [Referring to his experience as a Rhodes scholar in England during the late 1960s, 1992.]

10 Yes, the president should resign. He has lied to the American people, time and time again, and betrayed their trust. Since he has admitted guilt, there is no reason to put the American people through an impeachment. He will serve absolutely no purpose in finishing out his term. The only possible solution is for the president to save some dignity and resign. [Referring to Richard M. Nixon and his role in the Watergate scandal, 1974.]

HILLARY RODHAM CLINTON (1947–). *American lawyer and first lady*

1 Being a Cubs fan prepares you for life—and Washington. [1994; the Chicago Cubs baseball team has long been notorious for its losing ways.]

2 I read things and hear stories about me, and I go, "Ugh, I wouldn't like her either." [1995]

3 If I believed the polls, I wouldn't get up in the morning. [1991]

BARNETT COCKS (1907–1989). *English parliamentary official*

A committee is a cul-de-sac down which ideas are lured, and then quietly strangled.

JEAN COCTEAU (1889–1963). *French writer*

1 Mirrors should reflect a little before throwing back images.

2 Regret cannot come. Lie to follow. [Telegram canceling a visit.]

3 The instinct of nearly all societies is to lock up anybody who is truly free. First, they try to beat you up. If this fails, they try to poison you. If this fails too, they finish by loading honors on your head.

4 The worst tragedy for a poet is to be admired through being misunderstood.

WILLIAM SLOANE COFFIN (1924–). *American clergyman*

Even if you win the rat race, you're still a rat. [1950s; often attributed to Lily Tomlin.]

GEORGE M. COHAN (1878–1942). *American actor and playwright*

1 I don't care what you say about me, as long as you say *something* about me, and as long as you spell my name right.

2 When you are away from old Broadway, you are only camping out.

HARRY COHEN (1891–1958). *American film producer*
I don't have ulcers; I give them.

MICKEY COHEN (20th century). *American gangster*
"You killed at least one man. How many more?" [Mike Wallace] Well, I have killed no man, in the first place, that didn't deserve killing. [1957 television interview.]

ROY COHN (1927–1986). *American lawyer*
I don't want to know what the law is, I want to know who the judge is.

JEAN-BAPTISTE COLBERT (1619–1683). *French controller general of finance*
The art of taxation consists in so plucking the goose as to obtain the largest amount of feathers with the least possible amount of hissing.

SAMUEL TAYLOR COLERIDGE (1772–1834). *English poet*
1 Only the wise possess ideas; the greater part of mankind are possessed by them.
2 Plagiarists are always suspicious of being stolen from.
3 Summer has set in with its usual severity.

JOHN CHURTON COLLINS (1848–1908). *British critic*
1 Envy is the sincerest form of flattery. —See also C. C. Colton 3
2 In prosperity our friends know us; in adversity we know our friends.

C. C. COLTON (1780–1832). *English clergyman*
1 Expect not praise without envy until you are dead.
2 He that dies a martyr proves that he was not a knave, but by no means that he was not a fool.
3 Imitation is the sincerest flattery. —See also Fred Allen 16; John Churton Collins 1; Elbert Hubbard 19
4 Many speak the truth when they say that they despise riches and prefer-ment, but they mean the riches and preferment possessed by *other* men.
5 Men will wrangle for religion; write for it; fight for it; die for it; anything but—*live* for it.
6 Power multiplies flatterers, and flatterers multiply our delusions by hiding us from ourselves.
7 Some read to think, these are rare; some read to write, these are common; and some read to talk, and these form the great majority.
8 Some who profess to despise all flattery are nevertheless to be flattered by being told that they do despise it.
9 Success seems to be that which forms the distinction between confidence and conceit.
10 The hate, which we all bear with the most Christian patience, is the hate of those who envy us.
11 The poorest man would not part with health for money, but the richest would gladly part with all their money for health.
12 There is a paradox in pride—it makes some men ridiculous, but prevents others from becoming so.
13 True friendship is like sound health, the value of it is seldom known until it is lost.

14 Vice has more martyrs than virtue; and it often happens that men suffer more to be lost than to be saved. —See also Josh Billings 82

15 We ask advice, but we mean approbation.

16 When the million applaud you, seriously ask yourself what harm you have done; when they censure you, what good!

MARY COLUM (20th century). *American critic*

The only difference between the rich and other people is that the rich have more money. [Ernest Hemingway used Colum's quip, without attribution, in his 1936 short story "The Snows of Kilimanjaro."]

BARRY COMMONER (1917–). *American biologist*

If you can see the light at the end of the tunnel, you are looking the wrong way. —See also Robert Lowell 2

CHARLEY CONERLY (1921–). *American football player*

When you win, you're an old pro. When you lose, you're an old man. [Referring to the last part of his career as a professional athlete.]

CYRIL CONNOLLY (1903–1974). *English writer*

1 As repressed sadists are supposed to become policemen or butchers, so those with an irrational fear of life become publishers.

2 Better to write for yourself and have no public than to write for the public and have no self.

3 Everything is a dangerous drug to me except reality, which is unendurable.

4 He would not blow his nose without moralizing on conditions in the handkerchief industry. [On his onetime classmate George Orwell.]

5 Imprisoned in every fat man, a thin one is wildly signaling to be let out. [1945] —See also Kingsley Amis 4; George Orwell 26

6 It's only those who do nothing that make no mistakes.

7 Life is a maze in which we take the wrong turn before we have learnt to walk.

8 M is for Marx / And clashing of classes / And movement of masses / and massing of asses.

9 Our memories are card indexes consulted, and then put back in disorder by authorities whom we do not control.

10 Perfect fear casteth out love.

11 The bestseller is the golden touch of mediocre talent.

12 The dread of loneliness is greater than the fear of bondage, so we get married.

13 The man who is master of passions is Reason's slave.

14 There are many who dare not kill themselves for fear of what the neighbors will say.

15 We are all serving a life sentence in the dungeon of self.

16 We must select the illusion which appeals to our temperament and embrace it with passion, if we want to be happy.

17 Whom the gods wish to destroy they first call promising. —See also Bernard Levin 4; Joyce Carol Oates 3

JOSEPH CONRAD (1857–1924). *Polish-born British novelist*
A belief in a supernatural source of evil is not necessary; men alone are quite
  capable of every wickedness.

ALISTAIR COOKE (1908–). *English-born American journalist*
1 As always, the British especially shudder at the latest American linguistic
  vulgarity, and then they embrace it with enthusiasm two years later.
2 Canned music is like audible wallpaper.
3 He was at his best only when the going was good. [On Edward VIII, Duke
  of Windsor.]
4 The most flourishing factory of popular mythology since the Greeks. [On
  Hollywood.]

CALVIN COOLIDGE (1872–1933). *American president*
1 Business will either be better or worse.
2 Don't talk back to 'em. [On getting rid of unwelcome visitors.]
3 "How do you get exercise?" Having my picture taken.
4 I have never been hurt by anything I didn't say.
5 I think the American public wants a solemn ass as a president, and I think
  I'll go along with them.
6 If you don't say anything, you won't be called on to repeat it.
7 "Mr. President, I'm from Boston!" [Guest at a White House reception] You'll
  never get over it.
8 Never go out to meet trouble. If you will just sit still, nine cases out of ten
  someone will intercept it before it reaches you.
9 One rule of action more important than all others consists in never doing
  anything that someone else can do for you.
10 When more and more people are thrown out of work, unemployment results.
11 "You must talk to me, Mr. Coolidge. I made a bet today that I could get
  more than two words out of you." You lose.

GARY COOPER (1901–1961). *American actor*
1 *Gone with the Wind* is going to be the biggest flop in Hollywood history.
  I'm just glad it'll be Clark Gable who's falling flat on his face and not Gary
  Cooper. [After Gable's acceptance of the Rhett Butler role Cooper himself
  had turned down, 1938.]
2 There ain't never a horse that can't be rode; there ain't never a rider that
  can't be throwed.

ALAN COREN (1938–). *British writer*
Democracy consists of choosing your dictators after they've told you what
  you think it is you want to hear.

NOEL COWARD (1899–1973). *English actor and playwright*
1 A gentleman never heard the story before.
2 Certain women should be struck regularly, like gongs.
3 Dear 338171 (May I call you 338?). [Opening line of a letter to T. E.
  Lawrence, 1930.]
4 Every wise and thoroughly worldly wench / Knows there's always something fishy about the French!

5 He's completely unspoiled by failure.

6 I can take any amount of criticism, so long as it is unqualified praise.

7 I read the *Times,* and if my name is not in the obits, I proceed to enjoy the day.

8 "I'm not a suspicious woman, but I don't think my husband 'as been entirely faithful to me." [Wendle] "Whatever makes you think that?" [Pellet] "My last child doesn't resemble him in the least." [Wendle]

9 It's discouraging to think how many people are shocked by honesty, and how few by deceit.

10 Jan. 30, 1948: Gandhi has been assassinated. In my humble opinion, a bloody good thing but far too late. [Diary.]

11 Know your lines and don't bump into the furniture. [Advice to actors; attributed.] —See also Ronald Reagan 5

12 Mad dogs and Englishmen go out in the midday sun.

13 My idea of heaven? Tonight at 8:30! [When the theater curtain goes up.]

14 Never mind, dear, we're all made the same, though some more than others.

15 People are wrong when they say that the opera isn't what it used to be. It *is* what it used to be—that's what's wrong with it.

16 *Private Lives* connoted to the public mind cocktails, evening dress, repartee and irreverent allusions to copulation, thereby causing a gratifying number of respectable people to queue up at the box office. [Referring to his 1930 play.]

17 The House of Commons en bloc do it, / Civil Servants by the clock do it. —See also Cole Porter 1

18 The stately homes of England, / How beautiful they stand, / To prove the upper classes / Have still the upper hand. —See also Quentin Crisp 1; Virginia Woolf 3

19 Television is for appearing on, not for watching.

20 "What are your views on marriage?" Rather garbled.

WILLIAM COWPER (1731–1800). *English poet*

1 A priest, / A piece of mere church furniture at best.

2 Habit with him was all the test of truth, / "It must be right: I've done it from my youth."

3 His wit invites you by his looks to come, / But when you knock, it never is at home. [1782] —See also Alexander Pope 20

4 That thou mayest injure no man, dove-like be, / And serpent-like, that none may injure thee!

JAMES GOULD COZZENS (1903–1978). *American novelist*

1 A cynic is just a man who found out when he was about ten that there wasn't any Santa Claus, and he's still upset.

2 With politicians, the question is whether they're going to use you, or you're going to use them. To use them, you must begin by making them think they're using you.

QUENTIN CRISP (1908–1999). *English writer*

1 I became one of the stately homos of England. —See also Noel Coward 18

2 If one is not going to take the necessary precautions to avoid having parents, one must undertake to bring them up.

3 Life was a funny thing that happened to me on the way to the grave.

4 Marriage is but for a little while. It is alimony that is forever.

5 Never keep up with the Joneses. Drag them down to your level; it's cheaper.

6 Nothing shortens a journey so pleasantly as an account of misfortunes at which the hearer is permitted to laugh.

7 Sex is the last refuge of the miserable. —See also Samuel Johnson 64

8 The English think that incompetence is the same thing as sincerity.

9 The very purpose of existence is to reconcile the glowing opinion we hold of ourselves with the appalling things that other people think about us.

10 The young always have the same problem—how to rebel and conform at the same time. They have now solved this by defying their elders and copying one another.

11 There are three reasons for becoming a writer. The first is that you need the money; the second, that you have something to say that you think the world should know; and the third is that you can't think what to do with the long winter evenings.

12 There was no need to do any housework after all. After the first four years the dirt doesn't get any worse.

13 To know all is not to forgive all. It is to despise everybody.

14 Vice is its own reward.

OLIVER CROMWELL (1599–1658). *English soldier and statesman*

1 A man never rises higher than when he does not know where his path may lead him.

2 "Are you not proud that so many came to see the chosen of the Lord enter in triumph?" Three times as many would have come to see me hanged.

3 Mr. Lely, I desire you would use all your skill to paint my picture truly like me, and not flatter me at all, but remark all these roughnesses, pimples, warts and everything as you see me, otherwise I will not pay a farthing for it. [Popular version, "Paint me, warts and all."]

4 Put your trust in God, my boys, but mind to keep your powder dry.

MARIO M. CUOMO (1932–). *New York governor*

1 Ever since the Republican landslide on Nov. 8th, it's been getting dark outside a little earlier every day. You notice that? [Speech given soon after Democrat Cuomo's failed campaign for a third term as New York governor, 1994.]

2 You campaign in poetry. You govern in prose.

RICHARD M. DALEY (1902–1976). *Chicago mayor*

1 Gentlemen, get the thing straight for once and for all. The policeman isn't there to create disorder; the policeman is there to preserve disorder. [News conference during the 1968 Democratic National Convention in Chicago.]

2 We are proud to have with us the poet lariat of Chicago. [Introducing Carl Sandburg.]

3 We shall reach greater and great platitudes of achievement.

SALVADOR DALI (1904–1989). *Spanish painter*

1 Compared to contemporary painters, I am the most big genius of modern time, but modesty is not my specialty.

2 Each morning when I awake, I experience again a supreme pleasure—that of being Salvador Dali.

3 Liking money like I like it is nothing less than mysticism. Money is glory.

4 There is only one difference between a madman and me. I am not mad.

RODNEY DANGERFIELD (1922–). *American comedian*

1 At certain times I like sex—like after a cigarette.

2 Children! How times have changed! Remember thirty years ago when a juvenile delinquent was a kid with an overdue library book?

3 I get no respect. I was crossing the street and get hit by a mobile library. I was lying there in pain, screaming. The guy looked at me. He went, "Shh!"

4 I said to my mother-in-law last year, "My house is your house." The next day she sold it.

5 I told my psychiatrist that everyone hates me. He said I was being ridiculous—everyone hasn't met me yet.

6 I told my wife the truth, that I was seeing a psychiatrist. Then she told me the truth, that she was seeing a psychiatrist, two plumbers, and a bartender.

7 I was an ugly kid. My old man took me to the zoo. They thanked him for returning me.

8 I'm at the age where food has taken the place of sex in my life. In fact, I've just had a mirror put over my kitchen table.

9 My father gave me a bat for Christmas. The first time I tried to play with it, it flew away.

10 One woman I was dating said, "Come on over; there's nobody home." I went over—nobody was home.

11 We sleep in separate rooms, we have dinner apart, we take separate vacations—we're doing everything we can to keep our marriage together.

CLARENCE DARROW (1857–1938). *American lawyer*

1 Calvin Coolidge—the greatest man who ever came out of Plymouth Corner, Vermont.

2 Even if you do learn to speak correct English, whom are you going to speak it to?

3 Everybody makes his living along the lines of least resistance.

4 I don't believe in God because I don't believe in Mother Goose.

5 I have never wanted to see anybody die, but there were a few obituary notices I have read with pleasure.

6 I have suffered from being misunderstood, but I would have suffered a hell of a lot more if I had been understood.

7 My constitution was destroyed long ago; now I'm living under the bylaws.

8 The first half of our lives is ruined by our parents, and the second half by our children.

9 We know life is futile. A man who considers that his life is of very wonderful importance is awfully close to a padded cell.

10 When I was a boy, I was told that anybody could become president. I'm beginning to believe it.

11 Whenever I hear people discussing birth control, I always remember that I was the fifth.

CHARLES DARWIN (1809–1882). *English naturalist*

1 A mathematician is a blind man in a dark room looking for a black cat which isn't there.

2 I love fools' experiments; I am always making them.

BETTE DAVIS (1908–1989). *American actress*

1 Fasten your seat belts. It's going to be a bumpy night. [Joseph L. Mankiewicz's line spoken famously by Davis in the 1949 film *All About Eve*.]

2 Getting old ain't for sissies.

3 "How would you describe yourself in five words?" [Barbara Walters] I am just too much! [1987 television interview.]

4 I was thought to be "stuck up." I wasn't. I was just sure of myself. This is and always has been an unforgivable quality to the unsure.

5 I'd love to kiss ya, but I just washed my hair. [Her "favorite line" from one of her films.]

6 I'd love to redo *The Private Lives of Elizabeth and Essex* one more time. I'd feel more comfortable as the older queen, since I *am* an older queen. [1974; referring to the 1939 film.]

7 "I'm Ava Gardner, and I'm a great fan of yours." [Going up to Davis at a hotel in Madrid.] Of course you are, my dear. [Davis responded and swept on.]

8 It all started when I was told that I had a gift. The gods are Yankee traders. There are no gifts. Everything has a price, and in bitter moments I have been tempted to cry "Usury!"

9 She's the original good time that was had by all. [Referring to a Hollywood actress.]

10 The best time I ever had with Joan Crawford was when I pushed her down the stairs in *Whatever Happened to Baby Jane?*

11 To look back is to relax one's vigil.

12 Wave after wave of love flooded the stage and washed over me. This was the beginning of the one great durable romance of my life. [Recalling her first solo curtain call.]

13 When a man gives his opinion, he's a man. When a woman gives her opinion, she's a bitch. [Attributed.]

ELMER DAVIS (1890–1958). *American broadcast journalist*
1 The first and great commandment is, Don't let them scare you.
2 Yesterday afternoon, Senator —— wrestled with his conscience. He won.

SAMMY DAVIS, JR. (1925–1990). *American entertainer*
1 Being a star has made it possible for me to get insulted in places where the average Negro could never hope to get insulted.
2 Fame creates its own standard. A guy who twitches his lips is just another guy with a lip twitch—unless he's Humphrey Bogart.
3 Whenever you step outside, you're on, brother, you're on.

RICHARD DAWKINS (1941–). *English zoologist*
The essence of life is a statistical improbability on a colossal scale.

CLARENCE DAY (1874–1935). *American writer*
If you don't go to other men's funerals, they won't go to yours.

DOROTHY DAY (1897–1980). *American social reformer*
Don't call me a saint. I don't want to be dismissed that easily.

MOSHE DAYAN (1915–1981). *Israeli general and cabinet minister*
Whenever you accept our views, we shall be in full agreement with you.

DIZZY DEAN (1911–1974). *American baseball player*
It ain't bragging if you can do it.

SIMONE de BEAUVOIR (1908–1986). *French writer and philosopher*
Woman is shut up in a kitchen or in a boudoir, and astonishment is expressed that her horizon is limited. Her wings are clipped, and it is found deplorable that she cannot fly.

DANIEL DEFOE (1660–1731). *English writer*
1 Middle age is youth without its levity. / And age without decay.
2 Of all plagues with which mankind are curst, / Ecclesiastic tyranny's the worst.
3 Pleasure is a thief to business.
4 Things as certain as death and taxes can be more firmly believed. [*Political History of the Devil,* 1726.] —See also Margaret Mitchell 1
5 Wherever God erects a house of prayer, / The Devil always builds a chapel there; / And 'twill be found, upon examination, / The latter hast the largest congregation.

CHARLES de GAULLE (1890–1970). *French general and president*
1 A state worthy of the name has no friends—only interests.
2 Diplomats are useful only in fair weather. As soon as it rains they drown in every drop.
3 "General, all of my friends say you are deserting us. They want me to get you to change your Algerian policy. What should I do?" [Léon Delbecque, in great distress.] Change your friends.
4 Gentlemen, I am ready for the questions to my answers. [News conference.] —See also Ronald Reagan 4

5 How can you govern a country which has 246 kinds of cheese?

6 I might have had trouble saving France in 1946—I didn't have television then. [Referring to his leadership during the Algerian War, 1963.]

7 I respect only those who resist me, but I cannot tolerate them.

8 Old age is a shipwreck.

9 One cannot govern with "buts."

10 Politics are too serious a matter to be left to the politicians. —See also Georges Clemenceau 4

11 Since a politician never believes what he says, he is surprised when others believe him.

12 The better I get to know men, the more I find myself loving dogs.

13 The graveyards are full of indispensable men. —See also Elbert Hubbard 33

14 The worst calamity after a stupid general is an intelligent one.

15 Treaties are like roses and young girls. They last while they last.

16 When I want to know what France thinks, I ask myself.

STANTON DELAPLANE (1908–1988). *American journalist*
Proposed simplified tax form: How much money did you make last year? Mail it in.

JOHN DENHAM (1615–1669). *Irish poet*
Ambition is like love, impatient both of delays and rivals.

CHAUNCEY DEPEW (1834–1928). *New York senator*
If you will refrain from telling any lies about the Republican party, I'll promise not to tell the truth about the Democrats. —See also Adlai E. Stevenson 7

VITTORIO DE SICA (1901–1974). *Italian film director*
Moral indignation is in most cases 2 percent moral, 48 percent indignation, and 50 percent envy.

PETER DE VRIES (1910–1993). *American writer*
1 A suburban mother's role is to deliver children: obstetrically once, and by car forever after.

2 "Do you believe in astrology?" I don't even believe in astronomy.

3 Everybody hates me because I'm so universally liked.

4 Gluttony is an emotional escape, a sign that something is eating us.

5 I love being a writer. What I can't stand is the paperwork.

6 I write when I'm inspired, and I see to it that I'm inspired at nine o'clock every morning.

7 If you want my final opinion on the mystery of life and all that, I can give it to you in a nutshell. The universe is like a safe to which there is a combination. Unfortunately, the combination is locked up inside the safe.

8 It is not true that some people need less sleep than others. They simply sleep faster.

9 Life is a zoo in a jungle.

10 Marriage is to courting as humming is to singing.

11 Stan Waltz has decided to take unto himself a wife but hasn't decided yet whose.

12 That dark day when a man decides he must wear his belt under instead of over his cascading paunch.

13 The rich aren't like us—they pay less taxes.

14 The tuba is certainly the most intestinal of instruments, the very lower bowel of music.

15 There are times when parenthood seems like nothing but feeding the mouth that bites you.

16 They made love as though they were an endangered species.

17 We must love one another, but nothing says we have to like each other.

18 When I see something that makes absolutely no sense whatever, I figure there must be a damn good reason for it.

THOMAS ROBERT DEWAR (1864–1930). *British businessman*

1 Minds are like parachutes: they only function when open. [Attributed.]

2 Nothing deflates so fast as a punctured reputation.

3 The road to success is filled with women pushing their husbands along.

4 There are only two classes of pedestrians in these days of reckless motor traffic—the quick and the dead.

DIANA (Princess of Wales, 1961–1997). *English member of the royal family*

1 The things I do for England.

2 There were three of us in this marriage, so it was a bit crowded.

PHILIP K. DICK (1928–1982). *American writer*

1 Drug misuse is not a disease, it is a decision, like the decision to step out in front of a moving car. You would call that not a disease but an error of judgment.

2 Reality is that which, when you stop believing in it, doesn't go away.

CHARLES DICKENS (1812–1870). *English novelist*

1 Annual income twenty pounds, annual expenditure nineteen nineteen six, result happiness. Annual income twenty pounds, annual expenditure twenty pounds ought and six, result misery.

2 He had but one eye, and the popular prejudice runs in favor of two.

3 He'd make a lovely corpse. [1843] —See also Oliver Goldsmith 1

4 Here's the rule for bargains: "Do other men, for they would do you." That's the true business precept.

5 "If the law supposes that," said Mr. Bumble, "the law is a ass—a idiot."

6 In company with several other old ladies of both sexes.

7 It was a maxim with Foxey—our revered father, gentlemen—"Always suspect everybody."

8 "It's always best on these occasions to do what the mob do." "But suppose there are two mobs?" suggested Mr. Snodgrass. "Shout with the largest," replied Mr. Pickwick.

9 It's over and can't be helped, and that's one consolation, as they always says in Turkey, ven they cuts the wrong man's head off.

10 My life is one demd horrid grind!

11 Old Marley was as dead as a doornail.

12 Secret, and self-contained, and solitary as an oyster.

13 She still aims at youth, though she shot beyond it years ago.

14 The one great principle of the English law is, to make business for itself.

15 Train up a fig tree in the way it should go, and when you are old sit under the shade of it.

16 United Metropolitan Improved Hot Muffin and Crumpet Baking and Punctual Delivery Company.

17 Vices are sometimes only virtues carried to excess!

18 With affection beaming in one eye, and calculation shining out of the other.

EMILY DICKINSON (1830–1886). *American poet*

1 A little Madness in the Spring / Is wholesome even for the King.

2 Fame is a bee / It has a song— / It has a sting— / Ah, too, it has a wing.

3 How dreary—to be—Somebody! / How public—like a Frog— / To tell one's name—the livelong June— / To an admiring Bog!

4 Surgeons must be very careful / When they take the knife! / Underneath their fine incisions / Stirs the Culprit—*Life!*

5 The Brain—is wider than the Sky— / For—put them side by side— / The one the other will contain / With ease—and You—beside—

6 There are only two styles of portrait painting; the serious and the smirk.

7 To live is so startling, it leaves but little room for other occupations.

DIDEROT (1713–1784). *French philosopher*

The best doctor is the one you run for and can't find.

JOAN DIDION (1934–). *American writer*

1 A hoarder of secret sexual grievances, a wife.

2 California: the west coast of Iowa.

3 I have another cup of coffee with my mother. We get along very well, veterans of a guerrilla war we never understood.

4 That no one dies of migraine seems, to someone deep into an attack, an ambiguous blessing.

5 We are well advised to keep on nodding terms with the people we used to be, whether we find them attractive company or not. Otherwise they turn up unannounced and surprise us, come hammering on the mind's door at 4 A.M. of a bad night and demand to know who deserted them, who betrayed them, who is going to make amends.

HOWARD DIETZ (1896–1983). *American librettist and writer*

1 A day away from Tallulah Bankhead is like a month in the country.

2 I don't like composers who think. It gets in the way of their plagiarism.

PHYLLIS DILLER (1917–). *American comedienne*

1 Burt Reynolds once asked me out. I was in his room.

2 Cleaning your house / While your kids are still growing / Is like shoveling the walk / Before it stops snowing.

3 I'm at an age when my back goes out more than I do.

4 I've been asked to say a couple of words about my husband, Fang. How about "short" and "cheap."

5 I've buried a lot of ironing in the backyard.

6 Never go to bed mad—stay up and fight.

EVERETT DIRKSEN (1896–1969). *Illinois senator*
A billion here, a billion there, and pretty soon you're talking about real money.

WALT DISNEY (1901–1966). *American film producer*
I love Mickey Mouse more than any woman I've ever known.

BENJAMIN DISRAELI (1804–1881). *English novelist and prime minister*

1 A conservative government is an organized hypocrisy.

2 A government of statesmen or of clerks? Of humbug or of humdrum?

3 A jury consists of twelve persons chosen to decide who has the better lawyer.

4 A sophisticated rhetorician, inebriated with the exuberance of his own verbosity, and gifted with an egotistical imagination that can at all times command an interminable and inconsistent series of argument to malign his opponents, and glorify himself. [On Prime Minister William Ewart Gladstone.]

5 An author who speaks about his own books is almost as bad as a mother who talks about her own children.

6 An insular country subject to fogs, and with a powerful middle class, requires grave statesmen. [On England.]

7 Be frank and explicit. That is the right line to take, when you wish to conceal your own mind and to confuse the minds of others.

8 Every woman should marry—and no man. —See also H. L. Mencken 93

9 Everyone likes flattery; and when you come to Royalty you should lay it on with a trowel.

10 Gladstone made his conscience not his guide but his accomplice.

11 He has committed every crime that does not require courage. [On Daniel O'Connell.]

12 "How would you distinguish between a misfortune and a calamity?" If Gladstone fell into the Thames, that would be a misfortune; and if anybody pulled him out, that would be a calamity.

13 I am bound to furnish my antagonists with arguments but not with comprehension.

14 I have climbed to the top of the greasy pole. [After becoming prime minister.]

15 I never deny; I never contradict; I sometimes forget. [On his relations as prime minister with Queen Victoria.]

16 In politics, nothing is contemptible.

17 It seems to me a barren thing this conservatism—an unhappy crossbreed, the mule of politics that engenders nothing.

18 It's easier to be critical than correct.

19 Many thanks; I shall lose no time in reading it. [Acknowledging by letter the receipt of an unsolicited manuscript.]

20 "Mr. Disraeli, you will probably die by the hangman's noose or a vile disease." [William Ewart Gladstone] Sir, that depends upon whether I embrace your principles or your mistress.

21 My idea of an agreeable person is a person who agrees with me.

22 Never complain and never explain.

23 Next to knowing when to seize an opportunity, the most important thing in life is to know when to forgo an advantage.

24 No man is regular in his attendance at the House of Commons until he is married.

25 Palmerston is really an impostor, utterly exhausted, and at best only ginger-beer and not champagne, and now an old painted pantaloon, very deaf, very blind, and with false teeth, which would fall out of his mouth when speaking if he did not hesitate and halt so in his talk.

26 Said Waldershare, "Sensible men are all of the same religion." "And pray what is that?" "Sensible men never tell."

27 The magic of first love is our ignorance that it can ever end.

28 The more you are talked about, the less powerful you are.

29 The nearest thing to a Tory in disguise is a Whig in office.

30 There are three kinds of lies: lies, damned lies, and statistics. [Attributed.]

31 This career of plundering and blundering. [On politics.]

32 Though I sit down now, the time will come when you will hear me. [First speech in the House of Commons, 1837.]

33 What we call public opinion is generally public sentiment.

34 When a man fell into his anecdotage, it was a sign for him to retire from the world.

35 When I meet a man whose name I can't remember, I give myself two minutes, then if it is a hopeless case, I always say, "and how is the old complaint?" [Spoken in his old age.]

36 When I want to read a novel, I write one.

37 You know who the critics are? The men who have failed in literature and art.

38 Yes, I am a Jew, and when the ancestors of the right honorable gentleman were brutal savages in an unknown island, mine were priests in the temple of Solomon. [Reply to a taunt from Daniel O'Connell.]

39 Youth is a blunder; manhood, a struggle; old age, a regret.

AUSTIN DOBSON (1840–1921). *English poet*

Time goes, you say? Ah no! / Alas, Time stays, *we* go.

E. L. DOCTOROW (1931–). *American novelist*

The philosophical conservative is someone willing to pay the price of other people's suffering for his principles.

BOB DOLE (1923–). *Kansas senator and Republican presidential nominee*

1 Contrary to reports that I took the loss badly, I slept like a baby—every two hours I woke up and cried. [On losing his bid for the Republican presidential nomination in 1988.]

2 History buffs probably noted the reunion at a Washington party a few weeks ago of three ex-presidents: Carter, Ford, and Nixon—See No Evil, Hear No Evil, and Evil. [1983]

3 Sen. McGovern was making a speech. He said, "Gentlemen, let me tax your memories." And Ted Kennedy jumped up and said, "Why haven't we thought of that before!"

J. P. DONLEAVY (1926–). *American-born Irish novelist*
But Jesus, when you don't have any money, the problem is food. When you have money, it's sex. When you have both, it's health you worry about, getting ruptured or something. If everything is simply jake, then you're frightened of death.

JOHN DONNE (1572–1631). *English clergyman and poet*
1 John Donne, Anne Donne, Un-done. [Letter to his wife Anne after being dismissed by his father-in-law.]
2 Poor intricated soul! Riddling, perplexed, labyrinthical soul!

FYODOR DOSTOYEVSKY (1821–1881). *Russian novelist*
1 Everything seems stupid when it fails.
2 Money is coined liberty.
3 The best definition of man is—a creature that walks on two legs and is ungrateful.

KIRK DOUGLAS (1916–). *American actor and writer*
1 "G" means the hero gets the girl. "R" means the villain gets the girl. And "X" means everybody gets the girl.
2 If you become a star, you don't change, everyone else does.
3 Life is like a B-picture script. It's that corny. If I had my life story offered to me to film, I'd turn it down.
4 My children didn't have my advantages: I was born into abject poverty.

MAUREEN DOWD (1952–). *American journalist*
1 A friendship between reporter and source lasts only until it is profitable for one to betray the other.
2 If you're famous enough, the rules don't apply. [Referring to celebrity-drenched Washington.]
3 Perpetual optimism is annoying. It is a sign that you are not paying attention. —See also Mal Hancock 14
4 The minute you settle for less than you deserve, you get even less than you settled for.
5 We are riveted by the soap operas of public lives. We admire the famous most for what makes them infamous: it reassures us that they are no better and no happier than all the people with their noses pressed hard against the glass.
6 Zingers should glow with intelligence as well as drip with contempt.

ARTHUR CONAN DOYLE (1859–1930). *English physician and writer*
1 Good old Watson! You're the one fixed point in a changing age. [Sherlock Holmes in *His Last Bow,* 1917.]
2 How often have I said to you that when you have eliminated the impossible, whatever remains, however improbable, must be the truth?
3 I never make exceptions. An exception disproves the rule.

4 It has long been an axiom of mine that the little things are infinitely the most important.

5 It is my belief, Watson, founded upon my experience, that the lowest and vilest alleys of London do not present a more dreadful record of sin than does the smiling and beautiful countryside.

6 London, that great cesspool into which all the loungers and idlers of the Empire are irresistibly drained.

7 Mediocrity knows nothing higher than itself, but talent instantly recognizes genius.

8 Now, Watson, the fair sex is your department.

9 There is but one step from the grotesque to the horrible.

PETER DRUCKER (1909–). *Austrian-born American management consultant and writer*
In all recorded history there has not been one economist who had to worry about where the next meal was coming from.

JOHN DRYDEN (1631–1700). *English poet*
1 All heiresses are beautiful.

2 Far more numerous was the herd of such, / Who think too little, and who talk too much.

3 Here lies my wife: / Here let her lie! / Now she's at rest, / And so am I. [Proposed epitaph.]

4 If by the people you understand the multitude, the *hoi polloi*, 'tis no matter what they think; they are sometimes in the right, sometimes in the wrong: their judgment is a mere lottery.

5 Men are but children of a larger growth.

6 No government has ever been, or can ever be, wherein time-servers and blockheads will not be uppermost.

7 Shadwell never deviates into sense.

ALEXANDRE DUMAS (1824–1895). *French novelist*
1 All generalizations are dangerous, even this one.

2 Nothing succeeds like success. —See also Anonymous 94; G. K. Chesterton 20; Bob Dylan 11; Christopher Lasch 2; Fran Lebowitz 30; George Bernard Shaw 79; Arnold Toynbee 3; Oscar Wilde 70; Walter Winchell 5

3 How is it that little children are so intelligent and men so stupid? It must be education that does it.

4 I prefer rogues to imbeciles, because they sometimes take a rest.

PATSI DUNN (1948–). *Australian educator, journalist, and political leader*
Man without God is like a fish without a bicycle. —See also Anonymous 6

FINLEY PETER DUNNE ("Mr. Dooley," 1867–1936). *American writer and humorist*
1 A fanatic is a man that does what he thinks the Lord would do if He knew the facts of the case.

2 A healthy man will never reform while he has the strength.

3 A lie with a purpose is one of the worst kind, and the most profitable.

4 A man never becomes an orator if he has anything to say.

5 A man that would expect to train lobsters to fly in a year is called a lunatic, but a man that thinks men can be turned into angels by an election is called a reformer and remains at large.

6 Alcohol is necessary for a man so that now and then he can have a good opinion of himself, undisturbed by the facts.

7 Don't jump on a man unless he's down.

8 Fight fair but don't forget the other lad may not know where the belt line is.

9 I don't think we enjoy other people's suffering, Hennessey. It isn't actually enjoyment. But we feel better for it.

10 I'm strong for any revolution that isn't going to happen in my day.

11 It must be a good thing to be good or everybody wouldn't be pretending he was.

12 Many a man that couldn't direct you to the drug store on the corner when he was thirty will get a respectful hearing when age has further impaired his mind.

13 The reformer doesn't understand that people would rather be wrong and comfortable than right in jail.

14 There are no friends at cards or world politics.

15 To most people a savage nation is one that doesn't wear uncomfortable clothes.

16 Trust everybody, but cut the cards.

17 We're a great people. We are that. And the best of it is, we know we are.

18 What's one man's news is another man's troubles.

19 When you build your triumphal arch to your conquering hero, Hennessey, build it out of bricks so the people will have something convenient to throw at him as he passes through.

WILL DURANT (1885–1981). *American historian*

1 I wonder if today's radicals will not be as reactionary as I am when they are as old as I am. You soon wear out your foolishness, it's just the measles of your intellectual growth.

2 Only little states are virtuous.

3 Sixty years ago I knew everything; now I know nothing. Education is a progressive discovery of our own ignorance.

4 To say nothing, especially when speaking, is half the art of diplomacy.

5 To speak ill of others is a dishonest way of praising ourselves.

LEO DUROCHER (1906–1991). *American baseball player and manager*

1 If he could cook, I'd marry him. [On his star player Willie Mays.]

2 If you lose, you're going to be fired; and if you win, you only put off the day you're going to be fired.

3 Nice guys finish last. [His actual words were, "The nice guys over there are in seventh place"; as manager of the first-place Brooklyn Dodgers, Durocher was pointing at the dugout of the floundering New York Giants when he said it, in 1946.]

4 Show me a good sportsman, and I'll show you a player I'm looking to trade.

WILL DURST (20th century). *American comedian*

1 Al Gore is a human dial tone, the product of reverse taxidermy, and the father of five - four kids and the Internet. The man needs strobe lights at press conferences to give the appearance of movement.

2 George W. Bush said there was no room in the Republican Party for racists. Boy, I knew there were a lot of them; I didn't think all the slots were full.

3 Hillary Clinton made $100,000 on a $1,000 investment. Screw the New York senatorship: put her in charge of Social Security!

4 Hillary Clinton should get the Nobel Peace Prize for not belting Bill with a lamp every time they're seen in public.

5 "How do we refer to Slobodan Milosevic?" The Serbian Strongman, which he should have known was not a good sign. "Strongman" is U.S. shorthand for "guy whose country we're about to bomb back to the Stone Age."

6 I'm all in favor of billionaires running for president instead of politicians. That way we eliminate the middle men. [Referring to Donald Trump's candidacy in 1999.]

7 If God has cable, we are the twenty-four-hour doofus network.

8 Jesse Ventura refereed a wrestling event and caused an outcry: the wrestlers were afraid the appearance of a politician would cheapen the sport. [Referring to the Minnesota governor.]

9 Patrick Buchanan doesn't believe in evolution and some say he is his own best argument.

10 Racism is so stupid. There's more than enough reasons to dislike people on an individual basis.

11 We pride ourselves on our ability to get a pizza to our door faster than an ambulance.

BOB DYLAN (1941–). *American singer and songwriter*

1 Ah, get born, keep warm, / Short pants, romance, learn to dance, / Get dressed, get blessed, / Try to be a success.

2 At midnight all the agents / And the superhuman crew / Come out and round up everyone / That knows more than they do.

3 Colleges are like old-age homes, except for the fact that more people die in colleges.

4 "Did you ever lie down on the tracks?" [Jonathan Cott] Not personally. I once knew someone who did. "What happened?" I lost track of him.

5 "Do you know what your songs are about?" [Interviewer] Yeah, some of them are about ten minutes long, others five or six.

6 Don't follow leaders, / Watch the parkin' meters.

7 I've been walking through the middle of nowhere, / Trying to get to heaven before they close the door.

8 If my thought-dreams could be seen, / They'd probably put my head in a guillotine.

9 Jesus, who's got time to keep up with the times? [1984 interview.]

10 Money doesn't talk, it swears.

11 Sucksess. [One-word placard used as a song prop in the 1967 documentary *Don't Look Back*.] —See also Anonymous 94; Alexandre Dumas 2

12 There is no right wing / or no left wing; / There is only up wing / an' down wing.

13 Twenty years of schoolin' / And they put you on the day shift.

14 Yipee! I'm a poet, and I know it. / Hope I don't blow it.

CLINT EASTWOOD (1930–). *American actor*

1 I hate imitation; I have a reverence for individuality. I got where I am by coming off the wall.

2 I've actually had people come up to me and ask me to autograph their guns.

ABBA EBAN (1915–). *South African–born Israeli diplomat*

1 His ignorance is encyclopedic.

2 History teaches us that men and nations behave wisely once they have exhausted all other alternatives.

3 Political leaders do not always mean the opposite of what they say.

MARIE von EBNER-ESCHENBACH (1830–1960). *Austrian novelist and poet*

1 Be the first to say what is self-evident, and you are immortal.

2 It's bad enough when married people bore one another, but it's much worse when only one of them bores the other.

3 To be content with little is difficult; to be content with much, impossible.

4 We don't believe in rheumatism and true love until after the first attack.

5 We generally learn how to wait when there is nothing more to wait for.

ANTHONY EDEN (1897–1977). *British prime minister*

1 Everybody is always in favor of general economy and particular expenditure.

2 We are not at war with Egypt. We are in an armed conflict. [Referring to the Suez War, 1956.]

THOMAS ALVA EDISON (1847–1931). *American inventor*

1 Everything comes to him who hustles while he waits.

2 Genius is one percent inspiration, ninety-nine percent perspiration. —See also Elbert Hubbard 32

3 I have not failed. I've just found 10,000 ways that won't work. [On his experiments with an invention.]

4 "Mr. Edison, please tell me what laboratory rules you want me to observe." [M. A. Rosanoff] Hell! there ain't no rules around here! We're trying to accomplish somep'n!

5 So far as religion of the day is concerned, it is a damned fake. Religion is all bunk. —See also Henry Ford 4

6 The reason a lot of people do not recognize opportunity is because it usually goes around wearing overalls looking like hard work.

7 They say Wilson has blundered. Perhaps he has, but I notice he usually blunders forward. [Referring to Woodrow Wilson.]

8 We don't know half of one millionth of one percent about anything.

9 When down in the mouth, remember Jonah: he came out all right.

EDWARD VIII (Duke of Windsor, 1894–1972). *English king*

The thing that impresses me most about America is the way parents obey their children.

OLIVER EDWARDS (1711–1791). *English lawyer*

You are a philosopher, Dr. Johnson. I have tried too in my time to be a philosopher; but, I don't know how, cheerfulness was always breaking in. [Remark to Samuel Johnson.]

BARBARA EHRENREICH (1941–). *American writer*

1 Even when uttered by Democrats, "middle class" often sounds like a mealy-mouthed way of saying, "Us, and not them," where them includes poor people, snake handlers and those with pierced tongues.

2 It used to be almost the first question (just after "Can you type?") in the standard female job interview: "Are you now, or have you ever, contemplated marriage, motherhood, or the violent overthrow of the US Government?"

3 Marriage probably originated as a straightforward food-for-sex deal among foraging primates. Compatibility was not a big issue, nor, or course, was there any tension over who would control the remote.

4 "Money does not bring happiness"—only the wherewithal, perhaps, to endure its absence.

5 The difference between a religion and a cult is chiefly a matter of size. Forty-eight people donning plastic bags and shooting themselves in the head is a "cult," while a hundred million people bowing before a flesh-hating elderly celibate is obviously a world-class religion.

6 We who officially value freedom of speech above life itself seem to have nothing to talk about but the weather.

7 While everything else in our lives has gotten simpler, speedier, more microwavable and user-friendly, child-raising seems to have expanded to fill the time no longer available for it.

JOHN EHRLICHMAN (1925–1998). *American lawyer and presidential assistant*

I think we ought to let him hang there. Let him twist slowly, slowly in the wind. [Telephone remark to John Dean, referring to L. Patrick Gray, Richard M. Nixon's nominee for FBI director.]

ALBERT EINSTEIN (1879–1955). *German-born American physicist*

1 As far as the laws of mathematics refer to reality, they are not certain, and as far as they are certain, they do not refer to reality.

2 Common sense is the deposit of prejudice laid down in the mind before the age of eighteen.

3 Everything should be made as simple as possible, but not simpler.

4 For an idea that does not at first seem insane, there is no hope.

5 God does not play dice with the universe.

6 God is subtle, but he is not malicious. [1921; in 1946 Einstein offered another version of his aphorism, "God is slick, but he ain't mean."]

7 I don't believe in mathematics.

8 I have just got a new theory of eternity. [While listening to a long-winded after-dinner speaker.]

9 I never think of the future. It comes soon enough.

10 If A is a success in life, then A equals x plus y plus z. Work is x; y is play; and z is keeping your mouth shut.

11 If my theory of relativity is proven correct, Germany will claim me as a German and France will declare that I am a citizen of the world. Should my theory prove untrue, France will say that I am a German and Germany will declare that I am a Jew. [1929]

12 If only I had known, I would have become a watchmaker. [Referring to his theories which eventually led to the development of the atom bomb; attributed.]

13 No wealth in the world can help humanity forward, even in the hands of the most devoted worker in this cause. Can anyone imagine Moses, Jesus, or Gandhi armed with the moneybags of Carnegie?

14 Not everything that counts can be counted, and not everything that can be counted counts.

15 One is born into a herd of buffaloes and must be glad if one is not trampled underfoot before one's time.

16 Only two things are infinite, the universe and human stupidity, and I'm not sure about the former.

17 The hardest thing in the world to understand is the income tax.

18 The secret to creativity is knowing how to hide your sources.

19 When a man sits with a pretty girl for an hour, it seems like a minute. But let him sit on a hot stove for a minute—and it's longer than any hour. That's relativity. [Explaining tongue-in-cheek his theory of relativity.]

DWIGHT D. EISENHOWER (1890–1969). *American general and president*

1 A lot more people beat me now. [When asked about his golf game after stepping down as president.]

2 An atheist is a guy who watches a Notre Dame–SMU football game and doesn't care who wins.

3 An intellectual is a man who takes more words than he needs to say more than he knows.

4 "Have you ever met Douglas MacArthur?" Not only have I met him, ma'am; I studied dramatics under him for five years in Washington and for four years in the Philippines.

5 I probably long ago used up my time; but you know, there is one thing about being the president, it is hard to tell him to sit down.

6 I think that people want peace so much that one of these days governments had better get out of the way and let them have it.

7 Oh, that lovely title, ex-president.

8 Things are more like they are now than they ever were before.

MAMIE EISENHOWER (1896–1979). *American first lady*

I can't speak for any other marriage, but the secret of our marriage is that we have absolutely nothing in common.

PAUL ELDRIDGE (1888–1982). *American writer*

1 Democracy stands between two tyrannies: the one which it has overthrown and the one into which it will develop.

2 He who knows himself trusts no one.

3 However deeply we plumb our vanity, we shall never touch bottom.

4 Like the greedy merchants of bazaars, if we get out of life what we ask for, we are unhappy for not having asked for more.

5 Moral indignation is one of envy's stylish disguises.

6 Our sole standard for individual sanity is our collective insanity.

7 Repentance is a respite between two sins.

8 Satan—God's scapegoat.

9 Sincerity is the last refuge of the inept. —See also Samuel Johnson 64

10 Statues invite hammers.

11 The amount of temptation required differentiates the honest from the dishonest.

12 The faults of others console us in our own.

13 The hand that feeds should be heavily gloved.

14 The ideals men die for often become the prejudices their descendants kill for.

15 The traitor is a hero defeated.

16 Those in power codify their privileges into laws.

17 Those whom we cannot exploit we denounce as selfish.

18 We admire martyrdom because nothing impresses us so profoundly as egotism carried to its logical conclusion.

19 We are flattered in proportion to our vanity.

20 We reward small virtues and big vices.

21 We tolerate when we have lost the power to persecute.

22 Written history is largely the glorification of the iniquities of the triumphant.

GEORGE ELIOT (Mary Ann Evans Cross, 1819–1880). *English novelist*

1 A difference of taste in jokes is a great strain on the affections.

2 Blessed is the man who, having nothing to say, abstains from giving us wordy evidence of the fact.

3 He was a cock who thought the sun had risen to hear him crow.

4 I have nothing to say against him, only it was a pity he couldn't have been hatched over again, and hatched different.

5 I'm not denying the women are foolish: God Almighty made them to match the men.

6 I've never any pity for conceited people, because I think they carry their comfort about with them.

7 It is better sometimes not to follow great reformers of abuses beyond the threshold of their homes.

8 It's easy finding reasons why other folks should be patient.

9 It's them as take advantage that get advantage in this world. Folks have to wait long before it's brought to them.

T. S. ELIOT (1888–1965). *American-born English poet*

1 Birth, and copulation, and death. / That's all the facts when you come to brass tacks.

2 Immature poets imitate; mature poets steal. [1920] —See also Igor Stravinsky 1; Lionel Trilling 1

3 Our literature is a substitute for religion, and so is our religion.

4 The years between 50 and 70 are the hardest. You are always being asked to do things, and yet you are not decrepit enough to turn them down.

LINDA ELLERBEE (1944–). *American broadcast journalist and writer*

1 I want to know why, if men rule the world, they don't stop wearing neckties.

2 Styles, like everything else, change. Style doesn't.

3 The first law of journalism is to confirm existing prejudice, rather than contradict it.

HAVELOCK ELLIS (1859–1939). *English physician and writer*

What we call "progress" is the exchange of one nuisance for another nuisance.

RALPH WALDO EMERSON (1803–1882). *American philosopher*

1 A foolish consistency is the hobgoblin of little minds.

2 A man complained that on his way home to dinner he had every day to pass through that long field of his neighbor's. I advised him to buy it, and it would never seem long again.

3 Alcott tells me that Mr. Hedge is to write an essay on the importance of a liturgy. I propose to add an essay on the importance of a rattle in the throat.

4 Cunning egotism. If I cannot brag of knowing something, then I brag of not knowing it. At any rate, brag.

5 Envy is the tax which all distinction must pay.

6 Few envy the consideration enjoyed by the oldest inhabitant.

7 How could the Children of Israel sustain themselves for forty days in the desert? Because of the sand-which-is there.

8 I knew a man scared by the rustle of his own hatband.

9 I wish to be approved, but as soon as any approves me I distrust him. [1840] —See also Abraham Lincoln 19

10 In Maine they have not a summer but a thaw.

11 In this world, if a man sits down to think, he is immediately asked if he has the headache.

12 It is as bad as going to Congress; none comes back innocent. —See also Kin Hubbard 30

13 Money often costs too much.

14 New York is a sucked orange.

15 Our senator was of that stuff that our best hope lay in his drunkenness, as that sometimes incapacitated him from doing mischief.

16 Our weathercock government.

17 People say law, but they mean wealth.

18 Rain, rain. The good rain like a bad preacher does not know when to leave off.

19 Solitude is impractical, and society fatal.

20 Strange that our government, so stupid as it is, should never blunder into a good measure.

21 Surely nobody would be a charlatan who could afford to be sincere.

22 Take egotism out, and you would castrate the benefactors.

23 Tennyson is a beautiful half a poet.

24 That bloated vanity called public opinion.

25 That which we call sin in others, is experiment for us.

26 The age has an engine, but no engineer.

27 The hater of property and of government takes care to have his warranty deed recorded, and the book written against fame and learning has the author's name on the title page.

28 The history of man is a series of conspiracies to win from nature some advantage without paying for it.

29 The louder he talked of his honor, the faster we counted our spoons. — See also Samuel Johnson 39

30 The religion of one age is the literary entertainment of the next.

31 The shield against the stingings of conscience is the universal practice of our contemporaries.

32 The trouble is, the more it resembles me, the worse it looks. [Commenting on a statue he was sitting for in 1879.]

33 The unsaid part is the best of every discourse.

34 Things are in the saddle and ride mankind.

35 We all know the rule of umbrellas—if you take your umbrella, it will not rain; if you leave it, it will.

36 We learn geology the morning after the earthquake.

37 We love flattery, even though we are not deceived by it, because it shows that we are important enough to be courted. —See also George Bernard Shaw 141

38 We wish to be self-sustained. We do not quite forgive a giver. The hand that feeds us is in some danger of being bitten.

39 What is a weed? A plant whose virtues have not yet been discovered.

40 What reason to think Charles I consented to his execution? They axed him whether he would or no.

41 When believers and unbelievers live in the same manner, I distrust the religion.

42 Which was the best age of philosophy? That in which there were yet no philosophers.

43 Whoso goes to walk alone, accuses the whole world; he declareth all to be unfit to be his companions; it is very uncivil, nay, insulting; Society will retaliate.

44 You will always find those who think they know what is your duty better than you know it.

NORA EPHRON (1941–). *American writer and screenwriter*

1 I am continually fascinated at the difficulty intelligent people have in distinguishing what is controversial from what is merely offensive.

2 I'll have what she's having. [Remark to a waiter by Estelle Reiner after observing Meg Ryan, at another table, acting out an orgasm, in the 1989 film *When Harry Met Sally.*]

3 If pregnancy were a book, they'd cut the last two chapters.

4 That's the truest sign of insanity—insane people are always sure they're just fine. It's only the sane people who are willing to admit they're crazy.

5 There is no reason to confuse television news with journalism.

EVAN ESAR (1899–1995). *American writer*

1 A fool and his money are soon parted, but how did they get together in the first place? —See also Anonymous 1

2 Adolescence begins when children stop asking questions—because they know all the answers.

3 All work and no pay makes a housewife.

4 All work and no play makes Jack a dull boy—and Jill a wealthy widow.

5 An inferiority complex is the only trait which enables us to see ourselves as others see us.

6 Compare what you want with what you have, and you'll be unhappy; compare what you have with what you deserve, and you'll be happy.

7 Early to bed and early to rise is the way of a girl before she gets wise. —See also James Thurber 4; Ted Turner 1

8 If at first you don't succeed, try reading the instructions. —See also Anonymous 56; W. C. Fields 24

9 Income taxes could be a lot worse; suppose we had to pay on what we think we're worth.

10 Life is a game played on us while we are playing other games.

11 Nothing ages your car as much as the sight of your neighbor's new one.

12 Some couples divorce because of a misunderstanding; others, because they understand each other too well.

13 Some people exercise by jumping to conclusions, some by sidestepping their responsibilities, but most people get it by running down their friends.

CLIFTON FADIMAN (1904–1999). *American literary critic and radio personality*

Experience teaches you that the man who looks you straight in the eye, particularly if he adds a firm handshake, is hiding something.

FAROUK I (1920–1965). *Egyptian king*

In a few years there will be only five kings in the world—the king of England and the four kings in a pack of cards. [After his forced abdication in 1952.]

WILLIAM FAULKNER (1897–1962). *American novelist*

1 Henry James was one of the nicest old ladies I ever met.

2 The writer's only responsibility is to his art. He will be completely ruthless if he is a good one. If a writer has to rob his mother, he will not hesitate; the "Ode on a Grecian Urn" is worth any number of old ladies.

3 This is a free country. Folks have a right to send me letters, and I have a right not to read them.

WILLIAM FEATHER (1889–1981). *American writer and publisher*

1 If people really liked to work, we'd still be plowing the ground with sticks and transporting goods on our backs.

2 Success makes us intolerant of failure, and failure makes us intolerant of success.

JULES FEIFFER (1929–). *American cartoonist*

1 I do something dumb on the job, I chalk it up to experience. I screw up a perfectly good relationship, I chalk it up to experience. I make promises I can't keep and get people mad at me, I chalk it up to experience. "Experience" is the recognition when you're about to do something stupid—that you've done it before and you'll do it again. [Cartoon balloons.]

2 I grew up to have my father's looks, my father's speech patterns, my father's posture, my father's walk, my father's opinions, and my mother's contempt for my father.

3 I told the doctor I was overtired, anxiety-ridden, compulsively active, constantly depressed, with recurring fits of paranoia. Turns out I'm normal.

4 I used to think I was poor. Then they told me I wasn't poor, I was needy. Then they told me it was self-defeating to think of myself as needy, I was deprived. Then they told me deprived was a bad image, I was underprivileged. Then they told me underprivileged was overused, I was disadvantaged. I still don't have a dime. But I sure have a great vocabulary.

5 In bygone days America had morality. Friends of our morality controlled governments in the Far East, the Middle East, Latin America and Africa. We sent our friends money, arms, technocrats and advisors in counterinsurgency, and with our support they dictated, killed, tortured and plundered until they were overthrown to be replaced by dictators, killers, torturers and plunderers who are not our friends. The collapse of morality.

ot fit in.

7 Some mornings I wake up in a panic, because I'm convinced I've forgotten all the basics. Forgotten how to sit up, forgotten how to walk, forgotten how to talk, forgotten how to eat, forgotten how to think. Until my wife turns over and asks me a question, and I answer with my first lie of the day—and I know I'm going to make it.

8 Vietnam. Czechoslovakia. The Black Revolution. Student uprisings. And all I really care about—is that I'm losing my hair. [1969]

LAWRENCE FERLINGHETTI (1919–). *American poet*

1 Automobilized America.
2 Goodbye I'm going / I'm selling everything / and giving away the rest / to the Good Will Industries. / It will be dark out there / with the Salvation Army Band. / And the mind its own illumination.
3 I see where Walden Pond has been drained / to make an amusement park.
4 Love is the strangest bird / that ever winged about the world.
5 Poetry is the sound of summer in the rain and of people laughing behind closed shutters down a narrow street.
6 The poet like an acrobat / climbs on rime / to a high wire of his own making.
7 Where do we catch the boat for Plato's Republic?

W. C. FIELDS (1880–1946). *American comedian and actor*

1 A Merry Christmas to all my friends except two.
2 A thing worth having is worth cheating for.
3 After two days in hospital, I took a turn for the nurse.
4 Anybody who hates dogs and loves whiskey can't be all bad. [Attributed.]
5 Business is an establishment that gives you the legal, even though unethical, right to screw the naïve—right, left, and in the middle.
6 Children should neither be seen nor heard from—ever again.
7 "Do married people live longer?" No, it just seems longer. [Attributed.]
8 "Do you like children?" I do if they're properly cooked!
9 Don't worry about your heart; it will last you as long as you live.
10 During one of my treks through Afghanistan, we lost our corkscrew and were compelled to live on food and water for several days.
11 Hell, I never vote for anybody. I always vote against.
12 Here lies W. C. Fields. I would rather be living in Philadelphia. [Self-epitaph.]
13 Horse sense is what a horse has that keeps him from betting on people.
14 I always start each day with a smile—and get it over with.
15 I am free of all prejudice. I hate everyone equally.
16 I exercise strong self-control. I never drink anything stronger than gin before breakfast.
17 I got Mark Hellinger so drunk last night that it took three bellboys to put me to bed.
18 I have never struck a woman. Never! Not even my dear old mother.

19 I have spent a lot of time searching through the Bible for loopholes.

20 I like thieves. Some of my best friends are thieves. Why, just last week we had the president of the bank over for dinner.

21 I must have a drink of breakfast.

22 I never met a kid I liked. —See also Will Rogers 22

23 I was in love with a beautiful blonde once, but she drove me to drink. That's the one thing I'm indebted to her for.

24 If at first you don't succeed, try, try again. Then quit. No use being a damn fool about it. —See also Anonymous 56; Evan Esar 8

25 Instead of a New Deal, we want a New Deck. The New Deal has never ripened. It is still a Raw Deal.

26 It ain't a fit night out for man or beast.

27 Last week I went to Philadelphia, but it was closed.

28 Never give a sucker an even break!

29 "Say, Mr. Fields, I read in the paper where you consumed two quarts of liquor a day. What would your father think about that?" [Charlie McCarthy] He'd think I was a sissy. [Radio skit.]

30 Some weasel stole the cork from my lunch.

31 The cost of living has gone up another dollar a quart.

32 There comes a time in the affairs of a man when he has to take the bull by the tail and face the situation.

33 There's not a man in America who at one time or another hasn't had a secret desire to boot a child in the ass. [Attributed.]

34 Thou shalt not kill anything less than a fifth.

35 Thou shalt not take the name of the Lord thy God in vain unless you've used up all the other four-letter words.

36 Water rusts pipes.

37 Women are like elephants to me. I like to look at 'em, but I wouldn't want to own one.

EVA FIGES (1932–). *German-born English writer*
Providing for one's family as a good husband and father is a watertight excuse for making money hand over fist.

CARRIE FISHER (1956–). *American actress and writer*
1 A comfortable quiet had settled between them. A silence that was like newly fallen snow.

2 Instant gratification takes too long.

3 The message about sex and relationships that she had gotten as a child was confused, contradictory. Sex was for men, and marriage, like lifeboats, was for women and children.

F. SCOTT FITZGERALD (1896–1940). *American novelist*
1 An author ought to write for the youth of his own generation, the critics of the next, and the schoolmasters of ever afterwards.

2 Draw your chair up to the edge of the precipice, and I'll tell you a story.

3 Ernest would always give a helping hand to a man on a ledge a little higher up. [On Ernest Hemingway.]

4 Every one suspects himself of at least one of the cardinal virtues, and this is mine: I am one of the few honest people that I have ever known. [*The Great Gatsby,* 1925.]

5 First you take a drink, then the drink takes a drink, then the drink takes you.

6 For a statesman—any schoolchild knows that hot air rises to the top.

7 He repeated to himself an old French proverb that he had made up that morning.

8 Her voice is full of money.

9 I have never wished there was a God to call on—I have often wished there was a God to thank.

10 In a real dark night of the soul it is always three o'clock in the morning.

11 Show me a hero, and I will write you a tragedy.

12 The victor belongs to the spoils.

13 There are no second acts in American lives.

14 You can stroke people with words.

ZELDA FITZGERALD (1900–1948). *American writer*

Mr. Fitzgerald seems to believe that plagiarism begins at home. [On husband F. Scott Fitzgerald's appropriation of material from her diaries and letters.]

BOB FITZSIMMONS (1863–1917). *English-born American boxer*

The bigger they come, the harder they fall. —See also Anonymous 110; James Thurber 15

ELROY FLECKER (1884–1915). *English poet and playwright*

The dead know only one thing: it is better to be alive.

ERROL FLYNN (1909–1959). *Australian-born American actor*

If there's anyone listening to whom I owe money, I'm prepared to forget it if you are. [Broadcast before leaving Australia in the 1930s.]

SAMUEL FOOTE (1720–1777). *English actor and playwright*

He is not only dull himself, but the cause of dullness in others. —See also William Shakespeare 10

MALCOLM S. FORBES (1919–1990). *American publisher*

1 Ambition is best not naked.

2 By the time we make it, we've had it.

3 How children survive being Brought Up amazes me.

4 Let your children go if you want to keep them.

5 "Money isn't everything," according to those who have it.

6 Only drips drop out.

7 Some days are for living. Others are for getting through.

8 Sure things seldom are.

9 The difference between the men and the boys is the price of their toys.

10 The line between idiosyncrasy and idiocy is money.

11 Those who have it don't need to flaunt it. —See also Mel Brooks 1

12 We were nosed out by a landslide. [Referring to his defeat in a gubernatorial election campaign.]

13 While alive, I lived. [Memorial plaque inscription.]

GERALD FORD (1913–). *American president*
1 Ronald Reagan doesn't dye his hair. He's just prematurely orange.
2 You don't need a lot of bureaucrats looking over your shoulder and telling you how to run your life or how to run your business. We are a people who declared our independence 200 years ago, and we are not about to lose it now to paper shufflers and computers.

HARRISON FORD (1942–). *American actor*
Hard work and a proper frame of mind prepare you for the lucky breaks that finally come along—or don't.

HENRY FORD (1863–1947). *American automotive industrialist*
1 An idealist is a person who helps other people to be prosperous.
2 Any customer can have a car painted any color he wants so long as it is black.
3 "Good bye, I'll see you in heaven." [John D. Rockefeller] You will if you get in. [Parting words after a 1935 visit when Rockefeller was ninety-six and Ford was seventy-two.]
4 History is more or less bunk. It's tradition. We don't want tradition. We want to live in the present, and the only history that is worth a tinker's dam is the history we make today. —See also Thomas Edison 5
5 What we call evil is simply ignorance bumping its head in the dark.
6 Whether you believe you can do a thing or not, you are right.
7 You can't build a reputation on what you're going to do.

E. M. FORSTER (1879–1970). *English novelist*
1 All men are equal—all men, that is to say, who possess umbrellas.
2 I distrust Great Men. They produce a desert of uniformity around them and often a pool of blood too, and I always feel a little man's pleasure when they come a cropper.
3 One always tends to overpraise a long book, because one has got through it.
4 To trust people is a luxury in which only the wealthy can indulge; the poor cannot afford it.

ANATOLE FRANCE (1844–1924). *French novelist*
1 Chance is perhaps God's pseudonym when He does not want to sign.
2 He flattered himself on being a man without any prejudices; and this pretension itself was a very great prejudice.
3 It is in the ability to deceive oneself that the greatest talent is shown.
4 Man is so made that he can only find relaxation from one kind of labor by taking up another.
5 Never lend books, for no one ever returns them; the only books I have in my library are books that other people have lent me.
6 Of all sexual aberrations, chastity is the strangest.
7 People who have no weaknesses are terrible; there is no way of taking advantage of them.
8 The absurdity of a religious practice may be clearly demonstrated without lessening the number of persons who indulge in it.

9 The books that everybody admires are those that nobody reads.

10 The law, in its majestic equality, forbids the rich as well as the poor to sleep under bridges, to beg in the streets, and to steal bread.

11 We reproach people for talking about themselves, but it is the subject they treat best. —See also Henry David Thoreau 14

12 Without lies humanity would perish of despair and boredom.

BENJAMIN FRANKLIN (1706–1790). *American printer, inventor, and statesman*

1 An infallible remedy for toothache: wash the root of an aching tooth in vinegar, and let it dry half an hour in the sun.

2 Here Skugg / Lies snug / As a bug / In a rug. [Epitaph for a pet squirrel.]

3 I have heard of some great man, whose rule it was, with regard to offices, never to ask for them, and never to refuse them; to which I have always added, in my own practice, never to resign them.

4 I scarce ever heard or saw the introductory words, "Without vanity I may say," etc., but some vain thing immediately followed.

5 Mankind are very odd creatures: one half censure what they practice, the other half practice what they censure; the rest always say and do as they ought.

6 Who is wise? He that learns from everyone. Who is powerful? He that governs his passions. Who is rich? He that is content. Who is that? Nobody.

FREDERICK II (Frederick the Great, 1712–1786). *Prussian king*

1 Diplomacy without arms is music without instruments.

2 I begin by taking. I shall find scholars afterwards to demonstrate my perfect right.

3 If I wished to punish a province, I would have it governed by philosophers.

4 If my soldiers were to begin to think, not one would remain in the ranks.

5 My people and I have an agreement. They *say* whatever they like, and I *do* whatever I like.

6 Politics and villainy are almost synonymous terms.

SIGMUND FREUD (1856–1939). *Austrian psychoanalyst*

1 A mother is only brought unlimited satisfaction by her relation to a son. Even a marriage is not made secure until the wife has succeeded in making her husband her child as well and in acting as a mother to him.

2 America is a mistake, a giant mistake. [Freud visited America in 1909.]

3 Do you know why psychiatrists go into their specialty? It is because they do not feel that they are normal, and they go into this work because it is a means of sublimation for this feeling—a means of assuring themselves that they are really normal. Society puts them in charge of the mentally abnormal, and so they feel reassured. [1930]

4 From an old man who greets in the Ruler the Hero of Culture. [Inscription in book sent as a gift to the Italian dictator Benito Mussolini, 1933.]

5 Girls hold their mother responsible for their lack of a penis and do not forgive her for their being thus put at a disadvantage.

6 He is cheerful, sure of himself and agreeable. He understands as much

about psychology as I do about physics, so we had a very pleasant talk. [Referring to Albert Einstein.]

7 Housekeeping and the care and education of children claim the whole person and practically rule out any profession. It seems a completely unrealistic notion to send women into the struggle for existence in the same way as men. Am I to think of my delicate, sweet girl as a competitor? [Letter to his fiancée Martha Bernays, 1883.] —See also Adolf Hitler

8 I am actually not at all a man of science, not an observer, not an experimenter, not a thinker. I am by temperament nothing but a conquistador—an adventurer, if you want it translated—with all the curiosity, daring, and tenacity characteristic of a man of this sort. [Letter, 1900.]

9 I have never done anything mean or malicious and cannot trace any temptation to do so, so I am not in the least proud of it. Why I—and incidentally my six adult children also—have to be thoroughly decent human beings is quite incomprehensible to me. [Letter, 1915.]

10 I looked very fine and made a favorable impression on myself. We drove there in a carriage the expenses of which we shared. R. was terribly nervous, I quite calm with the help of a small dose of cocaine. [Recounting the prelude to a dinner engagement at the home of one of his professors in Paris where Freud was studying medicine, letter to Martha Bernays, 1886.]

11 Jesus could even have been an ordinary deluded creature.

12 Naturally homosexuality is something pathological, it is an arrested development.

13 Our psychoanalysis has also had bad luck. No sooner had it begun to interest the world because of the war neuroses than the war comes to an end, and when for once we come across a source of wealth it immediately dries up. But bad luck is a regular accompaniment of life. Our kingdom is evidently not of this world. [Letter to Sandor Ferenczi, 1919.]

14 People who dream often, and with great enjoyment, of swimming, cleaving the waves, etc., have usually been bed-wetters.

15 Religious intolerance was inevitably born with the belief in one God.

16 The effect of the consolations of religion may be compared to that of a narcotic. —See also Karl Marx 5

17 The fact that women must be regarded as having little sense of justice is no doubt related to the predominance of envy in their mental life.

18 The great question that has never been answered and which I have not been able to answer, despite my thirty years of research into the feminine soul, is: What does a woman want?

19 The moment a man questions the meaning and value of life, he is sick, since objectively neither has any existence.

20 The worst egoist is the person to whom the thought has never occurred that he might be one.

21 We are certainly getting ahead; if I am Moses, then you are Joshua and will take possession of the promised land of psychiatry, which I shall only be able to glimpse from afar. [Letter to Carl G. Jung, 1909.]

22 Women in America lead the men around by the nose, make fools of them, and the result is a matriarchy. In Europe, things are different. Men take the lead. That is as it should be. [Remarks to a visitor, 1934.]

MILTON FRIEDMAN (1912–). *American economist*

1 Hell hath no fury like a bureaucrat scorned. —See also Dick Gregory 1; C. E. Montague

2 In a bureaucratic system, useless work drives out useful work.

3 Inflation is taxation without representation.

MAX FRISCH (1911–1991). *Swiss playwright and novelist*

Technology, the knack of so arranging the world that we need not experience it.

ERICH FROMM (1900–1980). *German-born American psychoanalyst*

1 In the nineteenth century the problem was that *God is dead;* in the twentieth century the problem is that *man is dead.*

2 The successful revolutionary is a statesman, the unsuccessful one is a criminal. —See also Artemus Ward 21

3 We are a herd believing that the road we follow must lead to a goal since we see everybody else on the same road. We are in the dark and keep up our courage because we hear everybody else whistle as we do.

DAVID FROST (1939–). *British broadcast journalist*

1 Dobkins, I just don't know what we'd do without you. But we're going to try.

2 He's turned his life around. He used to be depressed and miserable. Now he's miserable and depressed.

ROBERT FROST (1874–1963). *American poet*

1 A diplomat is a man who always remembers a woman's birthday but never remembers her age.

2 A jury consists of twelve persons chosen to decide who has the better lawyer.

3 A liberal is a man too broad-minded to take his own side in a quarrel.

4 And were an epitaph to be my story / I'd have a short one ready for my own. / I would have written of me on my stone: / I had a lover's quarrel with the world. [1941]

5 By working faithfully eight hours a day, you may eventually get to be a boss and work twelve hours a day.

6 Education is the ability to listen to almost anything without losing your temper or your self-confidence.

7 Forgive, O Lord, my little jokes on Thee / And I'll forgive Thy great big one on me.

8 Half the world is composed of people who have something to say and can't, and the other half who have nothing to say and keep on saying it.

9 Hell is a half-filled auditorium.

10 Home is the place where, when you have to go there, / They have to take you in.

11 If society fits you comfortably enough, you call it freedom.

12 It's a funny thing that when a man hasn't got anything on earth to worry about, he goes off and gets married.

13 The brain is a wonderful organ. It starts working the moment you get up in the morning, and does not stop until you get to the office.

14 The reason why worry kills more people than work is that more people worry than work.

15 The world is full of willing people: some willing to work, the rest willing to let them.

16 Writing free verse is like playing tennis with the net down.

CHRISTOPHER FRY (1907–). *British playwright*

1 I tell you, / Miss, I knows an undesirable character / When I see one; I've been one myself for years.

2 Where in this small-talking world can I find / A longitude with no platitude?

STEPHEN FRY (1957–). *British actor and writer*

1 At my age travel broadens the behind.

2 I don't need you to remind me of my age: I have a bladder to do that for me.

3 Sir Arthur Conan Doyle is said to have once left a dinner party raving about Oscar Wilde's gift as a conversationalist. "But you did all the talking," his companion pointed out. "Exactly!" Conan Doyle said.

4 You don't need a Harvard MBA to know that the bedroom and the boardroom are just two sides of the same ball game.

CARLOS FUENTES (1928–). *Mexican novelist and playwright*

There are years when nothing happens and years in which centuries happen.

F. BUCKMINSTER FULLER (1895–1983). *American inventor and designer*

1 How *do* we know that the people we meet are not computers programmed to simulate people?

2 The most important fact about Spaceship Earth: an instruction book didn't come with it.

PAUL FUSSELL (1924–). *American academic and writer*

1 "Have a nice day!" Thank you, but I have other plans.

2 What someone doesn't want you to publish is journalism; all else is publicity.

CLARK GABLE (1901–1960). *American actor*
The only reason they come to see me is that I know life is great—and they know I know it.

ZSA ZSA GABOR (1919–). *Hungarian-born American actress*
1 A man in love is incomplete until he has married. Then he's finished.
2 Getting divorced just because you don't love a man is almost as silly as getting married just because you do.
3 "How many husbands have you had?" You mean apart from my own?
4 Husbands are like fires: they go out when unattended.
5 I know nothing about sex, because I was always married.
6 You're never too young to be younger.

JOHN KENNETH GALBRAITH (1908–). *Canadian-born American economist*
1 A common scold. [On himself.]
2 Ed Stettinius was one of those far from exceptional people who give everyone else a glow of satisfaction from feelings of undeniable superiority. [On the secretary of state.]
3 Every feature and facet of every product having been studied for selling points, these are then described with talent, gravity and an aspect of profound concern as the source of health, happiness, social achievement, or improved community standing. Even minor qualities of unimportant commodities are enlarged upon with a solemnity which would not be unbecoming in an announcement of the combined return of Christ, and all the apostles. [On advertising.]
4 Few things are more tempting to a writer than to repeat, admiringly, what he has said before.
5 Financial genius consists almost entirely of avarice and a rising market.
6 Galbraith's law states that anyone who says he won't resign four times, will.
7 I always find the fiction that I am being done in by malign influences strangely agreeable.
8 In any great organization it is far, far safer to be wrong with the majority than to be right alone.
9 In considering economic behavior, humor is especially important for, needless to say, much of that behavior is infinitely ridiculous.
10 It is a far, far better thing to have a firm anchor in nonsense than to put out on the troubled seas of thought.
11 It is possible that people need to believe that they are unmanaged if they are to be managed effectively. —See also William Penn 1
12 Meetings are indispensable when you don't want to do anything. —See also Fred Allen 7
13 Modesty is a vastly overrated virtue.
14 Nothing is so admirable in politics as a short memory.
15 Nothing so develops the latent fatuousness in a community as a speculative boom.

16 Nothing so gives the illusion of intelligence as personal association with large sums of money.

17 One of my greatest pleasures in writing has come from the thought that perhaps my work might annoy someone of comfortably pretentious position. Then comes the saddening realization that such people rarely read.

18 Originality is something that is easily exaggerated, especially by authors contemplating their own work.

19 Politics is not the art of the possible. It consists in choosing between the disastrous and the unpalatable.

20 The experience of being disastrously wrong is salutary; no economist should be denied it, and not many are.

21 The modern conservative is engaged in one of man's oldest exercises in moral philosophy; that is, the search for a superior moral justification for selfishness.

22 The salary of the chief executive of the large corporation is not a market award for achievement. It is frequently in the nature of a warm personal gesture by the individual to himself.

23 There are few ironclad rules of diplomacy but to one there is no exception. When an official reports that talks were useful, it can safely be concluded that nothing was accomplished.

24 There are two classes of people who tell what is going to happen in the future: those who don't know, and those who don't know they don't know.

25 These are the days when men of all social disciplines and all political faiths seek the comfortable and the accepted; when the man of controversy is looked upon as a disturbing influence; when originality is taken to be a mark of instability; and when, in minor modification of the scriptural parable, the bland lead the bland.

26 Trickle-down theory—the less than elegant metaphor that if one feeds the horse enough oats, some will pass through to the road for the sparrows.

27 Under capitalism man exploits man. And under communism it is just the reverse.

28 Wealth is not without its advantages and the case to the contrary, although it has often been made, has never proved widely persuasive.

JOHN GALSWORTHY (1867–1933). *English novelist*
Idealism increases in direct proportion to one's distance from the problem.
  —See also William F. Buckley, Jr. 5

MOHANDAS K. GANDHI (1869–1948). *Indian spiritual leader*
1 "Did you feel inadequate, wearing only a loincloth and a shawl, when you met George V?" [Reporter] The King had enough on for both of us. [During a visit to England, 1930.]

2 I am very imperfect. Before you are gone you will have discovered a hundred of my faults, and if you don't, I will help you to see them. [Remark to Louis Fischer, 1942.]

3 "Mr. Gandhi, what do you think of Western civilization?" [Reporter] That would be a good idea. [England, 1930.]

GRETA GARBO (1905–1990). *Swedish actress*
I never said, "I want to be alone." I only said, "I want to be left alone." [1955 *Life* magazine interview; she had in fact said "I want to be alone" in the 1932 film *Grand Hotel,* and also in the 1929 silent film *The Single Standard.*]

ED GARDNER (1905–1963). *American radio personality*
Opera is when a guy gets stabbed in the back and, instead of bleeding, he sings.

HY GARDNER (1908–1989). American journalist
You know you're growing old when almost everything hurts, and what doesn't hurt doesn't work.

JAMES A. GARFIELD (1831–1881). *American president*
1 A pound of pluck is worth a ton of luck.
2 An Englishman who was wrecked on a strange shore and wandering along the coast came to a gallows with a victim hanging on it, and fell down on his knees and thanked God that he at last beheld a sign of civilization. — See also Voltaire 10

JOHN NANCE GARNER (1868–1967). *Texas Speaker of the House of Representatives and U.S. vice president*
The vice presidency isn't worth a pitcher of warm piss.

BILL GATES (1955–). *American computer industry leader*
1 I think business is very simple. Profit. Loss. Take the sales, subtract the costs, you get this big positive number. The math is quite straightforward.
2 640K ought to be enough for anybody. [1981]—See also Thomas Watson

JOHN GAY (1685–1732). *English poet and playwright*
1 That politician tops his part, / Who readily can lie with art.
2 Those who in quarrels interpose, / Must often wipe a bloody nose.
3 Where yet was ever found a mother, / Who'd give her booby for another?
4 Who friendship with a knave has made / Is judged a partner in the trade.

DAVID GEFFEN (1943–). *American record and film producer*
This is a town that doesn't just want you to fail, it wants you to die. [On Hollywood.]

BOB GELDOF (1954–). *American record producer*
Most people get into bands for three very simple rock 'n' roll reasons: to get laid, to get fame, and to get rich.

HENRY GELDZAHLER (20th century). *American cultural leader*
It is the theater God would have built if He had the money. [Testimony at hearings on the designation of Radio City Music Hall as a New York City landmark, 1978.]

WALTER GEORGE (1878–1957). *Georgia senator*
"You know the president is his own worst enemy." Not as long as I'm alive, he's not. [Referring to Franklin D. Roosevelt, 1938.]

J. PAUL GETTY (1892–1976). *American petroleum industry leader*
1 If you can actually count your money, then you're not really rich.

2 My formula for success? Rise early, work late, strike oil!

3 People who don't respect money don't have any.

4 The meek shall inherit the earth, but not the mineral rights.

EDWARD GIBBON (1737–1794). *English historian*

1 A portrait endowed with every merit excepting that of likeness to the original. [On Alexander Pope's translation of Homer.]

2 Corruption, the most infallible symptom of constitutional liberty.

3 It is always easy, as well as agreeable, for the inferior ranks of mankind to claim a merit from the contempt of that pomp and pleasure which fortune has placed beyond their reach.

4 Perhaps no human being was ever more perfectly exempt from the taint of malevolence, vanity, or falsehood. [On himself.]

5 The appellation of heretics has always been applied to the less numerous party.

6 The brutal insolence of Mr. Travis's challenge can only be excused by the absence of learning, judgment, and humanity. [Replying to a critic.]

7 The laws of probability, so true in general, so fallacious in particular.

8 The tediousness of an idle life.

9 The various modes of worship, which prevailed in the Roman world, were all considered by the people as equally true; by the philosopher as equally false; and by the magistrate as equally useful.

10 Twenty-two acknowledged concubines, and a library of sixty-two thousand volumes, attested the variety of his inclinations, and from the productions which he left behind him, it appears that the former as well as the latter were designed for use rather than ostentation. [Footnote:] By each of his concubines the younger Gordian left three or four children. His literary productions were by no means contemptible. [On the Roman emperor Gordian.]

11 Unprovided with original learning, unformed in the habits of thinking, unskilled in the arts of composition, I resolved—to write a book.

ANDRÉ GIDE (1869–1951). *French writer*

1 It is better to be hated for what you are than loved for what you are not.

2 It is only when proofs are lacking that people try to impose their opinions.

3 Other people's appetites easily appear excessive when one doesn't share them.

4 The true hypocrite is the one who ceases to perceive his deception, the one who lies with sincerity.

JOHN GIELGUD (1904–2000). *English actor and producer*

Dear Ingrid—speaks five languages and can't act in any of them. [On Ingrid Bergman.]

FRANK GIFFORD (1930–). *American football player and broadcaster*

Pro football is like nuclear warfare. There are no winners, only survivors.

W. S. GILBERT (1836–1911). *English librettist (Gilbert and Sullivan)*

1 I always voted at my party's call, / And I never thought of thinking for myself at all.

2 I have a left shoulder-blade that is a miracle of loveliness. People come miles to see it. My right elbow has a fascination that few can resist.

3 If you wish in this world to advance / Your merits you're bound to enhance; / You must stir it and stump it, / And blow your own trumpet, / Or, trust me, you haven't a chance.

4 She may very well pass for forty-three / In the dusk with a light behind her!

5 The House of Peers, throughout the war, / Did nothing in particular, / And did it very well.

6 The idiot who praises, with enthusiastic tone, / All centuries but this, and every country but his own.

7 When every one is somebody, / Then no one's anybody.

8 When I was a lad I served a term / As office boy to an Attorney's firm. / I cleaned the windows and I swept the floor, / And I polished up the handle of the big front door. / I polished up that handle so carefullee / That now I am the Ruler of the Queen's Navee! [*HMS Pinafore,* 1878.]

9 While Darwinian Man, though well-behaved, / At best is only a monkey shaved!

10 You've no idea what a poor opinion I have of myself— / and how little I deserve it.

HERMIONE GINGOLD (1897–1987). *English actress*
1 Contrary to popular belief, English women do not wear tweed nightgowns.
2 "Is your husband still alive?" It's a matter of opinion.

ALLEN GINSBERG (1926–1997). *American poet*
1 America I'm putting my queer shoulder to the wheel.
2 A naked lunch is natural to us / We eat reality sandwiches.
3 I've got no axiom to grind.

NIKKI GIOVANNI (1943–). *American poet and writer*
Baseball is the world's most tranquil sport. It is probably the only active sport where you are not seriously required to be alive to play.

JEAN GIRAUDOUX (1882–1944). *French playwright*
1 There's no better way of exercising the imagination than the study of law. No poet ever interpreted nature as freely as a lawyer interprets truth.
2 To have money is to be virtuous, honest, beautiful and witty. And to be without money is to be ugly, boring, stupid and useless.

RUDOLPH W. GIULIANI (1944–). *New York mayor*
On 106 occasions, bribes were offered or discussed. On 105 of those occasions, the public official involved accepted the bribe. And on the other occasion he turned it down because he didn't think the amount was enough. [From his report, as a government attorney, on the results of a statewide sting operation in New York involving an FBI agent who posed as a steel-products salesman, *The New York Times,* 12 August 1987.]

WILLIAM EWART GLADSTONE (1809–1898). *English prime minister*
1 A radical is a liberal in earnest.
2 All the world over, I will back the masses against the classes.
3 He has not a single redeeming defect. [On Benjamin Disraeli.]

4 If you want to succeed in politics, you must keep your conscience well under control. —See also Don Marquis 8

5 The first essential for a prime minister is to be a good butcher.

GEORGE GLASS (1910–1984). *American film executive*

An actor is a kind of a guy who if you ain't talking about him ain't listening. [Often attributed to Marlon Brando.]

JOHN GLENN (1921–). *American astronaut and Ohio senator*

It's hard to beat a day in which you are permitted the luxury of four sunsets. [Referring to his 1962 orbital space flight.]

JOHANN WOLFGANG von GOETHE (1749–1832). *German poet and playwright*

1 Fools and wise folk are alike harmless. It is the half-wise and the half-foolish, who are the most dangerous.

2 In politics, as on the sickbed, people toss from side to side, thinking they will be more comfortable.

3 Know myself? If I knew myself, I'd run away.

4 Modern poets add a lot of water to their ink.

5 When ideas fail, words come in very handy.

ROBERT F. GOHEEN (1919–). *American educator, university president, and ambassador*

If you feel that you have both feet planted on level ground, then the university has failed you. [1961]

ISAAC GOLDBERG (1887–1938). *American critic*

1 Diplomacy is to do and say / The nastiest thing in the nicest way.

2 We spend half our lives unlearning the follies transmitted to us by our parents, and the other half transmitting our own follies to our offspring.

OLIVER GOLDSMITH (1728–1774). *Irish-born British novelist, playwright, and poet*

1 He makes a very handsome corpse and becomes his coffin prodigiously. [1768] —See also Charles Dickens 3

2 There is no arguing with Johnson; for when his pistol misses fire, he knocks you down with the butt end of it. [On Samuel Johnson.]

BARRY GOLDWATER (1909–1998). *Arizona senator and Republican presidential nominee*

1 If he were any dumber, he'd be a tree. [On Senator William Scott.]

2 Since I'm only half Jewish, can I join if I only play nine holes. [On being blackballed by a Phoenix golf club.]

3 The income tax has created more criminals than any other single act of government.

SAMUEL GOLDWYN (1882–1974). *Polish-born American film producer*

1 A verbal contract isn't worth the paper it's written on.

2 Coffee is not my cup of tea.

3 Do you want to put my head in a moose?

4 Don't pay any attention to the critics—don't even ignore them!

5 Gentlemen, include me out. [Informing associates he was quitting their organization.]

6 I can answer you in two words: "im possible."

7 I don't care about that; it rolls off my back like a duck.

8 I don't care if my pictures don't make a dime, so long as everyone comes to see them.

9 I don't want any yes-men around me. I want everybody to tell me the truth even if it costs them their jobs.

10 I read part of the book all the way through.

11 I was always an independent, even when I had partners.

12 I'll believe in color television when I see it in black and white. [Attributed.]

13 I'll give it to you straight, Mike. About that property. I could give you a positive "yes," and I don't want to give you a positive "no." But Mike, I *will* give you a positive maybe. [Phone conversation with Michael Bessie, who for weeks had been trying to find out if Goldwyn was going to bid for the movie rights to his novel.]

14 If I could drop dead right now, I'd be the happiest man alive. [Attributed.]

15 If I was in this business for the business, I wouldn't be in this business. [Attributed.]

16 If people don't want to go to the picture, nobody can stop them. [Also attributed to Sol Hurok.] —See also Yogi Berra 6

17 It's more than magnificent; it's mediocre. [Attributed.]

18 It's spreading like wildflowers. [Attributed.]

19 Let's bring it up to date with some snappy nineteenth-century dialogue.

20 Never let that bastard back in my office again—unless I need him. [Attributed.]

21 Next time I want to send an idiot on some errand, I'll go myself. [Attributed.]

22 Pictures are for entertainment; messages should be delivered by Western Union. [1930s] —See also Brendan Behan 7

23 Spare no expense to make everything as economic as possible.

24 Tell me how did you love my picture?

25 That makes me so sore it gets my dandruff up.

26 That's the way with these directors, they're always biting the hand that lays the golden egg.

27 The H-bomb. It's dynamite.

28 The reason so many people showed up at his funeral was because they wanted to make sure he was dead. [Referring to Louis B. Mayer; attributed, but Goldwyn denied having said it.]

29 The wide screen will only make bad films twice as bad.

30 They didn't release that film; it escaped.

31 Too caustic? To hell with the cost. If it's a good picture, we'll make it.

32 We have passed a lot of water since then. [Attributed.]

33 We're dealing with facts, not realities. [Attributed.]

34 We're overpaying him, but he's worth it.

35 What we need is a new cliché. [Attributed.]

36 What we want is a story that starts with an earthquake and works its way up to a climax.

37 Why should people go out and pay to see bad movies when they can stay at home and see bad television for nothing?

38 You've gotta take the sour with the bitter. [Attributed.]

VERNON "LEFTY" GOMEZ (1909–1989). *American baseball player*

"Lefty, I don't think you're throwing as hard as you used to." [New York Yankee manager Joe McCarthy] You're wrong, Joe. I'm throwing twice as hard, but the ball isn't going as fast. [Toward the end of his career.]

ELLEN GOODMAN (1941–). *American journalist*

1 Statistically speaking, the Cheerful Early Riser is rejected more completely than a member of any other subculture, save those with boot odor.

2 The same people who tell us that smoking doesn't cause cancer are now telling us that advertising cigarettes doesn't cause smoking. [1986]

3 We want our children to fit in and to stand out. We rarely address the conflict between these goals.

PAUL GOODMAN (1911–1972). *American writer*

1 Few great men could pass Personnel.

2 When there is official censorship, it is a sign that speech is serious. When there is none, it is pretty certain that the official spokesmen have all the loudspeakers.

JACK GOULD (1919–1993). *American critic*

Mr. Presley has no discernible singing ability. His specialty is rhythm songs which he renders in an undistinguished whine; his phrasing, if it can be called that, consists of the stereotyped variations that go with a beginner's aria in a bathtub. For the ear he is an unutterable bore. [Referring to Elvis Presley, 1956.]

LEW GRADE (1906–1998). *British impresario*

1 All my shows are great. Some of them are bad, but they're all great.

2 When a little girl asked me what two and two make, I'm supposed to have answered, "It depends if you're buying or selling." Not true.

MARTHA GRAHAM (1894–1991). *American dancer and choreographer*

They never raised a statue to a critic.

CARY GRANT (1904–1986). *English-born American actor*

1 Everyone wants to be Cary Grant, even I want to be Cary Grant.

2 "How old Cary Grant?" [Inquiry by telegram] Old Cary Grant fine. How you? [Response by telegram.]

3 I pretended to be somebody I wanted to be until finally I became that person. Or he became me.

4 I think our young people are getting it all together. Not that I think you should be making love all the time—who can do it all the time? Though I *do* try.

5 Money talks, they say. But all it ever said to me was "good-bye."

ULYSSES S. GRANT (1822–1885). *American general and president*

1 Garfield has shown that he is not possessed of the backbone of an angleworm. [On President James A. Garfield.] —See also Theodore Roosevelt 4

2 "I disagree with your opinion about ——; he's been in ten campaigns." General, so has that mule yonder, but he's still a jackass.

3 I know only two tunes. One of them is "Yankee Doodle" and the other isn't.

4 The day we started was the first time the horse had ever been under saddle. I had, however, but little difficulty in breaking him, though for the first day there were frequent disagreements between us as to which way we should go, and sometimes whether we should go at all.

5 The truth is I am more of a farmer than a soldier. I take little or no interest in military affairs, and, although I entered the army thirty-five years ago and have been in two wars, in Mexico as a young lieutenant, and later, I never went into the army without regret and never retired without pleasure.

6 They tell me, my Lord, that your father was also a military man. [Remark to the Duke of Wellington's son during a European tour.]

7 Venice would be a fine city if it were only drained.

8 "What were your thoughts, General, in that sublime moment when you knew that at last Lee would surrender, and the heavens of your glory were about to open?" My dirty boots and wearing no sword.

ROBERT GRAVES (1895–1985). *English poet*

1 The remarkable thing about Shakespeare is that he is really very good, in spite of all the people who say he is very good.

2 There's no money in poetry, but then there's no poetry in money either.

HORACE GREELEY (1811–1872). *American editor*

1 I never said all Democrats were saloonkeepers. What I said was that all saloonkeepers are Democrats.

2 Tow-headed, and half-bald at that, slouching in dress; goes bent like a hoop, and so rocking in his gait that he walks down both sides of the street at once. [On himself.]

GRAHAM GREENE (1904–1991). *English novelist*

1 Fame is a powerful aphrodisiac. —See also Henry A. Kissinger 12

2 Sentimentality—that's what we call the sentiment we don't share.

ALAN GREENSPAN (1926–). *American economist and Federal Reserve System chairman*

1 I think where the confusion arises is the fact that you cannot view monetary policy as a sort of simple issue of, if the most probable outcome is coming out of this soft patch into moderate growth with low inflation, which I think is the most probable outcome, that is not the same statement as saying that you therefore, in the process of implementing monetary policy or formulating it, I should say, completely disregard what the upsides and downsides of a potential outcome may be. [Testimony before the Senate Banking Committee, 1996.]

2 I worry incessantly that I might be too clear.

3 Since I've become a central banker, I've learned to mumble with great coherence. If I seem unduly clear to you, you must have misunderstood what I said.

4 The buck starts here. [Desk sign in his office.] —See also Harry S. Truman 23

5 This is a town that is full of evil people. If you can't deal every day with having people trying to destroy you, you shouldn't even think of coming down here. [Advice to a New Yorker who was considering a top administrative appointment in Washington, 1994.]

GERMAINE GREER (1939–). *Australian writer*

1 Freud was the father of psychoanalysis. It had no mother.

2 Probably the only place where a man can feel really secure is in a maximum security prison, except for the imminent threat of release.

3 The sight of women talking together has always made men uneasy; nowadays it means rank subversion.

4 The tragedy of machismo is that a man is never quite man enough.

DICK GREGORY (1932–). *American comedian*

1 Hell hath no fury like a liberal scorned. —See also Milton Friedman 1; C. E. Montague

2 I happen to know quite a bit about the South. Spent twenty years there one night.

3 If they took all the drugs, nicotine, alcohol, caffeine off the market for six days, they'd have to bring out the tanks to control you.

4 If killing was the answer, we'd have solved all our problems a long time ago.

5 When the U.S. cavalry won, it was a great victory; when the Indians won, it was a massacre.

6 You've gotta say this for the white race—its self-confidence knows no bounds. Who else could go to a small island in the South Pacific where there's no poverty, no crime, no unemployment, no war and no worry—and call it a "primitive society"?

FULKE GREVILLE (1554–1628). *English poet*

1 Our companions please us less from the charms we find in their conversation than from those they find in ours.

2 People seldom speak ill of themselves, but when they have a good chance of being contradicted.

3 You must be a little out of the fashion to be well in it.

BOB GUCCIONE (20th century). *American publisher*

If I were asked for a one-line answer to the question, "What makes a woman good in bed?" I would say, "A man who is good in bed."

PHILIP GUEDALLA (1899–1944). *British historian and biographer*

1 Autobiography is an unrivaled vehicle for telling the truth about other people.

2 Biography is a very definite region bounded on the north by history, on the south by fiction, on the east by obituary, and on the west by tedium.

3 History repeats itself. Historians repeat each other. [Attributed.]

4 The twentieth century is only the nineteenth speaking with a slight American accent.

5 There is no Gibbon but Gibbon and Gibbon is his prophet. [On the historian Edward Gibbon.]

ARLO GUTHRIE (1947–). *American folk singer and songwriter*

I don't want a pickle, / Just want to ride on my motorsickle, / And I don't want a tickle, / 'Cause I'd rather ride on my motorsickle / And I don't want to die, / Just want a ride on my motorcycle.

WOODY GUTHRIE (1912–1967). *American folk singer and songwriter*

Some men will rob you with a six-gun, / Some with a fountain pen. ["Pretty Boy Floyd."]

WALTER HAGEN (1892–1969). *American golfer*

You're only here for a short visit. Don't hurry. Don't worry. And be sure to smell the flowers along the way.

H. R. HALDEMAN (1926–1993). *American advertising executive and presidential assistant*

1 Every president needs his son of a bitch, and I'm Nixon's.

2 Once the toothpaste is out of the tube, it is awfully hard to get it back in. [Remark to John Dean during the Watergate hearings, 1973.]

EDWARD EVERETT HALE (1822–1909). *American clergyman and Senate chaplain*

"Do you pray for the senators, Dr. Hale?" No, I look at the senators and pray for the country.

THOMAS CHANDLER HALIBURTON (1796–1865). *Canadian jurist and humorist*

A college education shows a man how little other people know.

LORD HALIFAX (George Saville, 1622–1695). *English statesman and essayist*

1 A man that should call everything by its right name would hardly pass the streets without being knocked down as a common enemy.

2 Education is what remains when we have forgotten all that we have been taught.

3 Ignorance makes most men go into a party, and shame keeps them from getting out of it.

4 In this age, when it is said of a man, "He knows how to live," it may be implied he is not very honest.

5 Most men's anger about religion is as if two men should quarrel for a lady they neither them care for.

6 Nothing has an uglier look to us than reason, when it is not on our side.

7 The best party is but a kind of a conspiracy against the rest of the nation.

8 The best qualification of a prophet is to have a good memory.

9 The vanity of teaching often tempts a man to forget he is a blockhead.

10 When the people contend for their liberty, they seldom get anything by their victory but new masters.

ALEXANDER HAMILTON (1755–1804). *American secretary of the treasury*

1 In times like these in which we live, it will not do to be overscrupulous.

2 Man—a reasoning rather than a reasonable animal.

WILLIAM HAMILTON (20th century). *American cartoonist*

1 I made my money the old-fashioned way—I inherited it. [Man to woman at a cocktail party, cartoon caption.]

2 I think older women with younger men threaten all the right people. [One woman to another at a cocktail party, cartoon caption.]

3 I took because I had what it took to take. [Man to woman in a cocktail lounge, cartoon caption.]

4 Millions is craft. Billions is art. [One man to another at a cocktail party, cartoon caption, 1994.]

5 The point is to get so much money that money's not the point anymore. [One young man to another at a cocktail lounge, cartoon caption.]

DASHIELL HAMMETT (1894–1961). *American novelist and screenwriter*

1 "I read where you were shot five times in the tabloids." [Myrna Loy] "It's not true. He didn't come anywhere near my tabloids." [William Powell, in the 1934 film *The Thin Man*.]

2 "Mr. Hammett, if you were in our position, would you allow your book in the United States Information Service libraries?" [Senator Joseph McCarthy] If I were you, Senator, I would not allow any libraries. [Testifying before a Senate committee chaired by McCarthy during the early 1950s, soon after Hammett's popular 1930 crime novel *The Maltese Falcon* had been removed from USIS libraries.]

CHRISTOPHER HAMPTON (1946–). *English playwright*

1 Asking a working writer what he thinks about critics is like asking a lamppost how it feels about dogs. [Attributed.]

2 I always divide people into two groups. Those who live by what they know to be a lie, and those who live by what they believe, falsely, to be the truth.

MAL HANCOCK (1937–1993). *American cartoonist*

1 A bromide a day keeps original thought away.

2 A pollyanna meets a curmudgeon: "Have a nice day!" "Drop dead!"

3 As soon as life starts making sense to me I know I'm in trouble.

4 Give me liberty or give me a benevolent dictatorship.

5 I keep forgetting. Am I in the groove, or in a rut?

6 I suppose that eating health food is the price one must pay for being healthy.

7 I wish my life had more "thrill of victory" and less "agony of defeat."

8 I'm my own cult of one.

9 I'm rich and getting richer. You're poor and getting poorer. See, I told you the system still works! [Cigar-smoking rich guy to poor guy in tatters, cartoon balloon.]

10 I'm searching for some temptation to give in to.

11 I've been an oppressor and I've been an oppressee. And believe me, being an oppressor is best! —See also Sophie Tucker 2

12 I've finally got my act together, only to discover that I've got a crummy act.

13 I've striven to become what I've become, only to discover that what I've become is not what I want to be.

14 If you're not outraged, you're not paying attention. —See also Maureen Dowd 3

15 Keep Your Eye on Everything! [Wall sign.]

16 Life is a joke of which I'm the butt!

17 Look, Janice, if God hadn't wanted us to live life in the fast lane, he wouldn't have created a fast lane for us to live in!

18 My mind is full of ideas whose times have not come.

19 Reality is the ultimate illusion.

20 Sure, history will judge him right, but you know what a crock history is!

21 The good news is the economy is doing better. The bad news is the bottom is about to fall out.

22 Thou Shalt Not Believe Thy Own Hype! [Wall sign.]

23 Truth is the accepted lie of the moment.

24 Unto Your Own Self Be Reasonably True! [Wall sign.]

25 Warning: Any Suggestion You Make May Be Used Against You. [Sign above suggestion box.]

26 What I lack in <u>know how</u>, I more than make up for in <u>know who</u>.

E. Y. "YIP" HARBURG (1898–1981). *American songwriter*

1 A virgin is the worst / Her method is reversed; / She'll lead a horse to water / And then let him die of thirst.

2 Did God who gave us flowers and trees, / Also provide the allergies?

3 "For what we are about to receive, / Oh Lord, 'tis Thee we thank," / Said the cannibal as he cut a slice / Of the missionary's shank.

4 She has eyes that men adore so / And a torso even more so.

5 When I'm not near the girl I love, / I love the girl I'm near. [1947]

6 Why should I write for posterity? / What, if I may be free / To ask a ridiculous question, / Has posterity done for me?

WARREN G. HARDING (1865–1923). *American president*

1 American business is not a monster, but an expression of the God-given impulse to create, and the savior and guardian of our happiness.

2 I don't know what to do or where to turn on this taxation matter. Somewhere there must be a book that tells all about it, where I could go to straighten it out in my mind. But I don't know where the book is, and maybe I couldn't read it if I found it! My God, this is a hell of a place for a man like me to be! [On the presidency.]

3 I have no trouble with my enemies. I can take care of my enemies all right. But my damn friends, my goddamn friends. They're the ones that keep me walking the floor nights!

THOMAS HARDY (1840–1928). *English novelist and poet*

1 A lover without indiscretion is no lover at all.

2 That man's silence is wonderful to listen to.

JOHN HARINGTON (1561–1612). *English writer and courtier*

1 My writings oft displease you: what's the matter? / You love not to hear truth, nor I to flatter.

2 Treason doth never prosper, what's the reason? / For if it prosper, none dare call it treason.

SYDNEY J. HARRIS (1917–1986). *English-born American journalist*

1 A cynic is not merely one who reads bitter lessons from the past, he is one who is prematurely disappointed in the future.

2 A "good marriage" is one in which the initial expectations were so low that no illusions could be shattered by the reality.

3 An avant-garde thinker is someone who is ready to repudiate his own ideas as soon as a sufficient number of the public begin to accept them.

4 Any philosophy that can be put "in a nutshell" belongs there.

5 Growth for the sake of growth is the ideology of the cancer cell.

6 Nobody can be so amusingly arrogant as a young man who has just discovered an old idea and thinks it is his own.

7 One of the oldest Russian proverbs remains as inexorably true in modern America: "No one is hanged who has money in his pocket." Or, one might say, capital punishment is only for those without capital. —See also Anonymous 109

8 People who think they're generous to a fault usually think that's their only fault.

9 The real danger is not that computers will begin to think like men, but that men will begin to think like computers.

10 The strong get stronger until they collapse; the weak get weaker until they rebel; then they change places and repeat the process. [Responding to a reader who wanted to know, in twenty-five words or less, "what was happening in the world."]

REX HARRISON (1908–1990). *English actor*

I'm now at the age where I've got to prove that I'm just as good as I never was.

PAUL HARVEY (1918–). *American broadcast journalist*

1 If there is a 50–50 chance that something can go wrong, then nine times out of ten it will.

2 In times like these, it helps to recall that there have always been times like these.

ORRIN G. HATCH (1934–). *Utah senator*

Capital punishment is our society's recognition of the sanctity of human life.

VÁCLAV HAVEL (1936–). *Czech president and writer*

There's always something suspect about an intellectual on the winning side.

IAN HAY (1876–1952). *British writer*

What do you mean, funny? Funny peculiar, or funny ha-ha?

HELEN HAYES (1900–1993). *American actress*

1 An actress's life is so transitory—suddenly you're a building. [On having a Broadway theater named after her, 1955.]

2 I was at a party feeling very shy because there were a lot of celebrities around. I was sitting in a corner alone and a very beautiful young man came up to me and offered me some salted peanuts. Handing them to me, he said, "I wish they were emeralds." That was the end of my heart; I never got it back. [On meeting her future husband.]

3 Stardom can be a gilded slavery.

W. B. "BILL" HAYLER (20th century). *American naval officer*

A collision at sea can ruin your entire day. [1960]

WILLIAM HAZLITT (1778–1830). *English essayist*

1 Cunning is the art of concealing our own defects, and discovering other people's.

2 It is essential to the triumph of reform that it should never succeed.

3 Man is the only animal that laughs and weeps; for he is the only animal that is struck with the difference between what things are, and what they ought to be.

4 People had much rather be thought to look ill than old: because it is possible to recover from sickness, but there is no recovering from age.

5 Political truth is libel; religious truth, blasphemy.

6 The garb of religion is the best cloak for power. —See also Aldous Huxley 3

7 The least pain in our little finger gives more concern and uneasiness than the destruction of millions of our fellow beings.

8 There are amiable vices and obnoxious virtues.

9 We are never so much disposed to quarrel with others as when we are dissatisfied with ourselves.

10 We as often repent the good we have done as the ill.

11 We can forgive anyone sooner than those who lower us in our own opinion.

12 Without the aid of prejudice and custom, I should not be able to find my way across the room.

WILLIAM RANDOLPH HEARST (1863–1951). *American publisher*

1 "Everything is quiet. There is no trouble here. There will be no war. I wish to return." [Frederic Remington in a wire from Cuba to the *New York Journal* in 1897.] You furnish the pictures, and I'll furnish the war. [Return wire; the Spanish-American War broke out the next year; attributed, but Hearst denied the exchange.]

2 Get in a lot of youngsters who don't know it can't be done. [On staffing an organization.]

3 It takes a good mind to resist education. [On formal schooling.]

4 Whatever begins to be tranquil is gobbled up by something that is not tranquil.

GEORG HEGEL (1770–1831). *German philosopher*

1 I may say with Christ that not only do I teach truth, but that I am myself truth. [Opening words of a lecture.]

2 Only one man ever understood me. And he didn't understand me. [Last words.]

3 We learn from history that we do not learn from history. —See also George Bernard Shaw 133

JASCHA HEIFETZ (1901–1987). *Lithuanian-born American violinist*

If I don't practice one day, I know it: two days, the critics know it: three days, the public knows it.

PIET HEIN (1905–1996). *Danish scientist and poet*

1 As eternity / is reckoned, there's a lifetime / in a second.

2 Here lies extinguished in his prime, / a victim of modernity: / but yesterday he hadn't time— / and now he has eternity. ["More Haste (inscription for a monument at the crossroads)," *Grooks,* 1966.]

3 If no thought / your mind does visit, / make your speech / not too explicit.

4 My faith in doctors / is immense. / Just one thing spoils it: / their pretense / of authorized / omniscience.

5 Philosophers / must ultimately find / their true perfection / in knowing all / the follies of mankind / —by introspection.

6 Problems worthy / of attack / prove their worth / by hitting back.

7 Shun advice / at any price— / that's what I call / good advice.

8 The human spirit sublimates / the impulses it thwarts; / a healthy sex life mitigates / the lust for other sports.

9 We don't discover what we can't achieve / until we make an effort not to try.

HEINRICH HEINE (1797–1856). *German poet and critic*

1 God will forgive me—that's his business!

2 I want there to be one man who will regret my death. [Bequeathing his entire estate to his wife with the single condition that she marry again.]

3 I've never met an ass that talked like a human being, but I've met many human beings who talked like asses.

4 It's too bad our public knows so little about poetry, almost as little, in fact, as our poets.

5 Merchants throughout the world have the same religion.

6 Money is the god of our time, and Rothschild is his prophet.

7 Ordinarily he was insane, but he had lucid moments when he was merely stupid. [Referring to an ambassador.]

8 We should forgive our enemies, but not before they've been hanged.

ROBERT A. HEINLEIN (1907–). *American writer*

1 It is better to copulate than never.

2 Obscurity is the refuge of incompetence. —See also Samuel Johnson 64

JOSEPH HELLER (1923–1999). *American novelist*

1 Catch-22 says they have a right to do anything we can't stop them from doing. [*Catch-22*, 1961.]

2 Clevinger was one of those people with lots of intelligence and no brains, and everyone knew it except those who soon found it out. In short, he was a dope.

3 Colonel Cathcart had courage and never hesitated to volunteer his men for any target available.

4 Fortunately, just when things were blackest, the war broke out.

5 General Peckem liked listening to himself talk, liked most of all listening to himself talk about himself.

6 Good God, how much reverence can you have for a Supreme Being who finds it necessary to include such phenomena as phlegm and tooth decay in His divine system of creation?

7 "Has it ever occurred to you that in your promiscuous pursuit of women you are merely trying to assuage your subconscious fears of sexual impotence?" "Yes, sir, it has." "Then why do you do it?" "To assuage my fears of sexual impotence."

8 He had decided to live forever or die in the attempt.

9 He was a long-limbed farmer, a God-fearing, freedom-loving, law-abiding rugged individualist who held that federal aid to anyone but farmers was creeping socialism.

10 He was a self-made man who owed his lack of success to nobody.

11 Hungry Joe collected lists of fatal diseases and arranged them in alphabetical order so that he could put his finger without delay on any one he wanted to worry about.

12 I'd like to see the government get out of war altogether and leave the whole field to private industry.

13 People who met him were always impressed by how unimpressive he was.

14 Prostitution gives her an opportunity to meet people. It provides fresh air and wholesome exercise, and it keeps her out of trouble.

15 Some men are born mediocre, some men achieve mediocrity, and some men have mediocrity thrust upon them. With Major Major it had been all three.

16 The Texan turned out to be good-natured, generous and likable. In three days no one could stand him.

17 There was only one catch and that was Catch-22, which specified that a concern for one's own safety in the face of dangers that were real and immediate was the process of a rational mind. If Orr flew more combat missions, he was crazy and didn't have to; but if he didn't want to he was sane and had to.

18 When I read something saying I've not done anything as good as *Catch-22*, I'm tempted to reply, "Who has?" [1993]

19 While none of the work we do is very important, it is important that we do a great deal of it.

LILLIAN HELLMAN (1907–1984). *American playwright*

1 People always sound so proud when they announce they know nothing of music.

2 Some people supply too many past victories or pleasures with which to comfort themselves, and other people cling to pains, real and imagined, to excuse what they have become.

3 Truth made you a traitor, as it often does in a time of scoundrels.

4 Well, people change and forget to tell each other. Too bad—causes so many mistakes.

ERNEST HEMINGWAY (1899–1961). *American novelist, short-story writer, and journalist*

1 All good books are alike in that they are truer than if they had really happened.

2 But did thee feel the earth move? [*For Whom the Bell Tolls,* 1940.]

3 "Exactly what do you mean by guts?" [Dorothy Parker] I mean grace under pressure.

4 He was just a coward and that was the worst luck any man could have.

5 I want to be Champion of the World, but I have that son of a bitch Tolstoy blocking me and when I get by him I run into Shakespeare.

6 I'm Ernie Hemorrhoid, the poor man's Pyle. [Referring to Ernie Pyle, America's foremost war correspondent during World War II; Hemingway himself had just signed on to cover the war in France.]

7 Nobody ever fielded 1000 if they tried for the hard ones.

8 Pardon me for not getting up. [Self-epitaph.]

9 The most essential gift for a good writer is a built-in, shock-proof, shit detector. This is the writer's radar and all great writers have had it.

O. HENRY (1862–1910). *American short-story writer*

1 It was beautiful and simple as all truly great swindles are.

2 Life is made up of sobs, sniffles and smiles, with sniffles predominating.

KATHARINE HEPBURN (1907–). *American actress*

1 He gives her class, and she gives him sex. [On Fred Astaire and Ginger Rogers.]

2 I don't care what is written about me so long as it isn't true.

3 I would have made a terrible parent. The first time my child didn't do what I wanted, I'd kill him.

A. P. HERBERT (1890–1971). *English writer and member of Parliament*

We have read with particular repugnance the record of the alleged god, Zeus, whose habit it was to assume the shape of swans, bulls, and other animals, and, thus disguised, to force his attentions upon defenseless females of good character.

OLIVER HERFORD (1864–1935). *English-born American writer and humorist*

1 A hair in the head is worth two in the brush.

2 Bigamy is one way of avoiding the painful publicity of divorce and the expense of alimony.

3 Darling: the popular form of address used in speaking to a person of the opposite sex whose name you cannot at the moment recall.

4 Diplomacy: lying in state.

5 I don't recall your name but your manners are familiar. [After being slapped on the back.]

6 Liar: one who tells an unpleasant truth.

7 Modesty: the gentle art of enhancing your charm by pretending not to be aware of it.

8 Only the young die good.

9 Tact: to lie about others as you would have them lie about you.

10 Wedding: a necessary formality before securing a divorce.

EDWARD S. HERMAN (1925–). *American academic and writer*

1 Great men: those who had a large impact on the world as measured by the number of corpses left in their wake.

2 Justice: the will of the stronger.

3 Law: the form. Law enforcement: the reality. Law and order: internal pacification.

4 Propaganda: their lies. Public information: our lies.

DON HEROLD (1889–1966). *American writer and cartoonist*
1 Babies are such a nice way to start people.
2 Doctors think a lot of patients are cured who have simply quit in disgust.
3 Genius is an infinite capacity for giving pains.
4 Gentlemen prefer blondes but take what they can get.
5 "The more articulate, the less said," is an old Chinese proverb which I just made up myself.
6 This is too deep for me. [Self-epitaph.]
7 Unhappiness is not knowing what we want and killing ourselves to get it.
8 When a fellow says, "Well, to make a long story short," it's already too late.
9 Women give us solace, but if it were not for women we should never need solace.

JIM HIGHTOWER (1943–). *American broadcast journalist and writer*
1 He was born on third base and thinks he hit a triple. [On George Bush.]
2 *If the Gods Had Meant Us to Vote, They Would Have Given Us Candidates.* [Book title, 2000.]
3 Money is the crack cocaine of politics. —See also Herb Caen 2; Jesse Unruh

LADY ALICE HILLINGDON (1857–1940). *English society figure*
I am happy now that Charles calls on my bedchamber less frequently than of old. As it is, I now endure but two calls a week, and when I hear his steps outside my door I lie down on my bed, close my eyes, open my legs and think of England.

PHILIP J. HILTS (20th century). *American journalist*
The top executives of the seven largest American tobacco companies testified in Congress today that they did not believe that cigarettes were addictive, but that they would rather their own children did not smoke. [Opening paragraph of a *New York Times* article, 15 April 1994.]

HIPPOCRATES (460?–377? B.C.). *Greek physician*
Life is short, the art long, opportunity fleeting, experience treacherous, judgment difficult.

ALFRED HITCHCOCK (1899–1980). *English film director*
1 Drama is life with the dull bits cut out.
2 For me the cinema is not a slice of life, but a piece of cake.
3 I didn't say actors are cattle. What I said was, actors should be *treated* like cattle.
4 One doesn't direct Cary Grant; one simply puts him in front of a camera.
5 Seeing a murder on television can help work off one's antagonisms. And if you haven't any antagonisms, the commercials will give you some.
6 Television has brought murder back into the home—where it belongs.
7 There is no terror in a bang, only in the anticipation of it.
8 We seem to have a compulsion these days to bury time capsules in order to give those people living in the next century or so some idea of what we are like. I have prepared one of my own. I have placed some rather large samples of dynamite, gunpowder, and nitroglycerin. My time capsule is set to go off in the year 3000. It will show them what we are really like.

ADOLF HITLER (1889–1945). *German dictator*

Her world is her husband, her family, her children and her home. We do not find it right when the woman presses into the world of the man. —See also Sigmund Freud 7

THOMAS HOBBES (1588–1679). *English philosopher*

Truth, which opposeth no man's profit, nor pleasure, is to all men welcome. [Closing words, *Leviathan,* 1651.]

RALPH HODGSON (1871–1962). *English poet*

Some things have to be believed to be seen.

JIMMY HOFFA (1913–1975). *American union leader*

1 I do to others what they do to me, only worse.

2 I may have faults, but being wrong ain't one of them.

ERIC HOFFER (1902–1983). *American longshoreman and writer*

1 A man by himself is in bad company.

2 Much of man's thinking is propaganda of his appetites.

3 One of the surprising privileges of intellectuals is that they are free to be scandalously asinine without harming their reputation.

4 People who bite the hand that feeds them usually lick the boot that kicks them.

5 Rudeness is the weak man's imitation of strength. —See also Henry A. Kissinger 5

6 Self-righteousness is a loud din raised to drown the voice of guilt within us.

7 Sensuality reconciles us with the human race. The misanthropy of the old is due in large part to the fading of the magic glow of desire.

8 Sometimes it seems that people hear best what we do not say.

9 The hardest arithmetic to master is that which enables us to count our blessings.

10 The less satisfaction we derive from being ourselves, the greater is our desire to be like others.

11 The search for happiness is one of the chief sources of unhappiness.

12 The so-called nonconformists travel in groups, and woe unto him who doesn't conform.

13 The weakness of a soul is proportionate to the number of truths which must be kept from it.

14 There are no chaste minds. Minds copulate wherever they meet.

15 To most of us nothing is so invisible as an unpleasant truth. Though it is held before our eyes, pushed under our noses, rammed down our throats—we know it not.

16 We can never have enough of that which we really do not want.

17 We know ourselves chiefly by hearsay.

18 We probably have a greater love for those we support than those who support us. Our vanity carries more weight than our self-interest.

RICHARD HOFSTADTER (1916–1970). *American historian*

1 There is a vital difference between the paranoid spokesman in politics and the clinical paranoiac: although they both tend to be overheated, over-

suspicious, overaggressive, grandiose, and apocalyptic in expression, the clinical paranoid sees the hostile and conspiratorial world in which he feels himself to be living as directed specifically against him; whereas the spokesman of the paranoid style finds it directed against a nation, a culture, a way of life whose fate affects not himself alone but millions of others.

2 Yesterday's avant-garde experiment is today's chic and tomorrow's cliché.

BEN HOGAN (1912–1997). *American golfer*
"I'm having trouble with my long putts." Why don't you try hitting your irons closer to the pin?

OLIVER WENDELL HOLMES (1809–1894). *American physician and writer*
1 Death tugs at my ear and says, "Live, I am coming."
2 Fame usually comes to those who are thinking of something else.
3 Humility is the first of the virtues—for other people.
4 I firmly believe that if the whole *materia medica,* as now used, could be sunk to the bottom of the sea, it would be better for mankind—and all the worse for the fishes.
5 I was always patient with those who thought well of me, and accepted all their tributes with something more than resignation.
6 It is the peculiarity of the bore that he is the last person to find himself out.
7 Life is a romantic business. It is painting a picture, not doing a sum.
8 Man has his will—but woman has her way!
9 Put not your trust in money, but put your money in trust.
10 The nullifier of civilization, who insisted on nibbling his asparagus at the wrong end. [On Henry David Thoreau.]
11 To be seventy years young is sometimes far more cheerful and hopeful than to be forty years old.
12 Why can't somebody give us a list of things that everybody thinks and nobody says, and another list of things that everybody says and nobody thinks?

OLIVER WENDELL HOLMES, JR. (1835–1935). *American Supreme Court chief justice*
1 A man who takes half a page to say what can be said in a sentence will be damned.
2 A second-class intellect, but a first-class temperament. [On Franklin D. Roosevelt, 1933.] —See also Tom Wicker 1
3 If a man is a minority of one, we lock him up.
4 Lawyers spend a great deal of their time shoveling smoke.
5 The mind of the bigot is like the pupil of the eye; the more light you pour upon it, the more it will contract.

HERBERT HOOVER (1874–1964). *American president*
1 Blessed are the young, for they shall inherit the national debt.
2 Every president should have the right to shoot two reporters a year—without explanation.
3 It was ironic that a man guilty of inciting hundreds of murders, in some of which he took a personal hand, had to be punished merely for failure to

pay taxes on the money he had made by murder. [On Chicago gangster Al Capone who, in 1931, was sentenced to an eleven-year prison term for tax evasion.]

4 Once upon a time, my political opponents honored me as possessing the fabulous intellectual and economic power by which I created a worldwide depression all by myself. [Referring to the depression which began during his presidency.]

5 "What do retired presidents do?" Madam, we spend our time taking pills and dedicating libraries.

6 Words without actions are the assassins of idealism.

J. EDGAR HOOVER (1895–1972). *American Federal Bureau of Investigation director*

I regret to say that we of the FBI are powerless to act in cases of oral-genital intimacy, unless it has in some way obstructed interstate commerce.

BOB HOPE (1903–). *English-born American comedian*

1 Bing doesn't pay an income tax anymore: he just asks the government what they need. [Referring to his friend Bing Crosby.]

2 I do benefits for all religions. I'd hate to blow the hereafter on a technicality.

3 I don't feel eighty. In fact, I don't feel anything till noon. Then it's time for my nap.

4 I don't know what people have got against Jimmy Carter. He's done nothing. [Campaign speech for Ronald Reagan, 1980.]

5 I love to go to Washington—if only to be near my money.

6 I see the Beatles have arrived from England. They were forty pounds overweight, and that was just their hair. [1964]

7 I think it's wonderful you could all be here for the forty-third anniversary of my thirty-ninth birthday. We decided not to light the candles this year— we were afraid Pan Am would mistake it for a runway.

8 If they liked you, they didn't applaud—they just let you live. [Recalling his vaudeville days.]

9 It's amazing how many people see you on TV. I did my first television show a month ago, and the next day five million television sets were sold. The people who couldn't sell theirs threw them away.

10 Middle age is when your age starts to show around your middle.

11 Money is paper blood.

12 My father told me all about the birds and the bees. The liar—I went steady with a woodpecker till I was twenty-one.

13 The audience was swell. They were so polite, they covered their mouths when they yawned.

14 The program is nearly over! I can feel the audience is still with me; but if I run faster, I can shake them off.

15 When she started to play, Steinway came down personally and rubbed his name off the piano. [On Phyllis Diller.]

16 You don't see me at Vegas or at the races throwing my money around. I've got a government to support.

17 You know you're getting old when the candles cost more than the cake.

HEDDA HOPPER (1890–1956). *American journalist*
Our town worships success, the bitch goddess whose smile hides a taste for blood. [On Hollywood.]

JUDY HORACEK (20th century). *Australian cartoonist*
In hell all the messages you ever left on answering machines will be played back to you. [Cartoon caption.]

A. E. HOUSMAN (1859–1936). *English poet*
1 And wherefore is he wearing such a conscience-stricken air? / Oh they're taking him to prison for the color of his hair.
2 Nature not content with denying him the ability to think, has endowed him with the ability to write.

SAM HOUSTON (1793–1863). *American soldier and Texas senator*
He has all the characteristics of a dog—except loyalty. [On Thomas Jefferson Green.]

ED HOWE (1853–1937). *American journalist and humorist*
1 A modest man is usually admired—if people ever hear of him.
2 Be careful, and you will save many men from the sin of robbing you.
3 Bravery is knowledge of the enemy's cowardice.
4 Doing business without advertising is like winking at a girl in the dark. You know what you are doing, but nobody else does.
5 Most people put off till tomorrow what they should have done yesterday. —See also Anonymous 90; Aldous Huxley 8; Mark Twain 87
6 The only way to amuse some people is to slip and fall on an icy pavement.
7 The way out of trouble is never as simple as the way in.
8 What is said behind your back is the community's estimate of you.
9 When a man has no reason to trust himself, he trusts in luck.
10 When a man says money can do everything, that settles it: he hasn't any.

WILLIAM DEAN HOWELLS (1837–1920). *American novelist*
Some people can stay longer in an hour than others do in a week.

ELBERT HUBBARD (1856–1915). *American writer, editor, publisher, and humorist*
1 An optimist is a fellow who believes what's going to be will be postponed.
2 Charity begins at home, and usually stays there.
3 Cooperation: doing what I tell you to do, and doing it quick.
4 Death: to stop sinning suddenly.
5 Do not take life too seriously—you will never get out of it alive. [1911]
6 Do your work with your whole heart and you will succeed—there is so little competition!
7 Dogma: a hard substance which forms in a soft brain.
8 Economics: the science of the production, distribution and use of wealth, best understood by college professors on half rations.

9 Editor: a person employed on a newspaper, whose business it is to separate the wheat from the chaff, and to see that the chaff is printed. [Often attributed to Adlai E. Stevenson.]

10 Every man is a damn fool for at least five minutes every day; wisdom consists of not exceeding the limit.

11 Fear: a club used by priests, presidents, kings and policemen to keep the people from recovering stolen goods.

12 Forecast: to observe that which has passed, and guess it will happen again.

13 Genius: the ability to act wisely without precedent—the power to do the right thing for the first time. A capacity for evading hard work.

14 Good people are only half as good, and bad people only half as bad, as other people regard them.

15 He who does not understand your silence will probably not understand your words. —See also Henry James 2

16 Heaven is always pictured as a community—never as made up of individuals who live in boxes, which they call homes, where they lock themselves in by locking others out.

17 I believe in the Motherhood of God.

18 If you want work well done, select a busy man—the other kind has no time.

19 Imitation: the sincerest form of insult. —See also Fred Allen 16; C. C. Colton 3

20 Last year we said, "Things can't go on like this." And they didn't: they got worse.

21 Life is just one damn thing after another. —See also Edna St. Vincent Millay 2

22 Mystic: a person who is puzzled before the obvious, but who understands the nonexistent.

23 On man's journey through life he is confronted by two tragedies: one when he wants a thing he cannot get; and the other when he gets a thing and finds he does not want it.

24 Poet: a person born with an instinct for poverty.

25 Poetry is the bill and coo of sex.

26 Pray that success does not come any faster than you are able to endure it.

27 Punishment: the justice that the guilty deal out to those who are caught.

28 Remember the weekday, to keep it holy.

29 Respectability: the dickey on the bosom of civilization.

30 Righteous indignation: your own wrath as opposed to the shocking bad temper of others.

31 Servility: a natural law, the violation of which makes one famous or poor.

32 Success is ten percent opportunity and ninety percent intelligent hustle. —See also Thomas Alva Edison 2

33 The graveyards are full of people the world could not do without. —See also Charles de Gaulle 13

34 The punishment of the liar is that he eventually believes his own lies. — See also Garry Wills 2

35 The reformer is a savior or a rebel, depending largely upon whether he succeeds or fails.

36 The world is moving so fast these days that the man who says it can't be done is generally interrupted by someone doing it.

37 There are three kinds of punishment: the punishment of God, the punishment of man, and the punishment of living in Buffalo.

38 This will never be a civilized country until we expend more money for books than we do for chewing gum.

39 To avoid criticism, do nothing, say nothing, be nothing.

40 To make mistakes is human, but to profit by them is divine.

41 Tradition: a clock that tells what time it was.

42 Truth lies at the end of a circle.

43 We credit ourselves for our successes; we blame others for our failures.

44 Whom the gods love die young no matter how long they live. —See also Ashley Montague 3

KIN HUBBARD (Frank McKinney Hubbard, 1868–1930). *American journalist and humorist*

1 A fool and his money are soon spotted. —See also Anonymous 1

2 A pessimist is usually a fellow that ain't got the goods.

3 A word to the wise is unnecessary.

4 After a fellow gets famous, it doesn't take long for someone to bob up that used to sit by him at school.

5 Boys will be boys, and so will a lot of middle-aged men.

6 Classical music is the kind that we keep thinking will turn into a tune.

7 Distant relatives are the best kind, and the further the better.

8 Everything comes to him who waits but a loaned book.

9 Fun is like life insurance: the older you get, the more it costs.

10 I'll say this for adversity: people seem to be able to stand it, and that's more than I can say for prosperity.

11 If everybody thought before they spoke there wouldn't be enough noise in this world to scare a jaybird.

12 If others could only see us as we think we are.

13 If you want to get rid of somebody, just tell him something for his own good.

14 Intelligent people are always on the unpopular side of anything.

15 It ain't what a man don't know that hurts him; it's what he knows that just ain't so.

16 It must be great to be rich and let the other fellow keep up appearances.

17 It seems like one of the hardest lessons to be learned in this life is where your business ends and somebody else's begins.

18 It's going to be fun to watch and see how long the meek can keep the earth after they inherit it.

19 It's no disgrace to be poor, but it might as well be.

20 It's pretty hard to tell what does bring happiness. Poverty and wealth have both failed.

21 It's what we learn after we think we know it all that counts.

22 Knowing all about baseball is just about as profitable as being a good whittler.

23 Lack of pep is often mistaken for patience.

24 More dogs than widows have died of grief.

25 Nobody can be as agreeable as an uninvited guest.

26 Nobody ever forgets where he buries a hatchet.

27 Nobody ever grew despondent looking for trouble.

28 Nobody ever listened to reason on an empty stomach.

29 Nobody kicks on being interrupted if it's by applause.

30 Now and then an innocent man is sent to the legislature. —See also Ralph Waldo Emerson 12

31 Of all the home remedies a good wife is the best.

32 Only one fellow in ten thousand understands the currency question, and we meet him every day. —See also George Burns 7

33 Some fellows get credit for being conservative when they're only stupid.

34 Some folks seem to have descended from the chimpanzee later than others.

35 Some people pay a compliment as if they expected a receipt.

36 Stew Nugent has decided to go to work till he can find something better to do.

37 The election isn't very far off when a candidate can recognize you from across the street.

38 The fellow that agrees with everything you say is either a fool or he is getting ready to skin you.

39 The fellow that owns his own home is always just coming out of a hardware store.

40 The fellow that says, "I may be wrong, but—," does not believe there can be any such possibility.

41 The only absolutely safe way to double your money is to fold it once and put it in your hip pocket.

42 The only way to entertain some folks is to listen to them.

43 The reason the way of the transgressor is hard is because it's so crowded.

44 The richer a relative is, the less he bothers you.

45 The wedding over at the Tilford Moots farm went off without a hitch Saturday night. The bridegroom didn't show up.

46 There seems to be an excess of everything but parking space and religion.

47 There's another advantage of being poor: a doctor will cure you faster.

48 There's few things as uncommon as common sense. —See also Voltaire 3

49 There's few things in this life that equal the sensation of being paid up.

50 There's lots of honest people who never had a good chance to be anything else.

51 There's one thing we ought to let folks find out for themselves, and that's how great we are.

52 There's some folks standing behind the president that ought to get around where he can watch 'em.

53 Very often the quiet fellow has said all he knows.

54 We all run in debt for things we wouldn't think of paying perfectly good money for.

55 We're all mighty unselfish when it comes to handing out advice we could use ourselves.

56 When a fellow says, "It ain't the money, but the principle of the thing," it's the money.

57 When some fellows take a vacation, everybody gets a rest.

58 When some folks don't know something mean about someone, they switch the subject.

59 Who recalls when folks got along without something if it cost too much?

60 Why doesn't the fellow who says, "I'm no speechmaker," let it go at that instead of giving a demonstration.

LANGSTON HUGHES (1902–1967). *American poet*

1 De lady I work for / Told her husband / She wanted a / Robe o' love— / But de damn fool / Give her / A fur coat! / Yes, / He did!

2 Folks, I'm telling you, / birthing is hard / and dying is mean— / so get yourself / a little loving / in between.

3 I swear to the Lord / I still can't see / Why Democracy means / Everybody but me. ["The Black Man Speaks," 1943.]

4 I went to San Francisco. / I saw the bridges high, / Spun across the water / Like cobwebs in the sky.

5 Just because I loves you / That's de reason why / My heart's a fluttering aspen leaf / When you pass by.

VICTOR HUGO (1802–1885). *French novelist and playwright*

1 Common sense is in spite of, not the result of education.

2 I had rather be hissed for a good verse than applauded for a bad one.

3 If you would civilize a man, begin with his grandmother. —See also William Ralph Inge 8

4 Indigestion is charged by God with enforcing morality on the stomach.

5 Kings are for nations in their swaddling clothes.

6 The peculiarity of prudery is to multiply sentinels in proportion as the fortress is less threatened.

HUBERT H. HUMPHREY (1911–1978). *Minnesota senator and U.S. vice president*

1 Behind every successful man stands a surprised mother-in-law.

2 It's not what they take away from you that counts: it's what you do with what you have left.

3 The right to be heard does not automatically include the right to be taken seriously.

4 We believe that to err is human. To blame it on someone else is politics.

JOHN HUNT (1775–1848). *English art critic*

Rembrandt is not to be compared in the painting of character with our extraordinary [sic] gifted English artist, Mr. Rippingille.

JAMES HURT (19th century). *American literary critic*

The sequence of ideas is commonplace to the point of banality, the ordinary coin of funeral oratory. [On Abraham Lincoln's *Gettysburg Address*, 1863.]

ROBERT M. HUTCHINS (1899–1977). *American educator and university chancellor*

1 We call Japanese soldiers fanatics when they die rather than surrender, whereas American soldiers who do the same thing are heroes. [1945]

2 We can put television in its proper light by supposing that Gutenberg's great invention had been directed at printing only comic books.

3 Whenever I feel like exercise, I lie down until the feeling passes.

ALDOUS HUXLEY (1894–1963). *English novelist and essayist*

1 Chastity: the most unnatural of all sexual perversions.

2 Facts do not cease to exist because they are ignored.

3 Idealism is the noble toga that political gentlemen drape over their will to power. —See also William Hazlitt 6

4 "It's like the question of the authorship of the *Iliad*," said Mr. Cardan. "The author of that poem is either Homer or, if not Homer, somebody else of the same name."

5 Lady Capricorn, he understood, was still keeping open bed.

6 Maybe this world is another planet's hell.

7 Most of one's life is one prolonged effort to prevent oneself thinking.

8 Never put off till tomorrow the fun you can have today. —See also Anonymous 90; Ed Howe 5; Mark Twain 87

9 Technological progress has merely provided us with more efficient means for going backwards.

10 The cinema acts far more effectively as the opium of the people than does religion. —See also Karl Marx 5

11 The only completely consistent people are dead.

12 Ye shall know the truth, and the truth shall make thee mad. —See also Herbert Agar 2

13 You never see animals going through the absurd and often horrible fooleries of magic and religion. Only man behaves with such gratuitous folly. It is the price he has to pay for being intelligent but not, as yet, quite intelligent enough.

T. H. HUXLEY (1825–1895). *English biologist*

1 If a little knowledge is dangerous, where is the man who has so much as to be out of danger?

2 Operationally, God is beginning to resemble not a ruler but the last fading smile of a cosmic Cheshire cat.

3 The great tragedy of Science—the slaying of a beautiful hypothesis by an ugly fact.

ADA LOUISE HUXTABLE (1921–). *American architecture critic*

1 It would be great if it wasn't awful. [On Marcel Breuer's design for a sky-scraper above New York's Grand Central Station.]

2 New York, thy name is irreverence and hyperbole. And grandeur.

3 This is born-dead, neo-penitentiary modern. [On Washington's Hirshhorn Museum.]

I

HAROLD L. ICKES (1874–1952). *American secretary of the interior*

The trouble with Senator Long is that he is suffering from halitosis of the intellect. That's presuming he has an intellect. [Referring to Huey Long.]

IVAN ILLICH (1926–). *Austrian-born American writer*

Any attempt to reform the university without attending to the system of which it is an integral part is like trying to do urban renewal in New York City from the twelfth story up.

WILLIAM RALPH INGE (1863–1954). *English theologian*

1 A nation is a society united by a delusion about its ancestry and by common hatred of its neighbors.

2 Democracy is a form of government which may be rationally defended, not as being good, but as being less bad than any other. [1919] —See also Winston Churchill 10

3 I think middle age is the best time, if we can escape the fatty degeneration of the conscience which often sets in at about fifty.

4 Many people believe they are attracted by God, or by Nature, when they are only repelled by man.

5 Originality is undetected plagiarism.

6 Public opinion, a vulgar, impertinent, anonymous tyrant who deliberately makes life unpleasant for anyone who is not content to be the average man.

7 Religion is caught, not taught.

8 The proper time to influence the character of a child is about a hundred years before he is born. —See also Victor Hugo 3

9 There are two kinds of fools: one says, "This is old, therefore it is good"; the other says, "This is new, therefore it is better."

10 Worry is the interest paid on trouble before it falls due.

ROBERT G. INGERSOLL (1833–1899). *American lawyer and lecturer*

1 Custom meets us at the cradle and leaves us only at the tomb.

2 Few rich men own their own property; the property owns them.

3 For the most part, colleges are places where pebbles are polished and diamonds are dimmed.

4 In all ages hypocrites, called priests, have put crowns on the heads of thieves, called kings.

5 It is a thousand times better to have common sense without education than to have education without common sense.

WASHINGTON IRVING (1783–1859). *American writer*

1 A sharp tongue is the only edged tool that grows keener with constant use.

2 I'm always at a loss to know how much to believe of my own stories.

3 There is a certain relief in change, even though it be from bad to worse; as I have found in traveling in a stage coach, that it is often a comfort to shift one's position and be bruised in a new place.

4 Whenever a man's friends begin to compliment him about looking young, he may be sure that they think he is growing old.

MOLLY IVINS (1936–). *American journalist*

1 Being slightly paranoid is like being slightly pregnant—it tends to get worse. [Referring to Ross Perot.]

2 If George W. Bush's IQ slips any lower, we'll have to water him twice a day. [Referring to the Texas governor and presidential candidate, 1999.]

3 The charm of Ronald Reagan is not just that he kept telling us screwy things, it was that he believed them all. No wonder we trusted him, he never lied to us.

4 With politicians, artful evasion is always preferable to the outright lie.

5 Wouldn't you think some sociologist would have done a comparative study by now to prove, as I have always suspected, that there is a higher proportion of Undeserving Rich than Undeserving Poor? [1992]

J

ANDREW JACKSON (1767–1845). *American president*

1 I can with truth say mine is a situation of dignified slavery. [Referring to the presidency.]

2 I have only two regrets: that I have not shot Henry Clay and hanged John C. Calhoun. [Last words.]

GLENDA JACKSON (1936–). *English actress*

The important thing in acting is to be able to laugh and cry. If I have to cry, I think of my sex life. If I have to laugh, I think of my sex life.

HOLBROOK JACKSON (1874–1948). *American writer*

1 Man is a dog's ideal of what God should be. —See also Anonymous 22

2 Suffer fools gladly. They may be right.

3 There are only two classes in society: those who get more than they earn, and those who earn more than they get. —See also Nicolas Chamfort 14

4 Why did Nature create man? Was it to show that she is big enough to make mistakes, or was it pure ignorance?

HENRY JAMES (1843–1916). *American-born British novelist*

1 I don't regret a single "excess" of my responsive youth—I only regret, in my chilled age, certain occasions and possibilities I didn't embrace.

2 I like people who understand what one says to them, and also what one doesn't say. —See also Elbert Hubbard 15

3 To become adopted as a national poet, it is not enough to discharge the undigested contents of your blotting-book into the lap of the public. [On Walt Whitman's *Drum-Taps,* 1865; James later disavowed his review as a "little atrocity... perpetrated... in the gross impudence of youth."]

WILLIAM JAMES (1842–1910). *American philosopher and psychologist*

1 A great many people think they are thinking when they are merely rearranging their prejudices. [Attributed.]

2 All new doctrine goes through three stages. It is attacked and declared absurd; then it is admitted as true and obvious but insignificant. Finally, its true importance is recognized and its adversaries claim the honor of having discovered it.

3 Hogamus, higamous / Man is polygamous / Higamus, Hogamous / Woman monogamous.

4 If merely "feeling good" could decide, drunkenness would be the supremely valid human experience.

5 Our science is a drop, our ignorance a sea.

6 The perfection of rottenness. [On his Harvard colleague George Santayana.]

7 There is no more miserable human being than one in whom nothing is habitual but indecision.

8 Whenever two people meet, there are really six people present. There is each man as he sees himself, each man as the other person sees him, and each man as he really is.

THOMAS JEFFERSON (1743–1826). *American president*

1 I really look with commiseration over the great body of my fellow citizens, who, reading newspapers, live and die in the belief that they have known something of what has been passing in the world in their time.

2 If the present Congress errs in too much talking, how can it be otherwise in a body to which the people send 150 lawyers, whose trade it is to question everything, yield nothing, and talk by the hour? That 150 lawyers should do business together ought not to be expected.

3 Never did a prisoner, released from his chains, feel such relief as I shall on shaking off the shackles of power. [Referring to the presidency.]

4 No person will have occasion to complain of the want of time who never loses any. It is wonderful how much may be done if we are always doing.

5 Nothing can now be believed which is seen in a newspaper. Truth itself becomes suspicious by being put into that polluted vehicle.

6 Perhaps an editor might begin a reformation in some such way as this. Divide his paper into 4 chapters, heading the 1st, Truths. 2d, Probabilities. 3d, Possibilities. 4th, Lies.

7 The man who never looks into a newspaper is better informed than he who reads them, inasmuch as he who knows nothing is nearer to truth than he whose mind is filled with falsehoods and errors.

8 The moment a person forms a theory, his imagination sees in every object only the traits which favor that theory.

9 The second office in the government is honorable and easy; the first is but a splendid misery. [Comparing the vice presidency with the presidency.]

10 Were it left to me to decide whether we should have a government without newspapers, or newspapers without a government, I should not hesitate a moment to prefer the latter.

11 When angry, count ten before you speak; if very angry, an hundred.

12 Whenever a man has cast a longing eye on offices, a rottenness begins in his conduct.

13 "You are replacing Benjamin Franklin as America's minister to France?" [Count de Vergennes] I succeed him; no one can replace him. [Soon after Jefferson's arrival in Paris, 1785.]

JEROME K. JEROME (1859–1927). *English writer and humorist*

1 Conceit is the finest armor a man can wear.

2 Everything has its drawbacks, as the man said when his mother-in-law died, and they came down upon him for the funeral expenses. —See also Gerald Brenan 3

3 I like work; it fascinates me; I can sit and look at it for hours.

4 It is always the best policy to speak the truth—unless, of course, you are an exceptionally good liar.

5 It is impossible to enjoy idling thoroughly unless one has plenty of work to do.

6 It is so pleasant to come across people more stupid than ourselves. We love them at once for being so.

7 We drink to one another's health and spoil our own.

DOUGLAS JERROLD (1803–1857). *English writer and humorist*

1 Earth is here so kind, that just tickle her with a hoe and she laughs with a harvest. [Referring to Australia.]

2 In this world, truth can wait; she's used to it.

3 Love's like the measles—all the worse when it comes late in life.

4 Some people are so fond of ill-luck that they run half-way to meet it.

5 Talk to him of Jacob's ladder, and he would ask the number of the steps.

JOHN XXIII (1881–1963). *Italian pope*

1 Anybody can be pope; the proof of this is that I have become one. [Letter to a young boy.]

2 Dear Professor, don't be disturbed. My bags are always packed. When the moment to depart arrives, I won't lose any time. [Remark to a visitor two days before his death.]

3 Here I am at the end of the road and at the top of the heap. [On becoming pope at age 77.]

4 "How many persons work at the Vatican?" Oh, no more than half of them!

5 It often happens that I wake up at night and begin to think of a serious problem and decide that I must tell the pope about it. Then I wake up completely and remember that I am the pope.

LYNDON B. JOHNSON (1908–1973). *American president*

1 A grandstanding little runt. [On Robert F. Kennedy.]

2 Being president is like being a jackass in a hailstorm: there's nothing to do but stand there and take it.

3 Boys, I may not know much, but I know the difference between chicken shit and chicken salad. [Referring to a speech by Richard M. Nixon.]

4 Did y'ever think, Ken, that making a speech on ee-conomics is a lot like pissing down your leg? It seems hot to you, but it never does to anyone else. [Remark to economist John Kenneth Galbraith.]

5 For the first time in history, profits are higher than ever before.

6 He's a nice guy, but he played too much football with his helmet off. [On Gerald Ford; attributed.]

7 I don't want loyalty, I want *loyalty*. I want him to kiss my ass in Macy's window at high noon and tell me it smells like roses. I want his pecker in my pocket. [On the importance of loyalty in the White House inner circle.]

8 I seldom think of politics more than eighteen hours a day.

9 "I understand you were born in a log cabin." [German Chancellor Ludwig Erhard during a visit to Johnson's Texas ranch.] No, no, no! You have me confused with Abe Lincoln. I was born in a manger. [Attributed.]

10 If one morning I walked on top of the water across the Potomac River, the headline that afternoon would read: PRESIDENT CAN'T SWIM.

11 If you can convince the lowest white man he's better than the best colored man, he won't notice you're picking his pocket. Hell, give him somebody to look down on, and he'll empty his pockets for you. [1960]

12 Jerry Ford is so dumb he can't fart and chew gum at the same time.

13 My daddy told me that if I didn't want to get shot at, I should stay off the firing lines. This is politics. —See also Harry S. Truman 13

14 People don't support you because they like you. You can count on a person's support only when you can do something for him or something to him.

15 This is a moment that I deeply wish my parents could have lived to share. My father would have enjoyed what you have so generously said of me—and my mother would have believed it. [Responding to introductory remarks before delivering a commencement address.]

16 "This is your helicopter, sir." [Air force corporal pointing to the helicopter Johnson was to board.] They're all my helicopters, son.

17 Well, it's probably better to have J. Edgar Hoover inside the tent pissing out, then outside pissing in. [On his decision to retain the aging FBI director.]

18 When I want your advice, I'll give it to you. [Remark to Vice President Hubert H. Humphrey; attributed.]

SAMUEL JOHNSON (Dr. Johnson, 1709–1784). *English writer, lexicographer, and conversationalist*

1 A cucumber should be well sliced, and dressed with pepper and vinegar, and then thrown out as good for nothing.

2 A fishing rod is a stick with a hook at one end and a fool at the other.

3 A man had rather have a hundred lies told of him than one truth which he does not wish should be told.

4 A man may be so much of everything that he is nothing of anything.

5 A man seldom thinks with more earnestness of anything than he does of his dinner.

6 A man who has not been in Italy is always conscious of an inferiority.

7 A news writer is a man without virtue who lies at home for his own profit. To these compositions is required neither genius nor knowledge, neither industry not sprightliness; but contempt of shame and indifference to truth are absolutely necessary.

8 A woman's preaching is like a dog's walking on his hinder legs. It is not done well; but you are surprised to find it done at all.

9 Abstinence is as easy to me as temperance would be difficult.

10 Advice always gives a temporary appearance of superiority.

11 All argument is against it, but all belief is for it. [On the existence of ghosts.]

12 All the arguments which are brought to represent poverty as no evil, show it to be evidently a great evil. You never find people laboring to convince you that you may live very happily upon a plentiful fortune.

13 Attack is the reaction; I never think I have hit hard unless it rebounds.

14 Be not too hasty to trust or to admire the teachers of morality: they discourse like angels, but they live like men.

15 Being in a ship is being in a jail, with the chance of being drowned.

16 Corneille is to Shakespeare as a clipped hedge is to a forest.

17 Depend on it that if a man talks of his misfortunes, there is something in them that is not disagreeable to him.

18 Depend upon it, Sir, when a man knows he is to be hanged in a fortnight, it concentrates his mind wonderfully.

19 Dictionaries are like watches, the worst is better than none, and the best cannot be expected to go quite true.

20 Envy desires not so much its own happiness as another's misery.

21 Every man has a right to utter what he thinks truth, and every other man has a right to knock him down for it.

22 Foote is quite impartial, for he tells lies of everybody. [Referring to Samuel Foote.]

23 He is gone, and we are going. [Remark to a woman whose son had just died.]

24 He that knows not whither to go, is in no haste to move.

25 He that tries to recommend Shakespeare by select quotations, will succeed like the pedant in *Hierocles,* who, when he offered his house to sale, carried a brick in his pocket as a specimen. —See also Jonathan Swift 13

26 "How did you come to define in your Dictionary *pastern* as the *knee* of a horse?" Ignorance, Madam, pure ignorance.

27 How is it that we hear the loudest yelps for liberty among the drivers of negroes? [1775]

28 I am very fond of the company of ladies; I like their beauty, I like their delicacy, I like their vivacity, and I like their silence.

29 I am willing to love all mankind, except an American.

30 I do not care to speak ill of any man behind his back, but I believe the gentleman is an attorney.

31 I hate a fellow whom pride, or cowardice, or laziness drives into a corner, and who does nothing when he is there but sit and growl; let him come out as I do, and bark.

32 I hate mankind, for I think myself one of the best of them, and I know how bad I am.

33 I have always been more afraid of failing than hopeful of success. —See also Larry Bird 1

34 I inherited a vile melancholy from my father, which has made me mad all my life, at least not sober.

35 I live in the crowds of jollity, not so much to enjoy company as to shun myself.

36 "I was pleased to see that you omitted vulgar words from your *Dictionary.*" How do you know, madam? You must have been looking for them.

37 I would not give half a guinea to live under one form of government rather than another. It is of no moment to the happiness of an individual.

38 I'll come no more behind your scenes, David; for the silk stockings and white bosoms of your actresses excite my amorous propensities. [Remark to actor-producer David Garrick.]

39 If he does really think that there is no distinction between virtue and vice, why, Sir, when he leaves our houses, let us count our spoons. —See also Ralph Waldo Emerson 29

40 If you are idle, be not solitary; if you are solitary, be not idle.

41 In lapidary inscriptions a man is not upon oath.

42 "Is not the Giant's Causeway in Dublin worth seeing?" [James Boswell] Worth seeing? yes; but not worth going to see.

43 It is a mortifying reflection for any man to consider what he has done compared with what he might have done.

44 It is better a man should be abused than forgotten.

45 It is better to live rich than to die rich.

46 It is nonsense to bolt a door with a boiled carrot. [When asked for an illustrative definition of nonsense.]

47 It was the triumph of hope over experience. [On an acquaintance's remarriage.]

48 Lexicographer: a writer of dictionaries, a harmless drudge.

49 Love is the wisdom of the fool and the folly of the wise.

50 Marriage has many pains, but celibacy has no pleasures.

51 Most schemes of political improvement are very laughable things.

52 Mrs. Montagu has dropped me. Now, Sir, there are people whom one should like very well to drop, but would not wish to be dropped by.

53 Much may be made of a Scotchman, if he be caught young.

54 Mutual cowardice keeps us at peace.

55 My diseases are an asthma and a dropsy, and what is less curable, seventy-five.

56 No man but a blockhead ever wrote, except for money.

57 No man is a hypocrite in his pleasures.

58 No man is much pleased with a companion who does not increase, in some respect, his fondness of himself. —See also Lady Blessington 5; Lord Chesterfield 15

59 No man practices so well as he writes. I have, all my life long, been lying till noon; yet I tell all young men, and tell them with great sincerity, that nobody who does not rise early will ever do any good.

60 No place affords a more striking conviction of the vanity of human hopes than a public library.

61 Nothing has more retarded the advancement of learning than the disposition of vulgar minds to ridicule and vilify what they cannot comprehend.

62 Oats: a grain which in England is generally given to horses, but in Scotland supports the people.

63 Of all the griefs that harass the distressed, / Sure the most bitter is a scornful jest.

64 Patriotism is the last refuge of a scoundrel. —See also Isaac Asimov; Ambrose Bierce 48; Quentin Crisp 7; Paul Eldridge 9; Robert A. Heinlein 2; Anthony Lewis 1; Oscar Wilde 10

65 Patron: One who countenances, supports, and protects—usually a writer. One who supports with insolence and is repaid with flattery.

66 Players, Sir! I look on them as no better than creatures set upon tables and joint-stools to make faces and produce laughter, like dancing dogs.

67 Politics are now nothing more than means of rising in the world.

68 Praise, like gold and diamonds, owes its value only to its scarcity.

69 Prepare for death, if here at night you roam, / And sign your will before you sup from home. ["London: A Poem," 1738.]

70 Promise, large promise, is the soul of an advertisement.

71 Read over your compositions, and wherever you meet with a passage which you think is particularly fine, strike it out. [Recalling an old tutor's dictum.]

72 Round numbers are always false.

73 Sir, I have found you an argument; but I am not obliged to find you an understanding.

74 Sir John, Sir, is a very unclubbable man.

75 Sir, the insolence of wealth will creep out.

76 Sir, you have but two topics, yourself and me. I am sick of both. [Remark to an acquaintance who had been pestering him with questions.]

77 That fellow seems to me to possess but one idea, and that is a wrong one.

78 The critics' profession has one recommendation peculiar to itself, that it gives vent to malignity without real mischief.

79 The forms of government are but various aspects of the same fraud.

80 The greatest part of mankind have no other reason for their opinions than that they are in fashion.

81 The Irish are a fair people—they never speak well of one another.

82 The noblest prospect which a Scotchman ever sees is the high road that leads him to England!

83 The sharp employ the sharp; verily, a man may be known by his attorney.

84 The two most engaging powers of an author: new things are made familiar, and familiar things are made new.

85 The value of statuary is owing to its difficulty. You would not value the finest head cut upon a carrot.

86 There are few ways in which a man can be more innocently employed than in getting money.

87 There is nothing more dreadful to an author than neglect, compared with which reproach, hatred and opposition are names of happiness. —See also Oscar Wilde 109

88 Thomas Gray was dull in a new way, and that made many people think him great.

89 Towering in the confidence of twenty-one.

90 Treating your adversary with respect is giving him an advantage to which he is not entitled.

91 Vanity inclines us to find faults anywhere rather than in ourselves.

92 We have less reason to be surprised or offended when we find others differ from us in opinion, because we very often differ from ourselves.

93 We know our will is free, and there's an end on't.

94 What I gained by being in France was learning to be better satisfied with my own country.

95 What is written without effort is in general read without pleasure.

96 Your manuscript is both good and original; but the part that is good is not original, and the part that is original is not good. —See also Harold Macmillan 3

HANNS JOHST (1890–1978). *German playwright*
When I hear the word culture, I reach for my revolver. [Often attributed to Hermann Goering.]

MOTHER JONES (Mary Harris Jones, 1830–1930). *Irish-born American labor leader*
1 I asked a man in prison once how he happened to be there and he said he had stolen a pair of shoes. I told him if he had stolen a railroad he would be a United States senator. —See also Theodore Roosevelt 3
2 "Who issued you a permit to speak on the streets?" [Judge] Patrick Henry, Thomas Jefferson, and John Adams.

ERICA JONG (1942–). *American writer*
1 Advice is what we ask for when we already know the answer but wish we didn't.
2 Charlie had that defensive contempt for homosexuals which people often have when their own sexuality is an embarrassment to them.
3 Divorce is my generation's coming of age ceremony—a ritual scarring that makes anything that happens afterward seem bearable.
4 Jealousy is all the fun you think they had.
5 Men have always detested women's gossip because they suspect the truth: their measurements are being taken and compared.
6 Solitude is un-American.
7 Sometimes, especially if we are too lucky or too successful or too pretty, our misery is the only thing that endears us to our friends.
8 There are no atheists on turbulent airplanes.
9 Where is Hollywood located? Chiefly between the ears. In that part of the American brain lately vacated by God.
10 Your morals are like roads through the Alps. They make these hairpin turns all the time.

BEN JONSON (1572–1637). *English playwright*
1 Honor? tut, a breath; / There's no such thing in nature: a mere term / Invented to awe fools.
2 I do honor the very flea of his dog.
3 Some men are born only to suck out the poison of books.

JANIS JOPLIN (1943–1970). *American singer*
1 Fourteen heart attacks and he had to die in my week. In *my* week. [Referring to President Eisenhower's death, which scratched her from the cover of *Newsweek*.]
2 On stage, I make love to 25,000 different people, then I go home alone.

BARBARA JORDAN (1936–1996). *American congresswoman*
1 The most important thing for Americans to know about Ross Perot is that the country would probably not self-destruct under his leadership. [During the 1992 presidential election campaign.]
2 The stakes are too high for government to be a spectator sport.

JOSEPH JOUBERT (1754–1824). *French moralist*
1 Children have more need of models than of critics. —See also James Baldwin 2

2 Mediocrity is excellence to the mediocre.
3 One of the evils of our literature is that our learned men have little wit, while our brilliant writers are not learned.

JAMES JOYCE (1882–1941). *Irish writer*
1 All moanday, tearsday, wailsday, thumpsday, frightday, shatterday till the fear of the Law.
2 Greater love than this no man hath that a man lay down his wife for his friend.
3 History, Stephen said, is a nightmare from which I am trying to awake.
4 I caught a cold in the park. The gate was open.
5 The Gracehoper was always jigging ajog, hoppy on akkant of his joyicity.

CARL G. JUNG (1875–1961). *Swiss psychiatrist*
1 Everything that the modern mind cannot define it regards as insane.
2 First it was passion, then it became duty, and finally an intolerable burden.
3 In the Middle Ages they spoke of the devil, today we call it a neurosis.
4 The more intelligent and cultured a man is, the more subtly he can humbug himself.

PAULINE KAEL (1919–1991). *American film critic*

1 At the end, Schwarzenegger makes his ritual preparations for the climactic showdown, decking himself out in leather, packing up an arsenal of guns, and, as he leaves his apartment, copping a quick look of satisfaction in the mirror. It's his only love scene.

2 From ingenue-goddess, she went right over the hill. [On Elizabeth Taylor.]

3 I sat screaming silently. [On the 1991 film *The Silence of the Lambs*.]

4 If you think it so easy to be a critic, so difficult to be a poet or a painter or film experimenter, may I suggest you try both? You may discover why there are so few critics, so many poets.

5 In show business there's not much point in asking yourself if someone really likes you or if he just thinks you can be useful to him, because there's no difference.

6 The words "Kiss Kiss Bang Bang," which I saw on an Italian movie poster, are perhaps the briefest statement imaginable of the basic appeal of movies. This appeal is what attracts us, and ultimately what makes us despair when we begin to understand how seldom movies are more than this.

7 To lambast a Ross Hunter production is like flogging a sponge.

8 Trash has given us an appetite for art.

FRANZ KAFKA (1883–1924). *Czech writer*

1 A book must be the ax for the frozen sea within us.

2 Every revolution evaporates, leaving behind only the slime of a new bureaucracy.

3 In the fight between you and the world, back the world!

4 My life is a hesitation before birth.

5 The meaning of life is that it stops.

6 There was once a community of scoundrels, that is to say, they were not scoundrels, but ordinary people.

HERMAN KAHN (1920–1983). *American physicist and strategist*

It is the hallmark of the expert professional that he doesn't care where he is going as long as he proceeds competently.

HENRY J. KAISER (1882–1967). *American industrialist*

1 Problems are only opportunities in work clothes.

2 When your work speaks for itself, don't interrupt.

ALPHONSE KARR (1808–1890). *French editor and novelist*

Some people are always grumbling because roses have thorns; I am thankful that thorns have roses.

STANLEY KAUFFMANN (1916–). *American film critic*

Batman Forever almost lives up to its title. I thought it would never end. [Complete review of the 1995 film.]

BOB KAUFMAN (1925–1986). *American poet*

1 Abomunists never carry more than fifty dollars in debts on them. ["Abomunist Manifesto," 1965.]

2 Cities should be built on one side of the street.

3 I am not anything that is anything I am not.

4 My navel is a button to push when I want inside out. / Am I not more than a mass of entrails and rough tissue?

5 Psychiatrists pretend not to know everything.

6 Reality is unrealizable while it exists.

7 *Solitudes Crowded with Loneliness.* [Book title, 1965.]

8 Way out people know the way out.

9 We shall demand that the government stop cluttering up our billboards with highways.

10 What of the answers / I must find questions for?

11 "Would You Wear My Eyes?" [Poem title, 1965.]

GEORGE S. KAUFMAN (1899–1961). *American playwright, radio personality, and humorist*

1 I saw the play under the worst circumstances: the curtain was up.

2 I'd rather be a poor winner than any kind of loser.

3 Office hours are from twelve to one with an hour off for lunch.

4 Over my dead body. [Self-epitaph.]

5 Posterity is just around the corner.

6 Satire is what closes Saturday night.

7 There was laughter in the back of the theater, leading to the belief that someone was telling jokes back there.

8 You've heard of people living in a fool's paradise? Well, Leonora has a duplex there. [On Leonora Corbett.]

CHARLES KEATING (1923–). *American banker*

One question, among the many others raised in recent weeks, had to do with whether my financial support in any way influenced several political figures to take up my cause. I want to say in the most forceful way that I can: I certainly hope so. [Keating was later sentenced to prison for his involvement in the savings and loans scandal which came to light during the late 1980s.]

GARRISON KEILLOR (1942–). *American writer, radio personality, and humorist*

1 I believe in looking reality straight in the eye and denying it.

2 I'm forty-six. I grew up in a gentler, slower time. When Ike was president, Christmases were years apart, and now it's about five months from one to the next.

3 It is our farewell performance, and I hope the first of many. [At New York's Radio City Music Hall, 1988.]

4 It reads like it was edited by two elderly sociologists, one of whom has been dead for many years. [On *The New York Times,* 1990.]

5 It was luxuries like air conditioning that brought down the Roman Empire. With air conditioning their windows were shut, they couldn't hear the barbarians coming.

6 Selective ignorance, a cornerstone of child rearing.

7 Some luck lies in not getting what you thought you wanted but getting what you have, which once you have it you may be smart enough to see is what you would have wanted had you known.

8 That's the news from Lake Wobegon, where all the women are strong, the men are good-looking, and all the children are above average. [His signature line.]

9 The funniest line in English is "Get it?" When you say that, everyone chortles.

10 They say such nice things about people at their funerals that it makes me sad to realize I'm going to miss mine by just a few days.

11 They turn on television in rest homes because after you've watched it a while, death doesn't seem so awful.

12 Years ago, manhood was an opportunity for achievement, and now it is a problem to be overcome.

13 You can no more become a Christian by going to church than you can become an automobile by sleeping in your garage.

14 Zeus: The God of wine and whooppee.

HELEN KELLER (1880–1968). *American writer and lecturer*
Our democracy is but a name. We vote? What does that mean? It means that we choose between two bodies of real, though not avowed, autocrats. We choose between Tweedledom and Tweedledee.

WALT KELLY (1913–1973). *American cartoonist*
1 We are confronted by insurmountable opportunities.
2 We have met the enemy and he is us. [His signature line.]

MURRAY KEMPTON (1917–1997). *American journalist*
1 Always pretend to be stupid; then when you have to show yourself smart, the display has the additional effect of surprise.
2 Every now and then, in the course of great events, the elements of tradition and innovation ally themselves and each one's weakness supplements the other and together they achieve the perfect debacle.
3 It is a function of government to invent philosophies to explain the demands of its own convenience.
4 The task of editorial writers is to come down out of the hills after the battle is over to shoot the wounded. [Attributed.]
5 To say that an idea is fashionable is to say, I think, that it has been adulterated to a point where it is hardly an idea at all.

FLORYNCE R. KENNEDY (1916–). *American lawyer*
1 Here I am a woman attorney being told I can't practice law in slacks by a judge dressed in drag. [1972]
2 If men could get pregnant, abortion would be a sacrament.
3 My parents gave us a fantastic sense of security and worth. By the time the bigots got around to telling us we were nobody, we already *knew* we were somebody.

4 The biggest sin is sitting on your ass.

JACQUELINE "JACKIE" KENNEDY (1929–1994). *American first lady and editor*

1 A newspaper reported I spend $30,000 a year buying Paris clothes and that women hate me for it. I couldn't spend that much unless I wore sable underwear.

2 History is what bitter old men write.

3 Minimum information with maximum politeness. [Guidelines for dealing with the press.]

4 Whenever I was upset by something in the papers, Jack always told me to be more tolerant, like a horse flicking away flies in the summer.

JOHN F. KENNEDY (1917–1963). *American president*

1 All free men, wherever they may live, are citizens of Berlin. And therefore, as a free man, I take pride in the words, "Ich bin ein Berliner." ["Berliner" means someone from Berlin, but "ein Berliner" refers to a pastry; the literal translation of what Kennedy said before a huge Berlin crowd on 26 June 1963 was "I am a jelly doughnut."]

2 Bobby wants to practice law, and I thought he ought to get a little experience first. [Commenting on the appointment of his brother as attorney general.]

3 Do you realize the responsibilities I carry? I'm the only person between Nixon and the White House. [Remark to a supporter during the 1960 presidential campaign.]

4 He could see nothing improper in writing to the president of the Bank of the United States—at the very time when the Senate was engaged in debate over a renewal of the Bank's charter—noting that "my retainer has not been received or refreshed as usual." [Referring to Massachusetts senator Daniel Webster, 1782–1852.]

5 "How did you become a hero in World War II?" It was involuntary. They sank my boat.

6 I am sorry to say that there is too much point to the wisecrack that life is extinct on other planets because their scientists were more advanced than ours.

7 I asked each senator about his preferences for the presidency, and ninety-six senators each received one vote.

8 I do not think it entirely inappropriate to introduce myself to this audience. I am the man who accompanied Jacqueline Kennedy to Paris, and I have enjoyed it. [His French-speaking wife was warmly greeted during their 1961 visit.]

9 I have just received the following telegram from my generous daddy. It says, "Dear Jack: Don't buy a single vote more than is necessary. I'll be damned if I'm going to pay for a landslide."

10 I think this is the most extraordinary collection of talent, of human knowledge, that has ever been gathered together at the White House—with the possible exception of when Thomas Jefferson dined alone. [Remark to Nobel Prize winners at a White House dinner.]

11 I understand that Tom Dewey has just joined Dick Nixon out on the Coast, to give him some last-minute strategy on how to win an election. [1960; in 1944 and 1948, Dewey had campaigned unsuccessfully as the Republican presidential nominee.]

12 My experience in government is that when things are noncontroversial, beautifully coordinated, and all the rest, it must be that there is not much going on.

13 No president was ever prayed over with such fervor. Evidently they felt that the country or I needed it—probably both. [Postscript in a letter to John Steinbeck shortly after the 1961 inauguration.]

14 Of course, I screwed around when I was younger, but you don't think I'd be crazy enough to do that now? [Remark to biographer Ralph G. Martin, 1959.]

15 Politics is like football. If you see daylight, go through the hole.

16 The United States has to move very fast to even stand still.

17 There is no city in the United States in which I get a warmer welcome and less votes than Columbus, Ohio.

18 Washington is a city of northern charm and southern efficiency.

19 When Herodotus found himself short on facts, he didn't hesitate to use his imagination, which may be why he is called the first historian.

20 When we got into office, the thing that surprised me most was to find that things were just as bad as we'd been saying they were. [After assuming the presidency.]

21 "Why do you want to become president?" Because that's where the power is! —See also Willie Sutton

JOSEPH P. KENNEDY (1888–1969). *American financier and ambassador*
1 He may be president, but he still comes home and swipes my socks.
2 With the money I spent, I could have elected my chauffeur. [Referring to his son John's congressional campaign in 1948.]

JACK KEROUAC (1922–1969). *American writer*
1 I drink eternally. Drink always and ye shall never die. Keep running after a dog, and he will never bite you; drink always before the thirst, and it will never come upon you.
2 I had nothing to offer anybody except my own confusion.
3 I haven't had time to work in weeks.
4 Walking on water wasn't built in a day.
5 We are beat, man. Beat means beatific, it means you get the beat.

CLARK KERR (1911–). *American educator and university president*
I find that the three major administrative problems on a campus are sex for the students, athletics for the alumni, and parking for the faculty.

JEAN KERR (1923–). *American playwright*
1 A poor person who is unhappy is in a better position than a rich person who is unhappy. Because the poor person has hope. He thinks money would help.
2 Being divorced is like being hit by a Mack truck. If you live through it, you start looking very carefully to the right and to the left.

3 Hope is the feeling you have that the feeling you have isn't permanent.

4 I'm tired of all this nonsense about beauty being only skin-deep. That's deep enough. What do you want—an adorable pancreas? —See also Saki 3

5 Life with Mary was like being in a telephone booth with an open umbrella—no matter which way you turned, you got it in the eye.

6 Marrying a man is like buying something you've been admiring for a long time in a shop window. You may love it when you get it home, but it doesn't always go with everything else in the house.

7 The average, healthy, well-adjusted adult gets up at seven-thirty in the morning feeling just plain terrible.

WALTER KERR (1913–1996). *American drama critic*

1 He had delusions of adequacy.

2 I will not say that *Portofino* is the worst musical *ever* produced, because I've only been seeing musicals since 1919. [Closing sentence of his review, 1956.]

3 Me no Leica. [On the 1951 play *I Am a Camera.*]

KEN KESEY (1935–). *American novelist*

1 About as big as the small end of nothing whittled to a point.

2 But it's the truth even if it didn't happen. [*One Flew over the Cuckoo's Nest,* 1962.]

CHARLES F. KETTERING (1876–1958). *American inventor*

1 If you have always done it that way, it is probably wrong.

2 Inventing is a combination of brains and materials. The more brains you use, the less material you need.

3 My interest is in the future because I am going to spend the rest of my life there.

JOHN MAYNARD KEYNES (1883–1946). *English economist*

1 If you owe your bank a hundred pounds, you have a problem; but if you owe your bank a million, it has.

2 *Long run* is a misleading guide to current affairs. In the *long run,* we are all dead.

3 "What do you think happens to Mr. Lloyd George when he is alone in the room?" [Lady Violet Bonham-Carter] When he is alone in the room, there is nobody there.

4 Worldly wisdom teaches us that it is better for the reputation that one should fail conventionally than to succeed unconventionally.

NIKITA KHRUSHCHEV (1894–1971). *Soviet premier*

1 I don't like the life here in New York. There is no greenery. It would make a stone sick.

2 If anyone believes our smiles involve the abandonment of the teachings of Marx, Engels, and Lenin, he deceives himself poorly. Those who wait for that must wait until a shrimp learns to whistle. [1955]

3 Literature plays an important role in our country, helping the Party to educate the people correctly, to instill in them advanced, progressive ideas

by which our Party is guided. And it is not without reason that writers in our country are called engineers of the human soul.

4 Politicians are the same all over: they promise to build a bridge even where there is no river.

FLORENCE KING (1936–). *American writer*

1 Democracy is the fig leaf of elitism.

2 Familiarity doesn't breed contempt, it is contempt.

3 In the South, Sunday morning sex is accompanied by church bells.

4 The more immoral we become in big ways, the more puritanical we become in little ways.

STEPHEN KING (1946–). *American writer and screenwriter*

1 He had a massive stroke. He died with his tie on. Do you think that could be our generation's equivalent of that old saying about dying with your boots on?

2 I was sitting one day and thinking about cannibalism, because that's what guys like me do and I thought, suppose a guy was washed up on a rocky island, how much of himself could he eat?

3 Sometimes, being a bitch is the only thing a woman has to hold onto.

HUGH KINGSMILL (1889–1949). *English writer*

1 A concern with the perfectibility of mankind is always a symptom of thwarted or perverted development.

2 Friends are God's apology for relations.

BARBARA KINGSOLVER (1955–). *American writer*

1 I personally am inclined to approach housework the way governments treat dissent: ignore it until it revolts. [*High Tide in Tucson,* 1996.]

2 Kids don't stay with you if you do it right. It's one job where, the better you are, the more surely you won't be needed in the long run.

3 School is about two parts ABCs to fifty parts Where Do I Stand in the Great Pecking Order of Humankind.

4 Some people bungee jump; I write.

5 The reason most people have kids is because they get pregnant.

6 Write a nonfiction book, and be prepared for the legion of readers who are going to doubt your facts. But write a novel, and get ready for the world to assume every word is true.

MICHAEL KINSLEY (1951–). *American journalist and editor*

1 A "gaffe" occurs not when a politician lies, but when he tells the truth.

2 The scandal in Washington is not what's illegal, but what's legal.

RUDYARD KIPLING (1865–1936). *English writer and poet*

1 A woman is only a woman, but a good cigar is a smoke.

2 San Francisco has only one drawback. 'Tis hard to leave.

3 The silliest woman can manage a clever man; but it takes a very clever woman to manage a fool.

4 Words are the most powerful drug used by mankind. —See also Karl Marx

5

LISA KIRK (1925–). *American singer*

A gossip is one who talks to you about others, a bore is one who talks to you about himself; and a brilliant conversationalist is one who talks to you about yourself.

HENRY A. KISSINGER (1923–). *German-born American secretary of state*

1 An expert is someone who is capable of articulating the interests of people with power.

2 "Do you prefer to be called Mr. Secretary or Dr. Secretary?" I do not stand on protocol. If you just call me Excellency, it will be okay.

3 Even a paranoid can have enemies.

4 Had matters gone as planned—and the tapes trickled out posthumously—Nixon would have managed the extraordinary feat of committing suicide after his own death.

5 Insolence is the armor of the weak. —See also Eric Hoffer 5

6 Moderation is a virtue only in those who are thought to have a choice.

7 My capacity to admire others is not my most fully developed trait.

8 "My rule in international affairs is: do unto others as they would do unto you." [Richard M. Nixon] Plus ten percent.

9 Nations rarely pay for services already rendered.

10 Ninety percent of the politicians give the other ten percent a bad reputation.

11 "Oh, Dr. Kissinger, thank you for saving the world." You're welcome.

12 Power is the ultimate aphrodisiac. —See also Graham Greene 1

13 That man is unfit to be president. [On Richard M. Nixon, 1968.]

14 The illegal we do immediately: the unconstitutional takes a little longer.

15 The nice thing about being a celebrity is that when you bore people, they think it's their fault. —See also Mary Wilson Little 2

16 There cannot be a crisis next week. My schedule is already full.

17 There is really very little of Machiavelli that can be accepted or used in the modern world.

18 Washington is like a Roman arena. Gladiators do battle, and the spectators determine who survives by giving the appropriate signal, just as in the Coliseum.

19 "You know, you look a lot like Henry Kissinger." A lot of people tell me that.

ERWIN KNOLL (1931–1994). *American editor*

1 A Marine Corps enlisted man who applied for conscientious-objector status on religious grounds was advised by his commanding officer, "If the Marine Corps wanted you to have a god, they would have issued you one."

2 Beulah Easton of Bloomington, Illinois, was sentenced to pay a $50 fine for criminal trespass after distributing copies of the Declaration of Independence at a shopping center. [1984]

3 Everything you read in the newspapers is absolutely true except for that rare story of which you happen to have firsthand knowledge. ["Knoll's Law of Media Accuracy."]

4   The Internal Revenue Service sent a registered letter to Lloyd Rummer advising him that his company, Empire Auto Parts, Colville, Washington, owed the government one cent.

5   The New York Department of Mental Hygiene produced and distributed a three-page illustrated memorandum on how to split an English muffin. [1984]

6   Walton C. Galinat, a research professor of genetics at the University of Massachusetts, developed a square ear of sweet corn "so it won't roll off the plate."

ARTHUR KOESTLER (1905–1983). *Hungarian-born British writer*

1   A writer's ambition should be to trade a hundred contemporary readers for ten readers in ten years' time and for one reader in a hundred years' time.

2   Creativity in science could be described as the act of putting two and two together to make five.

3   God seems to have left the receiver off the hook, and time is running out.

4   If the creator had a purpose in equipping us with a neck, he surely meant us to stick it out.

5   Nothing was ever discovered by looking for it.

6   Thou shalt not carry moderation unto excess.

7   Two half-truths do not a make a truth.

MICHAEL KORDA (1933–). *English-born American publisher*

1   The fastest way to succeed is to look as if you're playing by other people's rules, while quietly playing by your own.

2   The more people you yourself can put and keep on hold, the more successful you will seem.

ALFRED KORZYBSKI (1879–1950). *Polish-born American semanticist*
God may forgive your sins, but your nervous system won't.

KARL KRAUS (1874–1936). *Austrian journalist*

1   An original thinker is the person who is the first to steal an idea.

2   How is the world ruled and led to war? Diplomats lie to journalists and believe these lies when they see them in print.

3   Psychoanalysis is the disease of which it claims to be the cure. —See also George F. Will 7

4   The devil is an optimist if he thinks he can make people worse than they are.

5   The making of a journalist: no ideas and the ability to express them.

6   The psychiatrist unfailingly recognizes the madman by his excited behavior on being incarcerated.

7   The secret of the demagogue is to make himself appear as stupid as his audience so that they'll believe they're as smart as he is.

8   There are people who can never forgive a beggar for their not having given him anything.

KRIS KRISTOFFERSON (1936–). *American singer, songwriter, and actor*

1   Between the two of us, President Clinton and I have put to rest any myths about the intelligence of Rhodes scholars.

2 Freedom's just another word for nothing left to lose. ["Me and Bobby McGee," 1969 song cowritten with Fred Foster.]

IRVING KRISTOL (1920–). *American economist*

A neoconservative is a liberal who has been mugged by reality.

LOUIS KRONENBERGER (1904–1980). *American writer and critic*

1 It's the gossip columnist's business to write about what is none of his business.

2 Nothing so soothes our vanity as a display of greater vanity in others; it makes us vain, in fact, of our modesty.

3 The trouble with our age is that it is all signposts and no destination.

4 We might define an eccentric as a man who is a law unto himself, and a crank as one who, having determined what the law is, insists on laying it down to others.

BARBARA KRUGER (1945–). *American artist*

1 Fashion is everywhere and about everything. It is folly, vanity and the fun of it all. It is disguise, innuendo, and cunning. It is mean, gorgeous and ambitious, and definitely the last word for the next few seconds. [*Thinking of You,* 1999.]

2 I shop, therefore I am.

3 If you're so successful, why do you feel like a fake?

4 It's a small world, but not if you have to clean it.

5 Love is something you fall into.

JOSEPH WOOD KRUTCH (1893–1970). *American critic and naturalist*

1 Cats seems to go on the principle that it never does any harm to ask for what you want.

2 Logic is the art of going wrong with confidence.

3 The most serious charge which can be brought against New England is not Puritanism but February.

MILAN KUNDERA (1929–). *Czech novelist*

1 Optimism is the opium of the people. —See also Karl Marx 5

2 Women don't look for handsome men; they look for men with beautiful women.

IRV KUPCINET (1912–). *American journalist*

What can you say about a society that says God is dead and Elvis is alive?

JEAN de LA BRUYÈRE (1713–1762). *French moralist*

1 A man who knows how to make good bargains or finds his money increase in his coffers thinks presently that he has a good deal of brains and is almost fit to be a statesman.

2 A mixture of brandy and water spoils two good things.

3 A slave has but one master; an ambitious man has as many masters as there are people who may be useful in bettering his position.

4 All the wit in the world is lost upon him who has none.

5 As favor and riches forsake a man, we discover in him the foolishness they concealed.

6 If it is common to be strongly impressed by things that are scarce, why are we so little impressed by virtue?

7 It is a great misfortune neither to have enough wit to talk well nor enough judgment to be silent.

8 It is the glory and the merit of some men to write well, and of others not to write at all.

9 The best way of making your fortune is to let people clearly see that it is in their interest to promote yours.

10 The first thing men do when they have renounced pleasure, through decency, listlessness, or for the sake of health, is to condemn it in others.

11 The true spirit of conversation consists more in bringing out the cleverness of others than in showing a great deal of it yourself.

12 There are but two ways of rising in the world: either by your own industry or by the folly of others.

13 Those who make the worst use of their time are the first to complain of its brevity.

14 We seldom regret talking too little, but very often talking too much. This is a well-known maxim which everybody knows and nobody practices.

FIORELLO LA GUARDIA (1882–1947). *New York mayor*

1 Statistics are like alienists—they will testify for either side. [Alienist is an outdated word for psychiatrist.]

2 When I make a mistake, it's a beaut! [Referring to his appointment of a judge who turned out to be a fascist.]

CHARLES LAMB (1775–1834). *English essayist*

1 A poor relation is the most irrelevant thing in nature.

2 Anything awful makes me laugh. I misbehaved once at a funeral.

3 For thy sake, Tobacco, I / Would do anything but die.

4 He has left off reading altogether, to the great improvement of his originality.

5 How I like to be liked, and what I do to be liked!

6 I am determined my children shall be brought up in their father's religion, if they can find out what it is.

7 I have been trying all my life to like Scotchmen, and am obliged to desist from the experiment in despair.

8 In everything that relates to science, I am a whole encyclopedia behind the rest of the world.

9 My theory is to enjoy life, but the practice is against it.

10 Presents endear absents.

11 When my sonnet was rejected, I exclaimed: Damn the age; I will write for antiquity. —See also George Ade 2

12 Your borrowers of books—those mutilators of collections, spoilers of the symmetry of shelves, and creators of odd volumes.

ANNE LAMOTT (1954–). *American writer*

1 Again and again I tell God I need help, and God says, "Well, isn't that fabulous? Because I need help too. So you go get that old woman over there some water, and I'll figure out what we're going to do about *your* stuff."

2 Expectations are resentments under construction.

3 If you want to make God laugh, tell her your plans.

4 Lighthouses don't go running all over an island looking for boats to save; they just stand there shining.

5 Truth is always subversive.

ANN LANDERS (1918–). *American journalist*

1 More divorces start in the bedroom than in any other room in the house.

2 The best things in life aren't things.

3 Women complain about sex more often than men. Their gripes fall into two major categories: (1) Not enough, (2) Too much. [1968]

WALTER SAVAGE LANDOR (1775–1864). *English writer and poet*

1 Ambition is but avarice on stilts, and masked.

2 Despotism sits nowhere so secure as under the ensigns of Freedom.

3 We often stand in need of hearing what we know full well.

4 We talk on principle, but we act on interest.

ANDREW LANG (1844–1912). *Scottish writer*

He uses statistics as a drunken man uses lampposts—for support rather than illumination.

LAO-TZU (6th century B.C.). *Chinese philosopher*

Those who know do not talk, / And talkers do not know.

LEWIS H. LAPHAM (1935–). *American editor and writer*

1 A successful American politician is a smiling and accommodating fellow who learns to put a human face on the imperatives of property. [*Money and Class in America: Notes and Observations on the Civil Religion,* 1988]

2 Money always implies the promise of magic, but the effect is much magnified when, as now, people have lost faith in everything else.

3 The feasts of consumption become rituals of communion. The faithful consume goods and services as if they were partaking of the body and blood of Christ.

4 The national distrust of the contemplative temperament arises less from an innate Philistinism than from a suspicion of anything that cannot be counted, stuffed, framed or mounted over the fireplace in the den.

5 The trick in politics is to sustain the illusions of progress and change while preserving the freeze-frame of the status quo.

ADAIR LARA (1952–). *American journalist*

1 A pleasure deferred is a pleasure intensified.

2 Do unto others as others would have you do unto them.

3 Good looks build character, as there is so much more temptation to overcome.

4 Principles are our way of getting out of things we don't want to do.

5 The movie's just out. There's still time for you not to go see it. [On the 1999 film *Eyes Wide Shut*.]

6 We are never so certain of our knowledge as when we're dead wrong. —See also Oscar Wilde 102

RING LARDNER (1885–1933). *American writer and humorist*

1 "Are you lost, daddy," I asked tenderly. "Shut up," he explained. —See also Joe Namath

2 He gave her a look you could have poured on a waffle.

3 He looked at me as if I was a side dish he hadn't ordered.

4 Middle age: when you're home on Saturday night, the telephone rings, and you hope it's the wrong number.

5 The only exercise I get is when I take the studs out of one shirt and put them in another.

6 They gave each other a smile with a future in it.

PHILIP LARKIN (1922–1985). *English poet and novelist*

1 Far too many books rely on the classic formula of a beginning, a muddle, and an end.

2 Get stewed; books are a load of crap.

3 Sexual intercourse began / In nineteen sixty-three / (Which was rather late for me)— / Between the end of the Chatterly ban / And the Beatles' first LP.

FRANÇOIS de LA ROCHEFOUCAULD (1613–1680). *French writer*

1 As the stamp of great minds is to suggest much in few words, so, contrariwise, little minds have the gift of talking a great deal and saying nothing.

2 Envy is a monster which cannot endure the good fortune of others.

3 Everybody complains of his memory, but nobody of his judgment.

4 Few men are sufficiently discerning to appreciate all the evil they do.

5 Humility is often merely feigned submissiveness assumed in order to dominate others, an artifice of pride which stoops to conquer.

6 Hypocrisy is the homage that vice pays to virtue.

7 If we had no faults, we would not take so much pleasure in noticing them in others.

8 In the misfortune of our best friends, we always find something that is not displeasing.

9 It is easier to be wise for others than for oneself.

10 Lovers never weary of each other because they are always talking about themselves.

11 Many people despise money, but few hurry to give it away.

12 Mediocre minds usually dismiss anything beyond their understanding.

13 Most people judge others simply by how prosperous or popular they are.

14 Nature endowed us with pride to spare us the pain of knowing our imperfections.

15 No occurrences are so unfortunate that the shrewd cannot turn them to some advantage, nor so fortunate that the imprudent cannot turn them to their own disadvantage.

16 Nothing so much prevents our being natural as the desire to seem so.

17 Old people are fond of giving good advice; it consoles them for no longer being capable of setting a bad example.

18 One reason why so few people seem sensible and pleasant in conversation is that almost everybody is thinking about what he wants to say himself rather than about answering clearly what is being said to him.

19 Our virtues are often vices in disguise.

20 Philosophy easily triumphs over past ills and ills to come, but present ills triumph over philosophy.

21 Prudence and love are not made for each other: as love waxes, prudence wanes.

22 Quarrels would not last long if the fault were on one side only.

23 Self-love is the greatest of all flatterers.

24 Social life would not last long if men were not taken in by each other.

25 Some evil men would be less dangerous if there were no good in them at all.

26 Sometimes we think we dislike flattery, but it is only the way it is done that we dislike.

27 The most violent passions sometimes let us relax, but vanity keeps us always on the go.

28 The passions are the only orators who always convince.

29 The very clever know how to hide their cleverness.

30 There are fools with wit but never any with judgment.

31 There are reproaches that praise and praises that reproach.

32 True love is like ghosts, which everyone talks about but few have seen.

33 Unless they share our opinions, we seldom find people sensible.

34 Virtue would not go nearly so far if vanity did not keep her company.

35 We all have strength enough to endure the troubles of others. —See also Alexander Pope 10; William Shakespeare 5

36 We are held to our duty by laziness and timidity, but virtue usually gets the credit.

37 We are often more liked for our defects than for our qualities.

38 We find few guilty of ingratitude while we are still in a position to help them.

39 We love to see through others but dislike being seen through.

40 We often forgive those who bore us, but we cannot forgive those who find us boring.

41 We prefer to speak evil of ourselves rather than not speak of ourselves at all.

42 We promise according to our hopes and perform according to our fears.

43 We should not take offense when people hide the truth from us, since so often we hide it from ourselves.

[44] We should often blush at our noblest deeds if the world were to see all their underlying motives.

[45] We try to make virtues out of the faults we have no wish to correct.

[46] We would rather be with those we do good to than those who do good to us.

[47] What men call friendship is often just an arrangement for mutual gain.

[48] When we resist our passions, it is more on account of their weakness than our strength.

[49] With nothing are we so generous as advice.

CHRISTOPHER LASCH (1932–1994). *American writer*

[1] Bureaucratic propaganda is calculatedly obscure and unintelligible—qualities that commend it to a public that feels informed in proportion as it is befuddled.

[2] Nothing succeeds like the appearance of success. —See also Alexandre Dumas 2

HAROLD D. LASSWELL (1902–1978). *American political scientist*

The Republican and Democratic wings of the Republocratic party. [1936]

RALPH LAUREN (1939–). *American fashion designer*

I don't design clothes; I design dreams.

JOHANN KASPER LAVATER (1741–1801). *Swiss poet and philosopher*

[1] He that can jest at love has never loved.

[2] Too much gravity argues a shallow mind.

VERNON LAW (1930–). *American baseball player*

Experience is a hard teacher because she gives the test first, the lesson afterward.

D. H. LAWRENCE (1885–1930). *English novelist and poet*

[1] Be still when you have nothing to say; when genuine passion moves you, say what you've got to say, and say it hot.

[2] Curse the blasted, jelly-boned swines, the slimy, the belly-wriggling invertebrates, the miserable soddingrotters, the flaming sods, the sniveling, dribbling, dithering, palsied, pulse-less lot that make up England today. They've got white of egg in their veins, and their spunk is that watery it's a marvel they can breed. [1912]

[3] I can never decide whether my dreams are the result of my thoughts, or my thoughts the result of my dreams.

[4] It is only immoral / to be dead-alive, / sun-extinct / and busy / putting out the sun / in other people.

[5] Nothing but old fags and cabbage stumps of quotations from the Bible and the rest, stewed in the juice of deliberate, journalistic dirty-mindedness. [On James Joyce.]

[6] The wages of work is cash. / The wages of cash is want more cash. / The wages of want more cash is vicious competition. / The wages of vicious competition is—the world we live in.

[7] The world doesn't fear a new idea. It can pigeonhole any idea. But it can't pigeonhole a real new experience.

T. E. LAWRENCE (1888–1935). *British soldier and writer*
To have news value is to have a tin can tied to one's tail.

STEPHEN LEACOCK (1869–1944). *Canadian economist and humorist*

1 A sportsman is a man who, every now and then, simply has to get out and kill something. Not that he's cruel. He wouldn't hurt a fly. It's not big enough.

2 Advertising may be described as the science of arresting human intelligence long enough to get money from it.

3 Freedom of speech only exists in proportion to indifference to the thing spoken of.

4 I am a great believer in luck, and I find the harder I work the more I have of it.

5 I detest life-insurance agents; they always argue that I shall some day die, which is not so.

6 Lord Ronald said nothing; he flung himself from the room, flung himself upon his horse and rode madly off in all directions.

7 Many of us can still remember the social nuisance of the inveterate punster. This man followed conversation as a shark follows a ship.

8 Most people tire of a lecture in ten minutes; clever people can do it in five. Sensible people never go to lectures at all.

FRANK LEAHY (1908–1973). *American football coach*
Egotism is the anesthetic that dulls the pain of stupidity.

GUSTAVE LE BON (1841–1931). *French sociologist*
Many men easily do without truth but none is strong enough to do without illusions.

FRAN LEBOWITZ (1951–). *American writer*

1 A dog who thinks he is man's best friend is a dog who obviously has never met a tax lawyer.

2 A great many people in Los Angeles are on special diets that restrict their intake of synthetic foods. The reason for this appears to be a widely held belief that organically grown fruits and vegetables make the cocaine work faster.

3 A hobby is, of course, an abomination, as are all consuming interests and passions that do not lead directly to large, personal gain.

4 A plate bereft of a good cut of something rare is an affront to the serious diner, and while I have frequently run across the fellow who could, indeed, be described as a broccoli-and-potatoes man, I cannot say that I have ever really taken to such a person.

5 All God's children are not beautiful. Most of God's children are, in fact, barely presentable.

6 Ask your child what he wants for dinner only if he's buying.

7 Being a woman is of special interest only to aspiring male transsexuals. To actual women, it is simply a good excuse not to play football.

8 Being poor is like being a child. Being rich is like being an adult: you get to do whatever you want. Everyone is nice when they have to be; rich people are nice when they feel like it.

9 Bread that must be sliced with an ax is bread that is too nourishing.

10 Communism requires of its adherents that they arise early and participate in a strenuous round of calisthenics. To someone who wishes that cigarettes came already lit the thought of such exertion at any hour when decent people are just nodding off is thoroughly abhorrent.

11 Do not allow your children to mix drinks. It is unseemly and they use too much vermouth.

12 Don't bother discussing sex with small children. They rarely have anything to add.

13 Food is an important part of a balanced diet.

14 Food plays a crucial role in international politics. If there was no such thing as food, state dinners would be replaced by state bridge games and, instead of fasting, political activists would probably just whine.

15 Friendships are easy to get out of compared to love affairs, but they are not easy to get out of compared to, say, jail.

16 Generally speaking, it is inhumane to detain a fleeting insight.

17 Having been unpopular in high school is not just cause for book publication.

18 I am not the type who wants to go back to the land—I am the type who wants to go back to the hotel.

19 I figure you have the same chance of winning the lottery whether you play or not.

20 If you are truly serious about preparing your child for the future, don't teach him to subtract—teach him to deduct.

21 If you have a burning, restless urge to write or paint, simply eat something sweet and the feeling will pass.

22 In 1956 the population of Los Angeles was 2,243,901. By 1970 it had risen to 2,811,801, 1,650,917 of whom are currently up for a series.

23 INFALLIBLE BUT NOT INFLEXIBLE. [Pope Ron's motto emblazoned in red on his white cotton T-shirt, "At Home with Pope Ron," *Social Studies,* 1981.]

24 Large, naked, raw carrots are acceptable as food only to those who live in hutches eagerly awaiting Easter.

25 Life is something to do when you can't get to sleep.

26 Magazines all too frequently lead to books and should be regarded by the prudent as the heavy petting of literature.

27 Middle-aged women favor for daytime wear much the same apparel as do teenage girls, but after six they like to pretty up and generally lean toward prom clothes.

28 Never judge a cover by its book.

29 No animal should ever jump up on the dining-room furniture unless absolutely certain that he can hold his own in the conversation.

30 Nothing succeeds like address. —See also Alexandre Dumas 2

31 Our system of law is something less than captivating, for it consistently fails to deal with the three questions of greatest concern: 1. Is it attractive? 2. Is it amusing? 3. Does it know its place?

32 Perhaps one of the more noteworthy trends of our time is the occupation of buildings accompanied by the taking of hostages. The perpetrators of these deeds are generally motivated by political grievance, social injustice, and the deeply felt desire to see how they look on TV.

33 Polite conversation is rarely either.

34 Remember that as a teenager you are at the last stage in your life when you will be happy to hear that the phone is for you.

35 Stand firm in your refusal to remain conscious during algebra. In real life, I assure you, there is no such thing as algebra. ["Tips for Teens," *Social Studies,* 1981.]

36 Success didn't spoil me; I've always been insufferable.

37 That I am totally devoid of sympathy for, or interest in, the world of groups is directly attributable to the fact that my two greatest needs and desires— smoking cigarettes and plotting revenge—are basically solitary pursuits.

38 The best fame is a writer's fame: it's enough to get a table at a good restaurant, but not enough that you get interrupted when you eat.

39 The first step in having any successful war is getting people to fight it.

40 The only appropriate reply to the question "Can I be frank?" is "Yes, if I can be Barbara."

41 The opposite of talking isn't listening. The opposite of talking is waiting.

42 There is no such thing as inner peace. There is only nervousness or death.

43 To me the outdoors is what you must pass through in order to get from your apartment into a taxicab.

44 12:35 P.M.—The phone rings. I am not amused. This is not my favorite way to wake up. My favorite way to wake up is to have a certain French movie star whisper to me softly at two-thirty in the afternoon that if I want to get to Sweden in time to pick up my Nobel Prize for Literature I had better ring for breakfast. This occurs rather less often than one might wish. [Opening paragraph, *Metropolitan Life,* 1978.]

45 Wealth and power are much more likely to be the result of breeding than they are of reading.

46 "What do you think of George W. Bush?" [Pat Holt] Well, I didn't like the first one, and I like this one less. I am very opposed to the idea of sons, or daughters if there were any, taking the place of the parent. The point of a democracy is to avoid this type of thing. With the current crop of politicians, one from each family is more than enough. [Theater interview, 2000.]

47 "What is your favorite animal?" Steak.

48 "When are you at a loss for words?" When I'm writing.

STANISLAW J. LEC (1909–1966). *Polish writer*

1 Is it progress if a cannibal uses knife and fork?

2 "Oh to be old again," said a young corpse.

3 Puritans should wear fig leaves on their eyes.

4 The dispensing of injustice is always in the right hands.

5 The face of the enemy frightens me only when I see how much it resembles mine.

6 What do I believe? I believe in God, if he exists.

7 When smashing monuments, save the pedestals—they always come in handy.

8 Why do I write these short aphorisms? Because words fail me!

JOHN LE CARRÉ (1931–). *English novelist*
A committee is an animal with four back legs.

GYPSY ROSE LEE (1914–1970). *American burlesque entertainer*
1 God is love, but get it in writing.
2 I have everything now I had twenty years ago—except now it's all lower.
3 If a thing is worth doing, it is worth doing slowly—very slowly. —See also G. K. Chesterton 5
4 She's descended from a long line her mother listened to.

SPIKE LEE (1956–). *American film director*
I remember trying to join the Boy Scouts, and they told me I couldn't join because I wasn't Catholic. You can't help growing up thinking something is amiss.

URSULA K. LE GUIN (1929–). *American writer*
1 He had grown up in a country run by politicians who sent the pilots to man the bombers to kill the babies to make the world safer for children to grow up in.
2 Success is somebody's else's failure.
3 There are no right answers to wrong questions.
4 What sane person could live in this world and not be crazy?
5 When action grows unprofitable, gather information; when information grows unprofitable, sleep.

CHRISTOPHER LEHMANN-HAUPT (1934–). *American literary critic*
1 The only trouble with this book is that its covers are too close together. [On Florence King's *With Charity Toward None*, 1992.] —See also Ambrose Bierce 82
2 There is no medical proof that television causes brain damage—at least from over five feet away. In fact, TV is probably the least physically harmful of all the narcotics known to man. —See also Karl Marx 5
3 This isn't bad; it's awful. [On Joe McGinniss's *The Last Brother: The Rise and Fall of Teddy Kennedy*, 1993.]

TOM LEHRER (1928–). *American songwriter*
1 I wish people who have trouble communicating would just shut up.
2 It is a sobering thought that when Mozart was my age he had been dead for two years. [At age 37.]

JACK LEMMON (1925–). *American actor*
If you think it's hard to meet new people, try picking up the wrong golf ball.

V. I. LENIN (1870–1924). *Russian revolutionary leader*
Speaking the truth is a petty-bourgeois prejudice. A lie, on the other hand, is often justified by the end.

JOHN LENNON (1940–1980). *English singer and songwriter*
1 Life is what happens to you while you're busy making other plans.

2 People think the Beatles know what's going on. We don't. We're just doing it.

3 Reality leaves a lot to the imagination.

4 Would the people in the cheaper seats clap your hands. And the rest of you—if you'd just rattle your jewelry. [Remark to a Royal Variety Performance audience, 1963.]

JOHN LENNON (1940–1980) and **PAUL McCARTNEY** (1942–). *English singers and songwriters*

1 Eight days a week I love you.

2 Father McKenzie, writing the words / of a sermon that no one will hear.

3 I get by with a little help from my friends.

4 Lady Madonna, children at your feet, / Wonder how you manage to make ends meet.

5 You tell me it's the institution. / Well, you know, / You better free your mind instead.

JAY LENO (1950–). *American television talk-show host*

1 Experts are saying that President Bush's goal now is to politically humiliate Saddam Hussein. Why don't we just make him the next Democratic presidential nominee? [1991]

2 I went into a McDonald's yesterday and said, "I'd like some fries." The girl at the counter said, "Would you like some fries with that?"

ELMORE LEONARD (1925–). *American novelist*

"Why are your detective novels so popular?" I try to leave out the parts that people skip.

ALAN JAY LERNER (1918–1986). *American lyricist and screenwriter*

1 Coughing in the theater is not a respiratory ailment. It is a criticism.

2 I'm getting married in the morning! / Ding dong! The bells are gonna chime. / Pull out the stopper! / Let's have a whopper! / But get me to the church on time! ["Get Me to the Church on Time," *My Fair Lady,* 1956.]

3 It's often good to be interesting, but it's always interesting to be good.

4 *On a Clear Day You Can See Forever.* [Musical comedy title, 1965.]

5 That's quite a dress you almost have on.

6 "Why do people take an instant dislike to me?" [Andrew Lloyd Webber] Because it saves time.

MAX LERNER (1902–1992). *American journalist and writer*

I am neither an optimist nor pessimist, but a possibilist.

DAVID LETTERMAN (1947–). *American television talk-show host*

1 A recent survey showed that 25 percent of all New Yorkers had seen a dead person while living in the city. And what's more, 60 percent of them said they'd pay to see it again.

2 According to the *Rand McNally Places Rated Almanac,* the best place to live in America is the city of Pittsburgh. The city of New York came in twenty-fifth. Here in New York we really don't care too much. Because we know that we could beat up their city anytime.

3 Based on what you know about him in history books, what do you think Abraham Lincoln would be doing if he were alive today? (1) Writing his memoirs of the Civil War. (2) Advising the president. (3) Desperately clawing at the inside of his coffin.

4 Everyone has a purpose in life. Perhaps yours is watching television.

5 Fall is my favorite season in Los Angeles, watching the birds change color and fall from the trees.

6 I went to the beach a couple of times in New York City. Tough summer out there, but I was pretty excited. I found what I thought at the time was a very rare seashell. And I took it to a friend of mine who works in a museum. And I was really disappointed. It turned out to be just a human ear.

7 If you're planning to travel to New York City, do yourself a favor—this is a lot of fun—check into a Times Square hotel and take the Bible out of the nightstand there, if it hasn't already been stolen, of course. Then open up to the Ten Commandments and go to the window. On a good day you can check the Commandments off as you see them being broken.

8 It is not officially summer until Willie Nelson puts his hair up in a red bandanna.

9 Martin Levine has passed away at the age of seventy-five. Mr. Levine had owned a movie theater chain here in New York. The funeral will be held on Thursday, at 2:15, 4:20, 6:30, 8:40, and 10:50.

10 New York now leads the world's great cities in the number of people around whom you shouldn't make a sudden move.

11 Reasons why members of Congress deserve a pay raise: many big corporations are cutting back on bribes; nearly half the members have never been indicted.

12 This warning from the New York City Department of Health Fraud: be suspicious of any doctor who tries to take your temperature with his finger.

13 Tomorrow is "National Meat-Out Day." It's being sponsored by vegetarians—not exhibitionists.

14 Tourists—have some fun with New York's hard-boiled cabbies. When you get to your destination, say to your driver, "Pay? I was just hitchhiking."

15 Traffic signals in New York are just rough guidelines.

16 USA Today has come out with a new survey: apparently, three out of every four people make up 75 percent of the population.

17 Way too much coffee. But if it weren't for the coffee, I'd have no identifiable personality whatsoever.

18 You look into his eyes, and you get the feeling someone else is driving.

OSCAR LEVANT (1906–1972). *American pianist, actor, and humorist*

1 A pun is the lowest form of humor—when you don't think of it first.

2 Chutzpah enables a man who has murdered his mother and father to throw himself on the mercy of the court as an orphan. [Attributed.]

3 Do me a favor—don't do me a favor! [A favorite reply to anyone's offer of help.]

4 Happiness isn't something you experience; it's something you remember.

5 He uses music as an accompaniment to his conducting. [On Leonard Bernstein.]

6 I don't drink liquor. I don't like it. It makes me feel good.

7 I played myself. I was miscast. [On his role in a film.]

8 I treasure every moment I don't see her. [Attributed.]

9 I was once thrown out of a mental hospital for depressing the other patients.

10 I'm a study of a man in chaos in search of frenzy.

11 I've given up reading books; I find it takes my mind off myself.

12 In some situations I was difficult, in odd moments impossible, in rare moments loathsome, but at my best unapproachably great.

13 It is not what you are; it's what you don't become that hurts.

14 My behavior has been impeccable; I've been unconscious for the past six months.

15 My first wife divorced me on grounds of incompatibility, and besides, I think she hated me.

16 *Romance on the High Seas* was Doris Day's first picture; that was before she became a virgin.

17 Roses are red, violets are blue, / I'm schizophrenic, and so am I.

18 So little time, so little to do.

19 Strip away the phony tinsel of Hollywood and you'll find the real tinsel underneath.

20 Tell me, George, if you had to do it all over would you fall in love with yourself again? [Remark to George Gershwin.]

21 The first thing I do in the morning is brush my teeth and sharpen my tongue.

22 Underneath this flabby exterior is an enormous lack of character.

23 What the world needs is more geniuses with humility. There are so few of us left.

SAM LEVENSON (1911–1980). *American humorist and television personality*
1 Insanity is hereditary—you get it from your children.
2 My mother used to get up at 5 A.M. no matter what time it was.

LORD LEVERHULME (William Hesketh Lever, 1851–1925). *English manufacturer*
Half the money I spend on advertising is wasted, and the trouble is I don't know which half.

BERNARD LEVIN (1928–). *British journalist and writer*
1 The best headlines never fi
2 "The future is not what it was." The past is not getting any better either.
　—See also Walter Truett Anderson; Anonymous 118; Paul Valéry 7
3 The persistence of public officials varies inversely with the importance of the matter in which they are persisting.
4 Whom the mad would destroy, first they make gods. —See also Cyril Connolly 17; Joyce Carol Oates 3

ANTHONY LEWIS (1927–). *American journalist*

1   Beating up on "intellectuals" is the last refuge of demagogues. —See also Samuel Johnson 64

2   The press has its own version of Gresham's Law: the tendency, in the competition for readers, to let the scandalous and sensational drive out serious news.

C. S. LEWIS (1898–1963). *English scholar and writer*

1   She's the sort of woman who lives for others—you can always tell the others by their hunted expression.

2   The future is something which everyone reaches at the rate of sixty minutes an hour, whatever he does, whoever he is.

3   There are two kinds of people: those who say to God, "Thy will be done," and those to whom God says, "All right, then, have it your way."

4   This extraordinary pride in being exempt from temptation is like eunuchs boasting of their chastity.

5   This world is a great sculptor's shop. We are the statues and there is a rumor going round the shop that some of us are some day going to come to life.

JOE E. LEWIS (1902–1971). *American comedian*

1   A man is never drunk if he can lay on the floor without holding on.

2   I drink to forget I drink.

3   I went on a diet, swore off drinking and heavy eating, and in fourteen days I lost two weeks.

4   It doesn't matter if you're rich or poor, as long as you've got money.

5   You only live once—but if you work it right, once is enough.

SINCLAIR LEWIS (1885–1951). *American novelist*

1   Babbitt was not too unreasonably honest.

2   His name was George F. Babbitt. He was forty-six years old now, in April, 1920, and he made nothing in particular, neither butter nor shoes nor poetry, but he was nimble in the calling of selling houses for more than people could afford to pay.

3   Our American professors like their literature clear and cold and pure and very dead.

4   To George F. Babbitt, as to most prosperous citizens of Zenith, his motor car was poetry and tragedy, love and heroism. The office was his pirate ship but the car his perilous excursion ashore.

5   Writers have a rare power not given to anyone else; we can bore people long after we are dead.

WINDHAM LEWIS (1882–1957). *English novelist and critic*

1   Gertrude Stein's prose song is a cold, black suet pudding of fabulously reptilian length.

2   Hemingway invariably invokes a dull-witted, bovine, monosyllabic simpleton, a lethargic and stuttering dummy, a village idiot of few words and fewer ideas. [1934]

LIBERACE (1919–1987). *American pianist and entertainer*

1 I've done my bit for motion pictures. I've stopped making them.

2 My great virtue is that I have no vanity. People criticize me, but when they meet me nobody can help liking me.

3 When the reviews are bad, I tell my staff that they can join me as I cry all the way to the bank.

GEORG CHRISTOPH LICHTENBERG (1742–1799). *German scientist and critic*

1 A book is a mirror: if an ape looks into it, an apostle is unlikely to look out.

2 Among the greatest discoveries that the human mind has made in recent times belongs the art of judging books without having read them.

3 Does music make plants grow, or are there some plants that are musical?

4 How did you enjoy yourself with these people? Answer: very much, almost as much as I do when alone.

5 In England a man was charged with bigamy and his lawyer got him off by proving that his client had three wives.

6 In former days when the soul was still immortal.

7 Much reading has brought upon us a learned barbarism.

8 Nothing contributes more to peace of mind than the lack of any opinion whatever.

9 Perhaps in time the so-called Dark Ages will be thought of as including our own.

10 Resolved: to send out arrest warrants when someone has borrowed an idea from me and then appropriated it.

11 To make other people laugh is no great feat so long as one does not mind whether they are laughing at our wit or at us ourselves.

12 We are obliged to regard many of our original minds as crazy at least until we have become as clever as they are.

13 What astonished him was that cats had two holes cut in their furs exactly where their eyes were.

14 You can make a good living from soothsaying but not from truthsaying.

B. H. LIDDELL HART (1895–1970). *English military historian*

1 Haig was an honorable man according to his lights—but his lights were dim. [On Douglas Haig.] —See also David Lloyd George 4

2 History marches on the stomachs of statesmen.

3 To write true history is always offensive to those who have an interest in concealing it.

A. J. LIEBLING (1904–1963). *American journalist*

1 Freedom of the press is guaranteed only to those who own one.

2 People everywhere confuse what they read in newspapers with news.

ABRAHAM LINCOLN (1809–1865). *American president*

1 Abraham Lincoln, / His hand and pen, / He will be good, / But God knows when. [Doggerel written as a youngster.]

2 Abraham Lincoln is my name / And with my pen I wrote the same / I wrote in both haste and speed / And left it here for fools to read.

3 Better to remain silent and be thought a fool than to speak out and remove all doubt.

4 Common looking people are the best in the world: that is the reason the Lord makes so many of them. [From a dream Lincoln had in December 1863.] —See also H. L. Mencken 36; Kenneth Patchen 1

5 For people who like that sort of thing, that is about the sort of a thing they would like. [Responding to a young poet who had sent Lincoln some newly published poems with a request for his opinion of them.] —See also George Bernard Shaw 128

6 General Banks hasn't come up to my expectations. "Then, sir, why don't you remove him?" Well, one principal reason is that it would hurt General Banks' feelings very much!

7 Ha! T. R. Strong, but coffee are stronger. [Remark to Secretary of State William H. Seward who, while the two were walking together on Pennsylvania Avenue, had pointed out a new sign reading "T. R. Strong."]

8 He can compress the most words into the smallest ideas of any man I ever met. [On a lawyer colleague.] —See also Samuel Butler 9

9 He was now without means and out of business, but was anxious to remain with his friends who had treated him with so much generosity, especially as he had nowhere to go to. [From a third-person autobiographical sketch written after being defeated for office in 1832.]

10 Honest statesmanship is the wise employment of individual meannesses for the public good. [Attributed.]

11 How difficult it is to find a place for an officer of high rank when there is no place seeking him.

12 "How long should a man's legs be?" I should think a man's legs ought to be long enough to reach from his body to the ground.

13 I am on my way to Massachusetts, where I have a son at school, who, if report be true, already knows much more than his father.

14 I believe I shall never be old enough to speak without embarrassment when I have nothing to talk about.

15 I do the very best I know how—the very best I can; and I mean to keep doing so until the end. If the end brings me out all right, what is said against me won't amount to anything. If the end brings me out wrong, ten angels swearing I was right would make no difference.

16 I feel somewhat like the boy in Kentucky who stubbed his toe while running to see his sweetheart. The boy said he was too big to cry, and far too badly hurt to laugh. [When asked how he felt about his party's losses in a recent election, 1862.]

17 I have endured a great deal of ridicule without much malice; and have received a great deal of kindness, not quite free from ridicule.

18 I have not permitted myself, gentlemen, to conclude that I am the best man in the country; but I am reminded, in this connection, of a story of an old Dutch farmer, who remarked to a companion once that "it was not best to swap horses when crossing streams."

19 I have now come to the conclusion never again to think of marrying, and

for this reason: I can never be satisfied with anyone who would be block-head enough to have me. [After Mary Todd, his future wife, refused an earlier marriage proposal, 1838.] —See also Ralph Waldo Emerson 9; Groucho Marx 19

20 I hope you will perfectly easy about having nominated me; don't be troubled about it; I forgive you. [Parting words to an editor who claimed to have been the first to suggest his name for the presidency.]

21 I presume, sir, in painting your portrait, you took your idea of me from my principles, and not from my person. [Remark "in a merry voice" to an unnamed artist who had just spoken of his photo-based portrait of Lincoln.]

22 I remember a good story when I hear it, but I never invented anything original. I am only a retail dealer.

23 I was not very much accustomed to flattery, and it came the sweeter to me. I was rather like the Hoosier, with the gingerbread, when he said he reckoned he loved it better than any other man and got less of it.

24 I wish some of you would tell me the brand of whiskey that Grant drinks. I would like to send a barrel of it to my other generals. [Responding to criticism of Ulysses S. Grant, his highly successful, but allegedly hard-drinking general; attributed.]

25 If General —— had known how big a funeral he would have had, he would have died years ago. [On a recently deceased public figure known for his vanity.]

26 If to be at the head of Hell is as hard as what I have to undergo here, I could find it in my heart to pity Satan himself. [Referring to the presidency.]

27 It's a fortunate thing I wasn't born a woman, for I cannot refuse anything.

28 It's been my experience that folks who have no vices have very few virtues.

29 Maj. Gen. McClellan: I have just read your dispatch about sore-tongued and fatigued horses. Will you pardon me for asking what the horses of your army have done since the battle of Antietam that fatigues anything? [Telegram, 1862.]

30 Many a time have I stood on one side of the counter and sold whiskey to Mr. Douglas, but the difference between us now is this. I have left my side of the counter, but Mr. Douglas still sticks to his as tenaciously as ever. [Lincoln-Douglas debates, 1858.]

31 "Mr. Lincoln, how do you like being president of the United States?" [Visitor] You have heard the story, haven't you, about the man who was tarred and feathered and carried out of town on a rail? A man in the crowd asked him how he liked it. His reply was that if it was not for the honor of the thing, he would much rather walk.

32 "Mr. Lincoln, I wish you would say something to me that I will always remember." [Young girl among well-wishers at a White House reception following Lincoln's Second Inaugural Address.] I think you are the prettiest girl I have seen this evening.

33 My dear judge: The bearer of this is a young man who thinks he can be a lawyer. Examine him if you want to. I have done so and am satisfied. He's a good deal smarter than he looks to be.

34 My dear McClellan: If you don't want to use the army I should like to borrow it for a while.

35 My dear sir: I personally wish Jacob Freese, of New Jersey, to be appointed colonel for a colored regiment, and this regardless of whether he can tell the exact shade of Julius Caesar's hair.

36 My dear sir: The lady—bearer of this note—says she has two sons who want to work. Set them at it, if possible. Wanting to work is so rare a merit that it should be encouraged.

37 My father taught me to work; he did not teach me to love it.

38 My old father used to have a saying that "if you make a bad bargain, hug it the tighter"; and it occurs to me that if the bargain you have just closed can possibly be called a bad one, it is certainly the most pleasant one for applying that maxim to, which my fancy can, by any effort, picture. [Letter to his newly married friend Joshua Speed, 1842.]

39 Now, my man, go away, go away! I cannot meddle in your case. I could as easily bail out the Potomac River with a teaspoon as attend to all the details of the army. [Remark to a soldier with a petty grievance who had overstretched Lincoln's patience.]

40 Politicians are a set of men who have interests aside from the interests of the people, and who, to say the most of them, are, taken as a mass, at least one long step removed from honest men. I say this with the greater freedom because, being a politician myself, none can regard it as personal. [1837]

41 Stanton, I find a heap of fun in Artemus Ward's book. "Yes, but what do you think of that chapter where he makes fun of you?" [Secretary of War Edwin M. Stanton] Stanton, upon my life I could never see any humor in that chapter.

42 The trouble with Hooker is that he's got his headquarters where his hindquarters ought to be. [Referring to a dispatch from General Joseph Hooker headed "Headquarters in the Saddle."]

43 These capitalists generally act harmoniously, and in concert, to fleece the people. [Speech, 1837.]

44 We won't jump that ditch until we come to it.

45 "We're building a privy for General McClellan, a one-holer." [Soldier] Thank God it's a one-holer, for if it were a two-holer, before McClellan could make up his mind which to use, he would beshit himself.

46 Whatever fees we earn at a distance, if not paid before, we notice we never hear of after the work is done. We therefore, are growing a little sensitive on the point. [Referring to his law partnership with Judge Logan, letter, 1842.]

47 When I give away a government position, I find that I always make a hundred foes to one friend. —See also Louis XIV

48 When I hear a man preach, I like to see him act as if he were fighting bees.

49 When I was a boy, I spent considerable time along the Sangamon River. An old steamboat plied on the river, the boiler of which was so small that when they blew the whistle, there wasn't enough steam to turn the pad-

dle wheel. And when the paddle wheel went around, they couldn't blow the whistle. My friend Douglas reminds of that old steamboat; for when he talks he can't think, and when he thinks he can't talk. [Lincoln-Douglas debates, 1858.]

50 Whenever I hear anyone arguing for slavery, I feel a strong impulse to see it tried on him personally.

51 With educated people, I suppose, punctuation is a matter of rule; with me it is a matter of feeling. But I must say that I have a great respect for the semicolon; it is a useful little chap.

52 You can fool all the people some of the time and some of the people all the time, but you cannot fool all the people all of the time. [Attributed.] — See also Franklin P. Adams 4; Laurence J. Peter 55; James Thurber 23

53 "You never swear, Mr. President, do you?" Oh, I don't have to. You know I have Stanton in my cabinet.

54 "You're a two-faced liar." If I had another face, do you think I'd use this one?

ASSAR LINDBECK (20th century). *Swedish economist*
That is the true test of a brilliant theory. What first is thought to be wrong is later shown to be obvious. [1985]

WALTER LIPPMANN (1889–1974). *American journalist and writer*
1 He is an amiable man with many philanthropic impulses, but he is not the dangerous enemy of anything. He is a pleasant man who, without any important qualifications for the office, would like to be president. [On Franklin D. Roosevelt, 1932.]

2 Machiavelli has a worse name and more disciples than any political thinker who ever lived.

3 Men with faith can face martyrdom while men without it feel stricken when they are not invited to dinner.

4 Nobody has ever worked harder at inactivity, with such force of character, with such unremitting attention to detail, with such conscientious devotion to the task. Inactivity is a political philosophy and a party program with Mr. Coolidge.

5 Propaganda is that branch of lying which often deceives your friends without ever deceiving your enemies. [Attributed.]

6 The American's conviction that he must be able to look any man in the eye and tell him to go to hell, is the very essence of the free man's way of life.

7 The statistical method is of use only to those who have found it out.

8 When all think alike, no one thinks very much.

MARY WILSON LITTLE (19th century). *American writer*
1 He who devotes sixteen hours a day to hard study may become as wise at sixty as he thought himself at twenty.

2 The penalty of success is to be bored by the attention of people who formerly snubbed you. —See also Henry A. Kissinger 15

3 The tombstone is about the only thing that can stand upright and lie on its face at the same time.

DAVID LLOYD GEORGE (1863–1945). *British prime minister*
1 A fully-equipped duke costs as much to keep up as two dreadnoughts; and dukes are just as great a terror and they last longer. [1909]
2 A politician was a person with whose politics you did not agree. When you did agree, he was a statesman.
3 A young man who isn't a socialist hasn't got a heart; an old man who is a socialist hasn't got a head.
4 Brilliant to the top of his army boots. [On General Douglas Haig, inept commander of the British Expeditionary Force in France during World War I.] —See also B. H. Liddell Hart 1
5 He had sufficient conscience to bother him, but not sufficient to keep him straight. [On Ramsay MacDonald.]
6 He might make an adequate Lord Mayor of Birmingham in a lean year. [On Neville Chamberlain.]
7 It was the best I could do, seated as I was between Jesus Christ and Napoleon Bonaparte. [Referring to his difficulties with Woodrow Wilson and Georges Clemenceau at the Paris Peace Conference following World War I in 1919.]
8 Negotiating with de Valera is like trying to pick up mercury with a fork. [On the Irish prime minister Eamon de Valera.]
9 The world is becoming like a lunatic asylum run by lunatics. [1933]
10 This war, like the next war, is a war to end war. [Referring to World War I; attributed.]
11 When they circumcised Herbert Samuel, they threw away the wrong part.

DAVID LODGE (1935–). *English novelist*
Literature is mostly about having sex and not much about having children. Life is the other way round.

G. M. LOEB (1899–). *American investment adviser*
Every time you think you've got the key to the market, some SOB changes the lock.

VINCE LOMBARDI (1913–1970). *American football coach*
Football isn't a contact sport; it's a collision sport. Dancing is a contact sport.

RUSSELL B. LONG (1918–). *Louisiana senator*
A tax loophole benefits the other guy. If it benefits you, it's a tax reform.

ALICE ROOSEVELT LONGWORTH (1884–1980). *American socialite*
1 Father wanted to be the corpse at every funeral, the bride at every wedding, and the baby at every christening. [On Theodore Roosevelt.]
2 Harding was not a bad man, he was just a slob. [On Warren G. Harding.]
3 I have a simple philosophy: fill what's empty, empty what's full, and scratch where it itches.
4 If you can't say anything good about someone, sit right here by me. [Embroidered on a cushion in her home.]
5 Never trust a man who combs his hair straight from his left armpit. [On Douglas MacArthur.]

ANITA LOOS (1893–1981). *American writer*
The people I'm furious with are the women's liberationists. They keep getting up on soapboxes and proclaiming women are brighter than men. That's true, but it should be kept quiet or it ruins the whole racket.

SOPHIA LOREN (1934–). *Italian actress*
Everything you see I owe to spaghetti.

LOUIS XIV (1638–1715). *French king*
Every time I fill a vacant office I make a hundred malcontents and one ingrate. —See also Abraham Lincoln 47

JOE LOUIS (1914–1981). *American boxer*
He can run, but he can't hide. [On Billy Conn and their upcoming heavyweight title fight, 1946; Louis knocked him out.]

JAMES RUSSELL LOWELL (1819–1891). *American writer and diplomat*
1 Blessed is he who has nothing to say, and who cannot be persuaded to say it.
2 Democracy gives every man the right to be his own oppressor.
3 He seems to us to have been a man with so high a conceit of himself that he accepted without questioning, and insisted on our accepting, his defects and weaknesses of character as virtues and powers peculiar to himself. [On Henry David Thoreau.]
4 His more ambitious works may be defined as careless thinking carefully versified. [On Alexander Pope.]
5 I don't believe in princerple, / But O, I *du* in interest.
6 Mr. Carlyle's borrowing is mainly from his own former works. But he does this so often and so openly that we may at least be sure that he ceased growing a number of years ago, and is a remarkable example of arrested development. [On Thomas Carlyle.]
7 My gran'ther's rule was safer'n 'tis to crow: / Don't never prophesy—onless ye know.
8 The misfortunes that are hardest to bear are those that never come.
9 There is no good in arguing with the inevitable. The only argument available with an east wind is to put on your overcoat.

ROBERT LOWELL (1917–1977). *American poet*
1 If youth is a defect, it is one we outgrow too soon.
2 We feel the machine slipping from our hands, / As if someone else were steering; / If we see light at the end of the tunnel, / It's the light of the oncoming train. —See also Barry Commoner

VICTOR LOWNES (1929–). *American publisher*
What is a promiscuous person—it's usually someone who is getting more sex than you are.

E. V. LUCAS (1868–1938). *English essayist*
I have noticed that the people who are late are often so much jollier than the people who have to wait for them.

CLARE BOOTHE LUCE (1903–1987). *American playwright and ambassador*
1 Autobiography is mostly alibiography.
2 I am in my anecdotage.
3 I was wondering today what the religion of the country is, and all I could come up with was sex.
4 Much of what Mr. Wallace calls his global thinking is, no matter how you slice it, still globaloney. [On Vice President Henry A. Wallace, 1943.] —See also Al Smith 2
5 Nature abhors a virgin—a frozen asset.
6 No good deed goes unpunished.
7 The politicians were talking themselves red, white, and blue in the face.

MARTIN LUTHER (1483–1546). *German religious reformer*
Experience has proved the toad to be endowed with valuable qualities. If you run a stick through three toads, and, after having dried them in the sun, apply them to any pestilent tumor, they draw out all the poison, and the malady will disappear.

PETER LYNCH (1944–). *American investment manager*
I like to buy a company any fool can manage because eventually one will.

RUSSELL LYNES (1910–). *American editor*
1 It is always well to accept your own shortcomings with candor but to regard those of our friends with polite incredulity.
2 The only gracious way to accept an insult is to ignore it; if you can't ignore it, top it; if you can't top it, laugh at it; if you can't laugh at it, it's probably deserved.

MOMS MABLEY (1894–1975). *American comedienne*

1 A woman's a woman until the day she dies, but a man's only a man as long as he can.

2 They say you shouldn't say nothing about the dead unless it's good. He's dead. Good.

THOMAS BABINGTON MACAULAY (1800–1859). *English historian*

1 An acre in Middlesex is better than a principality in Utopia.

2 From the poetry of Lord Byron they drew a system of ethics compounded of misanthropy and voluptuousness—a system in which the two great commandments were to hate your neighbor and to love your neighbor's wife.

3 His imagination resembled the wings of an ostrich; it enabled him to run, though not to soar. When he attempted the highest flights, he became ridiculous; but while he remained in a lower region, he outstripped all competitors. [On John Dryden.]

4 Perhaps no person can be a poet, or can even enjoy poetry, without a certain unsoundness of mind.

5 The characteristic peculiarity of his intellect was the union of great powers with low prejudices. [On Samuel Johnson.]

6 The more I read about Socrates, the less I wonder that they poisoned him.

7 The Puritan hated bear-baiting, not because it gave pain to the bear, but because it gave pleasure to the spectators.

8 We know no spectacle so ridiculous as the British public in one of its periodical fits of morality.

GEORGE MacDONALD (1824–1905). *Scottish novelist and poet*

Here lie I, Martin Elginbrodde: / Hae mercy o' my soul, Lord God; / As I wad do, were I Lord God, / And ye were Martin Elginbrodde.

SHIRLEY MacLAINE (1934–). *American actress and writer*

1 I would rather have a president who does it to a woman than a president who does it to his country.

2 I've made so many movies playing a hooker that they don't pay me in the regular way anymore. They leave it on the dresser.

HAROLD MACMILLAN (1894–1986). *British prime minister*

1 A foreign secretary is always poised between a cliché and an indiscretion.

2 A man who trusts nobody is apt to be the kind of man whom nobody trusts.

3 As usual the Liberals offer a mixture of sound and original ideas. Unfortunately, none of the sound ideas is original and none of the original ideas is sound. —See also Samuel Johnson 96

4 At home, you always have to be a politician. When you are abroad, you almost feel yourself to be a statesman.

5 Churchill was fundamentally what the English call unstable—by which they mean anybody who has that touch of genius which is inconvenient in normal times.

6 He enjoys prophesying the imminent fall of the capitalist system and is prepared to play a part, any part, in its burial, except that of mute. [On Aneurin Bevan.]

7 I have never found, in a long experience of politics, that criticism is ever inhibited by ignorance.

8 Memorial services are the cocktail parties of the geriatric set.

9 When a line of action is said to be supported "by all responsible men," it is nearly always dangerous or foolish.

SALVADOR de MADARIAGA (1886–1978). *Spanish diplomat*

1 Considering how bad men are, it is wonderful how well they behave.

2 The Anglo-Saxon conscience does not prevent the Anglo-Saxon from sinning. It merely prevents him from enjoying it.

MADONNA (1958–). *American singer and actress*

1 I'm tough, I'm ambitious, and I know exactly what I want. If that makes me a bitch, OK.

2 You don't have to have a language in common with someone for a sexual rapport. But it helps if the language you don't understand is Italian.

MAURICE MAETERLINCK (1862–1949). *Belgian playwright and poet*
The living are the dead on holiday.

GUSTAV MAHLER (1860–1911). *Austrian composer*
Fortissimo at last? [On seeing Niagara Falls.]

NORMAN MAILER (1923–). *American novelist and journalist*

1 Alimony is the curse of the writing classes.

2 It all comes down to who does the dishes.

3 Most of the people who nourish themselves in the political life are in the game not to make history but to be diverted from the history which is being made.

4 Sentimentality is the emotional promiscuity of those who have no sentiment.

5 Success has been a lobotomy to my past.

6 The crudest of the great movies, but a great movie. [On Oliver Stone's 1991 film *JFK*.]

7 The function of socialism is to raise suffering to a higher level.

8 The horror of the Twentieth Century is the size of each new event, and the paucity of its reverberation.

9 There are four stages to a marriage. First there's the affair, then there's the marriage, then children and finally the fourth stage, without which you cannot know a woman, the divorce.

10 You can't be a serious writer of fiction unless you believe the story you are telling.

MALCOLM X (1925–1965). *American clergyman and human rights leader*

1 As long as you're south of the Canadian border, you're in the South.

2 "Conservatism" in America's politics means "Let's keep the niggers in their place." And "liberalism" means "Let's keep the *knee*-grows in their place—

but tell them we'll treat them a little better; let's fool them more, with more promises."

3 Give your brain as much attention as you do your hair, and you'll be a thousand times better off.

4 You show me a capitalist; I'll show you a bloodsucker.

ROBERT MANKOFF (1944–). *American cartoonist and cartoon editor*

1 Jitters on Wall Street today over rumors that Alan Greenspan said, "A rich man can as soon enter Heaven as a camel fit through the eye of a needle." [Television newscaster, cartoon caption, 1997.]

2 One question: if this is the Information Age, how come nobody knows anything? [Woman to man at a party, cartoon caption, 1998.]

MARYA MANNES (1904–). *American writer and critic*

1 Everybody likes to see somebody else get caught for the vices practiced by themselves.

2 Generosity with strings is not generosity: it is a deal.

3 Nobody objects to a woman being a good writer or sculptor or geneticist as long as she manages also to be a good wife, mother, good-looking, good-tempered, well-dressed, well-groomed, unaggressive.

4 Those who are in reality superior in intelligence can be accepted by their fellows only if they pretend they are not.

MAO TSE-TUNG (1893–1976). *Chinese Communist Party chairman*

The right to vote belongs only to the people, not to the reactionaries. The combination of these two aspects, democracy for the people and dictatorship over the reactionaries, is the people's democratic dictatorship.

HERBERT MARCUSE (1898–1979). *German-born American political philosopher*

Not every problem someone has with his girlfriend is necessarily due to the capitalist mode of production.

MALCOLM MARGOLIN (1940–). *American publisher and writer*

It is difficult to keep quiet if you have nothing to say.

DON MARQUIS (1878–1937). *American journalist and humorist*

1 A louse I used to know told me that millionaires and bums tasted about alike to him.

2 A Pharisee is a man who prays publicly and preys privately.

3 A prophet is not without honor save on his own planet.

4 An idea isn't responsible for the people who believe in it.

5 An optimist is a guy that has never had much experience.

6 Did you ever notice that when a politician does get an idea he usually gets it all wrong?

7 Happiness is the interval between periods of unhappiness.

8 Honesty is a good thing but it is not profitable to its possessor unless it is kept under control. —See also William Ewart Gladstone 4

9 I never think when I write; nobody can do two things at the same time and do them well.

10 If you make people think they're thinking, they'll love you; but if you really make them think, they'll hate you.

11 If you want to get rich from writing, write the sort of thing that's read by persons who move their lips when they're reading to themselves.

12 It's cheerio, my deario, that pulls a lady through.

13 Just because you have heard a thing so often that it bores you is no sign it isn't true.

14 Middle age: the time when a man is always thinking that in a week or two he will feel just as good as ever.

15 Now and then there is a person born who is so unlucky that he runs into accidents which started out to happen to somebody else.

16 One of the most important things to remember about infant care is: never change diapers in midstream.

17 Ours is a world where people don't know what they want and are willing to go through hell to get it.

18 Procrastination is the art of keeping up with yesterday.

19 Publishing a volume of poetry today is like dropping a rose petal down the Grand Canyon and waiting for the echo.

20 Some persons are likable in spite of their unswerving integrity.

21 The art of newspaper paragraphing is to stroke a platitude until it purrs like an epigram.

22 The chief obstacle to the progress of the human race is the human race.

23 The more conscious a philosopher is of the weak spots of his theory, the more certain he is to speak with an air of final authority.

24 The successful people are the ones who can think up things for the rest of the world to keep busy at.

25 There is always a comforting thought in time of trouble when it is not our trouble.

26 When a man tells you that he got rich through hard work, ask him: "Whose?"

THOMAS R. MARSHALL (1854–1925). *Indiana governor and U.S. vice president*

1 I come from Indiana, the home of more first-rate second-class men than any state in the Union.

2 Once there were two brothers. One ran away to sea, the other was elected vice president, and nothing was ever heard from either of them again.

3 What this country needs is a really good five-cent cigar. [1920] —See also Franklin P. Adams 5

MARTIAL (A.D. 42?–102). *Roman poet and epigrammatist*

1 If you would have him mourn, leave him nothing.

2 She has buried all her woman friends. Would that she became my wife's friend.

STEVE MARTIN (1945–). *American comedian and actor*

There is only one thing that would cause me to break up with her: if she caught me with another woman. I won't stand for that.

CHICO MARX (1891–1961). *American comedian and actor*

I wasn't kissing her. I was whispering in her mouth. [When his wife discovered him kissing a chorus girl.]

GROUCHO MARX (1895–1977). *American comedian, actor, and television personality*

1 An amateur thinks it's funny if you dress a man up as an old lady, put him in a wheelchair, and give the wheelchair a push that sends it spinning down a slope towards a stone wall. For a pro, it's got to be a real old lady.

2 Anyone who says he can see through women is missing a lot.

3 "Can I have a table near the floor?" Certainly, I'll have the waiter saw the legs off. [At a nightclub.]

4 "Closer, hold me closer!" [Woman] If I hold you any closer, I'll be in back of you!

5 Dear Junior: From the moment I picked up your book until the moment I put it down, I could not stop laughing. Someday I hope to read it. [Letter to Leo Rosten.]

6 Don't point that beard at me; it might go off.

7 Either he's dead or my watch has stopped.

8 Go and never darken my towels again. [Remark to a house guest.]

9 He may look like an idiot and talk like an idiot, but don't let that fool you: he really is an idiot.

10 I could dance with you until the cows come home. On second thought, I'd rather dance with the cows until you come home.

11 I find television very educational. Every time someone switches it on, I go into another room and read a good book.

12 I never forget a face, but in your case I'll make an exception.

13 "I'd like to say good-bye to your wife." [Leo Rosten at Marx's front door after dinner.] Who wouldn't? [Soon afterward the Marxes were divorced.]

14 I've had a perfectly wonderful evening. But this wasn't it.

15 If you continue to publish slanderous pieces about me, I shall feel compelled to cancel my subscription. [Letter to a magazine editor.]

16 "Is Groucho your real name?" No, I'm breaking it in for a friend.

17 Marriage, more than politics, makes strange bedfellows. —See also Anonymous 98; William Shakespeare 19; Charles Dudley Warner 2

18 One morning I shot an elephant in my pajamas. How he got in my pajamas I'll never know.

19 Please accept my resignation. I don't want to belong to any club that will accept me as a member. [Telegram to the Delaney Club in Los Angeles.] —See also Abraham Lincoln 19

20 Remember, men, we're fighting for this woman's honor; which is probably more than she ever did.

21 Room service? Send up a larger room!

22 Send two dozen roses to Room 424 and put "Emily, I love you" on the back of the bill.

23 She got her good looks from her father—he's a plastic surgeon.

24 Some people claim that marriage interferes with romance. There's no doubt about it. Anytime you have a romance, your wife is bound to interfere.

25 "Thank you, for all the enjoyment you've given the world!" [Clergyman] And I want to thank you for all the enjoyment you've taken out of it.

26 "This is a gala day for you." That's plenty. I don't think I could manage more than one gal a day.

27 When I came into my hotel room last night, I found a strange blonde in my bed. I would stand for none of her nonsense! I gave her exactly twenty-four hours to get out.

28 Whoever called it necking was a poor judge of anatomy.

29 Why don't you bore a hole in yourself and let the sap run out?

30 You go Uruguay and I'll go mine.

31 You're a disgrace to our family name of Wagstaff, if such a thing is possible.

32 You've got the brain of a four-year-old boy, and I bet he was glad to get rid of it.

KARL MARX (1818–1883). *German political philosopher*

1 All I know is that I am not a Marxist.

2 *Das Kapital* will not pay for the cigars I smoked writing it.

3 History repeats itself—first as tragedy, second as farce.

4 I hope the bourgeoisie, as long as they live, will have cause to remember my carbuncles. [Referring to the painful boils he endured while writing *Das Kapital*.]

5 Religion is the opium of the people. —See also Russell Baker 7; Sigmund Freud 16; Aldous Huxley 10; Rudyard Kipling 4; Milan Kundera 1; Christopher Lehmann-Haupt 2; W. Somerset Maugham 2; Edward R. Murrow 2; Friedrich Nietzsche 16; Edmund Wilson 1

JACKIE MASON (1931–). *American comedian*

1 Britain is the only country in the world where the food is more dangerous than the sex.

2 I always thought music was more important than sex—then I thought if I don't hear a concert for a year-and-a-half it doesn't bother me.

COTTON MATHER (1663–1728). *American clergyman*

That there is a devil is a thing doubted by none but such as are under the influences of the devil.

BRANDER MATTHEWS (1852–1929). *American educator and writer*

A highbrow is a person educated beyond his intelligence.

W. SOMERSET MAUGHAM (1874–1965). *English novelist, short-story writer, and playwright*

1 American women expect to find in their husbands a perfection that English women only hope to find in their butlers.

2 Art, unless it leads to right action, is no more than the opium of an intelligentsia. —See also Karl Marx 5

3 At a dinner party one should eat wisely but not too well, and talk well but not too wisely.

4 Dying is a very dull, dreary affair. My advice to you is to have nothing whatever to do with it. [Last words.]

5 Excess is exhilarating. It prevents moderation from acquiring the deadening effect of a habit.

6 For many years I have been described as a cynic: I told the truth.

7 From the earliest times the old have rubbed it into the young that they are wiser than they, and before the young had discovered what nonsense this was they were old too, and it profited them to carry on the imposture.

8 Impropriety is the soul of wit. —See also Dorothy Parker 2; William Shakespeare 3

9 It is a funny thing about life: if you refuse to accept anything but the best, you very often get it.

10 Like all weak men he laid an exaggerated stress on not changing one's mind.

11 Love is only the dirty trick played on us to achieve continuation of the species.

12 Love is what happens to a man and a woman who don't know each other.

13 Money is the sixth sense which enables you to enjoy the other five.

14 Most people have a furious itch to talk about themselves and are restrained only by the disinclination of others to listen. Reserve is an artificial quality that is developed in most of us as the result of innumerable rebuffs.

15 Old age is ready to undertake tasks that youth shirked because they would take too long.

16 Only the mediocre are always at their best.

17 People will sometimes forgive you the good you have done them, but seldom the harm they have done you.

18 Perhaps the only thing of which I was certain was that I was certain of nothing else.

19 Sentimentality is only sentiment that rubs you the wrong way.

20 Success. I don't believe it has any effect on me. For one thing I always expected it.

21 The most useful thing about a principle is that it can always be sacrificed to expediency.

22 The unfortunate thing about this world is that good habits are so much easier to give up than bad ones.

23 There are few minds in a century that can look upon a new idea without terror. Fortunately for the rest of us, there are very few new ideas about.

24 To do each day two things one dislikes is a precept I have followed scrupulously: every day I have got up and I have gone to bed.

25 Tolerance is only another name for indifference.

BILL MAULDIN (1921–). *American cartoonist*
I feel like a fugitive from th' law of averages. [One foot soldier to another during a bombardment, cartoon caption, 1945.]

ANDRÉ MAUROIS (1885–1967). *French novelist and biographer*
When you become used to never being alone, you may consider yourself Americanized.

LOUIS B. MAYER (1886–1957). *Russian-born American film producer*
Look out for yourself, or they'll pee on your grave.

EUGENE McCARTHY (1916–). *Minnesota senator*
1 Being in politics is like being a football coach. You have to be smart enough to understand the game and dumb enough to think it's important.
2 I would not want Jimmy Carter and his men put in charge of snake control in Ireland. [1976]
3 It is dangerous for a national candidate to say things that people might remember.
4 Nelson Rockefeller is reported to have said to Diego Rivera, who objected to making changes in the mural he was painting in the Rockefeller Center, "It's my wall."
5 The only thing that saves us from the bureaucracy is its inefficiency.

MARY McCARTHY (1912–1989). *American novelist and critic*
1 A truth is something that everyone can be shown to know and to have known, as people say, all along.
2 Bureaucracy, the rule of no one, has become the modern form of despotism.
3 Every word she writes is a lie, including "and" and "the." [On Lillian Hellman.]
4 Most people do not care to be taught what they do not already know; it makes them feel ignorant.
5 You mustn't force sex to do the work of love or love to do the work of sex.

JOHN McENROE (1959–). *American tennis player*
My greatest strength is that I have no weaknesses.

PHYLLIS McGINLEY (1905–1978). *Canadian poet and writer*
1 Seventy is wormwood / Seventy is gall / But it's better to be seventy / Than not alive at all.
2 The knowingness of little girls / Is hidden underneath their curls.

MIGNON McLAUGHLIN (1915–). *American writer*
1 A car is useless in New York, essential everywhere else. The same with good manners.
2 A good executive is one who makes people contentedly settle for less than they meant to get, in return for more than they meant to give.
3 Boredom is often the cause of promiscuity, and always its result.
4 Character is what emerges from all the little things you were too busy to do yesterday, but did anyway.
5 Every society honors its live conformists, and its dead troublemakers. [*The Neurotic's Notebook*, 1963.]
6 It's important to our friends to believe that we are unreservedly frank with them, and important to the friendship that we are not.
7 It's innocence when it charms us, ignorance when it doesn't.
8 Many are saved from sin by being so inept at it.
9 Most of us become parents long before we have stopped being children.

10 No one really listens to anyone else, and if you try it for a while you'll see why.

11 Our strength is often composed of the weakness we're damned if we're going to show.

12 The fear of being laughed at makes cowards of us all. —See also Leo Rosten 6; William Shakespeare 4

13 The neurotic longs to touch bottom, so at least he won't have *that* to worry about any more.

14 There are a handful of people whom money won't spoil, and we all count ourselves among them.

15 Things are never so bad that they can't get worse. But they're sometimes so bad they can't get better.

16 Traditions are group efforts to keep the unexpected from happening.

17 We cough because we can't help it, but others do it on purpose.

18 We'd all like a reputation for generosity, and we'd all like to buy it cheap.

19 We're all born brave, trusting, and greedy, and most of us remain greedy.

20 What you have become is the price you paid to get what you used to want.

MARSHALL McLUHAN (1911–1980). *Canadian communications theorist*

1 Movies in America have not developed advertising intervals simply because the movie itself is the greatest of all forms of advertisement for consumer goods.

2 On Spaceship Earth there are no passengers; everybody is a member of the crew.

3 The new electronic interdependence recreates the world in the image of a global village.

4 The supple, well-adjusted man is the one who has learned to hop into the meat grinder while humming a hit-parade tune.

MARGARET MEAD (1901–1977). *American anthropologist*

1 Always remember that you are absolutely unique—just like everyone else.

2 My grandmother wanted me to have an education, so she kept me out of school.

3 Never doubt that a small group of thoughtful, committed citizens can change the world; indeed, it's the only thing that ever does.

4 The first thing you do is scream. [On solving problems.]

5 Young people are moving away from feeling guilty about sleeping with somebody to feeling guilty if they are *not* sleeping with someone.

GOLDA MEIR (1898–1978). *Russian-born Israeli prime minister.*

1 Don't be so humble—you're not that great. [Remark to Moshe Dayan.]

2 It's not a sin to be seventy, but it's also no joke.

3 Let me tell you something that we Israelis have against Moses. He took us forty years through the desert in order to bring us to the one spot in the Middle East that has no oil!

4 Old age is like a plane flying through a storm. Once you're aboard, there's nothing you can do about it.

LORD MELBOURNE (William Lamb Melbourne, 1779–1848). *British prime minister*

1 I don't care what damned lie we must tell, but not a man of you shall leave this room until we have all agreed to tell the same damned lie. [At a cabinet meeting.]

2 I wish I was as cocksure of anything as Tom Macaulay is of everything. [Referring to the historian.]

3 Things have come to a pretty pass when religion is allowed to invade the sphere of private life. [Commenting on a sermon.]

HERMAN MELVILLE (1819–1891). *American novelist*

1 Better sleep with a sober cannibal than a drunken Christian.

2 I cherish the greatest respect towards everybody's religious obligations, never mind how comical.

3 It is better to fail in originality than to succeed in imitation.

4 Not seldom to be famous is to be widely known for what you are not.

5 Sin that pays its way can travel freely, and with a passport; whereas virtue, if a pauper, is stopped at all frontiers.

6 There are certain queer times and occasions in this strange mixed affair we call life when a man takes this whole universe for a vast practical joke.

H. L. MENCKEN (1880–1956). *American journalist, editor, and critic*

1 A bad artist almost always tries to conceal his incompetence by whooping up a new formula.

2 A bore is simply a nonentity who resents his humble lot in life, and seeks satisfaction for his wounded ego by forcing himself on his betters.

3 A celebrity is one who is known to many persons he is glad he doesn't know.

4 A cynic is a man who, when he smells flowers, looks around for a coffin.

5 A gentleman is one who never strikes a woman without provocation.
   —See also Fred Allen 2

6 A good politician, under democracy, is quite as unthinkable as an honest burglar.

7 A man is called a good fellow for doing things which, if done by a woman, would land her in a lunatic asylum.

8 A man may be a fool and not know it—but not if he is married.

9 A prohibitionist is the sort of man one wouldn't care to drink with—even if he drank.

10 A Puritan is someone who is deathly afraid that someone, somewhere, is having fun.

11 A Sunday school is a prison in which children do penance for the evil conscience of their parents.

12 Adultery: democracy applied to love.

13 All government, in its essence, is organized exploitation.

14 All men are frauds. The only difference between them is that some admit it. I myself deny it.

15 All the errors and incompetencies of the Creator reach their climax in man.

16 All we got to say on the proposition that *all men are created equal* is this: first, you and me is as good as anybody else, and maybe a damn sight better.

17 An idealist is one who, on noticing that a rose smells better than a cabbage, concludes that it is also more nourishing.

18 Anything is moral that furthers the main concern of the politician's soul, which is to keep his place at the public trough.

19 Archbishop: a Christian ecclesiastic of a rank superior to that attained by Christ.

20 Bachelors have consciences, married men have wives.

21 Bachelors know more about women than married men; if they didn't, they'd be married too.

22 Can the United States ever become genuinely civilized? Certainly it is possible. Even Scotland has made enormous progress since the Eighteenth Century, when, according to Macaulay, most of it was on the cultural level of Albania.

23 Congress's occasional mavericks, thrown in by miracle, last a session, and then disappear. The old congressman, the veteran of genuine influence and power, is either one who is so stupid that the ideas of the mob are his own ideas, or one so far gone in charlatanry that he is unconscious of his shame.

24 Conscience is a mother-in-law whose visit never ends.

25 Conscience: the inner voice which warns us someone may be looking.

26 Courtroom: a place where Jesus Christ and Judas Iscariot would be equals, with the betting odds in favor of Judas.

27 Democracy is a form of religion. It is the worship of the jackals by the jackasses.

28 Democracy is the art and science of running the circus from the monkey cage.

29 Democracy is the theory that the common people know what they want, and deserve to get it good and hard.

30 Doing good has come to be, like patriotism, a favorite device of persons with something to sell.

31 Every normal man must be tempted, at times, to spit on his hands, hoist the black flag, and begin slitting throats.

32 Every time I hear a man pound a table with his fist and loudly endorse common sense, I permit myself a large and long-range spit.

33 Franklin Roosevelt is a fraud from snout to tail.

34 Free verse: a device for making poetry easier to write and harder to read.

35 Friendship: a mutual belief in the same fallacies, mountebanks, hobgoblins and imbecilities.

36 God must love the poor, said Lincoln, or he wouldn't have made so many of them. He must love the rich or he wouldn't divide so much mazuma among so few of them. —See also Abraham Lincoln 4; Kenneth Patchen 1

37 Has civilization a motto? Then certainly it must be "Not *thy* will, O Lord, but *ours,* be done!"

38 He hated all pretension save his own pretension. [On Theodore Roosevelt.]

39 He marries best who puts it off until it is too late.

40 He writes the worst English that I have ever encountered. It reminds me of a string of wet sponges; it reminds me of tattered washing on the line; it reminds me of stale bean soup, of college yells, of dogs barking idiotically through endless nights. It is so bad that a sort of grandeur creeps into it. It drags itself out of the dark abysm of pish and crawls insanely up to the topmost pinnacle of posh. It is rumble and bumble. It is flap and doodle. It is balder and dash. [On Warren G. Harding.]

41 Historian: an unsuccessful novelist.

42 I believe that religion, generally speaking, has been a curse to mankind—that its modest and greatly overestimated services on the ethical side have been more than overborne by the damage it has done to clear and honest thinking.

43 I believe that the present organization of society, as bad as it is, is better than any other that has ever been proposed.

44 I've made it a rule never to drink by daylight and never to refuse a drink after dark.

45 If he became convinced tomorrow that coming out for cannibalism would get him the votes he so sorely needs, he would begin fattening a missionary in the White House backyard come Wednesday. [On Franklin D. Roosevelt, 1936.]

46 If there had been any formidable body of cannibals in the country, he would have promised to provide them with free missionaries fattened at the taxpayer's expense.

47 Immorality: the morality of those who are having a better time.

48 In America, religion is used as a club and a cloak by both politicians and moralists, all of them lusting for power and most of them palpable frauds.

49 In the main, there are two sorts of books: those that no one reads and those that no one ought to read.

50 Injustice is relatively easy to bear; what stings is justice.

51 It is a sin to believe evil of others, but it is seldom a mistake.

52 It is better to have a conscience than to be run over by a locomotive.

53 It is hard to believe that a man is telling the truth when you know that you would lie if you were in his place.

54 Lawyer: one who protects us against robbers by taking away the temptation.

55 Love is the triumph of imagination over intelligence.

56 Man is the yokel par excellence, the booby unmatchable, the king dupe of the cosmos.

57 Men have a much better time of it than women. For one thing, they marry later. For another thing, they die earlier.

58 Metaphysics is almost always an attempt to prove the incredible by an appeal to the unintelligible.

59 Never argue with a man whose job depends on not being convinced.

60 No healthy male ever really thinks or talks of anything save himself.

61 No man ever came to market with less seductive goods, and no man ever got a better price for what he had to offer. [On Calvin Coolidge.]

62 Nobody ever went broke underestimating the intelligence of the great masses of plain people. —See also Lord Chesterfield 16; Mark Twain 122

63 One horselaugh is worth a thousand syllogisms.

64 One of the things that makes a Negro unpleasant to white folks is the fact that he suffers from their injustice. He is thus a standing rebuke to them.

65 Opera in English is, in the main, just about as sensible as baseball in Italian.

66 Political revolutions do not often accomplish anything of genuine value; their one undoubted effect is simply to throw out one gang of thieves and put in another.

67 Politics, as hopeful men practice it in the world, consists mainly of the delusion that a change in form is a change in substance.

68 Popularity: the capacity for listening sympathetically when men boast of their wives and women complain of their husbands.

69 Puritanism: the haunting fear that someone, somewhere, may be happy.

70 Remorse: regret that one waited so long to do it.

71 Reviewing here in Baltimore is a hazardous occupation. Once I spoke harshly of an eminent American novelist, and he retaliated by telling a very charming woman that I was non compos penis. In time she came to laugh at him as a liar.

72 Say what you will about the Ten Commandments, you must always come back to the pleasant fact that there are only ten of them.

73 Self-respect: the secure feeling that no one, as yet, is suspicious.

74 Show me a Puritan and I'll show you a son-of-a-bitch.

75 Temptation is an irresistible force at work on a movable body.

76 The act of worship, as carried on by Christians, seems to me to be debasing rather than ennobling. It involves groveling before a Being who, if He really exists, deserves to be denounced instead of respected. [Attributed.]

77 The American people, taking one with another, constitute the most timorous, sniveling, poltroonish, ignominious mob of serfs and goosesteppers ever gathered under one flag in Christendom since the end of the Middle Ages. [1922]

78 The average man does not get pleasure out of an idea because he thinks it is true; he thinks it is true because he gets pleasure out of it.

79 The basic fact about human existence is not that it is a tragedy, but that it is a bore. It is not so much a war as an endless standing in line.

80 The booboisie.

81 The chief business of the nation, as a nation, is the setting up of heroes, mainly bogus.

82 The chief contribution of Protestantism to human thought is its massive proof that God is a bore.

83 The chief difference between free capitalism and state socialism seems to be this: that under the former a man pursues his own advantage openly,

frankly and honestly, whereas under the latter he does so hypocritically and under false pretenses.

84 The difference between a moral man and a man of honor is that the latter regrets a discreditable act even when it has worked.

85 The doctrine that the cure for the evils of democracy is more democracy is like saying that the cure for crime is more crime. —See also Al Smith 1

86 The first Rotarian was the first man to call John the Baptist Jack.

87 The great artists of the world are never Puritans, and seldom even ordinarily respectable.

88 The men the American people admire most extravagantly are the most daring liars; the men they detest most violently are those who try to tell them the truth.

89 The most dangerous man, to any government, is the man who is able to think things out for himself, without regard to the prevailing superstitions and taboos.

90 The most valuable of all human possessions, next to a superior and disdainful air, is the reputation of being well-to-do.

91 The objection to Puritans is not that they try to make us think as they do, but that they try to make us do as they think.

92 The older I grow, the more I distrust the familiar doctrine that age brings wisdom.

93 The only really happy folk are married women and single men. —See also Benjamin Disraeli 8

94 The saddest life is that of a political aspirant under democracy. His failure is ignominious and his success is disgraceful.

95 The truth that survives is simply the lie that is pleasant to believe.

96 The truth, to the overwhelming majority of mankind, is indistinguishable from a headache.

97 The typical politician is not only a rascal but also a jackass, so he greatly values the puerile notoriety and adulation that sensible men try to avoid.

98 The university president who cashiered every professor unwilling to support him for the first vacancy in the Trinity. [On Woodrow Wilson, 1920.]

99 The urge to save humanity is almost always a false front for the urge to rule it.

100 The whole aim of practical politics is to keep the populace alarmed (and hence clamorous to be led to safety) by an endless series of hobgoblins, most of them imaginary.

101 The worshipper is the father of the gods.

102 The worst of politicians is a great deal better company than most generals in the army, or writers of murder mysteries, or astrophysicists, and the best is a really superior and wholly delightful man—full of sound knowledge, competent and prudent, frank and courageous, and quite as honest as any American can be without being clapped into a madhouse.

103 Theology is the effort to explain the unknowable in terms of the not worth knowing.

104 There are no dull subjects. There are only dull writers.

105 There are some people who read too much: the bibliobibuli.

106 There is always an easy solution to every human problem—neat, plausible, and wrong.

107 To sum up: 1) The cosmos is a gigantic flywheel making 10,000 revolutions a minute. 2) Man is a sick fly taking a dizzy ride on it. 3) Religion is the theory that the wheel was designed and set spinning to give him the ride.

108 Truth: something somehow discreditable to someone.

109 Under democracy one party always devotes its chief energies to trying to prove that the other party is unfit to rule—and both commonly succeed, and are right.

110 Voting is simply a way of determining which side is the stronger without putting it to the test of fighting.

111 We must respect the other fellow's religion, but only in the sense and to the extent that we respect his theory that his wife is beautiful and his children smart.

112 When a husband's story is believed, he begins to suspect his wife.

113 When I hear a man applauded by the mob, I always feel a pang of pity for him. All he has to do to be hissed is to live long enough.

114 Wife: a former sweetheart.

KARL MENNINGER (1893–1990). *American psychiatrist*
"Neurotic" means he's not as sensible as I am, and "psychotic" means he's even worse than my brother-in-law.

YEHUDI MENUHIN (1916–1999). *American violinist*
The violinist is that peculiarly human phenomenon distilled to a rare potency—half tiger, half poet.

JOHNNY MERCER (1909–1976). *American songwriter*
You've got to ac-cent-tchu-ate the positive / Elim-my-nate the negative / Latch on to the affirmative / Don't mess with Mister In-between.

GEORGE MEREDITH (1828–1909). *English novelist*
1 Cynics are only happy in making the world as barren for others as they have made it for themselves.

2 I expect that Woman will be the last thing civilized by Man.

3 Kissing don't last; cookery do!

GRACE METALIOUS (1920–1964). *American novelist*
Funny, you don't look like a friend—ah, but they never do.

BETTE MIDLER (1944–). *American singer and actress*
1 After thirty, a body has a mind of its own.

2 There were some initial difficulties when the director first told me the disappointing news that if the film was to have any semblance of reality at all there would have to be moments when other people were on screen at the same time I was.

JOHN STUART MILL (1806–1873). *English philosopher*
1 Ask yourself whether you are happy, and you cease to be so.
2 His eminence was due to the flatness of the surrounding landscape.
3 It is better to be a human being dissatisfied than a pig satisfied; better to be Socrates dissatisfied than a fool satisfied.

EDNA ST. VINCENT MILLAY (1892–1950). *American poet and playwright*
1 It may be said of me by Harper & Brothers, that although I reject their proposals, I welcome their advances.
2 It's not true that life is one damn thing after another—it is one damn thing over and over. —See also Elbert Hubbard 21
3 My heart is warm with the friends I make, / And better friends I'll not be knowing; / Yet there isn't a train I wouldn't take / No matter where it's going.

ARTHUR MILLER (1915–). *American playwright*
Roslyn: "How do you find your way back in the dark?" Gay nods, indicating the sky before them: "Just head for that big star straight on. The highway's under it; take us right home."

HENRY MILLER (1891–1980). *American novelist*
1 Civilization is the arteriosclerosis of culture.
2 Life, as it is called, is for most of us one long postponement.
3 Life has to be given a meaning because of the obvious fact that it has no meaning.
4 Sex is one of the nine reasons for reincarnation. The other eight are unimportant.
5 The only law which is really lived up to wholeheartedly and with a vengeance is the law of conformity.
6 The study of crime begins with the knowledge of oneself.
7 To live without killing is a thought which could electrify the world, if men were only capable of staying awake long enough to let the idea soak in.

SPIKE MILLIGAN (1918–). *Irish entertainer and writer*
1 Contraceptives should be used on every conceivable occasion.
2 I'm a hero wid coward's legs. I'm a hero from the waist up.
3 Money couldn't buy friends, but you got a better class of enemy.
4 Some people are always late, like the late King George V.
5 Tank heaven the ground broke me fall.

GILBERT MILLSTEIN (20th century). *American restaurateur*
He speaks English with the flawless imperfection of a New Yorker.

A. A. MILNE (1882–1956). *English writer*
On Monday, when the sun is hot / I wonder to myself a lot: / Now is it true, or is it not, / That what is which and which is what?

COMTE de MIRABEAU (1749–1791). *French revolutionary leader*
This man will go far, he believes what he says. [On fellow-revolutionary Robespierre.]

ADRIAN MITCHELL (1932–). *English writer and poet*
Most people ignore most poetry / because / most poetry ignores most people.

MARGARET MITCHELL (1900–1949). *American novelist*

1 Death and taxes and childbirth! There's never any convenient time for any of them. [*Gone with the Wind,* 1936.] —See also Daniel Defoe 4

2 If we'd had as many soldiers as that, we'd have won the war! [Commenting on the large number of Confederate troops in the 1939 film adaptation of *Gone With the Wind*.]

3 It was the usual masculine disillusionment in discovering that a woman has a brain.

4 Life's under no obligation to give us what we expect. We take what we get and are thankful it's no worse than it is.

5 Until you've lost your reputation, you never realize what a burden it was or what freedom really is.

ROBERT MITCHUM (1917–1997). *American actor*
Kid, life's hard. But it's a lot harder if you're stupid.

WILSON MIZNER (1876–1933). *American screenwriter and humorist*

1 A fellow who is always declaring he's no fool usually has his suspicions.

2 Be nice to people on your way up because you'll meet 'em on your way down.

3 Failure has gone to his head.

4 He's the only man I ever knew who had rubber pockets so he could steal soup.

5 I hate careless flattery, the kind that exhausts you in your effort to believe it.

6 I respect faith, but doubt is what gets you an education.

7 If you steal from one author, it's plagiarism; if you steal from many authors, it's research.

8 Life's a tough proposition; the first hundred years are the hardest.

9 Money is the only substance which can keep a cold world from nicknaming a citizen "Hey, you!"

10 The best way to keep your friends is not to give them away.

11 The gent who wakes up and finds himself a success hasn't been asleep.

12 The man who won't loan money isn't going to have many friends—or need them.

13 The only sure thing about luck is that it will change.

14 There is something about a closet that makes a skeleton terribly restless.

15 To my embarrassment I was born in bed with a lady.

16 Visiting Hollywood is like taking a trip through a sewer in a glass-bottomed boat.

17 When a woman tells you her age, it's all right to look surprised, but don't scowl.

MOLIÈRE (1622–1672). *French playwright*

1 A learned fool is more foolish than an ignorant one.

2 All fashionable vices pass for virtues.

3 Here in Paris they hang a man first and try him afterwards. —See also Roy Bean

4 I prefer an accommodating vice to an obstinate virtue.

5 My doctor and I talk together; he prescribes remedies; I do not take them; I recover.

6 People can be induced to swallow anything, provided it is sufficiently seasoned with praise.

7 There's no praise to beat the sort you can put in your pocket.

8 We die only once, and it's for such a long time!

9 You may cure, or you may bury 'em, / but you always get your honorarium. [On physicians.]

MARILYN MONROE (1926–1962). *American actress*

1 "Did you really have nothing on in the calendar photograph?" I had the radio on.

2 Fame will go by and, so long, I've had you, fame. If it goes by, I've always known it was fickle. So at least it's something I experienced, but that's not where I live. [Last interview, 1962.]

3 Hollywood's a place where they'll pay you a thousand dollars for a kiss, and fifty cents for your soul.

ASHLEY MONTAGU (1905–1999). *English-born American anthropologist*

1 Human beings are the only creatures who are able to behave irrationally in the name of reason.

2 Scientists believe in proof without certainty: most people believe in certainty without proof.

3 The idea is to die young as late as possible. —See also Elbert Hubbard 44

LADY MARY WORTLEY MONTAGU (1689–1762). *English writer*
People wish their enemies dead—but I do not; I say, give them the gout, give them the stone!

C. E. MONTAGUE (1867–1928). *English novelist*
War hath no fury like a noncombatant. —See also Milton Friedman 1; Dick Gregory 1

MICHEL de MONTAIGNE (1532–1592). *French essayist*

1 Especially in an age as corrupt and ignorant as this, the good opinion of the people is a dishonor.

2 I have seen people rude by being over-polite.

3 I speak the truth, not the whole of it, but as much as I dare speak; and I dare less and less as I grow older.

4 Lucius Arruntius killed himself, he said, to escape both the future and the past.

5 No one is exempt from talking nonsense; the mistake is to do it solemnly.

6 Nothing is so firmly believed as what is least understood.

7 Old age puts more wrinkles in our minds than on our faces.

8 The man who makes it his business to please the multitude is never done.

9 The sun shines on their successes, and the earth hides their failures. [On physicians.]

10 The want of goods is easily repaired, but poverty of the soul is irreparable.

11 There is as much difference between us and ourselves as between us and others.

12 There is no man so good that if he placed all his actions and thoughts under the scrutiny of the laws, he would not deserve hanging ten times in his life.

13 Truth nowadays is not what is, but what others can be convinced of.

14 What is the use of learning, if understanding is absent?

15 When I play with my cat, who knows if I am not a pastime to her more than she is to me.

16 Your self-condemnation is always believed; your self-praise, never.

BARON de MONTESQUIEU (1689–1755). *French philosopher*

1 An author is a fool who, not content with having bored those who have lived in his own time, insists on boring future generations.

2 If triangles had made a god, it would have three sides.

GEORGE MOORE (1852–1933). *Irish novelist, poet, and playwright*

1 I am convinced that both my long age and exceptional health are to be explained by an obvious fact: I never touched a cigarette, a drink, or a girl until I was almost ten years old.

2 If there were no husbands, who would look after our mistresses?

3 The difference between my quotations and those of the next man is that I leave out the inverted commas.

J. P. MORGAN (1837–1913). *American financier*

1 A man always has two reasons for the things he does—a good one and the real one.

2 Anybody has a right to evade taxes if he can get away with it. No citizen has a moral obligation to assist in maintaining the government. If Congress insists on making stupid mistakes and passing foolish tax laws, millionaires should not be condemned if they take advantage of them.

3 Anyone who has to ask about the annual upkeep of a yacht can't afford one.

4 I don't know as I want a lawyer to tell me what I cannot do. I hire him to tell me how to do what I want to do.

5 "What should I do about my stocks? I can't sleep nights." I'd sell down to the sleeping point.

ROBERT F. MORGAN (1941–). *American psychologist*

1 Better moderate excess than excessive moderation.

2 Never trust a tree that says we're out of the woods.

ROBIN MORGAN (1941–). *American feminist and writer*

1 Don't accept rides from strange men, and remember that all men are as strange as hell.

2 Let it all hang out; let it seem bitchy, catty, dykey, frustrated, crazy, Solanesque, nutty, frigid, ridiculous, bitter, embarrassing, man-hating, libelous, pure, unfair, envious, intuitive, lowdown, stupid, petty, liberating;

we are the women that men have warned us about. [1970] —See also
Brendan Behan 6; Nicholas Von Hoffman

SAMUEL ELIOT MORISON (1887–1976). *American historian*
America was discovered accidentally by a great seaman who was looking for
something else. History is like that, very chancy.

CHRISTOPHER MORLEY (1890–1957). *American writer and poet*
1 High heels were invented by a woman who had been kissed on the
forehead.
2 Human being: an ingenious assembly of portable plumbing.
3 I suffer fools gladly, for I have always been on good terms with myself.
4 The secret of respectability is to ignore what you don't understand.
5 There are no precedents: You are the first You that ever was.
6 There are three ingredients in the good life: learning, earning, and
yearning.
7 There's so much to say, but your eyes keep interrupting me.

JOHN MORLEY (1838–1923). *English journalist and member of Parliament*
1 All religions die of one disease, that of being found out.
2 It is no light thing to have secured a livelihood on condition of going
through life masked and gagged.
3 Three things matter in a speech; who says it, how he says it, and what he
says—and, of the three, the last matters the least.
4 Where it is a duty to worship the sun, it is pretty sure to be a crime to examine the laws of heat.

ROBERT MORLEY (1908–1992). *English actor*
1 Beware of the conversationalist who adds "in other words." He is merely
starting afresh.
2 It is a great help for a man to be in love with himself. For an actor, it is absolutely essential.
3 Show me a man who has enjoyed his schooldays, and I'll show you a bully
and a bore.
4 What have I done to achieve longevity? Woken up each morning and tried
to remember not to wear my hearing aid in the bath.

TONI MORRISON (1931–). *American novelist*
1 As is the case of many misanthropes, his disdain for people led him into
a profession designed to serve them.
2 There is really nothing more to say—except *why*. But since *why* is difficult
to handle, one must take refuge in *how*.

LANCE MORROW (1939–). *American journalist*
The fundamental rule of the Age of Celebrity: "It doesn't matter what you are,
it only matters what people think you are."

BILL MOYERS (1934–). *American presidential assistant and broadcast
journalist*
1 Ideas are like great arrows, but there has to be a bow. And politics is the
bow of idealism.

2 Making it was the game, and money was the way of keeping score. [On the 1950s.]
3 Pollution of language spreads everywhere, like great globs of sludge crowding the shore of public thought.

DANIEL PATRICK MOYNIHAN (1927–). *New York senator*
1 Life is one day at a time. And thank God! I couldn't take much more.
2 The single most exciting thing you encounter in government is competence, because it's so rare.

MALCOLM MUGGERIDGE (1903–1990). *English writer and television personality*
1 An orgy looks particularly alluring seen through the mists of righteous indignation.
2 Good taste and humor are a contradiction in terms, like a chaste whore.
3 He was not only a bore, he bored for England. [On Anthony Eden.]
4 It has to be admitted that we English have sex on the brain, which is a very unsatisfactory place to have it.
5 Sex has become the religion of the most civilized portions of the earth. The orgasm has replaced the Cross as the focus of longing and the image of fulfillment.

JOHN MUIR (1838–1914). *Scottish-born American naturalist*
1 I am richer than Harriman. I have all the money I want and he hasn't. [Referring to financier A. E. Harriman.]
2 In this silent, serene wilderness the weary can gain a heart-bath in perfect peace.
3 One day's exposure to mountains is better than cartloads of books.
4 Solemn loveliness of the night. Vast star-garden of the Universe.

MARK MULLEIAN (1947–). *American artist*
"I don't believe in absolutes." Are you absolutely sure?

BRIAN MULRONEY (1939–). *Canadian prime minister*
I am not denying anything I did not say.

LEWIS MUMFORD (1895–1990). *American sociologist and social critic*
1 Every generation revolts against its fathers and makes friends with its grandfathers.
2 I'm a pessimist about probabilities; I'm an optimist about possibilities.
3 In creating the thinking machine, man has made the last step in submission to mechanization; and his final abdication before this product of his own ingenuity has given him a new object of worship: a cybernetic god. [1956]
4 Man is the leopard who knows how to change his spots.
5 One of the functions of intelligence is to take account of the dangers that come from trusting solely to the intelligence.
6 Our national flower is the concrete cloverleaf.
7 What Marshall McLuhan understands has long been familiar to students of technics: it is his singular gift for *mis*understanding both technology and man that marks his truly original contributions.

CLINT W. MURCHISON (1895–1969). *American financier*
Money is like manure. If you spread it around, it does a lot of good; but if you pile it up in one place, it stinks like hell.

MICHAEL MURPHY (20th century). *American investment newsletter publisher*
The stock market always will do whatever it has to do to embarrass the maximum number of people.

JIM MURRAY (20th century). *American sportswriter*
Willie Mays should play in handcuffs to even things out a bit.

EDWARD R. MURROW (1908–1965). *American broadcast journalist*
1 Anyone who isn't confused doesn't really understand the situation. [On the Vietnam War.] —See also Anonymous 67
2 If television and radio are to be used for the entertainment of all of the people all of the time, we have come perilously close to discovering the real opiate of the people. —See also Karl Marx 5
3 If we were to do the Second Coming of Christ in color for a full hour, there would be a considerable number of stations which would decline to carry it on the grounds that a Western or a quiz show would be more profitable. [1958]
4 The politician is trained in the art of inexactitude. His words tend to be blunt or rounded because if they have a cutting edge, they may later return to wound him.
5 This instrument can teach. It can illuminate. Yes, and it can even inspire. But it can do so only to the extent that humans are determined to use it to those ends. Otherwise, it is merely wires and lights in a box. [On television]

VLADIMIR NABOKOV (1899–1977). *Russian-born American writer and academic*

1 Human life is but a series of footnotes to a vast, obscure, unfinished masterpiece.

2 I read him for the first time in the early 40s, something about bells, balls, and bulls, and loathed it. [On Ernest Hemingway.]

3 I welcome Freud's "Woodrow Wilson" not only because of its comic appeal, which is great, but because that surely must be the last rusty nail in the Viennese Quack's coffin. [Complete letter to *Encounter*, February 1967.]

JOHN NAISBITT (1929–). *American futurist*

1 Leadership involves finding a parade and getting in front of it.

2 Trends, like horses, are easier to ride in the direction they are already going.

3 We are drowning in information but starved for knowledge.

JOE NAMATH (1943–). *American football player*

Till I was thirteen, I thought my name was "Shut Up." —See also Ring Lardner 1

NAPOLEON (1769–1821). *French general and emperor*

1 A husband may sue for a divorce on account of the wife's adultery. A wife may sue for divorce only in the case in which the husband introduces a permanent mistress into the marital household. [*Code Napoleon,* 1804.]

2 A silk stocking filled with mud. [On Talleyrand.]

3 Against attempts on my life, I trust in my luck, my good genius, and my guards.

4 Doctors will have more lives to answer for in the next world than even we generals.

5 Equality for women? That is madness. Women are our property; we are not theirs. They give us children and belong to us as the fruit-bearing tree belongs to the gardener.

6 I defy anyone to trick me. Men would have to be exceptional rascals to be as bad as I assume them to be.

7 I generally had to give in. [On his relationship with Josephine, 1816.]

8 I have been to a ball at Weimar. The Emperor Alexander dances, but I don't. Forty is forty. [Letter to Josephine.]

9 I like only those people who are useful to me, and only so long as they are useful.

10 I shall never tolerate the newspapers to say or do anything against my interests; they may publish a few little articles with just a little poison in them, but one fine morning somebody will shut their mouths. [Letter to his minister of police, Joseph Fouché, 1805.]

11 In China the sovereign is worshipped as a god. That I think is how it ought to be.

12 In politics, an absurdity is not an obstacle.

13 Metternich comes close to being a statesman: he lies very well.

14 Newspapers should be limited to advertising.

15 Nobody is so stupid as not to be good for something.

16 Rascality has limits, stupidity has not.

17 Religion is excellent stuff for keeping common people quiet.

18 The object of the Republic in prosecuting the war is to bring about a peace.

19 The police invent more than they discover.

20 To promise and not to keep your promise is the way to get on in the world.

21 We attach ourselves more readily to those whom we have benefited than to our benefactors.

22 What is most extraordinary and I believe unparalleled in history is that I rose from being a private individual to the astonishing height of power I possess without having committed a single crime.

23 When I need anyone, I don't make too fine a point of it; I would kiss his arse. —See also Winston Churchill 30; Margaret Thatcher 1

24 You, doctor, would promise life to a corpse if he would swallow your pills.

25 You may also dispense with comparing me to God. I am willing to believe that you wrote this without thinking; the phrase is so singularly lacking in respect to me.

26 You must be aware that making confidences is a part of diplomacy and that Count Cobenzl never confides anything except what he wants known. [Letter to his brother, who was in negotiations with the Austrian government.]

27 Your Majesty cannot suppose that I, of all people, desire war. [Letter to Frederick, king of Württemberg, 1811.]

OGDEN NASH (1902–1971). *American versifier and humorist*

1 A bit of talcum / Is always walcum.

2 At another year / I would not boggle, / Except that when I jog / I joggle.

3 Beneath this slab / John Brown is stowed. / He watched the ads, / And not the road.

4 Candy / Is dandy / But liquor / Is quicker.

5 Children aren't happy without something to ignore, / And that's what parents were created for.

6 God in His wisdom made the fly / And then forgot to tell us why. —See also Mark Twain 89

7 Happiness is having a scratch for every itch.

8 Here lies my past. Goodbye, I have kissed it. / Thank you kids. I wouldn't have missed it.

9 Here's a good rule of thumb: / Too clever is dumb.

10 I think that I shall never see / A billboard lovely as a tree. / Indeed, unless the billboards fall / I'll never see a tree at all.

11 Life is not having been told that the man has just waxed the floor.

12 Marriage is the alliance of two people, one of whom never remembers birthdays and the other never forgets them.

13 One would be in less danger / From the wiles of the stranger / If one's own kin and kith / Were more fun to be with.

14 Parsley / Is gharsley.

15 Professional men, they have no cares; / Whatever happens, they get theirs.

16 Progress might have been all right once, but it's gone on too long.

17 Some people's money is merited / And other people's is inherited.

18 The Bronx? / No thonx!

19 There is only one way to achieve happiness on this terrestrial ball, / And that is to have either a clear conscience, or none at all.

20 To keep your marriage brimming / With love in the wedding cup, / Whenever you're wrong, admit it; / Whenever you're right, shut up.

GEORGE JEAN NATHAN (1882–1958). *American editor and drama critic*

1 Art is the sex of the imagination.

2 Bad officials are elected by good citizens who do not vote.

3 He writes his plays for the ages—the ages between five and twelve. [On George Bernard Shaw.]

4 I drink to make other people interesting.

5 In the popular theater, a hero is one who believes that all women are ladies; a villain, one who believes that all ladies are women.

6 Opening night: the night before the play is ready to open.

7 The test of a real comedian is whether you laugh at him before he opens his mouth.

8 What passes for woman's intuition is often nothing more than man's transparency.

9 Women, as they grow older, rely more and more on cosmetics. Men, as they grow older, rely more and more on a sense of humor.

MARTINA NAVRATILOVA (1957–). *Czech-born American tennis player*

1 In Czechoslovakia there is no such thing as freedom of the press. In the United States, no such thing as freedom from the press. [1984] —See also Mark Twain 114

2 Whoever said, "It's not whether you win or lose that counts," probably lost.

PAUL NEWMAN (1925–). *American actor*

1 I have often thought that my tombstone might well read: "Here lies Paul Newman, who died a failure because his eyes suddenly turned brown."

2 To work as hard as I've worked to accomplish anything and then have some yo-yo come up and say, "Take off those dark glasses and let's have a look at those blue eyes," is really discouraging.

JACK NICHOLSON (1937–). *American actor*

"How do you feel about turning 55?" I feel exactly the same as I've always felt: a lightly reined-in voracious beast.

HAROLD NICOLSON (1886–1968). *English diplomat and writer*

1 One of the minor pleasures of life is to be slightly ill.

2 Only one person in a thousand is a bore, and he is interesting because he is one person in a thousand.

3 We are all inclined to judge ourselves by our ideals; others by their acts.

FRIEDRICH NIETZSCHE (1844–1900). *German philosopher*

1 After coming in contact with a religious man, I always have to wash my hands.

2 Beggars ought to be abolished: for one is vexed at giving to them and vexed at not giving to them.

3 I am, therefore I think. [Compare, "I think, therefore I am." Descartes, 1637.] —See also Ambrose Bierce 44

4 I don't give alms; I'm not poor enough for that.

5 "I have done that," says my memory. "I cannot have done that," says my pride. Eventually—memory yields.

6 I would believe only in a God who could dance.

7 Neighbors praise unselfishness because they profit from it.

8 No victor believes in chance.

9 Only the day after tomorrow belongs to me. Some are born posthumously.

10 So long as you are praised, think only that you are not yet on your own path but on that of another.

11 The advantage of a bad memory is that, several times over, one enjoys the same good things for the first time.

12 The bad conscience is an illness but an illness as pregnancy is an illness.

13 The state is never interested in truth, but rather always only in that truth that is useful to it, or, more precisely, in everything that is useful to it, be it truth, half-truth, or error.

14 The two great European narcotics: alcohol and Christianity. [1889] —See also Karl Marx 5

15 There has been only one Christian, and he died on the Cross.

16 This most brilliant self-outwitter. [On Socrates.]

17 What does not kill me makes me stronger.

18 Which is it? Is man one of God's blunders or is God one of man's?

19 Woman was God's second mistake.

ANAÏS NIN (1903–1977). *French novelist and diarist*

1 Electric flesh-arrows traversing the body. A rainbow of color strikes the eyelids. A foam of music falls over the ears. It is the gong of the orgasm.

2 Life shrinks or expands in proportion to one's courage.

DAVID NIVEN (1909–1983). *English actor*

The only laugh that man will probably ever get is for stripping off and showing his shortcomings. [Referring to a streaker who had disrupted the Academy Award ceremonies in 1973.]

RICHARD M. NIXON (1913–1994). *American president*

1 As I leave you, I want you to know—just think how much you're going to be missing. You won't have Nixon to kick around anymore, because, gentlemen, this is my last press conference. [Remarks to reporters after being defeated in his 1962 bid to become governor of California.]

2 By 1980 we will be self-sufficient and will not need to rely on foreign enemies, uh, energy. [Referring to the oil shortage in 1973.]

3 Capitalism works better than it sounds, while socialism sounds better than it works.

4 He was a far more complex and devious man than most people realized, and in the best sense of those words. [On Dwight D. Eisenhower.]

5 I call it the Madman Theory, Bob. I want the North Vietnamese to believe I've reached the point where I might do *anything* to stop the war. We'll just slip the word to them that, "for God's sake, you know Nixon is obsessed about Communists. We can't restrain him when he's angry—and he has his hand on the nuclear button"—and Ho Chi Minh himself will be in Paris in two days begging for peace. [Remarks to H. R. Haldeman, 1969.]

6 I don't give a shit what happens. I want you all to stonewall it, let them plead the Fifth Amendment, cover-up or anything else, if it'll save it—save the plan. That's the whole point. [Remarks to several close advisers during the Watergate scandal, 22 March 1973.]

7 I gave 'em a sword. And they stuck it in, and they twisted it with relish. And I guess if I had been in their position, I'd have done the same thing. [Referring to the Watergate scandal.]

8 Image is, I think, all-important in television. That's why, frankly, you should be more concerned about your makeup artist than your researcher, the one that blows your hair dry than what's between your ears. That's television.

9 In all of my years in public life I have never obstructed justice. [News conference, 17 November 1973.]

10 It helped people see I wasn't just that Tricky Dick, mean-spirited son of a bitch. [Referring to his brief appearance on the *Laugh-In* television program in 1968.]

11 Let us begin by committing ourselves to the truth—to see it like it is, and tell it like it is—to find the truth, to speak the truth, and to live the truth. [Presidential nomination acceptance speech, 1968.]

12 People in the media say they must look at the president with a microscope, but boy, when they use a proctoscope, that's going too far. [Television interview, 1984.]

13 People react to fear, not love—they don't teach that in Sunday School, but it's true. [1975]

14 We should respect Mexico's rights to chart its own independent course, provided the course is not antagonistic to our interests.

15 When the president does it, that means that it's not illegal. [David Frost television interview, 1977.]

16 You'll never make it in politics; you don't know how to lie. [Remark to adviser Leonard Garment.]

LOUIS NIZER (1902–1994). *American lawyer*

1 A graceful taunt is worth a thousand insults.

2 A speaker who does not strike oil in ten minutes should stop boring.

3 When a man points a finger at someone else, he should remember that four of his fingers are pointing at himself.

PEGGY NOONAN (1950–). *American presidential speechwriter and writer*

1 A speech is poetry: cadence, rhythm, imagery, sweep! A speech reminds us that words, like children, have the power to make dance the dullest beanbag of a heart.

2 Humor is the shock absorber of life; it helps us take the blows.

3 It was the worst inaugural address of our lifetime, and I think the only controversy will be between those who say it was completely and utterly banal and those who say, "Well, not completely and utterly." [On Bill Clinton's second inaugural address, 1997.]

4 The battle for the mind of Ronald Reagan was like the trench warfare of World War I: Never have so many fought so hard for such barren terrain.

OLIVER NORTH (1943–). *American marine officer, White House aide, and television personality*

I'm trusting in the Lord and a good lawyer. [Referring to charges made against him during the Irangate scandal, 1986.]

BILL NYE (1850–1896). *American writer, lecturer, and humorist*

Wagner's music is better than it sounds.

O

JOYCE CAROL OATES (1938–). *American writer and academic*
1 Nothing comes of so many things, if you have patience.
2 The worst cynicism: a belief in luck.
3 Those whom the gods wish to destroy, they first make famous. —See also Cyril Connolly 17; Bernard Levin 4

CONOR CRUISE O'BRIEN (1917–). *Irish historian, critic, and diplomat*
Those who can, gloat; those who can't, brood.

EDNA O'BRIEN (1932–). *Irish novelist*
1 I did not sleep. I never do when I am overhappy, overunhappy, or in bed with a strange man.
2 The vote, I thought, means nothing to women. We should be armed.

SEAN O'CASEY (1884–1964). *Irish playwright*
It's my rule never to lose me temper till it would be dethrimental to keep it.

FLANNERY O'CONNOR (1925–1964). *American novelist*
1 Everywhere I go I'm asked if I think the university stifles writers. My opinion is that they don't stifle enough of them. There's many a bestseller that could have been prevented by a good teacher.
2 It's hard to make your adversaries real people unless you recognize yourself in them—in which case, if you don't watch out, they cease to be adversaries.

AUSTIN O'MALLEY (1858–1932). *American writer*
1 A gentleman never heard the story before.
2 An Englishman thinks seated; a Frenchman, standing; an American, pacing; an Irishman, afterward.
3 Every April God rewrites the Book of Genesis.
4 If you keep your mouth shut, you'll never put your foot in it.
5 It is a mean thief, or a successful author that plunders the dead. [Referring to plagiarism.]
6 The perjurer's mother told white lies.
7 The statesman shears the sheep, the politician skins them.

EUGENE O'NEILL (1888–1953). *American playwright*
1 For de little stealin' dey gits you in jail soon or late. For de big stealin' dey makes you Emperor and puts you in de Hall o' Fame when you croaks. [*The Emperor Jones,* 1921.]
2 Life is perhaps most wisely regarded as a bad dream between two awakenings.
3 "What do you think of critics?" I love every bone in their heads.

P. J. O'ROURKE (1947–). *American writer and editor*
1 Because of their size, parents may be difficult to discipline properly.
2 Children must be considered in a divorce—considered valuable pawns in the nasty legal and financial contest that is about to ensue.
3 Cockroaches have been given a bad rap. They don't bite, smell, or get into your booze. Would that all houseguests were as well behaved.

4 Communism doesn't really starve or execute that many people. Mostly it just bores them to death.

5 Compared to the Clintons, Reagan is living proof that a Republican with half a brain is better than a Democrat with two.

6 Feminism is the result of a few ignorant and literal-minded women letting the cat out of the bag about which is the superior sex.

7 Humor is, by its nature, more truthful than factual.

8 I have only one firm belief about the American political system, and that is this: God is a Republican and Santa Claus is a Democrat.

9 I like to think of my behavior in the sixties as a "learning experience." Then again, I like to think of anything stupid I've done as a "learning experience." It makes me feel less stupid.

10 Liberals have invented whole college majors—psychology, sociology, women's studies—to prove that nothing is anybody's fault.

11 Like many men of my generation, I had an opportunity to give war a chance, and I promptly chickened out.

12 No drug, not even alcohol, causes the fundamental ills of society. If we're looking for the source of our troubles, we shouldn't test people for drugs, we should test them for stupidity, ignorance, greed, and love of power.

13 Republicans are the party that says government doesn't work, and then they get elected and prove it.

14 The French are sawed-off sissies who eat snails and slugs and cheese that smells like people's feet. Utter cowards who force their own children to drink wine, they gibber like baboons even when you try to speak to them in their own wimpy language.

15 The sport of skiing consists of wearing three thousand dollars' worth of clothes and equipment and driving 200 miles in the snow in order to stand around at a bar and get drunk.

16 There are a number of mechanical devices which increase sexual arousal, particularly in women. Chief among these is the Mercedes-Benz 380SL convertible.

17 There's one more terrifying fact about old people: I'm going to be one soon.

18 You can always reason with a German. You can always reason with a barnyard animal, too, for all the good it does.

19 You can't shame or humiliate modern celebrities. What used to be called shame and humiliation is now called publicity.

GEORGE ORWELL (1903–1950). *English essayist, novelist, and journalist*

1 All animals are equal, but some animals are more equal than others. [*Animal Farm,* 1945.]

2 Attlee reminds me of nothing so much as a recently dead fish, before it has had time to stiffen. [On Clement Attlee.]

3 Autobiography is only to be trusted when it reveals something disgraceful.

4 England resembles a family, a family with the wrong members in control.

5 He was an embittered atheist, the sort of atheist who does not so much disbelieve in God as personally dislike Him.

6 History consists of a series of swindles, in which the masses are first lured into revolt by the promise of Utopia, and then, when they have done their job, enslaved over again by new masters.

7 Humanity is divided into two classes: the self-seeking, hypocritical minority, and the brainless mob whose destiny is always to be led or driven, as one gets a pig back to the sty by kicking it on the bottom or by rattling a stick inside a swill bucket, according to the needs of the moment.

8 If the war didn't happen to kill you, it was bound to start you thinking.

9 If there is a wrong thing to do, it will be done, infallibly. [Diary, 18 May 1941.] —See also Anonymous 55

10 In the matter of drink, the only result of a century of "temperance" agitation has been a slight increase in hypocrisy.

11 It had been found necessary to make a readjustment of rations. Squealer always spoke of it as a "readjustment," never as a "reduction." [*Animal Farm.*]

12 It was the first time that I had seen a person whose profession was telling lies—unless one counts journalists.

13 Lenin is one of those politicians who win an undeserved reputation by dying prematurely.

14 Liberal: a power worshipper without the power.

15 Napoleon had commanded that once a week there should be held something called a Spontaneous Demonstration, the object of which was to celebrate the struggles and triumphs of Animal Farm.

16 Nationalism is power hunger tempered by self-deception.

17 On the whole, human beings want to be good, but not too good, and not all the time.

18 One could not even dignify him with the name of stuffed shirt. He was simply a hole in the air. [On Stanley Baldwin.]

19 Political language is designed to make lies sound truthful and murder respectable, and to give the appearance of solidity to pure wind. ["Politics and the English Language," 1946.]

20 Saints should always be judged guilty until they are proved innocent.

21 Serious sport has nothing to do with fair play. It is war minus the shooting.

22 The Catholic and the Communist are alike in assuming that an opponent cannot be both honest and intelligent. Each of them tacitly claims that "the truth" has already been revealed, and that the heretic, if he is not simply a fool, is secretly aware of "the truth" and merely resists it out of selfish motives.

23 The great enemy of clear language is insincerity. When there is a gap between one's real and one's declared aims, one turns, as it were instinctively to long words and exhausted idioms, like a cuttlefish squirting out ink. ["Politics and the English Language."] —See also John Ray

24 The secret of rulership is to combine a belief in one's infallibility with the power to learn from past mistakes.

25 The typical Socialist is a prim little man with a white-collar job, usually a secret teetotaler and often with vegetarian leanings, with a history of Non-

conformity behind him, and, above all, with a social position which he has no intention of forfeiting.

26 There's a thin man inside every fat man, just as they say there's a statue inside every block of stone. [1939] —See also Kingsley Amis 4; Cyril Connolly 5

27 To tell deliberate lies while genuinely believing in them, to forget any fact that has become inconvenient, and then, when it becomes necessary again, to draw it back from oblivion for just so long as it is needed. [On double-think, *Nineteen Eighty-Four,* 1949.]

28 WAR IS PEACE. FREEDOM IS SLAVERY. IGNORANCE IS STRENGTH. [The Party's slogans inscribed on the Ministry of Truth building, *Nineteen Eighty-Four.*]

29 Who controls the past controls the future: who controls the present controls the past. [*Nineteen Eighty-Four.*]

30 You can only get people to fight when everyone who remembers what the last war was like is beyond military age.

JOHN OSBORNE (1929–1994). *English playwright*
1 Don't clap too hard—it's a very old building.
2 Monarchy is the gold filling in a mouth of decay.
3 Never believe in mirrors or newspapers.
4 The schoolteacher is certainly underpaid as a childminder, but ludicrously overpaid as an educator.
5 They spend their time mostly looking forward to the past.

WILLIAM OSLER (1849–1919). *Canadian physician*
1 It is more important to know what kind of patient has the disease than what kind of disease the patient has.
2 One of the first duties of the physician is to educate the masses not to take medicine.
3 The desire to take medicine is one feature which distinguishes man, the animal, from his fellow creatures.
4 The greater the ignorance, the greater the dogmatism.
5 The natural man has only two primal passions, to get and to beget.

OVID (43 B.C.–A.D. 17?). *Roman poet*
1 Desire sways me one way, reason another. I see which is the better course, and I approve it; but still I follow the worse.
2 Truly now is the golden age; the highest honor comes by means of gold.
3 Whether a woman grants or withholds her favors, she always likes to be asked for them.

AMOS OZ (1939–). *Israeli novelist*
I will tell you that this nation of four million citizens is really an uneasy coalition of four million prime ministers, if not four million self-appointed prophets and messiahs. [On Israel.]

P

JACK PAAR (1918–). *American television talk-show host*

1 I am fond of Steve Allen, but not as much as he is.

2 She has the reputation of being outspoken—by no one!

VANCE PACKARD (1914–). *American writer and social critic*

1 Psychological obsolescence is created by the double-barreled strategy of (1) making the public style-conscious, and then (2) switching styles.

2 Rock 'n' roll might best be summed up as monotony tinged with hysteria.

3 The status seekers are people who are continually straining to surround themselves with visible evidence of the superior rank they are claiming.

MARCEL PAGNOL (1894–1974). *French playwright*

One has to look out for engineers—they begin with sewing machines and end up with the atomic bomb.

LEROY "SATCHEL" PAIGE (1906–1982). *American baseball player*

1 How old would you be if you didn't know how old you was?

2 How to Stay Young: 1. Avoid fried meats which angry up the blood. 2. If your stomach disputes you, lie down and pacify it with cool thoughts. 3. Keep the juices flowing by jangling around gently as you move. 4. Go very lightly on the vices, such as carrying on in society. The social ramble ain't restful. 5. Avoid running at all times. 6. Don't look back. Something might be gaining on you.

THOMAS PAINE (1737–1809). *English-born American political philosopher*

1 It has been the political career of this man to begin with hypocrisy, proceed with arrogance, and finish with contempt. [On John Adams.]

2 Moderation in temper is always a virtue, but moderation in principle is a species of vice.

3 Society in every state is a blessing, but government, even in its best state, is but a necessary evil; in its worst state, an intolerable one.

4 The story of the whale swallowing Jonah, though a whale is large enough to do it, borders greatly on the marvelous; but it would have approached nearer to the idea of a miracle if Jonah had swallowed the whale. [*The Age of Reason,* 1796.]

5 What at first was plunder assumed the softer name of revenue. [On taxes.]

BARBARA "BABE" PALEY (1915–1978). *American socialite*

You can never be too skinny or too rich. [Attributed.]

LORD PALMERSTON (Henry John Temple, 1784–1865). *British prime minister*

1 Die, my dear doctor? That is the last thing I shall do. [Last words.]

2 Dirt is not dirt, but only matter in the wrong place.

CHARLIE PARKER (1920–1955). *American jazz musician*

1 Don't play the saxophone. Let it play you.

2 Music is your own experience, your thoughts, your wisdom. If you don't live it, it won't come out of your horn.

DOROTHY PARKER (1893–1967). *American writer and humorist*

1 "Age before beauty." [Clare Booth Luce, standing aside.] Pearls before swine. [Attributed, but Luce denied the exchange.]

2 Brevity is the soul of lingerie. —See also W. Somerset Maugham 8; William Shakespeare 3

3 By the time you swear you're his, / Shivering and sighing, / And he vows his passion is / Infinite, undying— / Lady, make a note of this: / One of you is lying.

4 Good work, Mary. We all knew you had it in you. [Telegram to her friend Mary Sherwood who had just given birth.]

5 His voice was intimate, as the rustle of sheets.

6 Hollywood money isn't money. It's congealed snow, melts in your hand, and there you are.

7 How could they tell? [When informed of Calvin Coolidge's death in 1933.]

8 I require only three things of a man. He must be handsome, ruthless, and stupid.

9 If all the girls at Smith and Bennington were laid end to end, I wouldn't be surprised.

10 If, with the literate, I am / Impelled to try an epigram, / I never seek to take the credit; / We all assume that Oscar said it. [Referring to Oscar Wilde.]

11 It is our national joy to mistake the first-rate for the fecond rate.

12 It may be that this autobiography is set down in sincerity, frankness, and simple effort. It may be, too, that the Statue of Liberty is situated in Lake Ontario. [On Aimee Semple McPherson's autobiography.]

13 It serves me right for putting all my eggs in one bastard. [On her abortion.]

14 Just before they made S. J. Perelman, they broke the mold.

15 Life is a glorious cycle of song, / A medley of extemporania; / And love is a thing that can never go wrong; / And I am Marie of Romania.

16 Men seldom make passes at girls who wear glasses.

17 My soul is crushed, my spirit sore / I do not like me anymore, / I cavil, quarrel, grumble, grouse / I ponder on the narrow house / I shudder at the thought of men / I'm due to fall in love again.

18 One more drink, and I'd have been under the host.

19 Razors pain you; / Rivers are damp; / Acids stain you; / And drugs cause cramp. / Guns aren't lawful; / Nooses give; / Gas smells awful; / You might as well live.

20 She runs the gamut of emotions from A to B. [On Katharine Hepburn's performance in the 1933 play *The Lake.*]

21 She whose body's young and cool / Has no need of dancing school.

22 She wore a low but futile décolletage.

23 She would be kind to her inferiors if she could find any. [On Clare Booth Luce.]

24 That woman speaks eighteen languages, and can't say "no" in any of them.

25 The best way to keep children home is to make the home atmosphere pleasant—and let the air out of the tires.

26 *The House Beautiful* is the play lousy.

27 The only "ism" she believes in is plagiarism. [On a well-known writer.]

28 The two most beautiful words in the English language are "check enclosed."

29 There's a hell of a distance between wisecracking and wit. Wit has truth in it; wisecracking is simply calisthenics with words.

30 This is not a novel to be tossed aside lightly. It should be thrown with great force.

31 This is on me. [Self-epitaph.]

32 Why is it no one ever sent me yet / One perfect limousine, do you suppose? / Ah no, it's always just my luck to get / One perfect rose.

33 You can lead a horticulture, but you can't make her think.

34 You can't teach an old dogma new tricks.

C. NORTHCOTE PARKINSON (1909–1993). *English political scientist*
1 Expenditure rises to meet income.
2 Men enter local politics solely as a result of being unhappily married.
3 The Law of Triviality means that the time spent on any item of the agenda will be in inverse proportion to the sum of money involved.
4 The progress of science varies inversely with the number of journals published. ["Parkinson's Sixth Law."]
5 Work expands so as to fill the time available for its completion. ["Parkinson's Law."]

DOLLY PARTON (1946–). *American singer, songwriter, and actress*
1 I'm on a seafood diet—I see food, I eat it.
2 You have no idea how much it costs to make a person look this cheap.

BLAISE PASCAL (1623–1662). *French philosopher and mathematician*
1 All the unhappiness of men derives from one thing, that they cannot sit quietly in their own room.
2 Being favored by your master, are you less a slave?
3 I have made this letter longer than usual, because I lack the time to make it short.
4 I only believe in histories told by witnesses who have had their throats slit.
5 Men are so necessarily mad that not to be mad would be yet another form of madness.
6 Men never do evil so completely and cheerfully as when they do it from religious conviction.
7 There are only two kinds of men: the righteous who believe themselves sinners and sinners who believe themselves righteous.

KENNETH PATCHEN (1911–1972). *American poet*
1 God must have loved the People in Power, for he made them so very like their own image of Him. —See also Abraham Lincoln 4; H. L. Mencken 36
2 Oh lonesome's a bad place / To get crowded into.

LESTER PEARSON (1897–1972). *Canadian prime minister*
1 Diplomacy is letting someone else have your way.
2 Not only did he not suffer fools gladly; he did not suffer them at all. [On Dean Acheson.]
3 Politics is the skilled use of blunt objects.

SEAN PENN (1960–). *American actor and film director*
The difference between being a director and being an actor is the difference
  between being the carpenter banging the nails into the wood, and being
  the piece of wood the nails are being banged into.

WILLIAM PENN (1644–1718). *English-born American religious reformer*
1 Let the people think they govern, and they will be governed. —See also
  John Kenneth Galbraith 11
2 Silence is wisdom where speaking is folly.

SAMUEL PEPYS (1633–1703). *English civil servant and diarist*
1 Good God, what an age is this, and what a world is this, that a man cannot live without playing the knave and dissimulation.
2 I went out to Charing Cross, to see Major General Harrison hanged, drawn,
  and quartered; which was done there, he looking as cheerful as any man
  could in that condition.
3 It is pretty to see what money can do.
4 My wife, who, poor wretch, is troubled with her lonely life.
5 Saw a wedding in the church; and strange to say what delight we married
  people have to see these poor fools decoyed into our condition.

S. J. PERELMAN (1904–1979). *American writer, screenwriter, and humorist*
1 As for consulting a dentist regularly, my punctuality practically amounted
  to a fetish. Every twelve years I would drop whatever I was doing and
  allow wild Caucasian ponies to drag me to a reputable orthodontist.
2 Button-cute, rapier-keen, wafer-thin and pauper-poor. [On himself.]
3 For years I have let dentists ride roughshod over my teeth; I have been
  sawed, hacked, chopped, whittled, bewitched, bewildered, tattooed, and
  signed on again; but this is cuspid's last stand.
4 He was a short man, almost squat, with a vulpine smirk that told you, as
  soon as his image flashed on the screen, that no wife or bankroll must be
  left unguarded. [On Erich Von Stroheim.]
5 I loathe writing. On the other hand, I'm a great believer in money.
6 Look at me: I worked myself up from nothing to a state of extreme poverty.
7 Love is not the dying moan of a distant violin—it's the triumphant twang
  of a bedspring.
8 The publishers contend that you only advertise a book to any extent *after*
  it's beginning to sell, which is certainly Alice-in-Wonderland thinking.
9 This sinister dwarf who consumed nine weeks of my life has no peer in
  his chosen profession, which—stated very simply—is to humiliate and
  cheapen his fellow man, fracture one's self-esteem, convert everybody
  around him into lackeys, hypocrites and toadies, and thoroughly debase
  every relationship, no matter how casual. His enormity grows on you like
  some obscene fungus. [On film producer Mike Todd.]
10 You've got a sharp tongue in your head, Mr. Essick. Look out it doesn't cut
  your throat.

ROSS PEROT (1930–). *American electronics industry leader and Reform
  Party presidential nominee*
1 Money tends to make you stupid.

2 Our first president was a man who could not tell a lie. Two hundred years later, we have a president who cannot tell the truth. [On Bill Clinton.]

3 Power is wonderful, and absolute power is absolutely wonderful. —See also Lord Acton 2

4 Which one of the three candidates would you want your daughter to marry? [While campaigning for the presidency against George Bush and Bill Clinton in 1992.]

LAURENCE J. PETER (1919–1990). *Canadian academic and writer*

1 A censor is a man who knows more than he thinks you ought to.

2 A liberal calls it share-the-wealth; a conservative calls it soak-the-rich.

3 A modern child will answer you back before you've said anything.

4 A pessimist is a man who looks both ways before crossing a one-way street.

5 An archaeologist is a person whose career lies in ruins.

6 An economist is an expert who will know tomorrow why the things he predicted yesterday didn't happen today.

7 An ounce of image is worth a pound of performance.

8 Bureaucracy defends the status quo long past the time when the quo has lost its status.

9 Competence, like truth, beauty and contact lenses, is in the eye of the beholder. [*The Peter Principle,* 1969, cowritten with Raymond Hull.]

10 Competition in academia is so vicious because the stakes are so small.

11 Democracy is a process by which people are free to choose the man who will get the blame.

12 Education is a method whereby one acquires a higher grade of prejudices.

13 He laughs best whose laugh lasts. —See also Anonymous 41; Mary Pettibone Poole 3

14 History teaches us the mistakes we are going to make.

15 I hate people who are intolerant.

16 If you don't know where you are going, you will probably end up somewhere else. —See also Yogi Berra 7

17 Ignorance of one's ignorance is the greatest ignorance.

18 In a hierarchy every employee tends to rise to his level of incompetence; the cream rises until it sours.

19 In most hierarchies, supercompetence is more objectionable than incompetence.

20 In time, every post tends to be occupied by an employee who is incompetent to carry out its duties.

21 Irony is when you buy a suit with two pair of pants, and then burn a hole in the coat.

22 It's amazing how radical an unemployed conservative can become.

23 Legend: a lie that has attained the dignity of age.

24 Middle age is when it takes longer to rest than to get tired.

25 Middle age is when work is a lot less fun and fun is a lot more work.

26 Middle age is when you stop criticizing the older generation and start criticizing the younger one.

27 Negative predictions yield negative results; positive predictions yield negative results. ["Peter's Nonreciprocal Law of Predictions."]

28 No matter which direction you go, it's uphill and against the wind. ["Peter's Bicycling Law."]

29 Old age is when you know all the answers, but nobody asks you the questions.

30 Originality is the fine art of remembering what you hear but forgetting where you heard it.

31 Psychiatry enables us to correct our faults by confessing our parents' shortcomings.

32 See that the patron has something to gain by assisting you, or something to lose by not assisting you, to rise in the hierarchy.

33 Tact is the art of putting your foot down without stepping on anyone's toes.

34 Take your choice: talk about others and be a gossip or talk about yourself and be a bore.

35 Television has changed the American child from an irresistible force into an immovable object.

36 That's the problem with old age—there's not much future in it.

37 The fanatic goes through life with his mouth open and his mind closed.

38 The man with a clear conscience probably has a poor memory.

39 The modern class of youngsters are alike in many disrespects.

40 The most useful of all social graces is the ability to yawn with your mouth closed.

41 The past is a good place to visit, but I wouldn't want to live there. —See also Josh Billings 65

42 The problem with success is that its formula is the same as the one for ulcers.

43 The red light is always longer than the green light. ["Peter's Theory of Relativity."]

44 The reformer wants his conscience to be your guide.

45 The trouble with resisting temptation is that you may not get another chance.

46 The watchword for Side-Issue Specialists is Look after the molehills and the mountains will look after themselves.

47 There are two kinds of failures: those who thought and never did, and those who did and never thought.

48 There are two kinds of losers: the good loser and those who can't act.

49 Thomas Crapper invented the modern flush toilet.

50 Today if you're not confused, you're just not thinking clearly.

51 Two can live as cheaply as one if they both have good jobs.

52 When a patient is at death's door, it is the duty of the doctor to pull him through.

53 When two people go to bed together at the same time, the one that snores will fall asleep first. ["Peter's Primary Principle."]

54 Work is accomplished by those employees who have not yet reached their level of incompetence.

55 You can fool some of the people all of the time and all of the people some of the time, but you can make a damn fool of yourself any old time. —See also Abraham Lincoln 52

56 You can never really get away—you can only take yourself somewhere else. ["Peter's Theory of Self."]

WILLIAM L. PHELPS (1865–1943). *American educator and critic*
I divide all readers into two classes; those who read to remember and those who read to forget.

REGIS PHILBIN (1931–). *American television talk-show host*
Is that your final answer? [Tag line used in the television quiz show *Who Wants to Be a Millionaire?*, 1999.]

WENDELL PHILLIPS (1811–1884). *American lawyer and lecturer*
1 The Puritan's idea of Hell is a place where everybody has to mind his own business.
2 You can always get the truth from an American statesman after he has turned seventy, or given up all hope of the presidency.

PABLO PICASSO (1881–1973). *Spanish artist*
1 Computers are useless: they only give answers.
2 For those who know how to read, I have painted my autobiography.
3 I have contented these people with all the many bizarre things that have come into my head. And the less they understand, the more they admire it.
4 "I like your portrait of Gertrude Stein." Yes, everybody has said she doesn't not look like it, but that doesn't make any difference—she will.
5 I paint objects as I think them, not as I see them.
6 It takes a very long time to become young.
7 The world today doesn't make sense, so why should I paint pictures that do?
8 There are painters who transform the sun into a yellow spot, but there are others who, thanks to their art and intelligence, transform a yellow spot into the sun.
9 There's no such thing as a bad Picasso, but some are less good than others.
10 Today, as you know, I am famous and very rich. But when I am alone with myself, I haven't the courage to consider myself an artist, in the great and ancient sense of that word. I am only a public entertainer, who understands his age.
11 When I am finished painting, I paint again for relaxation.
12 When I was a child, my mother said to me, "If you become a soldier, you'll be a general. If you become a monk, you'll end up as the pope." Instead, I became a painter and wound up as Picasso.

MARGE PIERCY (1936–). *American novelist and poet*
Burning dinner is not incompetence but war.

ARTHUR WING PINERO (1855–1934). *English dramatist*
A financier is a pawnbroker with imagination.

ROBERT M. PIRSIG (1928–). *American writer*
The truth knocks on the door and you say, "Go away, I'm looking for the truth," and so it goes away. Puzzling. [*Zen and the Art of Motorcycle Maintenance: An Inquiry into Values*, 1974.]

PLATO (427?–347 B.C.). *Greek philosopher*
1 I have hardly ever known a mathematician who was capable of reasoning.
2 "Plato, malicious rumors about you are being spread throughout the city." No matter: I will live so that no one shall believe them.
3 Wise men talk because they have something to say: fools, because they have to say something.

GEORGE WASHINGTON PLUNKITT (1842–1924). *American political leader (New York's Tammany Hall)*
1 A politician who steals is worse than a thief. He is a fool. With the grand opportunities all around for a man with political pull, there's no excuse for stealin' a cent.
2 If my worst enemy was given the job of writin' my epitaph when I'm gone, he couldn't do more than write: "George W. Plunkitt. He Seen His Opportunities, and He Took 'Em."

GEORGES POMPIDOU (1911–1974). *French premier*
A statesman is a politician who places himself at the service of the nation. A politician is a statesman who places the nation at his service.

MARY PETTIBONE POOLE (20th century). *American writer*
1 A pessimist is a person who has not had enough experience to be a cynic.
2 Familiarity breeds.
3 He who laughs, lasts. —See also Anonymous 41; Laurence J. Peter 13
4 Tact is the ability to describe others as they see themselves.

ALEXANDER POPE (1688–1744). *English poet*
1 A brain of feathers and a heart of lead.
2 A man should never be ashamed to own he has been in the wrong, which is but saying, in other words, that he is wiser today than he was yesterday.
3 A wit with dunces, and a dunce with wits.
4 Amusement is the happiness of those that cannot think.
5 Authors are judged by strange capricious rules, / The great ones are thought mad, the small ones fools.
6 Blessed is the man who expects nothing, for he shall never be disappointed. —See also G. K. Chesterton 3
7 But we, brave Britons, foreign laws despised, / And kept unconquered, and uncivilized.
8 Eternal smiles his emptiness betray, / As shallow streams run dimpling all the way.
9 Fools are only laughed at; wits are hated.
10 I never knew any man in my life who could not bear another's misfortunes perfectly like a Christian. —See also François de La Rochefoucauld 35; William Shakespeare 5

11 Men must be taught as if you taught them not; / And things unknown proposed as things forgot.

12 Party is the madness of many for the gain of a few.

13 Sir, I admit your general rule / That every poet is a fool: / But you yourself may serve to show it, / That every fool is not a poet.

14 The bookful blockhead, ignorantly read, / With loads of learned lumber in his head.

15 The hungry judges soon the sentence sign, / And wretches hang that jurymen may dine.

16 This long disease, my life.

17 We may see the small value God has for riches by the people he gives them to.

18 When men grow virtuous in their old age, they only make a sacrifice to God of the devil's leavings.

19 Words are like leaves; and where they most abound, / Much fruit of sense beneath is rarely found.

20 You beat your pate, and fancy wit will come: / Knock as you please, there's nobody at home. [1732] —See also William Cowper 3

COLE PORTER (1891–1964). *American composer*

1 Birds do it, bees do it, / Even educated fleas do it. / Let's do it, let's fall in love. —See also Noel Coward 17

2 I get no kick from champagne; / Mere alcohol doesn't thrill me at all. / So tell me why should it be true, / That I get a kick out of you?

3 In olden days a glimpse of stocking / Was looked on as something shocking; / But now, heaven knows, / Anything goes. [1934]

4 You're the Nile, / You're the Tower of Pisa. / You're the smile / On the Mona Lisa. / I'm a worthless check, a total wreck, a flop. / But if, baby, I'm the bottom, / You're the top!

5 You're the top! You're the Coliseum. / You're the top! You're the Louvre Museum. / You're a melody / From a symphony by Strauss. / You're a Bendel bonnet, / A Shakespeare sonnet, / You're Mickey Mouse!

KATHERINE ANNE PORTER (1890–1980). *American novelist*

1 The pimple on the face of American literature. [On Truman Capote.]

2 Oh, poor Pearl Buck! She has no more bounce than a boiled potato.

EMILY POST (1872–1960). *American etiquette authority*

1 A little praise is not only merest justice but is beyond the purse of no one.

2 To do exactly as your neighbors do is the only sensible rule. [*Etiquette,* 1922.]

EZRA POUND (1885–1972). *American poet*

1 A dirty book worth reading. [On Henry Miller's *Tropic of Cancer,* 1934.]

2 Literature is news that STAYS news.

3 Mr. Eliot is at times an excellent poet and has arrived at the supreme Eminence among English critics largely through disguising himself as a corpse. [On T. S. Eliot.]

4 Mr. Wordsworth, a stupid man, with a decided gift for portraying nature in vignettes, never yet ruined anyone's morals, unless, perhaps, he has driven some susceptible persons to crime in a very fury of boredom. [On William Wordsworth.]

ANTHONY POWELL (1905–). *English novelist*

1 All men are brothers, but, thank God, they aren't all brothers-in-law.

2 Dinner at the Huntercombes' possessed only two dramatic features—the wine was a farce and the food a tragedy.

3 Growing old is like being increasingly penalized for a crime you haven't committed.

4 In this country it is rare for anyone, let alone a publisher, to take writers seriously.

5 Parents are sometimes a disappointment to their children. They don't fulfill the promise of their early years.

6 Self-love seems so often unrequited.

ENOCH POWELL (1912–). *British political leader*

History is littered with the wars which everybody knew would never happen.

ANTHONY PRICE (1928–). *English writer*

1 Publicity is like power, Major Butler—it's a rare man who isn't corrupted by it. —See also Lord Acton 2

2 The devil himself had probably re-designed hell in the light of information he had gained from observing airport layouts.

J. B. PRIESTLEY (1894–1984). *English writer and humorist*

1 Sometimes you might think that the machines we worship make all the chief appointments, promoting the human beings who seem closest to them.

2 The more we elaborate our means of communication, the less we communicate.

3 The real lost souls don't wear their hair long and play guitars. They have crew cuts, trained minds, sign on for research in biological warfare, and don't give their parents a moment's worry.

4 There was no respect for youth when I was young, and now that I am old there is no respect for age—I missed it coming and going.

MATTHEW PRIOR (1664–1721). *English poet and diplomat*

1 Cured yesterday of my disease, / I died last night of my physician.

2 'Tis remarkable that they / Talk most who have the least to say.

HERBERT V. PROCHNOW (1897–1998). *American economist, banker, and government official*

1 Straddling an issue is like straddling the middle of the road: you are liable to be hit from both sides.

2 The trouble with opportunity is that it always comes disguised as hard work.

3 Thomas Edison did not invent the first talking machine. He invented the first one you could shut off.

MARCEL PROUST (1871–1922). *French novelist*

1 As soon as he ceased to be mad he became merely stupid. There are maladies which we must not seek to cure, because they alone protect us from others that are more serious.
2 As soon as one becomes unhappy, one becomes moral.
3 It has been said that the highest praise of God consists in the denial of him by the atheist who finds creation so perfect that he can dispense with its creator.
4 It is seldom that one parts on good terms, because if one were on good terms one would not part.
5 One of those telegrams of which M. de Guermantes had wittily fixed the formula: "Cannot come, lie follows."
6 The rootedness of a habit is generally in proportion to its absurdity.
7 There is nothing like desire for preventing the things one says from having any resemblance to the things in one's mind.
8 To believe in medicine would be the height of folly, if not to believe in it were not a greater folly still.

DAVID PRYCE-JONES (1936–). *British writer*

When you're bored with yourself, marry, and be bored with someone else.

RICHARD PRYOR (1940–). *American comedian and actor*

1 God was a junkie, baby. He had to be a junkie to put up with all this, you know what I mean. You don't just walk about feeling nothing, behind all that is going on, man.
2 Now they're calling taking drugs an epidemic—that's 'cos white folks are doing it.

MARIO PUZO (1920–1999). *American novelist*

1 A lawyer with his briefcase can steal more than a hundred men with guns.
2 He's a businessman. I'll make him an offer he can't refuse. [*The Godfather,* 1969.]
3 Like many businessmen of genius he learned that free competition was wasteful, monopoly efficient.
4 Show me a gambler, and I'll show you a loser; show me a hero, and I'll show you a corpse.

DAN QUAYLE (1947–). *Indiana senator and U.S. vice president*

1 I was recently on a tour of Latin America, and the only regret I have was that I didn't study Latin harder in school so I could converse with those people.

2 It is wonderful to be here in the great state of Chicago.

3 It isn't pollution that's harming the environment. It's the impurities in our air and water that are doing it.

4 Republicans understand the importance of bondage between a mother and child.

5 What a waste it is to lose one's mind, or not to have a mind. How true that is.

ANNA QUINDLEN (1953–). *American journalist*

There's a character issue for Mr. Bush in this campaign. The clothes have no emperor. [On George Bush, 1992.]

FRANÇOIS RABELAIS (1483?-1553). *French physician and novelist*

1 As for you, little envious prigs, snarling, bastard, puny critics, you'll soon have railed your last: go hang yourselves!

2 How can I be able to govern others when I don't know how to govern myself!

3 I never drink without a thirst, if not a present thirst a future one. I forestall it, you see. I drink for the thirst to come.

4 I owe much; I have nothing; the rest I leave to the poor. [Last words.]

JOHN RANDOLPH (1773–1833). *American congressman*

Henry Clay is so brilliant yet so corrupt that, like a rotten mackerel by moonlight, he both shines and stinks. [John F. Kennedy called this "the most memorable sentence in the history of personal abuse."]

JEANNETTE RANKIN (1880–1973). *American congresswoman*

1 We're half the people; we should be half the Congress. [Referring to women.]

2 You can no more win a war than you can win an earthquake.

JOHN RAY (1628–1705). *English naturalist and proverb editor*

He that uses many words for the explaining any subject, does, like the cuttlefish, hide himself for the most part in his own ink. —See also George Orwell 23

SAM RAYBURN (1882–1961). *Texas Speaker of the House of Representatives*

If you want to get along, go along.

NANCY REAGAN (1923–). *American actress and first lady*

1 A woman is like a teabag. It's only when she's in hot water that you realize how strong she is.

2 I must say acting was good training for the political life which lay ahead for us.

RONALD REAGAN (1911–). *American president*

1 A hippie is someone who looks like Tarzan, walks like Jane, and smells like Cheetah.

2 All the waste in a year from a nuclear power plant can be stored under a desk. [1980]

3 Approximately 80 percent of our air pollution stems from hydrocarbons released by vegetation. So let's not go overboard in setting and enforcing tough emissions standards for man-made sources.

4 Before I refuse to take your questions, I have an opening statement. [News conference.] —See also Charles de Gaulle 4

5 Don't bump into the furniture and, in the kissing scenes, keep your mouth closed. [Advice to senators when the cameras are rolling, 1986.] —See also Noel Coward 11

6 Don't you cut me off. I am paying for this microphone. [Remark during a televised debate in the 1980 New Hampshire presidential primary; in the

1948 film *State of the Union,* Spencer Tracy had delivered a similar line, "Don't you shut me off, I'm paying for this broadcast."]

7 Government is like a baby: an alimentary canal with a big appetite at one end and no sense of responsibility at the other.

8 Government is not the solution to our problem; government is the problem.

9 Government programs, once launched, never disappear. Actually, a government bureau is the nearest thing to eternal life we'll ever see on this earth!

10 Government's view of the economy could be summed up in a few short phrases: if it moves, tax it; if it keeps moving, regulate it; and if it stops moving, subsidize it.

11 Honey, I forgot to duck. [Remark to his wife Nancy after being wounded in a 1981 assassination attempt; Reagan was repeating what Jack Dempsey had said to his wife over the phone after losing his heavyweight title to Gene Tunney in 1926.]

12 I always throw my golf club in the direction I'm going.

13 I hope you're all Republicans. [Remark to surgeons who were about to operate on him after the assassination attempt.]

14 I will not make age an issue of this campaign. I am not going to exploit for political purposes my opponent's youth and inexperience. [Televised presidential debate with Walter Mondale, 1984; Reagan was seventy-three, Mondale fifty-six.]

15 I've noticed that everybody who is for abortion has already been born.

16 Just remember, my best side is my right side—my far right side. [Remark to photographers.]

17 Middle age is when you're faced with two temptations, and you choose the one that will get you home by nine o'clock.

18 My fellow Americans. I am pleased to tell you I just signed legislation which outlaws Russia forever. The bombing begins in five minutes. [Off-the-cuff "joke" made while testing the microphone before a radio broadcast, 1984.]

19 Once you've seen one redwood, you've seen them all.

20 Politics is supposed to be the second oldest profession. I have come to realize that it bears a very close resemblance to the first.

21 Recession is when your neighbor loses his job. Depression is when you lose yours. And recovery is when Jimmy Carter loses his. [Presidential election campaign speech while the country was floundering economically, 1980.] —See also Harry S. Truman 15

22 Republicans think every day is July 4, and Democrats think every day is April 15.

23 Take care of the policy and the politics will take care of itself. [Attributed.]

24 There you go again! [Responding to Jimmy Carter's charge that Reagan, if elected president, would dismantle federal health support for the elderly, televised presidential debate, 1980.]

25 They are the moral equivalent of our founding Fathers and the brave men and women of the French Resistance. We cannot turn away from them, for the struggle here is not right versus left; it is right versus wrong. [On the Nicaraguan contras, speech, 1985.]

26 This fellow they've nominated claims he's the new Thomas Jefferson. Well, let me tell you something. I knew Thomas Jefferson. He was a friend of mine. And, Governor, you're no Thomas Jefferson. [On William Jefferson Clinton, who had just become the Democratic presidential nominee, 1992.] —See also Lloyd Bentsen

27 Walter Mondale accuses us of ad-libbing our foreign policy. Not true. We read it right off the three-by-five cards.

28 "What kind of governor will you be?" [Reporter] I don't know; I've never played a governor. [After being elected governor of California in 1967.]

29 You can tell a lot about a fellow's character by his way of eating jellybeans.

THOMAS BRACKETT REED (1839–1902). *Oregon Speaker of the House of Representatives*
"As for me, I would rather be right than be president." [William McK. Springer, quoting Henry Clay's famous quip, in a speech before Congress.] Well, the gentleman will never be either.

NIGEL REES (1944–). *English writer, quotation editor, and radio personality*
1 How come there's only one Monopolies Commission?
2 However sure you are that you have attributed a quotation correctly, an earlier source will be pointed out to you. ["Rees's Second Law of Quotations."]
3 When in doubt, ascribe all quotations to George Bernard Shaw. ["Rees's First Law of Quotations."]

ROBERT B. REICH (1946–). *American economist and secretary of labor*
1 Economic forecasters exist to make astrologers look good.
2 The global financial crisis is too important to be left entirely to central bankers and finance ministers. —See also Georges Clemenceau 4
3 Walking is an excellent exercise. At 65, my grandmother began walking five miles a day. She's now 100—and we have no idea where she is. [Repeating an old joke.]

JULES RENARD (1842–1910). *French writer*
1 Already, I am developing a taste for walking in cemeteries. [Journal entry a few months before his death.]
2 Be modest! It is the kind of pride least likely to offend.
3 I don't know if God exists, but it would be better for His reputation if He didn't.
4 Laziness: the habit of resting before fatigue sets in.
5 Our life seems like a trial run.

JAMES RESTON (1909–1995). *American journalist*
1 Among the minor tragedies in Washington in the last generation has been the triumph of good manners over honest convictions. [1970]

2 He inherited some good instincts from his Quaker forebears but by diligent hard work, he overcame them. [On Richard M. Nixon.]

3 Mr. Solzhenitsyn entitled his commencement address at Harvard "A World Split Apart," but for all its brilliant passages, it sounded like the wanderings of a mind split apart.

4 Never antagonize any group, no matter how small, if you can avoid it. If you have to choose between two groups, always choose to antagonize the one that is less vindictive and less organized. [Advice to politicians.]

5 Stick with the optimists. It's going to be tough enough even if they're right. [Advice to his grandson.]

6 The government is the only known vessel that leaks from the top.

PIERRE REVERDY (1889–1960). *French poet*
One is vain by nature, modest by necessity.

JOSHUA REYNOLDS (1723–1792). *English painter*
Few have been taught to any purpose who have not been their own teachers. We prefer those instructions which we have given ourselves, from our affection for the instructor.

FRANK RICH (1949–). *American journalist and critic*
1 One of the dullest memoirs ever to lay waste to a forest. [On *Barbara Bush: A Memoir*, 1994.]

2 The faster the rise, the steeper the fall. [On the "instant obsolescence" of celebrities.]

3 The play is one big piece of Swiss cheese, minus the cheese.

MICHEL PAUL RICHARD (1933–). *American writer*
Better to be pissed off than pissed on.

ANN RICHARDS (1933–). *Texas governor*
1 Poor George, he can't help it—he was born with a silver foot in his mouth. [On George Bush, 1988.]

2 You have got to prove your manhood down here whether you're a man or a woman. [On Texas.]

RALPH RICHARDSON (1902–1983). *English actor*
Acting is merely the art of keeping a large group of people from coughing.
    —See also Ethel Barrymore 3

DON RICKLES (1926–). *American comedian and actor*
1 Make yourself at home, Frank—hit somebody! [Onstage remark to Frank Sinatra, who was in the audience.]

2 Oh my god, look at you. Anybody else hurt in the accident?

JOAN RIVERS (1933–). *American comedienne*
1 Any woman who has a child who doesn't yell is a fool. When I was having my kid it was ARRRRGH. And that was just during conception.

2 Boy George is all England needs—another queen who can't dress.

3 Can we talk? [Her signature line.]

4 Edgar had a heart attack, and I'm to blame. We were making love, and I took the bag off my head.

5 Half of all marriages end in divorce—and then there are the really unhappy ones.

6 Having a baby is definitely a labor of love.

7 I hate housework! You make the beds, you do the dishes—and six months later you have to start all over again.

8 My mother could make anybody feel guilty—she used to get letters of apology from people she didn't even know.

9 She's got more chins than a Chinese phone book. [On Elizabeth Taylor.]

10 There is not one female comic who was beautiful as a little girl.

WILL ROGERS (1879–1935). *American actor, journalist, and humorist*

1 A government treaty gave Cherokees their land as long as the grass grows and the water flows. But when they discovered oil, they took it back because there was nothin' in the treaty about oil.

2 A remark generally hurts in proportion to its truth.

3 But shucks, we got the best politicians in this country that money can buy.

4 Buy land! They ain't making any more of it.

5 Calvin Coolidge didn't say much; and when he did, he didn't say much.

6 Communism is like Prohibition, it's a good idea but it won't work.

7 Congress is going to start tinkering with the Ten Commandments just as soon as they can find someone in Washington who has read them.

8 Diplomacy is the art of saying "Nice doggie?" till you can find a rock. [Attributed.]

9 Don't gamble! Take all your savings and buy some good stock and hold it till it goes up, then sell it. If it don't go up, don't buy it.

10 Don't take things too seriously, especially yourself. Just lead your life so you wouldn't be ashamed to sell the family parrot to the town gossip!

11 Even if you're on the right track, you'll get run over if you just sit there.

12 Everybody is ignorant, only on different subjects.

13 Everything is funny, as long as it is happening to somebody else.

14 Fanatical religion driven to a certain point is almost as bad as none at all, but not quite.

15 Half our life is spent trying to find something to do with the time we have rushed through life trying to save.

16 Here lies Will Rogers. Politicians turned honest and he starved to death. [Self-epitaph.]

17 Heroing is one of the shortest-lifed [*sic*] professions there is.

18 I am not a member of any organized party—I'm a Democrat.

19 I can remember way back when a liberal was someone who was generous with his own money.

20 I had just enough white in me to make my honesty questionable. [Rogers was part Cherokee.]

21 I never lack material for my humor column when Congress is in session.

22 I never met a man I didn't like. [His signature line.] —See also W. C. Fields 22

23 It's not politics that is worrying this country; it's the second payment.

24 Let advertisers spend the same amount of money improving their product that they do on advertising, and they wouldn't have to advertise it.

25 More men have been elected between sundown and sunup than ever were elected between sunup and sundown.

26 My forefathers didn't come over on the *Mayflower,* but they met the boat.

27 Our foreign dealings are an open book—generally a checkbook.

28 Politics has got so expensive that it takes lots of money to even get beat with.

29 Republicans take care of the big money, for big money takes care of them.

30 Some say, what is the salvation of the movies? I say, run 'em backwards. It can't hurt 'em and it's worth a trial.

31 Thank heavens we don't get all the government we pay for.

32 That's called diplomacy, doing just what you said you wouldn't.

33 The business of government is to keep the government out of business; that is, unless business needs government aid.

34 The income tax has made more liars out of the American people than golf has.

35 The more you read about this politics thing, you got to admit that each party is worse than the other. The one that's out always looks the best.

36 The movies are the only business where you can go out front and applaud yourself.

37 The only time people dislike gossip is when it's about them.

38 The stock market has spoiled more appetites than bad cooking.

39 The suckers haven't permanently deserted the stock market. They are merely waiting until the prices get too high again. [Attributed.]

40 There have been three great inventions since the beginning of time: fire, the wheel and central banking.

41 There is no credit to being a comedian, when you have the whole government working for you. All you have to do is report the facts. —See also Art Buchwald 6

42 There is nothing so stupid as an educated man, if you get him off the thing that he was educated in.

43 We can't all be heroes because somebody has to sit on the curb and clap as they go by.

44 We don't seem able to check crime, so why not legalize it and then tax it out of business?

45 What the country needs is dirtier fingernails and cleaner minds.

46 When you put down the good things you ought to have done, and leave out the bad things you did do—that's memoirs.

47 With Congress, every time they make a joke it's a law. And every time they make a law it's a joke.

48 You can't say civilization don't advance, for in every war they kill you a new way.

49 You take religion backed up by commerce and it's awful hard for a heathen to overcome.

ANDY ROONEY (1919–). *American broadcast journalist and writer*

1 Crossing the street in New York keeps old people young—if they make it.

2 In a conversation, keep in mind that you're more interested in what you have to say than anyone else is.

3 It's not so much that I write well—I just don't write badly very often, and that passes for good on television. [Referring to his essays on *60 Minutes*, 1969.]

4 Man has made a sewer of the river—and spanned it with a poem. [On the Verrazano Narrows Bridge linking Brooklyn and Staten Island; completed in 1964, it is the longest suspension bridge in the United States.]

5 The only people who say worse things about politicians than reporters do are other politicians.

6 Why would I or anyone else want to lay me down to sleep with my head on a pillowcase embossed with the signature of Yves Saint Laurent?

FRANKLIN D. ROOSEVELT (1882–1945). *American president*

1 A radical is a man with both feet firmly planted—in the air; a conservative is a man with two perfectly good legs who, however, has never learned to walk; a reactionary is a somnambulist walking backwards; a liberal is a man who uses his legs and his hands at the behest of his head.

2 Be sincere; be brief; be seated. [Advice to his son James on speechmaking.]

3 He may be a son of a bitch, but he's *our* son of a bitch. [On Nicaraguan dictator Anastasio Somoza, 1938.]

4 He was a sad man because he couldn't get it all at once. And nobody can. [On Abraham Lincoln and the presidency.]

5 "I don't like you, Mr. President, I don't like you at all." [Mrs. Cornelius Vanderbilt V] Well, Mrs. Vanderbilt, lots of people don't like me. You are in good company.

6 I have no expectation of making a hit every time I come to bat. What I seek is the highest possible batting average.

7 I'd like to see sixteen lions turned loose on the Congress. "Might not the lions make a mistake?" [Someone asked.] Not if they stayed there long enough. [At a time when Roosevelt's relations with the Congress were particularly bad.]

8 "I'd like to tell you some of the latest political jokes." [Will Rogers during a visit to the White House.] You don't have to; I appointed them.

9 Leon, are you laboring under the impression that I read these memoranda of yours? I can't even lift them. [Remark to a member of his administration.]

10 "Mr. President, what is your reaction to the change in the Italian government?" Reaction? "Yes, sir." I never have reactions. I am much too old. [News conference, 1943.]

11 Once upon a time there was a schoolteacher who, after describing heaven in golden terms, asked her class of small boys how many wanted to go to heaven. Every boy in the class held up his hand—except one. "Charlie," the teacher said, "why don't you want to go to heaven?" "Teacher," he said, "sure I want to go to heaven, but"—pointing to the rest of the boys in the room—"not with that bunch." [Speech.]

12 These Republican leaders have not been content with attacks on me, or on my wife, or on my sons. No, not content with that, they now include my little dog Fala. Well, of course I don't resent attacks, and my family doesn't resent attacks, but Fala does resent them. [Responding to charges that Roosevelt had sent a destroyer to transport his dog back home, radio speech during the presidential election campaign of 1944.]

13 "Will reporters be allowed to use the new swimming pool and play tennis on the White House courts?" [Reporter] Of course, and the children have a sand pile. You boys can play in it too, if you like.

THEODORE ROOSEVELT (1858–1919). *American president*

1 A Byzantine logothete. [On Woodrow Wilson.]

2 A filthy little atheist. [On Thomas Paine.]

3 A man who has never gone to school may steal from a freight car; but if he has a university education, he may steal the whole railroad. —See also Mother Jones 1

4 He has no more backbone than a chocolate éclair. [On President William McKinley, his predecessor.] —See also Ulysses S. Grant 1

5 He means well feebly. [On Kaiser Wilhelm II of Germany.]

6 "How does it feel, Colonel? The bullet, I mean?" It feels like rheumatism, only a lot worse. [While recuperating from wounds sustained during an assassination attempt, 1912.]

7 I am only an average man but, by George, I work harder at it than the average man.

8 I don't mind having to die. I've had my good time, and I don't mind having to pay for it. But to think that those swine will say that I'm out of the game. [Referring to his political enemies in a remark to a friend who had found him ailing in a New York hotel room a year before his death.]

9 I think there is only one quality worse than hardness of heart and that is softness of head.

10 I took the Canal Zone and let Congress debate, and while the debate goes on, the canal does, too.

11 I'm as strong as a bull moose, and you can use me to the limit.

12 In life, as in a football game, the principle to follow is: hit the line hard; don't foul and don't shirk, but hit the line hard!

13 It is only the warlike power of a civilized people that can give peace to the world.

14 Most fortunately, the hard, energetic, practical men who do the rough pioneer work of civilization in barbarous lands, are not prone to false sentimentality.

15 Speak softly and carry a big stick—you will go far. [Cited as "an old proverb" in a speech, 1901.]

16 The English and Dutch administrators of Malaysia have done admirable work; but the profit to the Europeans in those States has always been one of the chief elements considered; whereas in the Philippines our whole attention was concentrated upon the welfare of the Filipinos themselves, if anything to the neglect of our own interests. [1913]

17 The great virtue of my radicalism lies in the fact that I am perfectly ready, if necessary, to be radical on the conservative side.

18 The most successful politician is he who says what everybody is thinking most often and in the loudest voice.

19 The reactionary is always willing to take a progressive attitude on any issue that is dead.

20 The White House is a bully pulpit!

ELIHU ROOT (1845–1937). *American secretary of state*

You have made a very good start in life, and your friends have great hope for you when you grow up. [Tongue-in-cheek congratulatory note to Theodore Roosevelt on his 46th birthday.]

ROSEANNE (1952–). *American comedienne*

1 I figure when my husband comes home from work, if the kids are still alive, then I've done my job.

2 I'm not upset about my divorce. I'm only upset that I'm not a widow.

JEAN ROSTAND (1894–1977). *French biologist*

My pessimism goes to the point of suspecting the sincerity of the pessimists.

LEO ROSTEN (1908–1997). *American writer*

1 Biting dogs don't bark.

2 Eccentric: a man too rich to be called crazy.

3 Give a man enough rope, and he'll hang you.

4 Imperialism: the aims of your neighbor; opposite to your own aims, which is called foreign policy.

5 International conferences: social functions at which statesmen who know that something is wrong agree that nothing can be done about it. [1935]

6 It's imagination, and not just conscience, which doth make cowards of us all. —See also Mignon McLaughlin 12; William Shakespeare 4

7 It's very easy to find something you're not looking for.

8 New Deal: the wedding of good intentions to bad economics.

9 Opposites attract—almost as often as they repel.

10 Peace: time out.

11 Private banking: the process by which banks redistribute the national income, among themselves.

12 Rock music: hear today, deaf tomorrow.

13 Rules of war: the laws that make it illegal to hit below the toes.

14 The only thing I can say about W. C. Fields, whom I have admired since the day he advanced upon Baby LeRoy with an ice pick, is this: any man who hates dogs and babies can't be all bad. [Speech at a Hollywood dinner honoring Fields in 1939; in the November 1937 issue of *Harper's,* the quip "No man who hates dogs and children can be all bad" was ascribed to Byron Barnton, a journalist with *The New York Times.*]

15 With twice as much brain, he'd still be a half-wit.

JEAN-JACQUES ROUSSEAU (1712–1778). *French philosopher*

1 At first we do not know how to live; and when we know how to live it is too late.

2 I have resolved on an enterprise which has no precedent, and which, once complete, will have no imitator. My purpose is to display to my kind a portrait in every way true to nature, and the man I shall portray will be myself. [Opening sentences of his *Confessions*, 1781.]

3 I hate books: they teach us only to talk about what we do not know.

4 It is not the criminal things that are the hardest to confess, but the ridiculous and the shameful.

5 My enemies employ more ingenuity in persecuting me than would be required for governing Europe.

6 The ever-recurring law of necessity soon teaches a man to do what he does not like, so as to avert evils which he would dislike still more.

7 The value set by the general public on the various arts is in inverse ratio to their real utility.

HELEN ROWLAND (1875–1950). *American journalist and humorist*

1 A bachelor never quite gets over the idea that he is a thing of beauty and a boy forever.

2 A fool and her money are soon courted. —See also Anonymous 1

3 A husband is what is left of a lover after the nerve has been extracted.

4 A man loses his illusions first, his teeth second, and his follies last.

5 Before marriage a man will lie awake all night thinking about something you said; after marriage he'll fall asleep before you finish saying it.

6 It takes a woman twenty years to make a man of her son, and another woman twenty minutes to make a fool of him.

7 Love, the quest; marriage, the conquest; divorce, the inquest.

8 Some widows are bereaved; others, relieved.

9 When a man makes a woman his wife, it's the highest compliment he can pay her, and it's usually the last.

RITA RUDNER (1955–). *American comedienne*

1 I never know what to get my father for his birthday. Once I gave him a hundred dollars and said, "Buy yourself something that will make your life easier." So he went out and bought a present for my mother.

2 If you never want to see a man again, just tell him, "I love you, I want to marry you. I want to have your children": they leave skid marks.

3 My boyfriend and I broke up. He wanted to get married, and I didn't want him to.

4 When I meet a man, I ask myself, "Is this the man I want my children to spend weekends with?"

DAMON RUNYON (1884–1946). *American journalist and short-story writer*

1 All life is six to five against. —See also Tom Stoppard 7

2 I do not approve of guys using false pretenses on dolls, except, of course, when nothing else will do.

3 My boy, always try to rub up against money, for if you rub up against money long enough, some of it may rub off on you.

4 The best way to be a bum and make a living is to be a sportswriter.

5 The race is not always to the swift, nor the battle to the strong, but that's the way to bet.

DEAN RUSK (1909–1994). *American secretary of state*

1 I wouldn't make the slightest concession for moral leadership. It's much overrated.

2 One of the best ways to persuade others is with your ears—by listening to them.

3 We're eyeball to eyeball, and I think the other fellow just blinked. [During the Cuban Missile Crisis, 1962.]

JOHN RUSKIN (1819–1900). *English art critic and writer*

1 An artist should be fit for the best society and keep out of it.

2 He thinks by infection, catching an opinion like a cold.

3 The art of becoming "rich" is not absolutely nor finally the art of accumulating much money for ourselves, but also of contriving that our neighbors shall have less. In accurate terms, it is "the art of establishing the maximum inequality in our own favor."

4 When a man is wrapped up in himself, he makes a pretty small package.

BERTRAND RUSSELL (1872–1970). *English mathematician and philosopher*

1 A great many people enjoy a war provided it's not in their neighborhood.

2 An honest politician will not be tolerated by a democracy unless he is very stupid.

3 Aristotle could have avoided the mistake of thinking that women have fewer teeth than men by the simple device of asking Mrs. Aristotle to keep her mouth open while he counted.

4 Democracy, as conceived by politicians, is a form of government, that is to say, it is a method of making people do what their leaders wish under the impression that they are doing what they themselves wish.

5 Ethics is in origin the art of recommending to others the sacrifices required for cooperation with oneself.

6 Every man, wherever he goes, is encompassed by a cloud of comforting convictions, which move with him like flies on a summer day.

7 I am firm; you are obstinate; he is a pig-headed fool.

8 I can only say that, while my own opinions as to ethics do not satisfy me, other people's satisfy me still less.

9 If one man offers you democracy and another offers you a bag of grain, at what stage of starvation will you prefer the grain to the vote?

10 Invariably Gladstone earnestly consulted his conscience, and invariably his conscience earnestly gave him the convenient answer. [On William Ewart Gladstone.]

11 It is illegal in England to state in print that a wife can and should derive sexual pleasure from intercourse. [1927]

12 It is obvious that "obscenity" is not a term capable of exact legal definition; in the practice of the courts, it means "anything that shocks the magistrate."

13 It is the fate of rebels to found new orthodoxies.

14 Man is a credulous animal, and must believe *something;* in the absence of good grounds for belief, he will be satisfied with bad ones.

15 Man is a rational animal—so at least I have been told. Throughout a long life, I have looked diligently for evidence in favor of this statement, but so far I have not had the good fortune to come across it.

16 Mathematics may be defined as the subject in which we never know what we are talking about, nor whether what we are saying is true.

17 More cranks take up unfashionable errors than unfashionable truths.

18 Most of the greatest evils that man has inflicted upon man have come through people feeling quite certain about something which, in fact, was false.

19 Most people would die sooner than think; in fact, they do.

20 My German engineer, I think is a fool. He thinks nothing empirical is knowable—I asked him to admit that there was not a rhinoceros in the room, but he wouldn't. [Referring to the philosopher Ludwig Wittgenstein.]

21 Next to enjoying ourselves, the next greatest pleasure consists in preventing others from enjoying themselves.

22 No one gossips about other people's secret virtues.

23 Not a gentleman; dresses too well. [On Anthony Eden.]

24 Organizations are of two kinds: those which aim at getting something done and those which aim at preventing something from being done.

25 Our great democracies still tend to think that a stupid man is more likely to be honest than a clever man, and our politicians take advantage of this prejudice by pretending to be even more stupid than nature made them.

26 Patriots always talk of dying for their country, and never of killing for their country.

27 Really high-minded people are indifferent to happiness, especially other people's.

28 The belief in the goodness of God is inversely proportional to the evidence.

29 The fact that an opinion has been widely held is no evidence whatever that it is not utterly absurd; indeed in view of the silliness of the majority of mankind, a widespread belief is more likely to be foolish than sensible.

30 The infliction of cruelty with a good conscience is a delight to moralists. That is why they invented Hell.

31 The megalomaniac differs from the narcissist by the fact that he wishes to be powerful rather than charming, and seeks to be feared rather than loved. To this type belong many lunatics and most of the great men in history.

32 The place of the father in the modern suburban family is a very small one, particularly if he plays golf.

33 The trouble with the world is that the stupid are cocksure and the intelligent full of doubt.

34 The truth is—and it's merciful—that in memory, humiliations and failures tend to vanish and successes are magnified.

35 The whiter my hair becomes, the more ready people are to believe what I say.

36 The whole conception of "sin" is one which I find very puzzling, doubtless owing to my sinful nature.

37 There's a Bible on that shelf there. But I keep it next to Voltaire—poison and antidote.

38 To die for one's beliefs is to put too high a price on conjecture. [Attributed.]

39 To fear love is to fear life, and those who fear life are already three parts dead.

40 We believe, first and foremost, what makes us feel that we are fine fellows.

41 We have two kinds of morality side by side: one which we preach but do not practice, and another which we practice but seldom preach.

42 We must be skeptical even of our skepticism.

43 When we pass in review the opinions of former times which are now recognized as absurd, it will be found that nine times out of ten they were such as to justify the infliction of suffering.

44 You mustn't exaggerate, young man. That's always a sign that your argument is weak.

GEORGE HERMAN "BABE" RUTH (1895–1948). *American baseball player*

Why not, I had a better year than he did. [Remark, during the Depression, to a reporter who had objected to Ruth's demanding $80,000 for the 1931 season, $5,000 more than President Herbert Hoover's salary.]

LOUIS A. SAFIAN (20th century). *American writer*
There are more important things than money—the only trouble is they all cost money.

WILLIAM SAFIRE (1929–). *American presidential speechwriter and journalist*

1 A pundit is an expert on nothing but an authority on everything.

2 Americans of all political persuasions are coming to the sad realization that our First Lady—a woman of undoubted talents who was a role model for many in her generation—is a congenital liar. [On Hillary Rodham Clinton, 1996.]

3 Appeasement does not always lead to war; sometimes it leads to surrender.

4 Cover your ass—the bureaucrat's method of protecting his posterior from posterity.

5 Create your own constituency of the infuriated. [Formula for writing a successful newspaper column.]

6 I'm a right-wing Republican; I'm conservative veering toward reactionary. The big moment of my year comes in October when daylight savings ends, and you can actually turn back the clock.

7 If I've told you once, I've told you a thousand times: resist hyperbole.

8 Limousine Liberal: one who takes up hunger as a cause but has never felt a pang; who will talk at length about the public school system but sends his children to private schools.

9 Never use a long word when a diminutive one will do.

10 News expands to fill the time and space allocated to its coverage.

11 Republican: an advocate of a democratic form of government, as a Democrat is an advocate of a republican form of government.

12 The reason pandas have reduplicating names like Ling-Ling and Hsing-Hsing is that they can't hear well and zoo keepers have to call them twice.

13 The trick in eating crow is to pretend it tastes good.

14 The truest truism in politics is: you can't beat Somebody with Nobody. [On elections.]

15 Whenever "whom" is required, recast the sentence. This keeps a huge section of the hard disk of your mind available for baseball averages.

16 Whose side is God on in the 1992 presidential race? His side.

MORT SAHL (1927–). *American comedian*

1 A conservative doesn't want anything to happen for the first time; a liberal feels it should happen, but not now.

2 I used to go out exclusively with actresses and other female impersonators.

3 Liberals feel unworthy of their possessions; conservatives feel they deserve everything they've stolen.

4 You haven't lived until you've died in California.

SAKI (H. H. Munro, 1870–1916). *Burmese-born British short-story writer*

1 A little inaccuracy sometimes saves tons of explanation.

2 All decent people live beyond their incomes nowadays, and those who aren't respectable live beyond other people's. A few gifted individuals manage to do both. [1911]

3 Beauty is only sin deep. —See also Jean Kerr 4; Herbert Spencer 3

4 But, good gracious, you've got to educate him first. You can't expect a boy to be vicious till he's been to a good school.

5 Every profession has its secrets: if it hadn't, it wouldn't be a profession.

6 I think she must have been very strictly brought up. She's so desperately anxious to do the wrong thing correctly.

7 The cook was a good cook, as cooks go; and as good cooks go, she went.

8 The people of Crete unfortunately make more history than they can consume locally.

9 The young have aspirations that never come to pass, the old have reminiscences of what never happened.

10 Waldo is one of those people who would be enormously improved by death.

11 We all know that prime ministers are wedded to the truth, but like other married couples they sometimes live apart.

12 You're looking nicer than usual, but that's so easy for you.

J. D. SALINGER (1919–). *American novelist and short-story writer*

1 Half the time, if you really want to know the truth, when I'm horsing around with a girl I have a helluva lot of trouble just finding what I'm looking for, for God's sake, if you know what I mean. Take this girl that I just missed having sexual intercourse with, that I told you about. It took me about an hour just to get her goddam brassière off. By the time I did get it off, she was about ready to spit in my eye.

2 I am a kind of paranoiac in reverse. I suspect people of plotting to make me happy.

3 I'm the most terrific liar you ever saw in your life. It's awful. If I'm on my way to the store to buy a magazine, even, and somebody asks me where I'm going, I'm liable to say I'm going to the opera. It's terrible.

4 If you really want to hear about it, the first thing you'll probably want to know is where I was born, and what my lousy childhood was like, and how my parents were occupied and all before they had me, and all that David Copperfield kind of crap, but I don't feel like going into it, if you want to know the truth. [Opening words, *The Catcher in the Rye*, 1951.]

5 "Life *is* a game, boy. Life *is* a game that one plays according to the rules." "Yes, sir. I know it is. I know it." Game my ass. Some game. If you get on the side where all the hot-shots are, then it's a game, all right—I'll admit that. But if you get on the *other* side, where there aren't any hot-shots, then what's a game about it? Nothing. No game.

6 Sally said I was a sacrilegious atheist. I probably am. The thing that Jesus *really* would've liked would be the guy that plays the kettle drums in the orchestra.

7 Sex is something I really don't understand too hot. You never know *where* the hell you are. I keep making up these sex rules for myself, and then I break them right away.

8 Take most people, they're crazy about cars. They worry if they get a little scratch on them, and they're always talking about how many miles they get to a gallon. I'd rather have a goddam horse. A horse is at least *human,* for God's sake.

9 That's the thing about girls. Every time they do something pretty, even if they're not much to look at, or even if they're sort of stupid, you fall half in love with them, and then you never know *where* you are.

10 What really knocks me out is a book that, when you're all done reading it, you wish the author that wrote it was a terrific friend of yours and you could call him up on the phone whenever you felt like it. That doesn't happen much though.

GEORGE SAND (Amandine Aurore Lucile Dupin Dudevant, 1804–1876). *French novelist*

Vanity is the quicksand of reason.

CARL SANDBURG (1874–1965). *American poet and biographer*

1 A baby is God's opinion that life should go on.

2 A politician should have three hats: one for throwing in the ring, one for talking through, and one for pulling rabbits out of if elected.

3 "How are crops this year?" / "Not so good for a good year / but not so bad for a bad year."

4 "How do you do, my farmer friend?" / "Howdy." / "Nice looking country you have here." / "Fer them that likes it." / "Live here all your life?" / "Not yit."

5 I am an idealist. I don't know where I'm going, but I'm on my way.

6 I was up day and night with Lincoln for years. I couldn't have picked a better companion. [On the writing of his multivolume biography of Abraham Lincoln.]

7 In these times you have to be an optimist to open your eyes when you awake in the morning.

8 Money is power, freedom, a cushion, / the root of all evil, the sum of blessings.

9 Poetry is the achievement of the synthesis of hyacinths and biscuits.

10 Slang is a language that rolls up its sleeves, spits on its hands and goes to work.

11 Sometime they'll give a war and nobody will come.

12 The drama of politics is only the people running around trying to change one gang of bandits for another gang of bandits.

13 The history of the world and its peoples in three words—"Born, troubled, died."

14 The past is a bucket of ashes.

15 This old anvil laughs at many broken hammers. / There are men who can't be bought.

16 To never see a fool, you lock yourself in your room and smash the looking glass.

17 Why does a hearse horse snicker / Hauling a lawyer away?

GEORGE SANDERS (1906–1972). *British actor*

1 An actor is not quite a human being—but then, who is?

2 Dear World, I am leaving you because I am bored. I feel I have lived long enough. I am leaving you with your worries in this sweet cesspool. Good luck. [Suicide note.]

ADAM SANDLER (1966–). *American comedian and actor*

I was in New Hampshire with my family at a pizza place. The kid working there goes, "Hey, you look like Adam Sandler." I said, "Yeah, I know." He goes, "What's your name?" I go, "Adam Sandler." And he goes, "Whoa, that's a coincidence."

GEORGE SANTAYANA (1863–1952). *Spanish-born American philosopher*

1 Fanaticism consists in redoubling your effort when you have forgotten your aim.

2 Fashion is something barbarous, for it produces innovation without reason and imitation without benefit.

3 Few revolutionists would be such if they were heirs to a baronetcy.

4 It is a great advantage for a system of philosophy to be substantially true.

5 It is easier to make a saint out of a libertine than out of a prig.

6 Music is essentially useless, as life is.

7 Mysticism is not a religion but a religious disease.

8 Sanity is madness put to good use.

9 Skepticism is the chastity of the intellect.

10 Society is like the air, necessary to breathe but insufficient to live on.

11 The fact of having been born is a bad augury for immortality.

12 The world is a perpetual caricature of itself; at every moment it is the mockery and the contradiction of what it is pretending to be.

13 There is no cure for birth and death save to enjoy the interval.

14 Those who cannot remember the past are condemned to repeat it.

15 To call war the soil of courage and virtue is like calling debauchery the soil of love.

FATHER GUIDO SARDUCCI (20th century). *American comedian*

Five-Minute University teaches you in five minutes what the average college student remembers five years after he or she's out of school. Say, if you want to take Spanish, what I teach you is "Cómo está usted?" That means "How are you?" And the response is "Muy bien." That means "Very well." And believe me, if you took two years of college Spanish, five years after you're out of school, "Cómo está usted" and "Muy bien" is about all you're gonna remember. So in my school that's all you learn. Economics? "Supply and demand." That's it!

JEAN-PAUL SARTRE (1905–1980). *French philosopher*

1 Freedom is what you do with what's been done to you.

2 Hell is other people.

3 I confused things with their names: that is belief.

4 Like all dreamers, I mistook disenchantment for truth.

5 Man is a useless passion.

6 My grandmother believed in nothing. Her skepticism alone kept her from being an atheist.

7 The game of the Nazis and their collaborators was to blur ideas. The Pétain regime called itself a revolution, and things reached such a point of absurdity that one day the following headline appeared in the *Gerbe:* "The motto of the National Revolution is—hold fast." [1946]

8 The world could get along very well without literature; it could get along even better without man.

DOROTHY L. SAYERS (1893–1957). *British writer*

1 As I grow older and older / And totter towards the tomb / I find that I care less and less / Who goes to bed with whom.

2 I always have a quotation for everything—it saves original thinking.

FRIEDRICH von SCHILLER (1759–1805). *German poet and playwright*
Against stupidity, the gods themselves struggle in vain.

PHYLLIS SCHLAFLY (1924–). *American writer*
The claim that American women are downtrodden and unfairly treated is the fraud of the century. The truth is that American women have never had it so good. Why should we lower ourselves to "equal rights" when we already have the status of special privilege?

ARTHUR M. SCHLESINGER, JR. (1917–). *American historian and presidential assistant*

1 Economists are about as useful as astrologers in predicting the future (and, like astrologers, they never let failure on one occasion diminish certitude on the next).

2 Political campaigns tend to be exercises in progressive degeneration.

3 The first rule of democracy is to distrust all leaders who begin to believe their own publicity.

4 The statesman who is surest that he can divine the future most urgently invites his own retribution.

ARTHUR SCHOPENHAUER (1788–1860). *German philosopher*

1 Anyone can sympathize with another's sorrow, but to sympathize with another's joy is the attribute of an angel.

2 Envy is the moving spirit of that alliance everywhere made by mediocrity against individual eminence.

3 Every evening we are poorer by a day.

4 Every nation mocks at other nations, and all are right.

5 Freedom of the press is to the machinery of the state what the safety valve is to the steam engine.

6 If there is nothing to cause me misery, I am tormented by the thought that there must be something hidden from me.

7 It is a source of consolation to look back upon those great misfortunes which never happened.

8   Many learned persons have read themselves stupid.

9   Many people try to conceal their poverty of thought under a flood of verbiage.

10 Should you ever intend to dull the wits of a young man and to incapacitate his brains for any kind of thought whatever, then you cannot do better than give him Hegel to read.

11 The closing years of life are like the end of a masquerade party, when the masks are dropped.

12 The main difference between youth and age is that while the one has a short past and a long future before it, the case is just the opposite with the other.

13 The man who comes into the world with the notion that he is really going to instruct it in matters of the highest importance, may thank his stars if he escapes with his whole skin.

14 The state is never interested in truth, but rather always only in that truth that is useful to it, or, more precisely, in everything that is useful to it, be it truth, half-truth, or error.

15 There is no absurdity so palpable but that it may be firmly planted in the human head if you only begin to inculcate it before the age of five, by constantly repeating it with an air of great solemnity.

16 What makes people hard-hearted is this, that each man has, or fancies he has, as much as he can bear of his own troubles.

17 Who writes for fools is always sure of a large audience.

PATRICIA SCHROEDER (1940–). *American congresswoman*

1   Compassion is not measured by how many people are on food stamps.

2   "Have you ever committed adultery?" No, but then most congresswomen don't have twenty-five-year-old lifeguards throwing themselves at their feet around this place.

3   I was cooking breakfast this morning for my kids, and I thought, "He's just like a Teflon frying pan: nothing sticks to him." [On Ronald Reagan's ability to take criticism, 1984.]

4   Washington is awash in post-war testosterone. [Following the Gulf War victory in 1991.]

BUDD SCHULBERG (1914–). *American novelist and screenwriter*

1   A powder-puff punch and a glass jaw—that's a great combination!

2   Do it to him before he does it to you.

3   Going through a life with a conscience is like driving your car with the brakes on. [Spoken by Sammy Glick in Schulberg's 1941 novel *What Makes Sammy Run.*]

CHARLES M. SCHULZ (1922–2000). *American cartoonist*

1   "After you've died, do you get to come back?" [Linus] "If they stamp your hand." [Charlie Brown, in the comic strip *Peanuts.*]

2   Daytime is so you can see where you're going. Nighttime is so you can lie in bed worrying. [Sally]

3 Good grief, Charlie Brown. [Catchphrase.]

4 *Happiness Is a Warm Puppy*. [Book title, 1962.]

5 "I apologize for being late to your party." [Charlie Brown on the phone] "I didn't even know you weren't here." [Host]

6 I can't live without that blanket. I can't face life unarmed.

7 I love mankind—it's people I can't stand.

8 Jogging is very beneficial. It's very good for your legs and your feet. It's also very good for the ground. It makes it feel needed.

9 "Life is difficult, isn't it, Charlie Brown?" [Lucy] "Yes, it is, but I've developed a new philosophy: I only dread one day at a time!"

10 More health tips: eat lots of fruits and vegetables, get plenty of exercise and learn to duck. [Snoopy]

11 Never try to lick ice cream off a hot sidewalk!

12 No problem is too big to run away from.

13 Nothing takes the taste out of peanut butter quite like unrequited love.

14 There's no heavier burden than a great potential. [Linus]

15 You are a foul ball in the line drive of life. [Lucy]

16 "You got sort of nervous when she walked by, didn't you, Charlie Brown?" [Linus] "What makes you think I got nervous?" "You tied your peanut butter sandwich in a knot."

E. F. SCHUMACHER (1911–1971). *German-born British economist*
It is amazing how much theory we can do without when work actually begins.

JOSEPH A. SCHUMPETER (1883–1950). *Austrian-born American economist*

1 Democracy is the surrogate faith of intellectuals deprived of religion.

2 The question that is so clearly in many potential parents' minds: "Why should we stunt our ambitions and impoverish our lives in order to be insulted and looked down upon in our old age?"

3 When I was a young man, I wanted to be three things: I wanted to be the world's greatest horseman, the world's greatest economist, and the world's greatest lover. Unfortunately, I never became the world's greatest horseman. [Attributed.]

H. NORMAN SCHWARZKOPF (1934–). *American general*
As far as Saddam Hussein being a great military strategist, he is neither a strategist, nor is he schooled in the operational art, nor is he a tactician, nor is he a general, nor is he a soldier. Other than that, he's a great military man. [Referring to the Iraqi leader's military role during the Gulf War, 1991.]

ALBERT SCHWEITZER (1875–1965). *German physician, theologian, musician, and philosopher*

1 Happiness? That's nothing more than health and a poor memory.

2 In case my life should end with the cannibals, I hope they will write on my tombstone, "We have eaten Dr. Schweitzer. He was good to the end."

3 The tragedy of man is what dies inside himself while he still lives. —See also Seneca the Younger 8

HAZEL SCOTT (1920–1981). *Trinidad-born American pianist, singer, and actress*

1 Any woman who has a lot to offer the world is in trouble.

2 Who ever walked behind anyone to freedom? If we can't go hand in hand, I don't want to go.

FLORIDA SCOTT-MAXWELL (1884–1979). *American writer and suffragist*

No matter how old a mother is, she watches her middle-aged children for signs of improvement.

TOM SEAVER (1944–). *American baseball player*

There's a fine line between being brave and being stupid.

PETE SEEGER (1919–). *American folk singer and songwriter*

Do you know the difference between education and experience? Education is when you read the fine print; experience is what you get when you don't.

ERICH SEGAL (1937–). *American novelist*

Love means not ever having to say you're sorry. [Closing line in *Love Story*, 1970; in the screen version of the novel "never" replaced "not ever."]

SENECA THE YOUNGER (4? B.C.–A.D. 65). *Roman philosopher and statesman*

1 If the number of our diseases surprises you, count our cooks.

2 Many men would have arrived at wisdom had they not believed themselves to have arrived there already.

3 No one becomes a laughingstock who laughs at himself.

4 Socrates, it is said, when once he received a box on the ear, merely declared that it was too bad that a man could not tell when he ought to wear a helmet while taking a walk.

5 Successful crime is called virtue.

6 The coward calls himself cautious; the miser, thrifty.

7 The sins of others we keep before our eyes; our own, behind our backs.

8 The worst evil of all is to leave the ranks of the living before one dies. — See also Albert Schweitzer 3

9 To know how many are envious of you, count your admirers.

10 We check manslaughter and isolated murders; but what of war and the much-vaunted crime of slaughtering whole peoples?

11 When you want to be praised sincerely, why be indebted to someone else for it? Praise yourself.

MACK SENNETT (1880–1960). *Canadian-born American film producer*

1 There are only a handful of possible jokes. The chief members of this joke band may be said to be: the fall of dignity and mistaken identity.

2 We never make fun of religion, politics, race or mothers. A mother never gets hit with a custard pie. Mothers-in-law, yes. But mothers, never!

WILLIAM SHAKESPEARE (1564–1616). *English playwright and poet*

1 A politician, one that would circumvent God. [*Hamlet.*]

2 Away, you scullion! You rampallion! You fustilarian! I'll tickle your catastrophe. [*Henry IV, Pt. 2.*]

3 Brevity is the soul of wit. [*Hamlet.*] —See also W. Somerset Maugham 8; Dorothy Parker 2

4 Conscience does make cowards of us all. [*Hamlet.*] —See also Mignon McLaughlin 12; Leo Rosten 6

5 Everyone can master a grief but he that has it. [*Much Ado About Nothing.*] —See also François de La Rochefoucauld 35; Alexander Pope 10

6 Have more than thou showest, / Speak less than thou knowest, / Lend less than thou owest. [*King Lear.*]

7 He jests at scars that never felt a wound. [*Romeo and Juliet.*]

8 He ploughed her, and she cropped. [*Antony and Cleopatra.*]

9 Honorificabilitudinitatibus. [*Love's Labour's Lost.*] —See also Lewis Carroll 12

10 I am not only witty in myself, but the cause that wit is in other men. [*Henry IV, Pt. 2.*] —See also Samuel Foote

11 I do desire we may be better strangers. [*As You Like It.*]

12 I wasted time, and now doth time waste me. [*Richard II.*]

13 If it be now, 'tis not to come; if it be not to come, it will be now; if it be not now, yet it will come: the readiness is all. [*Hamlet.*]

14 It is a custom more honored in the breach than the observance. [*Hamlet.*]

15 It is a wise father that knows his own child. [*The Merchant of Venice.*]

16 Let me have no lying: it becomes none but tradesmen. [*The Winter's Tale.*]

17 Look, he's winding up the watch of his wit, by and by it will strike. [*The Tempest.*]

18 "Master, I marvel how the fishes live in the sea." [3rd Fisherman] "Why, as men do a-land; the great ones eat up the little ones." [1st Fisherman, *Pericles.*]

19 Misery acquaints a man with strange bedfellows. [*The Tempest.*] —See also Anonymous 98; Groucho Marx 17; Charles Dudley Warner 2

20 My bounty is as boundless as the sea, / My love as deep; the more I give to thee, / The more I have, for both are infinite. [*Romeo and Juliet.*]

21 O monstrous world! Take note, take note, O world, to be direct and honest is not safe. [*Othello.*]

22 Some rise by sin, and some by virtue fall. [*Measure for Measure.*]

23 Still you keep o' the windy side of the law. [*Twelfth Night.*]

24 Suit the action to the word, the word to the action. [*Hamlet.*]

25 The eagle suffers little birds to sing. [*Titus Andronicus.*]

26 The fashion wears out more apparel than the man. [*Much Ado About Nothing.*]

27 The first thing we do, let's kill all the lawyers. [*Henry VI, Pt. 2.*]

28 There was never yet philosopher that could endure the toothache patiently. [*Much Ado About Nothing.*]

29 There's hope a great man's memory may outlive his life half a year. [*Hamlet.*]

30 They have a plentiful lack of wit. [*Hamlet.*]

31 This fellow is wise enough to play the fool. [*Twelfth Night.*]

32 Though I am not naturally honest, I am so sometimes by chance. [*The Winter's Tale.*]

33 Though this be madness, yet there is method in't. [*Hamlet.*]

34 Unbidden guests are often welcomest when they are gone. [*Henry VI, Pt. 1.*]

35 "What do you read, my lord?" [Polonius] "Words, words, words." [Hamlet, *Hamlet.*]

36 "What's the news?" [Hamlet] "None, my lord, but that the world's grown honest." [Rosencrantz] "Then is doomsday near: but your news is not true." [Hamlet, *Hamlet.*]

37 When I tell him, he hates flatterers, he says he does, being then most flattered. [*Julius Caesar.*]

38 When my love swears that she is made of truth / I do believe her, though I know she lies. [Sonnet.]

39 When sorrows come, they come not single spies, but in battalions. [*Hamlet.*]

40 Words are grown so false, I am loath to prove reason with them. [*Twelfth Night.*]

41 You are not worth the dust which the rude wind blows in your face. [*King Lear.*]

GEORGE BERNARD SHAW (1856–1950). *Anglo-Irish playwright and critic*

1 A doctor's reputation is made by the number of eminent men who die under his care.

2 A drama critic is someone who leaves no turn unstoned.

3 A government which robs Peter to pay Paul can always depend on the support of Paul.

4 A learned man is an idler who kills time by study.

5 A man of great common sense and good taste—meaning thereby a man without originality or moral courage.

6 A man who never missed an occasion to let slip an opportunity.

7 A perpetual holiday is a good working definition of hell.

8 A pessimist is a man who thinks everybody is as nasty as himself, and hates them for it.

9 A true journalist is fact-proof.

10 All professions are conspiracies against the laity.

11 All very serious revolutionary propositions begin as huge jokes. Otherwise they would be stamped out by the lynching of their first exponents.

12 An Englishman does everything on principle. He fights you on patriotic principles; he robs you on business principles; he enslaves you on imperial principles.

13 An Englishman thinks he is moral when he is only uncomfortable.

14 Anarchism is a game at which the police can beat you.

15 Assassination is the extreme form of censorship.

16 Baseball has the great advantage over cricket of being sooner ended.

17 Beware of the man whose god is in the skies.

18 Celibacy is a worse failure than marriage.

19 Christianity never got any grip of the world until it virtually reduced its claims on the ordinary citizen's attention to a couple of hours every seventh day, and let him alone on weekdays.

20 Critics, like other people, see what they look for, not what is actually before them.

21 Cusins is a very nice fellow, certainly: nobody would ever guess that he was born in Australia.

22 Dancing is a perpendicular expression of a horizontal desire.

23 Decadence can find agents only when it wears the mask of progress.

24 Decency is indecency's conspiracy of silence.

25 Democracy is a device that insures we shall be governed no better than we deserve.

26 Democracy substitutes selection by the incompetent many for appointment by the corrupt few.

27 Do not do unto others as you would they should do unto you. Their tastes may not be the same.

28 "Do you really never drink any wine at all?" [Winston Churchill] I am hard enough to keep in order as it is.

29 Each generation thinks the world is progressing because it is always moving. But a pendulum moves.

30 England and America are two countries divided by the same language. [Attributed.] —See also Oscar Wilde 130

31 Englishmen never will be slaves; they are free to do whatever the government and public opinion allow them to do.

32 Every man over forty is a scoundrel.

33 Everything happens to everybody sooner or later if there is time enough.

34 Fashions are only induced epidemics.

35 Few people think more than two or three times a year; I have made an international reputation for myself by thinking once or twice a week.

36 First love is only a little foolishness and a lot of curiosity.

37 Fools are more dangerous than rogues.

38 Gambling promises the poor what property performs for the rich.

39 "Have you no morals, man?" [Pickering] "Can't afford them, Governor. Neither could you if you was as poor as me." [Alfred Doolittle, in the 1912 play *Pygmalion*.]

40 He knows nothing, and he thinks he knows everything. That points clearly to a political career.

41 He who can, does. He who cannot, teaches.

42 He who would reform himself must first reform society. —See also Josh Billings 67

43 He's a devout believer in the department of witchcraft called medical science.

44 Home is the girl's prison and the woman's workhouse.

45 I am a beer teetotaler, not a champagne teetotaler. I don't like beer.

46 I am a millionaire. That is my religion.

47 I have never thought much of the courage of a lion tamer; inside the cage he is, at least, safe from other men.

48 I have to live for others and not for myself: that's middle-class morality.

49 I often quote myself; it adds spice to my conversation.

50 I see plenty of good in the world working itself out as fast as the idealists will allow it.

51 I would have been bored silly if I hadn't been there myself.

52 "I'm a brigand: I live by robbing the rich." [Mendoza] "I'm a gentleman: I live by robbing the poor." [Tanner, in the 1903 play *Man and Superman.*]

53 If a great man could make us understand him, we should hang him.

54 If all economists were laid end to end, they would not reach a conclusion.

55 If I were not a gloriously successful person, in England they would have dismissed me as an Irishman and in America as a socialist. [Shaw was born in Dublin and moved to England at 20.]

56 If parents would only realize how they bore their children.

57 If you rebel against high-heeled shoes, take care to do it in a very smart hat.

58 In heaven an angel is nobody in particular.

59 In literature the ambition of the novice is to acquire the literary language; the struggle of the adept is to get rid of it.

60 It is dangerous to be sincere unless you are also stupid.

61 It is greatly to Mrs. Patrick Campbell's credit that, bad as the play was, her acting was worse.

62 It is nearly 50 years since I was assured by a conclave of doctors that if I did not eat meat, I should die of starvation.

63 Kings are not born: they are made by universal hallucination.

64 Lack of money is the root of all evil. [Attributed; compare Paul's aphorism in I Timothy 6:10, "The love of money is the root of all evil."]

65 Leave it to the coward to make a religion of his cowardice by preaching humility.

66 Liberty means responsibility. That's why most men dread it.

67 Life is not meant to be easy, my child; but take courage: it can be delightful.

68 Madam, if I gave you a million pounds, would you have sexual intercourse with me? [Shaw to a woman at a dinner party.] "I think I would." [The woman replied after a pause.] Would you do it for a fiver? "Sir, what kind of woman do you think I am?" I thought we had established that, and were merely haggling over the price. [Attributed.]

69 Man is the only animal which esteems itself rich in proportion to the number and voracity of its parasites.

70 Marriage is popular because it combines the maximum of temptation with the maximum of opportunity.

71 Marriage is the most licentious of human institutions. That is the secret of its popularity.

72 Martyrdom, sir, is what these people like: it is the only way in which a man can become famous without ability.

73 Men have to do some awfully mean things to keep up their respectability.

74 Miss Warren is a great devotee of the Gospel of Getting On.

75 My capers are part of a bigger design than you think: Shakespeare, for instance, is to me one of the Towers of the Bastille, and down he must come. [Letter, 1897.]

76 My own education operated by a succession of eye-openers each involving the repudiation of some previously held belief.

77 My specialty is being right when other people are wrong.

78 My way of joking is to tell the truth. It's the funniest joke in the world.

79 Nothing succeeds like failure. —See also G. K. Chesterton 20; Alexandre Dumas 2

80 "One look at you, Mr. Shaw, and I know there's famine in the land." [Alfred Hitchcock] One look at you, Mr. Hitchcock, and I know who caused it. [The oversized and the undersized sizing each other up.]

81 Our ideals, like the gods of old, are constantly demanding human sacrifices.

82 Our middle classes, who are comfortable and irresponsible at other people's expense, are neither ashamed of that condition nor even conscious of it.

83 Our prejudices are so deeply rooted that we never think of them as prejudices but call them common sense.

84 Our professed devotion to political principles is only a mask for our idolatry of eminent persons.

85 Patriotism is your conviction that this country is superior to all other countries because you were born in it.

86 People always exaggerate the value of the things they haven't got.

87 People become attached to their burdens sometimes more than the burdens are attached to them.

88 Poverty is mainly the result of organized robbery and oppression (politely called Capitalism).

89 Power does not corrupt men; fools, however, if they get into a position of power, corrupt power. —See also Lord Acton 2

90 Put an Irishman on the spit, and you can always get another Irishman to turn him.

91 Revolutions have never lightened the burden of tyranny; they have only shifted it to another shoulder.

92 Self-denial is not a virtue: it is only the effect of prudence on rascality.

93 Self-sacrifice enables us to sacrifice others without blushing.

94 Smokers and non-smokers cannot be equally free in the same railway carriage.

95 Success covers a multitude of blunders.

96 Take care to get what you like or you will be forced to like what you get.

97 That is the use of money: it enables us to get what we want instead of what other people think we want.

98 The art of government is the organization of idolatry.

99 The characteristics that make a man eminent in one class ruin him in another. If you are a clerk, take care not to behave like a duke.

100 The fickleness of the women whom I love is only equaled by the infernal constancy of the women who love me.

101 The golden rule is that there are no golden rules.

102 The more things a man is ashamed of, the more respectable he is.

103 The most awful thing that one can do is to tell the truth. It's all right in my case because I am not taken seriously.

104 The nation's morals are like its teeth: the more decayed they are, the more it hurts to touch them.

105 The nauseous sham goodfellowship our democratic public men get up for shop use.

106 The 100 percent American is 99 percent idiot.

107 The only thing which provokes laughter is another's distress.

108 The people who get on in this world are the people who get up and look for the circumstances they want, and, if they don't find them, make them.

109 The power of accurate observation is commonly called cynicism by those who have not got it.

110 The reasonable man adapts himself to the world: the unreasonable one persists in trying to adapt the world to himself. Therefore all progress depends on the unreasonable man.

111 The savage bows down to idols of wood and stone: the civilized man to idols of flesh and blood.

112 The secret of being miserable is to have leisure to bother about whether you are happy or not.

113 The things most people want to know about are usually none of their business. [Attributed.]

114 The trouble with her is that she lacks the power of conversation but not the power of speech.

115 The true artist will let his wife starve, his children go barefoot, his mother drudge for his living at seventy, sooner than work at anything but his art.

116 The truth is the one thing nobody will believe.

117 There are two tragedies in life. One is to lose your heart's desire. The other is to gain it. —See also Oscar Wilde 53

118 There is a fashion in operations, as there is in sleeves and skirts.

119 There is no satisfaction in hanging a man who does not object to it.

120 There is only one religion, though there are a hundred versions of it.

121 This is the true joy in life, the being used for a purpose recognized by yourself as a mighty one; the being thoroughly worn out before you are thrown on the scrap heap; the being a force of Nature instead of a feverish, selfish, little clod of ailments and grievances complaining that the world will not devote itself to making you happy. [Epistle dedicatory to the 1903 play *Man and Superman*.]

122 Those who try to make life one long holiday find that they need a holiday from that too.

123 "Thou art a rare noodle, Master. Do what was done last time is thy rule, eh?" [Joan of Arc at her trial] "Thou wanton: dost thou dare call me noodle?" [Canon de Courcelles responding in anger, in the 1923 play *Saint Joan*.]

124 Titles distinguish the mediocre, embarrass the superior, and are disgraced by the inferior.

125 To a person with a toothache, even if the world is tottering, there is nothing more important than a visit to a dentist.

126 To live like a drone on the labor and service of others is to be a lady or a gentleman.

127 Under existing circumstances wealth cannot be enjoyed without dishonor or forgone without misery.

128 Very nice sort of place, Oxford, I should think, for people that like that sort of place. —See also Abraham Lincoln 5

129 Virtue is insufficient temptation.

130 We all bully as much as we dare.

131 We are told that when Jehovah created the world he saw that it was good. What would he say now?

132 We have not lost faith, but we have transferred it from God to the medical profession.

133 We learn from experience that men never learn anything from experience. —See also Georg Hegel 3

134 We must be thoroughly democratic, and patronize everybody without distinction of class.

135 We want a few mad people now. See where the sane ones have landed us!

136 We were not fairly beaten, my lord. No Englishman is ever fairly beaten.

137 Well, sir, you never can tell. That's a principle in life with me, sir, if you'll excuse my having such a thing, sir.

138 What God hath joined together no man ever shall put asunder: God will take care of that.

139 What is all human conduct but the daily and hourly sale of our souls for trifles?

140 What is life but a series of inspired follies?

141 What really flatters a man is that you think him worth flattering. —See also Ralph Waldo Emerson 37

142 What we call law and order is machinery for robbing the poor under legal forms.

143 When a man teaches something he does not know to somebody who has no aptitude for it and gives him a certificate of proficiency, the latter has undergone the education of a gentleman.

144 When a man wants to murder a tiger, he calls it sport: when the tiger wants to kill him, he calls it ferocity.

145 When a stupid man is doing something he is ashamed of, he always declares that it is his duty.

146 When a thing is funny, search it for a hidden truth.

147 When elephants fight, it's the grass that suffers.

148 When we want to read of the deeds that are done for love, whither do we turn? To the murder column.

149 Where there is no knowledge, ignorance calls itself knowledge.

150 Why, except as a means of livelihood, a man should desire to act on the stage when he has the whole world to act in, is not clear to me.

151 With the single exception of Homer, there is no eminent writer, not even Sir Walter Scott, whom I can despise so entirely as I despise Shakespeare when I measure my mind against his. It would be a relief to me to dig him up and throw stones at him. [1896]

152 "You have the greatest brain in the world, and I have the most beautiful body; so we ought to produce the most perfect child." [Unidentified woman proposing in a letter that she and Shaw have a child out of wedlock.] What if the child inherits my body and your brains? [Shaw wrote back.]

153 You must not suppose, because I am a man of letters, that I never tried to earn an honest living.

154 You must not tell lies because if you do you will find yourself unable to believe anything that is told to you.

155 Youth is a wonderful thing. What a crime to waste it on children!

FULTON J. SHEEN (1895–1979). *American bishop*
1 Baloney is flattery so thick it cannot be true; blarney is flattery so thin we like it.
2 Jealousy is the tribute mediocrity pays to genius.
3 The big print giveth and the fine print taketh away.

WILLIAM SHENSTONE (1714–1764). *English poet*
1 A fool and his words are soon parted. —See also Anonymous 1
2 We hate those faults most in others which we are guilty of ourselves.

PHILIP H. SHERIDAN (1831–1888). *American general*
If I owned Texas and Hell, I'd rent out Texas and live in Hell.

RICHARD SHERIDAN (1751–1816). *Irish playwright*
1 A wise woman will always let her husband have her way.
2 He is indebted to his memory for his jests and to his imagination for his facts.
3 I am, Sir, a Practitioner in Panegyric, or to speak more plainly—a Professor of the Art of Puffing, at your service—or anybody else's. [Spoken by Puff in *The Critic,* 1779.]
4 There is no possibility of being witty without a little ill-nature; the malice of a good thing is the barb that make it stick.

WILLIAM TECUMSEH SHERMAN (1820–1891). *American general*
1 "General, three members of the press were killed today by artillery fire." Good! Now we'll have news from hell before breakfast.
2 If forced to choose between the penitentiary and the White House for four years, I would say the penitentiary, thank you.
3 Vox populi, vox humbug! [Voice of the people, voice of humbug!]

GEORGE P. SHULTZ (1920–). *American secretary of state*
1 Don't just do something, stand there.
2 If I were married to her, I'd be sure to have dinner ready when she got home. [On Margaret Thatcher.]

SIMONE SIGNORET (1921–1985). *French actress*
He bore no grudge against those he had wronged. [On film producer Jack Warner.]

NEIL SIMON (1927–). *American playwright*
1 Housewife. You know, sleep-in maid.
2 It's like paradise, with a lobotomy. [On Los Angeles.]
3 The thought of death has now become a part of my life. I read the obituaries every day just for the satisfaction of not seeing my name there.
4 You're welcome to take a bath. You look like the second week of the garbage strike.

ALAN SIMPSON (1931–). *Wyoming senator*
Do you folks know the difference between a horse race and a political campaign? In a horse race, the whole horse runs.

UPTON SINCLAIR (1878–1968). *American novelist and social reformer*
It is difficult to get a man to understand something when his salary depends upon his not understanding it.

EDITH SITWELL (1887–1964). *English poet and writer*
1 I am one of those unhappy persons who inspire bores to the highest flights of their art.
2 I have often wished I had time to cultivate modesty, but I am too busy thinking about myself.
3 The aim of flattery is to soothe and encourage us by assuring us of the truth of an opinion we have already formed about ourselves.

RED SKELTON (1913–1997). *American comedian and actor*
1 I have a sixth sense, but not the other five. If I wasn't making money, they'd put me away.
2 Well, it only proves what they always say—give the public something they want to see, and they'll come out for it. [On the crowd attending the funeral of film producer Harry Cohen; attributed.]

ADAM SMITH (1723–1790). *Scottish economist and philosopher*
1 People of the same trade seldom meet together, even for merriment and diversion, but the conversation ends in a conspiracy against the public, or in some contrivance to raise prices.
2 There is no art which one government sooner learns from another than that of draining money from the pockets of the people.

AL SMITH (1872–1944). *New York governor*
1 All the ills of democracy can be cured by more democracy. —See also H. L. Mencken 85
2 No matter how thin you slice it, it's still baloney. [On the New Deal, 1936.] —See also Clare Booth Luce 4
3 "Tell 'em what's on your mind, Al. It won't take long." [Heckler during one of Smith's speeches] Stand up, pardner, and I'll tell 'em what's on both our minds. It won't take any longer.

HORACE SMITH (1779–1849). *English writer and humorist*

An absurdity is anything advanced by our opponents, contrary to our own practice, or above our comprehension.

LOGAN PEARSALL SMITH (1865–1946). *English writer and critic*

1 All reformers, however strict their social conscience, live in houses just as big as they can pay for.

2 An improper mind is a perpetual feast.

3 Don't laugh at a youth for his affectations; he is only trying on one face after another to find his own.

4 He who goes against fashion is himself its slave.

5 How can they say my life isn't a success? Have I not for more than sixty years got enough to eat and escaped being eaten?

6 I cannot forgive my friends for dying; I do not find these vanishing acts of theirs at all amusing.

7 I might give up my life for my friend, but he had better not ask me to do up a parcel.

8 If you eradicate a fault, you leave room for a worse one to take root and flourish.

9 If you want to be thought a liar, always tell the truth.

10 It is the wretchedness of being rich that you have to live with rich people.

11 Married women are kept women, and they are beginning to find it out.

12 Most people sell their souls and live with a good conscience on the proceeds.

13 People say that life is the thing, but I prefer reading.

14 Solvency is entirely a matter of temperament and not of income.

15 Thank heavens! The sun has gone in, and I don't have to go out and enjoy it.

16 The denunciation of the young is a necessary part of the hygiene of older people, and greatly assists the circulation of their blood.

17 There are few sorrows, however poignant, in which a good income is of no avail.

18 There are two things to aim at in life: first, to get what you want; and, after that, to enjoy it. Only the wisest of mankind achieve the second.

19 Those who set out to serve both God and Mammon soon discover that there is no God.

20 To suppose, as we all suppose, that we could be rich and not behave as the rich behave, is like supposing that we could drink all day and keep absolutely sober.

21 What I like in a good author is not what he says, but what he whispers.

22 What is more mortifying than to feel that you have missed the plum for want of courage to shake the tree?

23 When they come downstairs from their ivory towers, idealists are apt to walk straight into the gutter.

STEVIE SMITH (Florence Margaret Smith, 1902–1971). *English poet and novelist*

People who are always praising the past / And especially the times of faith as best / Ought to go and live in the Middle Ages / And be burnt at the stake as witches and sages.

SYDNEY SMITH (1771–1845). *English clergyman*

1 Among the smaller duties of life, I hardly know any one more important than that of not praising where praise is not due.

2 Daniel Webster struck me much like a steam engine in trousers.

3 He has occasional flashes of silence, that make his conversation perfectly delightful. [On Thomas Babington Macaulay.]

4 I am going to pray for you at St. Paul's, but with no very lively hope of success.

5 I like him and his wife; he is so ladylike, and she is such a perfect gentleman.

6 I never read a book before reviewing it; it prejudices a man so.

7 In composing, as a general rule, run your pen through every other word you have written; you have no idea what vigor it will give your style.

8 In this world the salary or reward is always in the inverse ratio of the duties performed.

9 It would be an entertaining change in human affairs to determine everything by minorities; they are almost always in the right.

10 Marriage resembles a pair of shears, so joined that they cannot be separated; often moving in opposite directions, yet always punishing anyone who comes between them.

11 The observances of the church concerning feasts and fasts are tolerably well kept since the rich keep the feasts and the poor keep the fasts.

12 There are very few who would not rather be hated than laughed at.

13 There is not the least use in preaching to anyone unless you chance to catch them ill.

14 What a pity it is we have no amusements in England but vice and religion!

15 What you don't know would make a great book.

16 When I am in the pulpit, I have the pleasure of seeing my audience nod approbation while they sleep.

WALTER "RED" SMITH (1905–1982). *American sportswriter*

Writing a column is easy. I just sit down at the typewriter, open a vein and bleed it out.

TOBIAS SMOLLETT (1721–1771). *Scottish novelist*

1 Hark, ye Clinker, you are a most notorious offender. You stand convicted of sickness, hunger, wretchedness, and want. [*Humphrey Clinker*, 1771.]

2 I am pent up in frowsy lodgings, where there is not room enough to swing a cat.

3 I think for my part one half of the nation is mad—and the other not very sound.

C. P. SNOW (1905–1980). *English physicist and writer*

1 Civilization is hideously fragile and there's not much between us and the horrors underneath, just about a coat of varnish.

2 Technology is a queer thing. It brings you great gifts with one hand, and it stabs you in the back with the other.

GARY SNYDER (1930–). *American poet*

1 Three-fourths of philosophy and literature is the talk of people trying to convince themselves that they really like the cage they were tricked into entering.

2 Ultimately, cities may exist only as joyous tribal gatherings and fairs, to dissolve after a few weeks.

SOCRATES (470?–399 B.C.). *Greek philosopher*

1 Although I do not suppose that either of us knows anything really beautiful and good, I am better off than he is—for he knows nothing, and thinks that he knows; I neither know nor think that I know.

2 I have a sufficient witness to the truth of what I say—my poverty.

3 I was really too honest a man to be a politician and live.

4 Whether you choose marriage or celibacy, you'll repent it.

5 Why do you wonder that traveling does not help you, seeing that you always take yourself with you? The reason which set you wandering is ever at your heels.

STEPHEN SONDHEIM (1930–). *American composer and lyricist*

My father is a bastard / My ma's an S.O.B. / My grandpa's always plastered / My grandma pushes tea / My sister wears a moustache / My brother wears a dress / Goodness gracious, that's why I'm a mess. ["Gee, Officer Krupke," in the 1957 musical *West Side Story*.]

SUSAN SONTAG (1933–). *American writer*

1 He who despises himself esteems himself as a great self-despiser.

2 I envy paranoids; they actually feel people are paying attention to them.

3 Interpretation is the revenge of the intellect upon art.

4 Religion is probably, after sex, the second oldest resource which human beings have available to them for blowing their minds.

5 The camera makes everyone a tourist in other people's reality, and eventually in one's own.

THOMAS SOWELL (1930–). *American economist*

There are only two ways of telling the complete truth—anonymously and posthumously.

HERBERT SPENCER (1820–1903). *English philosopher*

1 A clever theft was praiseworthy among the Spartans; and it is equally so among Christians, provided it be on a sufficiently large scale.

2 A jury is composed of twelve men of average ignorance.

3 The saying that beauty is only skin deep is but a skin-deep saying. —See also Saki 3

4 The ultimate result of shielding men from the effects of folly is to fill the world with fools.

5 To play billiards well is a sign of an ill-spent youth.

6 With family governments, as with political ones, a harsh despotism itself generates a great part of the crimes it has to repress.

OSWALD SPENGLER (1880–1936). *German historian*

1 As for the modern press, the sentimentalist may beam with contentment when it is constitutionally "free"—but the realist merely asks at whose disposal it is.

2 Man is a beast of prey. I shall say it again and again. All the would-be moralists and social-ethics people who claim or hope to be "beyond all that" are only beasts of prey with their teeth broken.

3 Socialism is nothing but the capitalism of the lower classes.

4 The stupidity of a theory has never impeded its influence.

5 What is truth? For the multitude, that which it continually reads and hears. What the Press wills, is true. Its commanders evoke, transform, interchange truths. Three weeks of press-work, and the "truth" is acknowledged by everybody.

BARUCH SPINOZA (1632–1677). *Dutch philosopher*

1 To an envious man nothing is more delightful than another's misfortune, and nothing more painful than another's success.

2 What Paul says about Peter tells us more about Paul than about Peter.

BRUCE SPRINGSTEEN (1949–). *American singer and songwriter*

1 "57 Channels, Nothing's On." [Song title.]

2 If you're an artist, you try to keep an ear to the ground and an ear to your heart.

3 Remember, nobody wins unless everybody wins.

MADAME de STAËL (1766–1817). *French writer*

1 Talleyrand resembles the toy-men whose heads are of cork and their legs of lead: throw them how you will, they always land on their feet.

2 The more I see of man, the more I like dogs.

3 There never was so great a man made out of such small materials. [On the Duke of Wellington.]

4 Wit consists in knowing the resemblance of things which differ, and the difference of things which are alike.

JOSEPH STALIN (1879–1953). *Soviet premier*

1 A sincere diplomat is like dry water or wooden iron.

2 A single death is a tragedy; a million deaths is a statistic.

3 "Can't you do something to encourage religion and the Catholics in Russia? It would help me so much with the Pope." [French foreign minister Pierre Laval] Oho! The Pope! How many divisions has *he* got? [1935]

GERTRUDE STEIN (1874–1946). *American writer*

1 Everybody gets so much information all day long that they lose their common sense.

2 I like familiarity. In me it does not breed contempt. Only more familiarity.

3 If a thing can be done, why do it?

4 In America everybody is, but some are more than others.

5 Nobody has done anything to develop the English language since Shakespeare, except myself, and Henry James perhaps a little.

6 What is the answer? [Deathbed question to her friend Alice B. Toklas, who gave no response] In that case, what is the question?

7 What was the use of my having come from Oakland? There is no there there. —See also Herb Caen 8

JOHN STEINBECK (1902–1968). *American writer*

1 A red is any son-of-a-bitch who wants thirty cents when we're payin' twenty-five. [*The Grapes of Wrath,* 1939.]

2 Coney Island: where the surf is one-third water and two-thirds people.

3 Little presses write to me for manuscripts and when I write back that I haven't any, they write to ask if they can print the letter saying I haven't any.

4 Man, unlike any other thing organic or inorganic in the universe, grows beyond his work, walks up the stairs of his concepts, emerges ahead of his accomplishments.

5 The profession of book writing makes horse racing seem like a solid, stable business.

6 Where does discontent start? You are warm enough, but you shiver. You are fed, yet hunger gnaws you. You have been loved, but your yearning wanders in new fields. And to prod all these there's time, the Bastard Time.

GLORIA STEINEM (1934–). *American feminist and writer*

1 A man can be called ruthless if he bombs a country to oblivion. A woman can be called ruthless if she puts you on hold.

2 For the reader who has put away comic books, but isn't yet ready for editorials in the *Daily News.* [On Jacqueline Susann's 1968 novel *Valley of the Dolls.*]

3 "How come you never got married?" [Roseanne] Just lucky.

4 I have yet to hear a man ask for advice on how to combine marriage and a career.

5 I'm going to make a button, "The truth will set you free, but first it will piss you off."

6 Self-esteem isn't everything; it's just that there's nothing without it.

7 She is a water bug on the surface of life.

8 Some of us are becoming the men we wanted to marry.

9 Someone once asked me why women don't gamble as much as men do, and I gave the common-sensical reply that we don't have as much money. That was a true but incomplete answer. In fact, women's total instinct for gambling is satisfied by marriage.

10 The same big TV antenna dwarfed each roof, as though life here could only be bearable if lived elsewhere in the imagination.

11 Writing is the only thing that, when I do it, I don't feel I should be doing something else.

STENDHAL (1783–1842). *French writer*

1 All religions are founded on the fear of the many and the cleverness of the few.

2 God's only excuse is that he doesn't exist.

3 Respected people are only rascals who have had the good fortune not to be caught in the act.

CASEY STENGEL (1890–1975). *American baseball player and manager*

1 Being with a woman all night never hurt no professional baseball player. It's staying up all night looking for a woman that does him in.

2 Good pitching will always stop good hitting and vice-versa.

3 He threw the ball as far from the bat and as close to the plate as possible. [On Leroy "Satchel" Paige.]

4 "How are you?" Not bad. Most people my age are dead. You could look it up.

5 I guess this means they fired me. I'll never make the mistake of being seventy years old again. [On being fired as manager of the New York Yankees in 1960.]

6 I know I'm a better manager when Joe DiMaggio is in center field.

7 Managing is getting paid for home runs someone else hits.

8 Play every game as if your job depended on it. It just might.

9 The secret of managing is to keep the guys who hate you away from the guys who are undecided.

10 There comes a time in every man's life, and I've had many of them.

11 They didn't give him a cake. They were afraid he'd drop it. [Remark at a New York Mets team party celebrating the birthday of Marv Throneberry, its notoriously weak-fielding first baseman.]

GEORGE STEPHANOPOULOS (1961–). *American presidential assistant and broadcast journalist*

The word politics comes from the Greek: poli, meaning many, and tics, meaning bloodsuckers.

ADLAI E. STEVENSON (1900–1965). *Illinois governor and Democratic presidential nominee*

1 A beauty is a woman you notice; a charmer is one who notices you.

2 A funny thing happened to me on the way to the White House. [After his defeat in the presidential election of 1952.]

3 A liberal will hang you from a lower branch.

4 A lie is an abomination unto the Lord and a very present help in trouble. [Quoting a young boy who had merged two verses from the Bible.]

5 A politician approaches every question with an open mouth.

6 Eggheads of the world unite; you have nothing to lose but your yolks.

7 I have been thinking that I would make a proposition to my Republican friends: that if they will stop telling lies about the Democrats, we will stop telling the truth about them. —See also Chauncey Depew

8 I suppose flattery hurts no one, that is, if he doesn't inhale. —See also Josh Billings 16

9 In America any boy may become president; I suppose it's just one of the risks he takes.

10 Man does not live by words alone, despite the fact that sometimes he has to eat them.

11 Man is a strange animal; he doesn't like to read the handwriting on the wall until his back is up against it.

12 My definition of a free society is a society where it is safe to be unpopular.

13 Nixon is the kind of politician who would cut down a redwood tree, then mount the stump for a speech on conservation.

14 Nixon's farm policy is vague, but he is going a long way toward solving the corn surplus by his speeches.

15 Power corrupts, but lack of power corrupts absolutely. —See also Lord Acton 2

16 Protocol, alcohol, and Geritol. [On the social life of a diplomat.]

17 The government must be the trustee for the little man because no one else will be. The powerful can usually help themselves—and frequently do.

18 The hardest thing about any political campaign is how to win without proving that you are unworthy of winning.

19 The way of the egghead is hard.

20 To the victor belong the toils. [A variant of William L. Marcy's "To the victor belong the spoils."]

ROBERT LOUIS STEVENSON (1850–1894). *Scottish writer*

1 All sorts of allowances are made for the illusions of youth, and none for the disenchantments of age.

2 I regard you with an indifference closely bordering on aversion.

3 If we take matrimony at its lowest, we regard it as a sort of friendship recognized by the police.

4 Man is a creature who lives not upon bread alone, but principally by catchwords.

5 Most of our pocket wisdom is conceived for the use of mediocre people, to discourage them from ambitious attempts, and generally console them in their mediocrity.

6 My body which my dungeon is, / And yet my parks and palaces.

7 Old and young, we are all on our last cruise.

8 The cruellest lies are often told in silence.

9 The presence of people who refuse to enter in the great handicap race for sixpenny pieces, is at once an insult and a disenchantment for those who do.

CASKIE STINNETT (1911–). *American writer*

A diplomat is a person who can tell you to go to hell in such a way that you actually look forward to the trip.

JENNIFER STONE (1933–). *American writer and broadcast journalist*

1 Integrity pays, but not in cash.

2 Marriage was the loneliest I got—being without the one you're with.

3 We see things as we are not as they are.

TOM STOPPARD (1937–). *Czech-born English playwright*

1 A circle is the longest distance to the same point.

2 A foreign correspondent is someone who flies around from hotel to hotel and thinks the most interesting thing about any story is the fact that he has arrived to cover it.

3 Eternity's a terrible thought. I mean, where's it all going to end?

4 Every exit is an entrance somewhere else.

5 It's an interesting view of atheism, as a sort of crutch for those who can't stand the reality of God. —See also Lily Tomlin 4

6 It's not the voting that's democracy; it's the counting.

7 Life is a gamble at terrible odds. If it was a bet, you wouldn't take it. —See also Damon Runyon 1

8 Skill without imagination is craftsmanship and gives us many useful objects such as wickerwork picnic baskets. Imagination without skill gives us modern art.

9 The idea of god is slightly more plausible than the alternative proposition that, given enough time, some green slime could write Shakespeare's sonnets.

10 The media. It sounds like a convention of spiritualists.

11 "Tomorrow is another day, McKendrick." [Anderson] "Tomorrow, in my experience, is usually the same day."

12 War is capitalism with the gloves off, and many who go to war know it but they go to war because they don't want to be a hero.

13 "Where do you get your ideas from?" If I knew, I'd go there.

REX STOUT (1886–1975). *American writer*

There are two kinds of statistics: the kind you look up and the kind you make up.

LIONEL STRACHEY (1864–1927). *English writer*

1 To be patriotic, hate all nations but your own; to be religious, all sects but your own; to be moral, all pretenses but your own.

2 When humor is meant to be taken seriously, it's no joke.

LYTTON STRACHEY (1880–1932). *English writer*

1 Discretion is not the better part of biography.

2 If this is dying, I don't think much of it. [Last words.]

3 Johnson's aesthetic judgments are almost invariably subtle, or solid, or bold; they have always some good quality to recommend them—except one: they are never right. [On Samuel Johnson.]

IGOR STRAVINSKY (1882–1971). *Russian-born American composer*

1 A good composer does not imitate; he steals. [1967] —See also T. S. Eliot 2; Lionel Trilling 1

2 A plague on eminence! I hardly dare cross the street anymore without a convoy.

3 My childhood was a period of waiting for the moment when I could send everyone and everything connected with it to hell.

4 To see Balanchine's choreography is to hear music with one's eyes.

5 Too many pieces of music finish too long after the end.

BARBRA STREISAND (1942–). *American singer and actress*
Success to me is having ten honeydew melons and eating only the top half
of each one.

WILLIE SUTTON (20th century). *American bank robber*
"Why do you rob banks?" Because that's where the money is. [Attributed, but
Sutton denied having said it.] —See also John F. Kennedy 21

HANNEN SWAFFER (1879–1962). *English journalist*
Freedom of the press in Britain means freedom to print such of the propri-
etor's prejudices as the advertisers don't object to.

GLORIA SWANSON (1899–1983). *American actress*

1 At the London airport a few years ago I was interviewed for ten minutes
before I discovered the interviewer thought I was Tallulah Bankhead. And
Miss Bankhead had already been dead for three months—if you can believe *The New York Times*.

2 Writing the story of your own life, I now know, is an agonizing experience,
a bit like drilling your own teeth.

JONATHAN SWIFT (1667–1745). *Anglo-Irish clergyman and writer*

1 A nice man is a man of nasty ideas.

2 Censure is the tax a man pays to the public for being eminent. —See also
George Washington 4

3 Complaint is the largest tribute Heaven receives, and the sincerest part of
our devotion.

4 Every man desires to live long, but no man would be old.

5 Felicity, the possession of being well-deceived, the serene peaceful state
of being a fool among knaves. [*A Tale of a Tub*, 1704.]

6 Fine words! I wonder where you stole them.

7 He had been eight years upon a project for extracting sunbeams out of cu-
cumbers, which were to be put into vials hermetically sealed, and let out
to warm the air in raw inclement summers. [*Gulliver's Travels*, 1726.]

8 I am as old as my tongue and a little older than my teeth.

9 I am now trying an experiment very frequent among modern authors;
which is to write upon nothing; when the subject is utterly exhausted, to
let the pen still move on; by some called the ghost of wit, delighting to
walk after the death of its body.

10 I cannot but conclude the bulk of your natives to be the most pernicious
race of little odious vermin that nature ever suffered to crawl upon the surface of the earth. [*Gulliver's Travels*.]

11 I hate and detest that animal called man; although I heartily love John,
Peter, Thomas, and so forth.

12 I have been assured by a very knowing American of my acquaintance in
London that a young healthy child well-nursed is at a year old a most delicious, nourishing, and wholesome food, whether stewed, roasted, baked,

or boiled, and I make no doubt that it will equally serve in a fricassee, or a ragout. [A *Modest Proposal for preventing the Children of poor People in Ireland, from being a Burden to their Parents or Country; and for making them beneficial to the Publick,* 1729.]

13 I have heard of a man who had a mind to sell his house, and therefore carried a piece of brick in his pocket, which he showed as a pattern to encourage purchasers. —See also Samuel Johnson 25

14 I must complain the cards are ill shuffled till I have a good hand.

15 If a man makes me keep my distance, the comfort is he keeps his at the same time.

16 It is a miserable thing to live in suspense; it is the life of a spider.

17 It is useless for us to attempt to reason a man out of a thing he has never been reasoned into.

18 Judges are picked out from the most dexterous lawyers who are grown old or lazy: and having been biased all their lives against truth and equity, lie under such a fatal necessity of favoring fraud, perjury, and oppression, that I have known several of them refuse a large bribe from the side where justice lay, rather than injure the faculty by doing anything unbecoming their nature or their office.

19 May you live all the days of your life.

20 Promises and pie crust are made to be broken.

21 Punning is a talent which no man affects to despise but he that is without it.

22 Satire is a sort of glass, wherein beholders do generally discover everybody's face but their own.

23 She wears her clothes as if they were thrown on her with a pitchfork.

24 Taverns are places where madness is sold by the bottle.

25 That's as well said as if I had said it myself.

26 The best doctors in the world are Doctor Diet, Doctor Quiet, and Doctor Merryman.

27 The stoical scheme of supplying our wants by lopping off our desires, is like cutting off our feet when we want shoes.

28 There are few wild beasts more to be dreaded than a talking man having nothing to say.

29 There is nothing in this world constant, but inconstancy.

30 We are so fond of each other because our ailments are the same.

31 We have just enough religion to make us hate, but not enough to make us love one another.

32 What religion is he of? Why, he is an Anythingarian.

33 When a true genius appears in the world, you may know him by this sign, that the dunces are all in confederacy against him.

34 When you have done a fault, be always pert and insolent, and behave yourself as if you were the injured person.

HERBERT BAYARD SWOPE (1882–1959). *American editor*

I cannot give you the formula for success, but I can give you the formula for failure, which is: try to please everybody.

J. M. SYNGE (1871–1909). *Irish playwright*

"A man who is not afraid of the sea will soon be drowned," he said, "for he
will be going out on a day he shouldn't. But we do be afraid of the sea,
and we do only be drowned now and again."

THOMAS S. SZASZ (1920–). *Hungarian-born American psychiatrist*

1 Beware of the psychoanalyst who analyzes jokes rather than laughs at
   them.

2 Delusion: belief said to be false by someone who does not share it.

3 If you talk to God, you are praying; if God talks to you, you have
   schizophrenia.

4 Psychoanalysis is a religion disguised as a science: As Abraham received
   the Laws of God from Jehovah to whom he claimed to have had special
   access, so Freud received the Laws of Psychology from the Unconscious
   to which he claimed to have had special access.

5 Those who suffer from and complain of their own behavior are usually
   classified as "neurotic"; those whose behavior makes others suffer, and
   about whom others complain, are usually classified as "psychotic."

6 Treating addiction to heroin with methadone is like treating addiction to
   scotch with bourbon.

7 When a man says he is Jesus or makes some other claim that seems to us
   outrageous, we call him psychotic and lock him up in the madhouse. Freedom of speech is only for normal people.

TACITUS (A.D. 56?–120?). *Roman historian*
Necessity reforms the poor; and satiety, the rich.

ROBERT A. TAFT (1889–1953). *Ohio senator*
You really have to get to know Dewey to dislike him. [On Thomas E. Dewey, two-time Republican presidential nominee.]

RABINDRANATH TAGORE (1861–1941). *Indian poet*
We read the world wrong and say that it deceives us.

CHARLES MAURICE de TALLEYRAND (1754–1838). *French foreign minister*

1 An important art of politicians is to find new names for institutions which under old names have become odious to the public.

2 He has a profound contempt for human nature. Of course, he is much given to introspection.

3 If you wish to appear agreeable in society, you must consent to be taught many things you know already.

4 Never speak ill of yourself! You can count on your friends for that.

5 Never trust first impulses! They are always good.

6 She's intolerable, but that's her only fault.

7 Society is divided into two classes: the shearers and the shorn. It's best to be on the side of the shearers.

8 Speech was given to man to conceal his thoughts.

9 To avoid being called a flirt, she always yielded easily.

10 "What is all this about non-intervention?" [Napoleon] Sire, it means about the same as intervention.

11 "You are a thief, a coward, a man without honor. To you nothing is sacred; you would sell your own father!" [Napoleon] What a pity that so great a man should be so ill-bred!

12 You can do everything with bayonets, Sire, except sit on them.

A. J. P. TAYLOR (1906–1990). *English historian*

1 All change in history, all advance, comes from the nonconformists. If there had been no troublemakers, no dissenters, we should still be living in caves.

2 Like most of those who study history, he learned from the mistakes of the past how to make new ones. [On Napoleon III.]

3 There is nothing more agreeable in life than to make peace with the Establishment—and nothing more corrupting.

ELIZABETH TAYLOR (1932–). *English-born American actress*

1 I, along with the critics, have never taken myself seriously.

2 I am wonderful playing bitches.

3 I don't *love* acting; I love chocolate.

4 I've only slept with the men I've been married to. How many women can make that claim?

5 If someone's dumb enough to offer me a million dollars to make a picture, I'm certainly not dumb enough to turn it down.

6 Some of my best leading men have been dogs and horses.

7 Success is a great deodorant: it takes away all your past smells.

SHIRLEY TEMPLE (1928–). *American actress and ambassador*
I stopped believing in Santa Claus when I was six. Mother took me to see him in a department store, and he asked for my autograph.

WILLIAM MAKEPEACE THACKERAY (1811–1863). *English novelist*

1 A clever, ugly man every now and then is successful with the ladies, but a handsome fool is irresistible.

2 Even when I am reading my lectures I often think to myself, "What a humbug you are," and I wonder the people don't find it out.

3 "How to Live Well on Nothing a Year." [Chapter title in *Vanity Fair,* 1848.]

4 I never know whether to pity or congratulate a man on coming to his senses.

5 If a man's character is to be abused, there's nobody like a relative to do the business.

6 Remember, it is as easy to marry a rich woman as a poor woman.

7 To love and win is the best thing; to love and lose, the next best.

8 When I walk with you, I feel as if I had a flower in my buttonhole.

9 Yes, I am a fatal man, Madame Fribsbi. To inspire hopeless passion is my destiny.

MARGARET THATCHER (1925–). *British prime minister*

1 By 1990 I had learned that I had to defer to him in conversation and not to stint the praise. If that was what was necessary to secure Britain's interests and influence, I had no hesitation in eating a little humble pie. [Referring to President George Bush.] —See also Winston Churchill 30; Napoleon 23

2 I am painted as the greatest little dictator, which is ridiculous—you always take some consultations.

3 I'm extraordinarily patient, provided I get my own way in the end.

4 If you are guided by opinion polls, you are not practicing leadership—you are practicing followership.

5 In politics, if you want anything said, ask a man. If you want anything done, ask a woman.

6 It is exciting to have a real crisis on your hands, when you have spent half your political life dealing with humdrum issues like the environment. [Speech during the Falklands War, 1982.]

7 Mr. Neil Kinnock, in all his years as Opposition Leader, never let me down. Right to the end, he struck every wrong note.

8 No one would remember the Good Samaritan if he'd only had good intentions. He had money as well.

9 Poor dear, there's nothing between his ears. [On Ronald Reagan.]

10 We have become a grandmother. [After the birth of her grandson.]

11 We shall not be diverted from our course. To those waiting with bated breath for that favorite media catch phrase, the U-turn, I have only this to say: "You turn if you want; the lady's not for turning." [Speech, 1980.]

DYLAN THOMAS (1914–1953). *Welsh poet*

1 An alcoholic is somebody you don't like who drinks as much as you do.

2 Dylan talked copiously, then stopped. "Somebody's boring me," he said, "I think it's me."

3 "I must dust the blinds and then I must raise them." [Mr. Pritchard] "And before you let the sun in, mind it wipes its shoes." [Mrs. Ogmore-Pritchard]

4 Mr. Kipling stands for everything in this cankered world which I would wish were otherwise. [On Rudyard Kipling.]

5 The land of my fathers. My fathers can have it. [Referring to Wales.]

6 When I take up assassination, I shall start with the surgeons in this city and work up to the gutter.

7 Will you take this woman Matti Richards to be your awful wedded wife?

HELEN THOMAS (1920–). *American journalist*

1 Anybody who runs for public office today has got to know his or her life will be an open book. I've decided that if you want to run for public office you have to decide at the age of five and live accordingly.

2 "Do you think Newt Gingrich will self-destruct?" Hope springs eternal.

3 You didn't tell a lie, you just left a big hole in the truth.

4 You're only as good as your last story.

HUNTER S. THOMPSON (1939–). *American writer*

1 Any political party that can't cough up anything better than a treacherous brain-damaged old vulture like Hubert Humphrey deserves every beating it gets. They don't hardly make 'em like Hubert any more—but just to be on the safe side, he should be castrated anyway. [*Fear and Loathing on the Campaign Trail,* 1973.]

2 He has the integrity of a hyena and the style of a poison toad. [On Richard M. Nixon.]

3 I hate to advocate drugs, alcohol, violence, or insanity to anyone, but they've always worked for me.

4 Sex without love is as hollow and ridiculous as love without sex.

5 When you start stealing from your own work, you're in bad trouble. [On self-plagiarism.]

ROY HERBERT THOMSON (1894–1976). *Canadian-born British publisher*

I buy newspapers to make money to buy more newspapers to make more money. As for editorial content, that's the stuff you separate the ads with.

HENRY DAVID THOREAU (1817–1862). *American philosopher*

1 Beware of all enterprises that require new clothes, and not rather a new wearer of clothes.

2 Books which even make us dangerous to existing institutions—such call I good books.

3 City life: millions of people being lonesome together.

4 Dr. Josiah Bartlett handed me a paper today, desiring me to subscribe for a statue to Horace Mann. I declined, and said that I thought a man ought not any more to take up room in the world after he was dead.

5 Every generation laughs at the old fashions, but follows religiously the new.

6 For many years I was self-appointed inspector of snowstorms and rainstorms, and did my duty faithfully, though I never received one cent for it.

7 "Have you made your peace with God?" I am not aware that we ever quarreled. [On his deathbed.]

8 I believe that what so saddens the reformer is not his sympathy with his fellows in distress, but, though he be the holiest son of God, is his private ail. Let this be righted, let the spring come to him, the morning rise over his couch, and he will forsake his generous companions without apology.

9 I have always been regretting that I was not as wise as the day I was born.

10 I have received no more than one or two letters in my life that were worth the postage.

11 I have three chairs in my house: one for solitude, two for friendship, three for company.

12 I have traveled a good deal in Concord.

13 I heard one boy say to another in the street today, "You don't know much more than a piece of putty."

14 I should not talk so much about myself if there were anybody else whom I knew as well. —See also Anatole France 11

15 I went to the store the other day to buy a bolt for our front door, for, as I told the storekeeper, the Governor was coming here. "Aye," said he, "and the Legislature too." "Then I will take two bolts," said I. He said that there had been a steady demand for bolts and locks of late, for our protectors were coming.

16 If a man does not keep pace with his companions, perhaps it is because he hears a different drummer. Let him step to the music that he hears, however measured or far away.

17 If I knew for a certainty that a man was coming to my house with the conscious design of doing me good, I should run for my life.

18 If I regret anything it is very likely to be my good behavior. What demon possessed me that I behaved so well?

19 If the race had never lived through a winter, what would they think was coming?

20 If words were invented to conceal thought, newspapers are a great improvement on a bad invention.

21 In Boston yesterday an ornithologist said significantly, "If you held the bird in your hand —"; but I would rather hold it in my affections.

22 It is an interesting question how far men would retain their relative rank if they were divested of their clothes.

23 It is enough if I please myself with writing; I am then sure of an audience.

24 Men have become the tools of their tools.

25 One world at a time. [Whispered response, on his deathbed, to a friend who wanted to talk with him about "the next world."]

26 People are less careful to avoid evil than its appearance.

27 Princes and magistrates are often styled serene, but what is their turbid serenity to that ethereal serenity which the bluebird embodies? His Most Serene Birdship!

28 Some circumstantial evidence is very strong, as when you find a trout in the milk.

29 Thank God, men cannot as yet fly, and lay waste the sky as well as the earth!

30 The bluebird carries the sky on his back.

31 The day after never, we will have an explanation.

32 The lawyer's truth is not Truth, but consistency or a consistent expediency.

33 The mass of men lead lives of quiet desperation. An unconscious despair is concealed even under what are the games and amusements of mankind.
—See also James Thurber 11

34 The rich man is always sold to the institution which makes him rich. Absolutely speaking, the more money, the less virtue.

35 The stupid you have always with you.

36 The youth gets together his materials to build a bridge to the moon, or perchance a palace or temple on the earth, and at length the middle-aged man concludes to build a woodshed with them.

37 There are few men who do not love better to give advice than to give assistance.

38 We are eager to tunnel under the Atlantic and bring the old world some weeks nearer to the new; but perchance the first news that will leak through into the broad, flapping American ear will be that the Princess Adelaide has the whooping cough. [On the prospect of a transatlantic cable, 1854.]

39 We are paid for our suspicions by finding what we suspected.

40 What does education often do? It makes a straight-cut ditch of a free, meandering brook.

41 What I got by going to Canada was a cold.

42 What is the use of a house if you haven't got a tolerable planet to put it on?

43 What men call social virtues, good fellowship, is commonly but the virtue of pigs in a litter, which lie close together to keep each other warm.

44 When a dog runs at you, whistle for him.

45 You must not blame me if I talk to the clouds.

JAMES THURBER (1894–1961). *American writer, cartoonist, and humorist*

1 A husband should not insult his wife publicly, at parties. He should insult her in the privacy of the home.

2 All right, have it your own way—you heard a seal bark. [Cartoon caption.]

3 Ashes to ashes, and clay to clay, if the enemy doesn't get you, your own folks may.

4 Early to rise and early to bed makes a male healthy and wealthy and dead.
—See also Evan Esar 7; Ted Turner 1

5 He fell down a great deal during this period, because of a trick he had of walking into himself.

6 Humor is emotional chaos remembered in tranquillity.

7 "I hope you didn't think it was too blood and thirsty." [Samuel Goldwyn] Not only did I think so, but I was horror and struck. [Referring to a Goldwyn film based on a Thurber story.]

8 I myself have accomplished nothing of excellence except a remarkable and, to some of my friends, unaccountable expertness in hitting empty ginger ale bottles with small rocks at a distance of thirty paces.

9 It is better to have loafed and lost than never to have loafed at all.

10 Let the meek inherit the earth—they have it coming to them.

11 Nowadays most men lead lives of noisy desperation. —See also Henry David Thoreau 33

12 One martini is all right, two is too many, three is not enough.

13 Seeing is deceiving. It's eating that's believing.

14 She used to be no better than she ought to be, but she is now.

15 The battle is sometimes to the small, for the bigger they are the harder they fall. —See also Anonymous 110; Bob Fitzsimmons

16 The play had one fault: it was kind of lousy. [Attributed.]

17 The trouble with the lost generation is that it doesn't get lost enough.

18 There is no safety in numbers, or in anything else.

19 We all have flaws, and mine is being wicked.

20 Well, if I called the wrong number, why did you answer the phone? [Cartoon caption.] —See also Anonymous 145

21 While he was no dumber than an ox, he was not any smarter.

22 With sixty staring me in the face, I have developed inflammation of the sentence structure and a definite hardening of the paragraphs.

23 You can fool too many of the people too much of the time. —See also Abraham Lincoln 52

ALEXIS de TOCQUEVILLE (1805–1859). *French historian and political leader*

1 Democracy and socialism have nothing in common but one word: equality. But notice the difference: while democracy seeks equality in liberty, socialism seeks equality in restraint and servitude.

2 Despots themselves do not deny that freedom is excellent, only they desire it for themselves alone.

3 Everybody I see about me seems bent on teaching his contemporaries, by precept and example, that what is useful is never wrong. Will nobody undertake to make them understand how what is right may be useful? [*Democracy in America,* 1835–1840.]

4 The desire of acquiring the comforts of the world haunts the imagination of the poor, and the dread of losing them that of the rich.

ALVIN TOFFLER (1928–). *American writer*

1 In New Zealand, the vacuity of mainstream politics prompted one protester to change his name to Mickey Mouse and enter himself as a candidate. So many others did likewise—adopting names like Alice in Wonderland—that Parliament rushed through a law banning anyone from running for office if he or she had legally changed a name within six months prior to an election. [1972]

2 Loneliness is now so widespread it has become, paradoxically, a shared experience.

3 The illiterate of the 21st century will not be those who cannot read and write, but those who cannot learn, unlearn, and relearn.

LEO TOLSTOY (1828–1910). *Russian novelist*

1 He who has money has in his pocket those who have none.

2 I sit on a man's back, choking him and making him carry me, and yet assure myself and others that I am very sorry for him and wish to lighten his load by all possible means—except by getting off his back.

3 It is easier to write ten volumes of philosophy than to put one principle into practice.

4 Life has become a burden to me of late. I see that I have begun to understand too much.

5 The difference between reactionary repression and revolutionary repression is the difference between cat shit and dog shit.

LILY TOMLIN (1939–). *American comedienne and actress*

1 For fast-acting relief, try slowing down.

2 If love is the answer, could you rephrase the question?

3 Is this the party to whom I am speaking? [Signature line in her role as Ernestine, a telephone operator, on Rowan and Martin's *Laugh-In* television program, 1969.]

4 Reality is a crutch for people who can't deal with drugs. —See also Tom Stoppard 5

5 Sometimes I feel like a figment of my own imagination.

6 The best mind-altering drug is truth.

7 Things are going to get a lot worse before they get worse.

8 We're all in this together—by ourselves.

ARTURO TOSCANINI (1867–1957). *Italian conductor*

1 Assassins! [Rebuking his entire orchestra after a disappointing rehearsal.]

2 God tells me how the music should sound, but *you* stand in the way. [Bitter remark to a musician during a rehearsal.]

3 I kissed my first woman and smoked my first cigarette on the same day. I have never had time for tobacco since.

4 Madame, there you sit with that magnificent instrument between your legs, and all you can do is scratch it. [Remark to a cellist; also attributed to Thomas Beecham.]

5 "Nuts to you!" [Shouted by a musician at Toscanini who had just ordered him to leave a rehearsal.] It's too late to apologize.

6 With one more drop of blood perhaps we can come a little nearer to what Beethoven wanted. [During a rehearsal of the Ninth Symphony.]

ARNOLD J. TOYNBEE (1889–1975). *English historian*

1 America is a large, friendly dog in a very small room. Every time it wags its tail, it knocks over a chair.

2 Man cannot live by technology alone.

3 Nothing fails like success when you rely on it too much. —See also Alexandre Dumas 2

SPENCER TRACY (1900–1967). *American actor*

1 "I'm afraid I'm a little tall for you, Mr. Tracy." [Katharine Hepburn] Don't worry, I'll soon cut you down to my size.

2 There were times when my pants were so thin, I could sit on a dime and know if it was heads or tails.

G. M. TREVELYAN (1876–1962). *English historian*

1 He may be a genius in mathematics—as to that I'm no judge; but about politics he is a perfect goose. [On Bertrand Russell.]

2 Once in every man's youth there comes the hour when he must learn, what no one ever yet believed save on the authority of his own experience, that the world was not created to make him happy.

LEE TREVINO (1939–). *American golfer*

The older I get, the better I used to be.

CALVIN TRILLIN (1935–). *American literary critic*

1 Harvard Law School is an institution that each fall takes five hundred of our brightest, most idealistic young people and in three years transforms them into Wall Street moneygrubbers.

2 Health food makes me sick.

3 In modern America, anyone who attempts to write satirically about the events of the day finds it difficult to concoct a situation so bizarre that it may not actually come to pass while his article is still on the presses.

4 Math was my worst subject because I could never persuade the teacher that my answers were meant ironically.

5 They said that there is definitely a distinction between real life and the movies, despite the fact that President Reagan once mentioned as an example of inspiring patriotism a heroic act that turned out to have been from a World War II bomber movie starring Dana Andrews.

6 Years ago, I discovered that I could keep the plane I was flying on from crashing by refusing to adjust my watch to the new time zone until we were on the ground, and I have used that method ever since.

LIONEL TRILLING (1905–1975). *American literary critic*

1 Immature artists imitate. Mature artists steal. [1960] —See also T. S. Eliot 2; Igor Stravinsky 1

2 We who are liberal and progressive know that the poor are our equals in every sense except that of being equal to us. [*The Liberal Imagination,* 1950.]

GARRY TRUDEAU (1948–). *American cartoonist*

1 Criticizing a political satirist for being unfair is like criticizing a nose guard for being physical.

2 Sometimes a man in serving God can only do as angels do, and wing it.

3 This is the only country where failure to promote yourself is widely considered arrogant.

PIERRE ELLIOTT TRUDEAU (1919–). *Canadian prime minister*

1 Living next to you is like sleeping with an elephant. No matter how friendly and even-tempered the beast, one is affected by every twitch and grunt. [On the United States, speech in Washington, 1969.]

2 The Hon. Member disagrees. I can hear him shaking his head.

HARRY S. TRUMAN (1884–1972). *American president*

1 A politician is a man who understands government, and it takes a politician to run a government. A statesman is a politician who's been dead ten or fifteen years.

2 About the meanest thing you can say about a man is that he means well.

3 All the president is, is a glorified public relations man who spends his time flattering, kissing and kicking people to get them to do what they are supposed to do anyway.

4 He's a good man. The only trouble was, he had a lot of damn fool Republicans around him. [On Dwight D. Eisenhower.]

5 I am going to make a common-sense, intellectually honest campaign. It will be a novelty, and it will win. [Diary, 1948.]

6 I am the president of the most powerful nation in the world. I take orders from nobody, except photographers. [Remark to foreign dignitaries.]

7 I fired General Douglas MacArthur because he wouldn't respect the authority of the president. That's the answer to that. I didn't fire him because he was a dumb son of a bitch, although he was, but that's not against the law for generals. If it was, half to three quarters of them would be in jail.

8 I have found the best way to give advice to your children is to find out what they want, and then advise them to do it. —See also Josh Billings 92

9 I have just read your lousy review buried in the back pages. You sound like a frustrated old man who never made a success, an eight-ulcer man on a four-ulcer job, and all four ulcers working. I have never met you, but if I do you'll need a new nose and plenty of beefsteak and perhaps a supporter below. [Letter to *Washington Post* critic Paul Hume, who, the previous day, had panned a singing recital by Truman's daughter Margaret, 1950.]

10 I never give 'em hell. I just tell the truth, and they think it's hell. [Explaining his "give 'em hell" campaign speeches.]

11 I wonder how far Moses would have gone if he had taken a poll in Egypt? What would Jesus Christ have preached if he had taken a poll in the land of Israel?

12 If you can't convince them, confuse them.

13 If you can't stand the heat, stay out of the kitchen! [Friend Harry Vaughan's saying which Truman popularized.] —See also Lyndon B. Johnson 13

14 If you want a friend in Washington, get a dog.

15 It's a recession when your neighbor loses his job; it's a depression when you lose your own. —See also Ronald Reagan 21

16 Leadership is the ability to get other people to do what they don't want to do and like it.

17 "Mr. President, have you read any columns in which you found any truth at all?" [Reporter] Not lately!

18 "Mr. President, have you seen any flying saucers?" [Reporter] Only in the newspapers.

19 "Mr. President, the first thing Jefferson did on taking office was to release eleven newspaper publishers from prison." [Reporter] Yes. I think he made a mistake on that.

20 My choice early in life was either to be a piano player in a whorehouse or a politician. And to tell the truth, there's hardly any difference.

21 Nixon is a shifty-eyed, goddamn liar, and people know it. He's one of the few in the history of this country to run for high office talking out of both sides of his mouth at the same time and lying out of both sides.

22 Some of the presidents were great and some of them weren't. I can say that because I wasn't one of the great presidents, but I had a good time trying to be one. [1959]

23 The buck stops here. [Desk sign in the Oval Office.] —See also Alan Greenspan 4

24 The finest prison in the world. [On the White House.] —See also Bill Clinton 7

25 When I first came to Washington, for the first six months I wondered how the hell I ever got here. For the next six months, I wondered how the hell the rest of them ever got here. [Truman was elected to the U.S. Senate in 1934.]

26 Whenever a fellow tells me he's bipartisan, I know he's going to vote against me.

27 Why, this fellow doesn't know any more about politics than a pig knows about Sunday. [On Dwight D. Eisenhower, 1952.]

28 Within the first few months I discovered that being a president is like riding a tiger. A man has to keep on riding or be swallowed. [Opening words of his *Memoirs,* 1956.]

DONALD J. TRUMP (1946–). *American real estate investor*

1 As long as you're going to be thinking anyway, think big!

2 Sometimes your best investments are the ones you don't make.

3 I play to people's fantasies. A little hyperbole never hurts. People want to believe that something is the biggest and the greatest and the most spectacular. I call it truthful hyperbole. It's an innocent form of exaggeration— and a very effective form of promotion.

4 The point is you can't be too greedy.

BARBARA W. TUCHMAN (1912–1989). *American historian*

1 Bureaucracy, safely repeating today what it did yesterday, rolls on as ineluctably as some vast computer, which once penetrated by error, duplicates it forever.

2 The fact of being reported increases the apparent extent of a deplorable development by a factor of ten.

3 Wooden-headedness consists of assessing a situation in terms of preconceived, fixed notions while ignoring or rejecting any contrary signs. It is acting according to wish while not allowing oneself to be confused by the facts.

DICK TUCK (20th century). *American political leader*

The people have spoken—the bastards! [After losing his campaign for the California state legislature, 1974.]

JERRY TUCKER (1941–). *American political scientist*

1 Bigot: someone who hates different people than I do.

2 Committee: a structured decision-making body in which the level of collective judgment is lower than that of any individual member.

3 Competition: a contest conducted according to rules made by the defending champion.

4 Emotion: the human spirit experienced in the flesh.

5 Expert: someone who knows practically everything about next to nothing.

6 Humor: the ability to laugh at any mistake you survive.

7 Optimist: one who believes things are so bad they're bound to get better.

8 Victim: someone who trusts too much in luck or human kindness.

SOPHIE TUCKER (1884–1966). *Russian-born American entertainer*

1 From birth to 18 a girl needs good parents. From 18 to 35 she need good looks. From 35 to 55, good personality. From 55 on, she needs good cash.

2 I've been rich and I've been poor. Believe me, honey, rich is better. [Her signature line.] —See also Mal Hancock 12

TED TURNER (1938–). *American media industry leader*

1 Early to bed, early to rise, work like hell, and advertise. —See also Evan Esar 7; James Thurber 4

2 If I only had a little humility, I would be perfect.

3 If you're only going to have ten rules, I don't know if adultery should be one of them. [Referring to the Ten Commandments.]

DESMOND TUTU (1931–). *South African bishop*

When the missionaries first came to Africa, they had the Bible and we had the land. They said "let us pray." We closed our eyes. When we opened them, we had the Bible and they had the land.

MARK TWAIN (Samuel Clemens; 1835–1910). *American writer, lecturer, and humorist*

1 A baby is an inestimable blessing and bother.

2 A banker is a fellow who lends his umbrella when the sun is shining and wants it back the minute it begins to rain.

3 A mistake is not a crime, it is only a miscarriage of judgment.

4 A swell house with all the modern inconveniences.

5 All kings is mostly rapscallions.

6 All religions issue Bibles against Satan, and say the most injurious things against him, but we never hear his side.

7 All you need in this life is ignorance and confidence, then success is sure.

8 Although this work is a History, I believe it to be true. [Opening words of his 1905 essay "3,000 Years Among the Microbes."]

9 Always do right. This will gratify some people, and astonish the rest.

10 Always obey your parents, when they are present. [Advice to children.]

11 An ethical man is a Christian holding four aces.

12 An uneasy conscience is a hair in the mouth.

13 April 1: this is the day upon which we are reminded of what we are on the other three hundred and sixty-four.

14 As to the adjective: when in doubt, strike it out.

15 Barring that natural expression of villainy which we all have, the man looked honest enough.

16 Be careless in your dress if you must, but keep a tidy soul.

17 Be good & you will be lonesome. [Frontispiece caption in *Following the Equator,* 1897.] —See also Josh Billings 26

18 By trying we can easily learn to endure adversity. Another man's, I mean.

19 Can any plausible excuse be found for the crime of creating the human race? [Annotation in his copy of Charles Darwin's *Journal of Researches.*]

20 Cheer up! The worst is yet to come.

21 Church ain't shucks to a circus.

22 Classic: a book which people praise and don't read.

23 Do right and you will be conspicuous.

24 Don't go around saying the world owes you a living. The world owes you nothing. It was here first.

25 Don't part with your illusions. When they are gone, you may still exist, but you will have ceased to live.

26 Each nation knowing it has the only true religion and the only sane system of government, each despising all the others, each an ass and not suspecting it.

27 Everybody's private motto: it's better to be popular than right.

28 Fame is a vapor; popularity an accident; the only earthly certainty is oblivion.

29 Familiarity breeds contempt—and children.

30 Few sinners are saved after the first twenty minutes of a sermon.

31 Few things are harder to put up with than the annoyance of a good example.

32 Fleas can be taught nearly anything that a Congressman can.

33 Get money. Get it quickly. Get it in abundance. Get it in prodigious abundance. Get it dishonestly if you can, honestly if you must.

34 Golf is a good walk spoiled.

35 Good breeding consists in concealing how much we think of ourselves and how little we think of the other person.

36 Good friends, good books and a sleepy conscience: this is the ideal life.

37 Habit is habit, and not to be flung out of the window by any man, but coaxed downstairs a step at a time.

38 Hain't we got all the fools in town on our side? And ain't that a big enough majority in any town?

39 Have a place for everything and keep the thing somewhere else. This is not advice, it is merely custom.

40 He was a preacher and never charged nothing for his preaching, and it was worth it, too.

41 Heaven for climate, hell for society. [1901] —See also J. M. Barrie 4

42 His money is twice tainted: 'taint yours and 'taint mine.

43 History shows us that the Moral Sense enables us to perceive morality and how to avoid it, and that the Immoral Sense enables us to perceive immorality and how to enjoy it.

44 Honesty *was* the best policy.

45 How often we recall, with regret, that Napoleon once shot at a magazine

editor and missed him and killed a publisher. But we remember, with charity, that his intentions were good.

46 Human nature is the same everywhere: it deifies success, it has nothing but scorn for defeat.

47 I admire him, I frankly confess it; and when his time comes I shall buy a piece of the rope for a keepsake. [On the British colonialist Cecil Rhodes.]

48 I asked Tom if countries always apologized when they had done wrong, and he says: "Yes; the little ones does."

49 I don't give a damn for a man that can spell a word only one way.

50 I have made it a rule never to smoke more than one cigar at a time.

51 I have never let my schooling interfere with my education. [Attributed.]

52 I have no race prejudice, and I think I have no color prejudices, nor caste prejudices. All I care to know is that a man is a human being—that is enough for me; he can't be any worse.

53 I never could make a good impromptu speech without several hours to prepare it.

54 I refused to attend his funeral, but I wrote a very nice letter explaining that I approved of it. [On hearing of a corrupt politician's death.]

55 I was born modest; not all over, but in spots.

56 I was sorry to have my name mentioned as one of the great authors, because they have a sad habit of dying off. Chaucer is dead. Spenser is dead, so is Milton, so is Shakespeare, and I am not feeling very well myself.

57 I would rather go to bed with Lillian Russell stark naked than Ulysses S. Grant in full military regalia. [Attributed.]

58 I'm opposed to millionaires, but it would be dangerous to offer me the position.

59 I'm pushing sixty. That's enough exercise for me.

60 If a person offends you and you are in doubt as to whether it was intentional or not, do not resort to extreme measures. Simply watch for your chance and hit him with a brick.

61 If there was two birds setting on a fence, he would bet you which one would fly first.

62 If you don't like the weather in New England, just wait a few minutes.

63 If you pick up a starving dog and make him prosperous, he will not bite you. This is the principal difference between a dog and a man.

64 In all matters of opinion our adversaries are insane.

65 In statesmanship get the formalities right, never mind about the moralities.

66 In the first place God made idiots. This was for practice, then he made school boards.

67 In truth you are always consistent, always yourself, always an ass.

68 It ain't those parts of the Bible that I can't understand that bother me, it is the parts that I do understand.

69 It could probably be shown by facts and figures that there is no distinctly native American criminal class except Congress.

70 It has always been my rule never to smoke when asleep, and never to refrain when awake.

71 It is a wise child that knows its own father, and an unusual one that unreservedly approves of him.

72 It is better to deserve honors and not have them than to have them and not deserve them.

73 It is by the goodness of God that in our country we have those three unspeakably precious things: freedom of speech, freedom of conscience, and the prudence never to practice either of them.

74 It is easier to stay out than to get out.

75 It takes a heap of sense to write good nonsense.

76 It takes your enemy and your friend, working together, to hurt you to the heart; the one to slander you and the other to get the news to you.

77 It used to be a good hotel, but that proves nothing—I used to be a good boy.

78 It were not best that we should all think alike; it is difference of opinion that makes horse races.

79 It's better to keep your mouth shut and appear stupid than to open it and remove all doubt.

80 Kipling is a stranger to me, but he is a most remarkable man—and I am the other one. Between us, we cover all knowledge: he knows all that can be known, and I know the rest.

81 Let us be thankful for the fools. But for them the rest of us could not succeed. —See also Josh Billings 17

82 Let us endeavor so to live that when we come to die even the undertaker will be sorry.

83 Life would be infinitely happier if we could only be born at the age of eighty and gradually approach eighteen.

84 Man: a creature made at the end of the week's work when God was tired.

85 Man is the only animal that blushes. Or needs to.

86 Name the greatest of all the inventors: Accident.

87 Never put off till tomorrow what you can do the day after tomorrow just as well. —See also Anonymous 90; Ed Howe 5; Aldous Huxley 8

88 Never waste a lie; you never know when you may need it.

89 Nothing is made in vain, but the fly comes near to it. —See also Ogden Nash 6

90 Nothing so needs reforming as other people's habits.

91 Obscurity and a competence—that is the life that is best worth living.

92 October. This is one of the peculiarly dangerous months to speculate in stocks. The others are, July, January, September, April, November, May, March, June, December, August, and February.

93 Often, the less there is to justify a custom, the harder it is to get rid of it.

94 Persons attempting to find a motive in this narrative will be prosecuted; persons attempting to find a moral in it will be banished; persons attempting to find a plot in it will be shot. ["Notice" to readers of *The Adventures of Huckleberry Finn,* 1884.]

95 Principles have no real force except when one is well fed.

96 Public servants: persons chosen by the people to distribute the graft.

97 Senator: person who makes laws in Washington when not doing time.

98 Silver City: prostitution, gambling, and drunken debauchery. I could tell at first glance it was no place for a young Presbyterian. So I didn't long remain one.

99 Simplified spelling is all right, but, like chastity, you can carry it too far.

100 Such is the human race. Often it does seem such a pity that Noah and his party didn't miss the boat.

101 Suppose I am a crook, and suppose I am a congressman, but I repeat myself.

102 The calamity that comes is never the one we had prepared ourselves for.

103 The coldest winter I ever spent was a summer in San Francisco. [Attributed.]

104 The difference between the *almost right* word and the *right* word is really a large matter—'tis the difference between the lightning bug and the lightning.

105 The first half of life consists of the capacity to enjoy without the chance; the last half consists of the chance without the capacity.

106 The human race is a race of cowards; and I am not only marching in the procession but carrying a banner.

107 The man with a new idea is a crank until the idea succeeds.

108 The principle of give and take is the principle of diplomacy—give one and take ten.

109 The real yellow peril: gold.

110 The report of my death was an exaggeration. [Countering a journalist's cable from London to New York reporting Twain's death, 1897.]

111 The universal brotherhood of man is our most precious possession—what there is of it.

112 The world consists of the dangerously insane and such that are not.

113 There ain't no way to find out why a snorer can't hear himself snore.

114 There are laws to protect the freedom of the press's speech, but none that are worth anything to protect the people from the press. [1873] —See also Martina Navratilova 1

115 There are many humorous things in the world; among them, the white man's notion that he is less savage than the other savages.

116 There are many scapegoats for our blunders, but the most popular one is Providence.

117 There are no grades of vanity, there are only grades of ability in concealing it.

118 There are several good protections against temptations, but the surest is cowardice.

119 There are those who scoff at the schoolboy, calling him frivolous and shallow. Yet it was a schoolboy who said, "Faith is believing what you know ain't so."

120 There are two times in a man's life when he should not speculate: when he can't afford it, and when he can.

121 There is no sadder sight than a young pessimist, except an old optimist.

122 There isn't any way to libel the intelligence of the human race. —See also H. L. Mencken 62

123 There was things which he stretched, but mainly he told the truth. . . . *The Adventures of Tom Sawyer* is mostly a true book; with some stretchers, as I said before.

124 There's always something about your success that displeases even your best friends.

125 They spell it Vinci and pronounce it Vinchy; foreigners always spell better than they pronounce.

126 Thrusting my nose firmly between his teeth, I threw him heavily to the ground on top of me. —See also Artemus Ward 2

127 To be good is noble, but to show others how to be good is nobler and less trouble.

128 To cease smoking is the easiest thing. I ought to know. I've done it a thousand times.

129 To John Smith. It is said that a man to whom a book is dedicated always buys a copy. If this is true in this instance, a princely affluence is about to descend upon the author. [Dedication to *The Celebrated Jumping Frog of Calaveras County, and Other Sketches,* 1867.]

130 Training is everything. The peach was once a bitter almond; cauliflower is nothing but cabbage with a college education.

131 Truth is mighty and will prevail. There is nothing the matter with this, except that it ain't so.

132 Truth is more of a stranger than fiction. —See also Lord Byron 25

133 Truth *is* stranger than fiction, because fiction is obliged to stick to possibilities; truth isn't. —See also Lord Byron 25

134 Virtue has never been as respectable as money.

135 Water taken in moderation cannot hurt anybody.

136 We have a criminal jury system which is superior to any in the world; and its efficiency is only marred by the difficulty of finding twelve men every day who don't know anything and can't read.

137 We ought never to do wrong when people are looking.

138 What a good thing Adam had. When he said a good thing, he knew nobody had said it before.

139 What is the difference between a taxidermist and a tax collector? The taxidermist takes only your skin.

140 What marriage is to morality, a properly conducted, licensed liquor traffic is to sobriety.

141 Whatever a man's age, he can reduce it several years by putting a bright-colored flower in his buttonhole.

142 When angry, count to four; when very angry, swear.

143 When I was a boy of fourteen, my father was so ignorant I could hardly stand to have the old man around. But when I got to be twenty-one, I was astonished at how much the old man had learned in seven years. [Attributed, but not found in his writings; Twain was fourteen when his father died.]

144 When in doubt, tell the truth.

145 When redheaded people are above a certain social grade, their hair is auburn.

146 When some men discharge an obligation, you can hear the report for miles around.

147 When you cannot get a compliment in any other way, pay yourself one.

148 Wrinkles should merely indicate where the smiles have been.

149 You can straighten a worm, but the crook is in him and only waiting.

150 You want to be very careful about lying; otherwise you are nearly sure to get caught. ["Advice to youth."]

KENNETH TYNAN (1927–1980). *English drama critic*

1 A good drama critic is one who perceives what is happening in the theater of his time. A great drama critic also perceives what is not happening.

2 A good many inconveniences attend play-going in any large city, but the greatest of them is usually the play itself.

3 Something between bland and grandiose: blandiose perhaps. [On Ralph Richardson's voice.]

U

JESSE UNRUH (1922–1983). *American political leader*

Money is the mother's milk of politics. —See also Herb Caen 2; Jim Hightower 3

JOHN UPDIKE (1932–). *American novelist and critic*

1 Appealingness is inversely proportional to attainability.

2 Being naked approaches being revolutionary; going barefoot is mere populism.

3 Now that I am sixty, I see why the idea of elder wisdom has passed from currency.

4 One out of three hundred and twelve Americans is a bore, and a healthy male adult bore consumes each year one and half times his own weight in other people's patience.

5 Possession diminishes the perception of value, immediately.

6 Sex is like money; only too much is enough.

7 The Bible is like a once fearsome lion that, now toothless and declawed, can be petted and teased.

8 The moment when the finished book or, better yet, a tightly packed carton of finished books arrives on my doorstep is the moment of truth, of culmination; its bliss lasts as much as five minutes, until the first typographical error or production flaw is noticed.

9 The odds on God's existence is precisely 10000000 to 1.

10 We live down here among shadows, shadows among shadows.

PETER USTINOV (1921–). *English actor and playwright*

1 A diplomat these days is nothing but a headwaiter who's allowed to sit down occasionally.

2 As for being a general, well, at the age of four with paper hats and wooden swords we're all generals. Only some of us never grow out of it.

3 British education is probably the best in the world, if you can survive it. If you can't, there is nothing left for you but the diplomatic corps.

4 Critics search for ages for the wrong word which, to give them credit, they eventually find.

5 Her virtue was that she said what she thought; her vice, that what she thought didn't amount to much. [On Hollywood gossip columnist Hedda Hopper.]

6 I do not believe that friends are necessarily the people you like best; they are merely the people who got there first.

7 I grew a beard for Nero, in *Quo Vadis,* but Metro-Goldwyn-Mayer thought it didn't look real, so I had to wear a false one.

8 If Botticelli were alive today, he'd be working for *Vogue.*

9 Laughter would be bereaved if snobbery died.

10 Parents are the bones on which children sharpen their teeth.

11 People who reach the top of the tree are only those who haven't got the qualifications to detain them at the bottom.

12 Sex is conversation carried out by other means.

PAUL VALÉRY (1871–1945). *French writer*

1 A man who is "of sound mind" keeps the inner madman under lock and key.

2 A poem is never finished, only abandoned.

3 God created man and, finding him not sufficiently alone, gave him a companion to make him feel his solitude more keenly.

4 Law is the interlude between acts of force.

5 Politics is the art of preventing people from taking part in affairs which properly concern them.

6 Talent without genius comes to little. Genius without talent is nothing.

7 The future is not what it used to be. —See also Walter Truett Anderson; Anonymous 118; Bernard Levin 2

8 The painter should not paint what he sees, but what will be seen.

NORM VAN BROCKLIN (1926–1983). *American football player*

If I ever needed a brain transplant, I'd choose a sportswriter because I'd want a brain that had never been used.

JOHN VANBRUGH (1664–1726). *English playwright*

O Fortune—Fortune—thou art a bitch.

WILLIAM HENRY VANDERBILT (1821–1885). *American railroad industry leader*

When I want to buy up any politicians, I always find the anti-monopolists the most purchasable. They don't come so high.

HARRIET VAN HORNE (1920–). *American journalist and critic*

1 Cooking is like love. It should be entered into with abandon or not at all.

2 Joan Crawford would have made an exemplary prison matron, possibly at Buchenwald.

3 There are days when any electrical appliance in the house, including the vacuum cleaner, seems to offer more entertainment possibilities than the TV set.

THORSTEIN VEBLEN (1857–1929). *American economist*

1 Conspicuous waste and conspicuous leisure are reputable because they are evidence of pecuniary strength; pecuniary strength is reputable because, in the last analysis, it argues success and superior force.

2 Invention is the mother of necessity.

3 The highest achievement in business is the nearest approach in getting something for nothing.

4 What is spoken of as safe and sane business reduces itself in the main to a sagacious use of sabotage.

JESSE VENTURA (1951–). *Minnesota governor and wrestler*

1 Organized religion is a sham and a crutch for weak-minded people who need strength in numbers. It tells people to go out and stick their noses in other people's business.

2 These are people who live on the razor's edge and defy death and do things where people die. They're not going to consider grabbing a woman's breast or buttock a major situation. That's much ado about nothing. [Referring to the scandal in which U.S. Navy aviators groped female officers at a 1991 Tailhook convention in Las Vegas, *Playboy* interview, 1999.]

3 Win if you can, lose if you must, but always cheat.

GORE VIDAL (1925–). *American novelist, critic, and screenwriter*

1 A genius with the IQ of a moron. [On Andy Warhol.]

2 A lack of talent is not enough. [On the Cockettes, a San Francisco drag troupe.]

3 A triumph of the embalmer's art. [On Ronald Reagan.]

4 A wise career choice. [On Truman Capote's death.]

5 Half of the American people have never read a newspaper. Half never voted for president. One hopes it is the same half.

6 He is a bad novelist and a fool. The combination usually makes for great popularity in the U.S. [On Aleksandr Solzhenitsyn.]

7 He will lie even when it is inconvenient, the sign of a true artist. [On Richard M. Nixon.]

8 I am, at heart, a tiresome nag complacently positive that there is no human problem which could not be solved if people would simply do as I advise.

9 I suspect that our own faith in psychiatry will seem as touchingly quaint to the future as our grandparents' belief in phrenology seems now to us.

10 I'm all for bringing back the birch, but only between consenting adults.

11 It is not enough to succeed. Others must fail.

12 It is the spirit of the age to believe that any fact, no matter how suspect, is superior to any imaginative exercise, no matter how true.

13 It's a country evenly divided between conservatives and reactionaries. [On America.]

14 Looks and sounds not unlike Hitler, but without the charm. [On William F. Buckley, Jr.]

15 Never have children, only grandchildren.

16 Paradise is wherever I am.

17 Persuading the people to vote against their own best interests has been the awesome genius of the American political elite from the beginning.

18 Reality is something the human race doesn't handle very well.

19 Style is knowing who you are, what you want to say, and not giving a damn.

20 That long wrangling for supremacy which is called marriage.

21 There is nothing more debasing than the work of those who do well what is not worth doing at all. —See also Alexander Woollcott 6

22 This is not at all bad, except as prose. [On Herman Wouk's 1974 novel *Winds of War.*]

23 What a nightmare, to wake up in the morning and realize that you are John Simon. [Simon is a literary critic.]

24 What other culture could have produced someone like Hemingway and *not* seen the joke?

[25] Whenever a friend succeeds, a little something in me dies.

[26] You get a better class of person at orgies, because people have to keep in trim more. There is an awful lot of going round holding in your stomach, you know. Everybody is very polite to each other. The conversation isn't very good, but you can't have everything.

KING VIDOR (1894–1982). *American film director*

Take it from me, marriage isn't a word. It's a *sentence!*

EDMUND H. VOLKART (1919–). *American writer*

[1] Ballot, *n.* In democracies, the means by which the lesser of two or more political evils is transformed into the "people's choice."

[2] Expert, *n.* A modern seer, often self-styled, whose pronouncements are received as if emanating from an oracle. A "recognized expert" is one whose pronouncements are closest to conventional wisdom.

[3] Fairness, *n.* That impartiality and equity of treatment that everyone approves of, so long as their own interests are not threatened.

[4] Quack, *n.* A person who dishonestly pretends to be a physician, as distinguished from an M.D. who honestly pretends to be one.

[5] Respectability, *n.* The social status of people whose sins haven't quite caught up with them.

[6] Tyranny, *n.* The arbitrary or excessive use of power, which all governments practice as both a right and a duty; they differ only in the amount of velvet in the glove, if there is a glove at all.

VOLTAIRE (1694–1778). *French philosopher*

[1] All history is an agreed-upon fiction.

[2] All styles are good, except the tiresome kind.

[3] Common sense is not so common. —See also Kin Hubbard 48

[4] Doctors pour drugs of which they know little, to cure diseases of which they know less, into human beings of whom they know nothing.

[5] England has 42 religions and only two sauces.

[6] Englishmen! You want to kill me because I am a Frenchman! Am I not punished enough, in not being an Englishman? [Spoken to an angry Francophobic London crowd which was shouting for his death; they cheered his words and escorted him to safety, 1727.]

[7] God created sex. Priests created marriage.

[8] He denounced the world in revenge for his complete lack of success in it.

[9] I have never made but one prayer to God, a very short one: "O Lord, make my enemies ridiculous." And God granted it.

[10] I know I am among civilized men because they are fighting so savagely. —See also James A. Garfield 2

[11] "If God did not exist, it would be necessary to invent him." I am rarely satisfied with my lines, but I own that I have a father's tenderness for that one.

[12] Illusion is the first of all pleasures.

[13] In England it is a good thing to kill an admiral from time to time to encourage the others.

[14] In the great game of life, one begins as a dupe and ends as a rogue.

15 In this world we run the risk of having to choose between being either the anvil or the hammer.

16 Is there anyone so wise as to learn by the experience of others?

17 It is dangerous to be right in matters on which the established authorities are wrong.

18 It is difficult to free fools from the chains they revere.

19 It is forbidden to kill; therefore all murderers are punished unless they kill in large numbers and to the sound of trumpets.

20 It is the final proof of God's omnipotence that he need not exist in order to save us.

21 Men will always be mad, and those who think they can cure them are the maddest of all.

22 Once the people begin to reason, all is lost.

23 Originality is nothing but judicious imitation.

24 Our wretched species is so made that those who walk on the beaten path always throw stones at those who teach a new path.

25 Prejudices are what fools use for reason.

26 The art of government consists in taking as much money as possible from one class of citizens and giving it to the other.

27 The art of medicine consists of amusing the patient while nature cures the disease.

28 The more truly learned he became, the more he doubted all he knew.

29 The multitude of books is making us ignorant.

30 The only reward to be expected from literature is contempt if one fails and hatred if one succeeds.

31 The secret of being a bore is to tell everything.

32 The truths of religion are never so well understood as by those who have lost their power of reasoning.

33 To believe in God is impossible; not to believe in Him is absurd.

34 To succeed in chaining the multitude you must seem to wear the same fetters.

35 To succeed in the world it is not enough to be stupid, you must also be well-mannered.

36 We use ideas merely to justify our evil, and speech merely to conceal our ideas.

37 When he who hears doesn't know what he who speaks means, and when he who speaks doesn't know what he himself means—that is philosophy.

38 When it is a question of money, everybody is of the same religion.

NICHOLAS VON HOFFMAN (1929–). *American writer*

We Are the People Our Parents Warned Us Against. [Book title, 1968.] —See also Brendan Behan 6; Robin Morgan 2

JANE WAGNER (1935–). *American writer and humorist*

1 All my life I've always wanted to be somebody. But I see now I should have been more specific. [*The Search for Signs of Intelligent Life in the Universe,* 1986, a one-woman comedy show performed by Lily Tomlin.]

2 As soon as humankind began to discover the truth about itself, we began to find ways to cover up that truth. But maybe that's for the best: Our ability to delude ourselves may be an important survival tool.

3 At the moment you are most in awe of all there is about life that you don't understand, you are closer to understanding it all than at any other time.

4 Did you know, the RNA/DNA molecule can be found throughout space in many galaxies—only everybody spells it different?

5 Having everything can sometimes make you stop wanting anything. It's called "Rich People's Burn-Out."

6 I even worry about reflective flea collars. Oh, sure, drivers can see them glow in the dark, but so can the fleas.

7 I made some studies, and reality is the leading cause of stress amongst those in touch with it. I can take it in small doses, but as a lifestyle I found it too confining.

8 I personally think we developed language because of our deep inner need to complain.

9 I refuse to be intimidated by reality any more. After all, what is reality anyway? Nothin' but a collective hunch.

10 I woke up in the nut house. They were hookin' me up. One thing they don't tell you about shock treatments, for months afterwards you got flyaway hair. And it used to be my best feature.

11 I'm getting my act together; throwing it in your FACE. I want to insult every member of the human race. I'm Agnus Angst. I don't kiss ass. I don't say thanks.

12 If I can be of service to humankind's progress, the loss of my mind is a small price to pay. I just think I should have been consulted.

13 If I'd known what it would have been like to have it all, I might have been willing to settle for less.

14 If we don't take in air every few minutes, we die, but the air we are taking in is killing us. I rush to my Behavior Modification Center, hoping they can help me cut down on my habit of *breathing.*

15 Never underestimate the power of the human mind to forget. The other day, I forgot where I put my house keys—looked everywhere, then I remembered I don't have a house. I forget more important things, too, like the meaning of life. I forget that. It'll come to me, though. Let's just hope when it does, I'll be in. [Spoken by Trudy, the bag lady.]

16 No matter how cynical you become, it's never enough to keep up.

17 One thing I have no worry about is whether God exists. But it has occurred to me that God has Alzheimer's and has forgotten we exist.

18 We import ethnic clothing, mostly from South America. And no, don't say it; I don't think we're exploiting cheap labor, so much as I think we're giving work to people who would be out of work, if we weren't exploiting cheap labor. Oh, Edie, I know what you're thinking, but it's hard to be politically conscious and upwardly mobile at the same time.

19 What goes up must come down. But don't expect it to come down where you can find it. Murphy's Law applied to Newton's.

20 You are what you think. Jeez, that's frightening.

21 You don't know what it's like! Hyperactive twins! When they turned three, my doctor prescribed Ritalin—I wouldn't dream of giving a drug to my children, but it does help when I take it myself.

22 You'd think by now evolution could've at least evolved us to the place where we could change ourselves.

JOHN WAIN (1925–1994). *English writer*
Poetry is to prose as dancing is to walking.

ALICE WALKER (1944–). *American writer*
1 I think it pisses God off if you walk by the color purple in a field somewhere and don't notice it. [*The Color Purple,* 1982.]

2 The long-term accommodation that protects marriage and other such relationships is forgetfulness.

HORACE WALPOLE (1717–1797). *English writer*
1 History makes one shudder and laugh by turns.

2 I never knew but one woman who would not take gold, and she took diamonds.

3 It was said of old Sarah, Duchess of Marlborough, that she never put dots over her i's, to save ink.

4 Lesson to the Indiscreet. They who say all they think, and tell all they know, put others on their guard and prevent themselves from being told anything of consequence.

5 Spring has set in with its usual severity.

6 The more one learns of Johnson, the more preposterous assemblance he appears—of strong sense, of the lowest bigotry and prejudices, of pride, brutality, fretfulness and vanity—and Boswell is the ape of most of his faults without a grain of his sense. It is the story of a mountebank and his zany. [On Samuel Johnson and his biographer James Boswell.]

7 The wisest prophets make sure of the event first.

8 This world is a comedy to those that think, a tragedy to those that feel.

BARBARA WALTERS (1931–). *American television personality*
1 A great many people think that polysyllables are a sign of intelligence.

2 Parents of young children should realize that few people, and maybe no one, will find their children as enchanting as they do.

3 Success can make you go one of two ways. It can make you a prima donna, or it can smooth the edges, take away the insecurities, let the nice things come out.

ARTEMUS WARD (1834–1867). *American writer, lecturer, and humorist*

1   Be sure and vote at least once in all elections.

2   By a sudden and adroit movement I placed my left eye against his fist.
—See also Mark Twain 126

3   Canada has politicians, and I expect they don't differ from our politicians,
some of them being gifted and talented liars, no doubt.

4   Did you ever have the measles and, if so, how many?

5   He is dreadfully married. He's the most married man I ever saw in my life.

6   I am happiest when I am idle. I could live for months without performing
any kind of labor, and at the expiration of that time I should feel fresh and
vigorous enough to go right on in the same way for numerous more months.

7   I girded up my loins and fled the scene.

8   I have abstrained from having any sentimunts or principles. My pollertics,
like my religion, bein of a exceedin accomodatin character. [As originally
published.]

9   I have already given two cousins to the war, and I stand ready to sacrifice
my wife's brother rather than not see the rebellion crushed. And if worse
comes to worse I'll shed every drop of blood my able-bodied relations has
got to prosecute the war. [Referring to the Civil War.]

10 I have always sustained a good moral character. I was never a railroad director in my life.

11 I have been gradually growing more and more respectable every year. I
love my children and never mistake another man's wife for my own.

12 I now bid you a welcome adoo.

13 I prefer temperance hotels, although they sell worse liquor than any other
kind of hotels.

14 I'm not a politician and my other habits are good.

15 Let us all be happy and live within our means, even if we have to borrow
the money to do it with.

16 Shakespeare wrote good plays, but he wouldn't have succeeded as a Washington correspondent of a New York daily paper. He lacked the requisite
fancy and imagination.

17 The female woman is one of the greatest institutions of which this land can
boast.

18 The Puritans nobly fled from a land of despotism to a land of freedom,
where they could not only enjoy their own religion, but prevent everybody
else from enjoying his.

19 The sun has a right to "set" where it wants to, and so, I may add, has a hen.

20 Thrice is he armed that hath his quarrel just—and four times he who gets
his fist in fust.

21 Traitors are an unfortunate class of people. If they wasn't, they wouldn't
be traitors. They conspire to bust up a country—they fail, and they're traitors. They bust her, and they become statesmen and heroes. —See also
Erich Fromm 2

22 Why is this thus? What is the reason of this thusness?

SELA WARD (1957–). *American actress*
I don't know that I have the courage not to have plastic surgery.

ANDY WARHOL (1927–1987). *American artist*
1 *Heaven and Hell Are Just One Breath Away.* [Title of his last artwork.]
2 I am a deeply superficial person.
3 I'd ask around ten or fifteen people for suggestions. Finally one lady friend asked the right question. "Well, what do you love most?" That's how I started painting money.
4 If you want to know all about Andy Warhol, just look at the surface: of my paintings and films and me, and there I am. There's nothing behind it.
5 In the future everybody will be world famous for fifteen minutes. [1968; years later he said, "I'm bored with that line. I never use it anymore. My new line is, 'In fifteen minutes, everybody will be famous.'"]
6 It would be very glamorous to be reincarnated as a giant ring on Elizabeth Taylor's finger.
7 Publicity is like eating peanuts. Once you start you can't stop. —See also Orson Welles 2
8 She's gone to Bloomingdale's. [Referring to his mother's death.]
9 That's what show business is for—to prove that it's not what you are that counts, it's what they think you are.

CHARLES DUDLEY WARNER (1829–1900). *American writer and editor*
1 Blessed be agriculture—if one does not have too much of it.
2 Politics makes strange bedfellows. [1871] —See also Anonymous 98; Groucho Marx 17; William Shakespeare 19
3 Public opinion is stronger than the legislature, and nearly as strong as the Ten Commandments.
4 The chief effect of talk on any subject is to strengthen one's own opinion.
5 The thing generally raised on city land is taxes.
6 There is but one pleasure in life equal to that of being called on to make an after-dinner speech, and that is not being called on to make one.
7 We are half-ruined by conformity, but we should be wholly ruined without it.
8 What small potatoes we all are, compared with what we might be!

HARRY M. WARNER (1881–1958). *Polish-born American film producer*
Who the hell wants to hear actors talk? [On talking films shortly before their introduction, 1927.]

JACK WARNER (1892–1978). *Canadian-born American film producer*
1 An explosive little broad with a sharp left. [On Bette Davis.]
2 What can you do with a guy with ears like that? [Commenting on Clark Gable after seeing his screen test and turning him down for a role in the 1930 film *Little Caesar.*] —See also Anonymous 80

GEORGE WASHINGTON (1732–1799). *American general and president*
1 Ay! I am fairly out and you are fairly in! See which of us will be happiest! [Remark to his successor John Adams, at the White House, 1797.]
2 My movements to the chair of government will be accompanied by feel-

ings not unlike those of a culprit, who is going to the place of his execution. [On taking office as president.]

3 Wherever and whenever one person is found adequate to the discharge of a duty by close application thereto, it is worse executed by two persons, and scarcely done at all if three or more are employed therein. [Letter, 1792.]

4 Why should I expect to be exempt from censure, the unfailing lot of an elevated station? —See also Jonathan Swift 2

THOMAS WATSON (1874–1956). *American business machine industry leader*

I think there is a world market for maybe five computers. [1943] —See also Bill Gates 2

EVELYN WAUGH (1903–1966). *English novelist*

1 All this fuss about sleeping together. For physical pleasure I'd sooner go to my dentist any day.

2 Anyone who has been to an English public school will always feel comparatively at home in prison.

3 "I often think," he continued, "that we can trace almost all the disasters of English history to the influence of Wales!"

4 Manners are especially the need of the plain. The pretty can get away with anything.

5 Only when one has lost all curiosity has one reached the age to write an autobiography.

6 Other nations use "force"; we Britons alone use "might."

7 Punctuality is the virtue of the bored.

8 Randolph Churchill went into hospital to have a lung removed. It was announced that the trouble was not "malignant." It was a typical triumph of modern science to find the only part of Randolph that was not malignant and remove it.

9 We cherish our friends not for their ability to amuse us, but for ours to amuse them.

JOHN WAYNE (1907–1979). *American actor*

1 I figured I needed a gimmick, so I dreamed up the drawl, the squint, and a way of moving which meant to suggest that I wasn't looking for trouble but would just as soon throw a bottle at your head as not.

2 My favorite four-letter words are "hard work."

3 Talk low, talk slow, and don't say too much. [Advice to actors.]

4 They have a right to work wherever they want to—as long as they have dinner ready when you get home.

SIMONE WEIL (1909–1943). *French writer*

Official history is a matter of believing murderers on their own word.

CHAIM WEIZMANN (1874–1952). *Israeli president*

1 Einstein explained his theory to me every day, and on my arrival I was fully convinced that he understood it. [During a transatlantic crossing.]

2 Miracles do happen, but one has to work very hard for them.

ORSON WELLES (1915–1985). *American writer, actor, and film director*

1   I don't say we all ought to misbehave, but we ought to look as if we could.

2   I hate television. I hate it as much as peanuts. But I can't stop eating peanuts. —See also Andy Warhol 7

3   I started from the top and worked my way down. [Referring to his career in Hollywood.]

4   The Swiss had brotherly love, they had five hundred years of democracy and peace, and what did that produce? The cuckoo clock. [Written and spoken by Welles in the 1949 film *The Third Man*; later he was told that credit for the cuckoo clock belonged to the Bavarians.]

5   This is the biggest electric train set any boy ever had. [Referring to the RKO studios.]

6   When you are down and out, something always turns up—and it's usually the noses of your friends.

DUKE OF WELLINGTON (Arthur Wellesley; 1769–1852). *British general and prime minister*

1   Next to a battle lost, the greatest misery is a battle won.

2   There are no manifestos like cannon and musketry.

3   "Was there anything you'd like my sermon to be about?" [Vicar] Yes, about ten minutes. [Attributed.]

4   When I reflect upon the characters and attainments of some of the general officers of this army, I tremble; and, as Lord Chesterfield said of the generals of his day, "I only hope that when the enemy reads the list of their names he trembles as I do."

CAROLYN WELLS (1869–1942). *American writer*

1   A guilty conscience is the mother of invention.

2   A tutor who tooted the flute, / Tried to teach two young tooters to toot; / Said the two to the tutor, / "Is it harder to toot or / To tutor two tooters to toot?"

3   Every dogma must have its day.

4   I cannot speak well enough to be unintelligible.

5   Invitation is the sincerest flattery.

6   They borrow books they will not buy, / They have no ethics or religions; / I wish some kind Burbankian guy / Would cross my books with homing pigeons.

H. G. WELLS (1866–1946). *English writer*

1   Bah! The thing is not a nose at all, but a bit of primordial chaos clapped on to my face.

2   Human history becomes more and more a race between education and catastrophe.

3   I launched the phrase "the war to end war"—and that was not the least of my crimes.

4   In England we have come to rely upon a comfortable time-lag of fifty years or a century intervening between the perception that something ought to be done and a serious attempt to do it.

5 Lies are the mortar that bind the savage individual man into the social masonry.

6 Moral indignation is jealousy with a halo.

7 The more I think about you, the more it comes home to me what an unmitigated Middle Victorian ass you are! [To George Bernard Shaw.]

JESSAMYN WEST (1902–1984). *American novelist and poet*
Fiction reveals truths that reality obscures.

MAE WEST (1893–1980). *American actress*

1 A hard man is good to find.

2 A man in the house is worth two in the street.

3 All discarded lovers should be given a second chance, but with someone else.

4 An ounce of performance is worth pounds of promises.

5 Between two evils, I always pick the one I never tried before.

6 Beulah, peel me a grape.

7 Come up and see me sometime, and bring La Guardia. [Referring to New York mayor Fiorello La Guardia, soon after he had described her show as indecent.]

8 Don't fight over me, boys—there's plenty to go around.

9 Find 'em, fool 'em, 'n forget 'em. [Referring to men; a variant of a well-known dictum, 1933.]

10 Give a man a free hand, and he'll run it all over you.

11 "Goodness, what beautiful diamonds!" [Hatcheck girl] Goodness had nothing to do with it, dearie.

12 He who hesitates is a damned fool.

13 He's the kind of man who picks his friends—to pieces.

14 His mother should have thrown him away and kept the stork.

15 "How do you do, Miss West?" [Red Skelton] How do you do what? [Radio skit.]

16 How tall are you, son? "Ma'am, I'm six feet seven inches." Let's forget the six feet and talk about the seven inches.

17 I always say, keep a diary, and some day it'll keep you.

18 I generally avoid temptation unless I can't resist it.

19 I like a man who takes his time.

20 I like to know what I'm doing. [On the mirrored ceiling over her bed.]

21 I only like two kinds of men: domestic and imported.

22 I used to be Snow White, but I drifted.

23 I wrote the story myself. It's about a girl who lost her reputation and never missed it.

24 Is that a gun in your pocket, or are you just glad to see me?

25 It's better to be looked over than overlooked.

26 It's not the men in my life that counts; it's the life in my men.

27 It's not what I do, but the way I do it. It's not what I say, but the way I say it.

28 Love conquers all things, except poverty and toothaches.

29 Marriage is a great institution, but I'm not ready for an institution yet.

30 Men like women with a past—because they hope history will repeat itself.
31 "O Miss West, I've heard so much about you." Yeah, but you can't prove a thing.
32 Save a boyfriend for a rainy day—and another, in case it doesn't rain.
33 She may be good for nothing, but she's not bad for nothing.
34 She's one of the finest women who ever walked the streets.
35 She's the kind of girl who climbed the ladder of success, wrong by wrong.
36 "Ten men are waiting to see you." I'm feeling a little tired today; one of those fellows will have to go home.
37 The best way to hold a man is in your arms.
38 There's no one in the world quite like Bill—Thank God! [On W. C. Fields.]
39 To err is human—but it feels divine.
40 Too much of a good thing can be wonderful.
41 When I'm good, I'm very, very good; but when I'm bad, I'm better.
42 When women go wrong, men go right after them.
43 You ought to get out of those wet clothes and into a dry Martini.
44 You're never too old to grow younger.

REBECCA WEST (1892–1983). *English novelist and critic*

1 Every other inch a gentleman.
2 I myself have never been able to find out precisely what feminism is: I only know that people call me a feminist whenever I express sentiments that differentiate me from a doormat.
3 If I wanted life to be easy, I should have gotten born in a different universe.
4 If the whole human race lay in one grave, the epitaph on its headstone might well be: "It seemed a good idea at the time."
5 It is queer how it is always one's virtues and not one's vices that precipitate one into disaster.
6 Journalism—an ability to meet the challenge of filling space.
7 The reward for total abstinence from alcohol seems, illogically enough, to be the capacity for becoming intoxicated without it.
8 There are two kinds of imperialists—imperialists and bloody imperialists.

EDITH WHARTON (1862–1937). *American novelist and short-story writer*

1 Inkstands and teacups are never as full as when one upsets them.
2 Life is the saddest thing there is, next to death.
3 Mrs. Bart had no tolerance for scenes which were not of her own making.

JAMES McNEILL WHISTLER (1834–1903). *American painter*

1 "By the way, I passed your house last night." [Young aristocrat] Thank you!
2 Fear I may not be able to reach you in time for the ceremony. Don't wait. [Telegram to Oscar Wilde, whose wedding he was about to miss, 1884.]
3 "I wish I had said that." [Oscar Wilde, after hearing Whistler make a witty remark.] You will, Oscar, you will.
4 I'm lonesome; they are all dying. I have hardly a warm personal enemy left.
5 If other people are going to talk, conversation becomes impossible.

6 "Why were you born in an unfashionable place like Lowell, Massachusetts?" The explanation is quite simple: I wished to be near my mother.

7 "Your picture is not up to your mark; it is not good this time." [Art critic] You shouldn't say it is not good. You should say you do not like it; and then, you know, you're perfectly safe. Now come and have something you do like—have some whiskey.

E. B. WHITE (1899–1985). *American writer*

1 A candidate could easily commit political suicide if he were to come up with an unconventional thought during a presidential tour.

2 A good farmer is nothing more nor less than a handy man with a sense of humus.

3 Democracy is the recurrent suspicion that more than half of the people are right more than half of the time.

4 I arise in the morning torn between a desire to improve (or save) the world and a desire to enjoy (or savor) the world. This makes it hard to plan the day.

5 "It's broccoli, dear." [Mother] "I say it's spinach, and I say the hell with it." [Daughter, cartoon caption.]

6 No one should come to New York to live unless he is willing to be lucky.

7 Not even a collapsing world looks dark to a man who is about to make his fortune.

8 Rich, ornate prose is hard to digest, generally unwholesome, and sometimes nauseating. [*The Elements of Style,* 1959.]

9 "What are the sources of your short stories?" Oh, I never look under the hood.

WILLIAM ALLEN WHITE (1868–1944). *American editor and writer*

1 He has a handshake like a ten-cent pickled mackerel in brown paper. [On Woodrow Wilson.]

2 Liberty is the only thing you cannot have unless you give it to others.

3 My advice to the women's clubs of America is to raise more hell and fewer dahlias.

4 With a pig's eyes that never look up, with a pig's snout that loves muck, with a pig's brain that knows only the sty, and with a pig's squeal that cries only when he is hurt, he sometimes opens his pig's mouth, tusked and ugly, and lets out the voice of God, railing at the whitewash that covers the manure about his habitat. [On H. L. Mencken, 1928.]

ALFRED NORTH WHITEHEAD (1861–1947). *English mathematician and philosopher*

1 A rule of men over women remained an established feature of highly civilized societies. It survived as a hangover from barbarism.

2 As society is now constituted, a literal adherence to the moral precepts scattered throughout the Gospels would mean sudden death.

3 Ideas won't keep. Something must be done about them.

4 Nothing is more curious than the self-satisfied dogmatism with which

mankind at each period of its history cherishes the delusion of the finality of its existing modes of knowledge.

5 The concept of "God" is the way in which we understand this incredible fact—that what cannot be, yet is.

6 The great English Universities, under whose direct authority school children are examined in plays of Shakespeare, to the certain destruction of their enjoyment, should be prosecuted for soul murder.

7 The safest general characterization of the European philosophical tradition is that it consists of a series of footnotes to Plato.

8 The "silly" question is the first intimation of some totally new development.

9 The tragedy of the world is that those who are imaginative have but slight experience, and those who are experienced have feeble imaginations.

10 The truth of a society is what cannot be said.

11 What is morality in any given time or place? It is what the majority then and there happen to like, and immorality is what they dislike.

12 Wherever there is a creed, there is a heretic round the corner or in his grave.

KATHARINE WHITEHORN (1928–). *English writer*

1 No nice men are good at getting taxis.

2 The best career advice to give the young is "Find out what you like doing best and get someone to pay you for doing it."

3 The great rule is not to talk about money with people who have much more or much less than you.

WALT WHITMAN (1819–1891). *American poet*

1 Do I contradict myself? / Very well then I contradict myself, / (I am large, I contain multitudes.)

2 Everybody is writing, writing, writing—worst of all, writing poetry. It'd be better if the whole tribe of the scribblers—every damned one of us—were sent off somewhere with tool chests to do some honest work.

3 He most honors my style who learns under it to destroy the teacher.

4 I call to the world to distrust the accounts of my friends, but listen to my enemies, as I myself do.

5 I sound my barbaric yawp over the roofs of the world.

6 I'm as bad as the worst but, thank God, I am as good as the best.

7 Is it the prophet's thought I speak, or am I raving?

8 Lobbiers are the born freedom sellers of the earth.

9 Manhattan crowds, with their turbulent musical chorus! / Manhattan faces and eyes forever for me.

10 Money-making is our magician's serpent, remaining today sole master of the field. The best class we show, is but a mob of fashionably dressed speculators and vulgarians.

11 O damnation, damnation! thy other name is school-teaching.

12 People who serve you without love get even behind your back.

13 Respectability has no use for me: I suppose the distaste is mutual.

14 The best politics that could happen for our republic would be the abolition of politics.

15 The true America, heir / of the past so grand, / To build a grander future.

CHARLOTTE WHITTON (1896–1975). *Ottawa mayor*
Whatever women do, they must do twice as well as men to be thought half as good. Luckily, this is not difficult. [After being elected mayor of Ottawa.]

TOM WICKER (1926–). *American journalist*
1 A first-class intellect, but a second-class temperament. [On Richard M. Nixon, 1994.] —See also Oliver Wendell Holmes, Jr. 2

2 Government expands to absorb revenue and then some.

3 The only thing you can say about the 1970 elections is that the Democrats picked up nine seats in the House and the Republicans one and a half senators. If you wonder how there can be a half-senator, you haven't met some of those fellows.

NORBERT WIENER (1894–1964). *American mathematician*
A conscience which has been bought once will be bought twice.

ELLA WHEELER WILCOX (1850–1919). *American writer*
Laugh, and the world laughs with you; / Weep, and you weep alone; / For the sad old earth must borrow its mirth, / But has trouble enough of its own.

OSCAR WILDE (1854–1900). *Anglo-Irish playwright*
1 A gentleman never hurts anyone's feelings unintentionally.

2 A little sincerity is a dangerous thing, and a great deal of it is absolutely fatal.

3 A man cannot be too careful in the choice of his enemies.

4 A poet can survive everything but a misprint.

5 A sentimentalist is simply one who desires to have the luxury of an emotion without paying for it.

6 A thing is not necessarily true because a man dies for it.

7 After a good dinner one can forgive anybody, even one's own relations.

8 All women become like their mothers—that is their tragedy; no man does—that's his. —See also Alan Bennett 2

9 Always forgive your enemies—nothing annoys them so much.

10 Ambition is the last refuge of the failure. —See also Samuel Johnson 64

11 An excellent man; he has no enemies, and none of his friends like him. [On George Bernard Shaw, 1896.]

12 An idea that is not dangerous is unworthy of being called an idea at all.

13 Any preoccupation with ideas of what is right and wrong in conduct shows an arrested intellectual development.

14 Anybody can sympathize with the sufferings of a friend, but it requires a very fine nature to sympathize with a friend's success.

15 Brute reasoning is hitting below the intellect.

16 Charity, dear Miss Prism, charity! None of us is perfect. I myself am peculiarly susceptible to draughts. [*The Importance of Being Earnest,* 1895.]

17 Children begin by loving their parents; as they grow older they judge them; sometimes they forgive them.

18 Conscience and cowardice are really the same thing. Conscience is the trade name of the firm. That is all.

19 Cynicism is merely the art of seeing things as they are instead of as they ought to be.

20 Democracy means simply the bludgeoning of the people by the people for the people.

21 Divorces are made in heaven.

22 Do you really think, Arthur, that it is weakness that yields to temptation? I tell you that there are terrible temptations that it requires strength, strength and courage, to yield to.

23 Either that wallpaper goes, or I do. [On his deathbed.]

24 Experience is the name everyone gives to their mistakes.

25 Fastidiousness is the ability to resist a temptation in the hope that a better one will come along.

26 Fathers should neither be seen nor heard. That is the only proper basis for family life.

27 For what is Truth? In matters of religion, it is simply the opinion that has survived.

28 "Have you anything to declare?" [A New York customs inspector] Nothing, nothing but my genius!

29 He had the sort of face that, once seen, is never remembered.

30 He has one of those terribly weak natures that are not susceptible to influence.

31 He hasn't a single redeeming vice.

32 He knew the precise psychological moment when to say nothing.

33 He was always late on principle, his principle being that punctuality is the thief of time.

34 I am always astonishing myself. It is the only thing that makes life worth living.

35 I beg your pardon, I didn't recognize you—I've changed a lot.

36 I can believe anything, provided that it is quite incredible.

37 I can resist everything except temptation.

38 I dislike arguments of any kind. They are always vulgar, and often convincing.

39 I dislike modern memoirs. They are generally written by people who have either entirely lost their memories, or have never done anything worth remembering.

40 I have no money at all: I live, or am supposed to live, on a few francs a day. Like dear St. Francis of Assisi I am wedded to Poverty: but in my case the marriage is not a success. [While living in France after his release from prison in 1899.]

41 I hope you have not been leading a double life, pretending to be wicked and being really good all the time. That would be hypocrisy.

42 I like men who have a future and women who have a past.

43 I love acting. It is so much more real than life.

44 I love hearing my relations abused. It is the only thing that makes me put up with them at all. Relations are simply a tedious pack of people, who haven't the remotest knowledge of how to live, nor the smallest instinct about when to die.

45 I love talking about nothing. It is the only thing I know anything about.

46 I must decline your invitation owing to a subsequent engagement.

47 I never came across anyone in whom the moral sense was dominant who was not heartless, cruel, vindictive, log-stupid and entirely lacking in the smallest sense of humanity.

48 I never travel without my diary. One should always have something sensational to read in the train.

49 I sometimes think that God in creating man somewhat overestimated His ability. —See also Woody Allen 30; Anonymous 31

50 I usually say what I really think. A great mistake nowadays. It makes one so liable to be misunderstood.

51 In America the young are always ready to give to those who are older than themselves the full benefits of their inexperience.

52 In the old days men had the rack. Now they have the Press.

53 In this world there are only two tragedies. One is not getting what one wants, and the other is getting it. —See also George Bernard Shaw 117

54 It is absurd to divide people into good and bad. People are either charming or tedious.

55 It is only shallow people who do not judge by appearances.

56 It is very vulgar to talk like a dentist when one isn't a dentist. It produces a false impression.

57 Life imitates Art far more than Art imitates Life.

58 Life is never fair, and perhaps it is a good thing for most of us that it is not.

59 Life's aim, if it has one, is simply to be always looking for temptations. There are not nearly enough. I sometimes pass a whole day without coming across a single one. It is quite dreadful. It makes one so nervous about the future.

60 M. Zola is determined to show that if he has not genius, he can at least be dull. [On French novelist Émile Zola.]

61 Man is a rational animal who always loses his temper when he is called upon to act in accordance with the dictates of reason.

62 Meredith is a prose Browning, and so is Browning.

63 Misfortunes one can endure; they come from outside, they are accidents. But to suffer for one's own faults—ah! there is the sting of life.

64 Modern journalism justifies its own existence by the great Darwinian principle of the survival of the vulgarest.

65 Morality is simply the attitude we adopt towards people whom we personally dislike.

66 Murder is always a mistake—one should never do anything one cannot talk about after dinner.

67 My own business bores me to death; I prefer other people's.

68 Never speak disrespectfully of Society, Algernon. Only people who can't get into it do that.

69 Nothing spoils a romance so much as a sense of humor in the woman— or the want of it in a man.

70 Nothing succeeds like excess. —See also Alexandre Dumas 2

71 Nowadays people know the price of everything and the value of nothing.

72 Nowadays, with our modern mania for morality, everyone has to pose as a paragon of purity, incorruptibility, and all the other seven deadly virtues.

73 One can always recognize women who trust their husbands: they look so thoroughly unhappy.

74 One can survive everything nowadays, except death, and live down anything except a good reputation.

75 One must have a heart of stone to read the death of Little Nell without laughing. [On the heroine in Charles *Dickens's The Old Curiosity Shop,* 1841.]

76 One should always be a little improbable.

77 One should always be in love. That is the reason one should never marry.

78 One should always play fairly—when one has the winning cards.

79 Only the shallow know themselves.

80 Philosophy teaches us to bear with equanimity the misfortunes of others.

81 Questions are never indiscreet; answers sometimes are.

82 Rich bachelors should be heavily taxed. It is not fair that some men should be happier than others.

83 She is a peacock in everything but beauty.

84 She wore far too much rouge last night, and not quite enough clothes. That is always a sign of despair in a woman.

85 Sir, it is your duty to get married. You can't be always living for pleasure.

86 Some cause happiness wherever they go; others whenever they go.

87 Talk to every woman as if you loved her, and to every man as if he bored you, and at the end of your first season you will have the reputation of possessing the most perfect social tact.

88 The amount of women in London who flirt with their own husbands is perfectly scandalous. It looks so bad. It is simply washing one's clean linen in public.

89 "The Book of Life begins with a man and a woman in a garden." [Lord Illingworth] "It ends with Revelations." [Mrs. Allonby, in *A Woman of No Importance,* 1893]

90 The books that the world calls immoral are books that show the world its own shame.

91 The difference between literature and journalism is that journalism is unreadable, and literature is not read.

92 The English public is wonderfully tolerant. It forgives everything except genius.

93 The English public takes no interest in a work of art until it is told that the work in question is immoral.

94 The old believe everything, the middle-aged suspect everything, the young know everything.

95 The one charm of marriage is that it makes a life of deception absolutely necessary for both parties.

96 The only difference between the saint and the sinner is that every saint has a past, and every sinner has a future.

97 The only thing that consoles man for the stupid things he does is the praise he always gives himself for doing them.

98 The only thing to do with good advice is pass it on. It is never of any use to oneself.

99 The only way to get rid of temptation is to yield to it. —See also Honoré de Balzac 5

100 The public have an insatiable curiosity to know everything, except what is worth knowing.

101 The real tragedy of the poor is that they can afford nothing but self-denial.

102 The things one feels absolutely certain about are never true. —See also Adair Lara 6

103 The world has grown suspicious of anything that looks like a happily married life.

104 The world is a stage, but the play is badly cast.

105 There are moments when art almost attains the dignity of manual labor.

106 There is always something ridiculous about the emotions of people whom one has ceased to love.

107 There is no sin except stupidity.

108 There is one thing worse than an absolutely loveless marriage. A marriage in which there is love, but on one side only.

109 There is only one thing in the world worse than being talked about, and that is not being talked about. —See also Samuel Johnson 87

110 They are so pleased to find out other people's secrets. It distracts public attention from their own.

111 Thirty-five is a very attractive age. London society is full of women of the very highest birth who have, of their own free choice, remained thirty-five for years.

112 To be good, according to the vulgar standard of goodness, is obviously quite easy. It merely requires a certain amount of sordid terror, a certain lack of imaginative thought, and a certain low passion for middle-class respectability.

113 To be natural is such a difficult pose to keep up.

114 To get back my youth I would do anything in the world, except take exercise, get up early, or be respectable.

115 To love oneself is the beginning of a lifelong romance.

116 To recommend thrift to the poor is both grotesque and insulting. It is like advising a man who is starving to eat less.

117 To the small part of ignorance we arrange and classify we give the name knowledge.

118 We are all in the gutter, but some of us are looking at the stars.

119 We are never more true to ourselves than when we are inconsistent.

120 We have really everything in common with America nowadays, except, of course, language. —See also George Bernard Shaw 30

121 What a pity that in life we only get our lessons when they are of no use to us.

122 What consoles one nowadays is not repentance, but pleasure. Repentance is quite out of date.

123 When people agree with me, I always feel that I must be wrong.

124 Whenever people talk to me about the weather, I always feel quite certain that they mean something else.

125 With an evening coat and a white tie, anybody, even a stockbroker, can gain a reputation for being civilized.

126 Women are meant to be loved, not understood.

127 Work is the curse of the drinking classes.

128 Work is the refuge of people who have nothing better to do.

129 Young men want to be faithful, and are not: old men want to be faithless and cannot.

130 Young people, nowadays, imagine that money is everything, and when they grow older they know it is.

BILLY WILDER (1906–). *Austrian-born American film director and screen-writer*

1 France is the only country where the money falls apart, and you can't tear the toilet paper.

2 Hindsight is always twenty-twenty.

3 I have ten commandments. The first nine are, thou shalt not bore. The tenth is, thou shalt have the right of final cut.

4 I would worship the ground you walk on, Audrey, if only you lived in a better neighborhood. [While courting his future wife.]

5 Television is a twenty-one inch prison. I'm delighted with it because it used to be that films were the lowest form of art. Now we have something to look down on.

6 "We can't get married at all; I'm a man." [Jack Lemmon in the role of Gerry, who had been posing as a woman.] "Well, nobody's perfect." [Joe E. Brown as Osgood, "her" dim-witted suitor, closing lines in the 1959 film *Some Like It Hot,* coscripted with I. A. L. Diamond.]

7 You have Van Gogh's ear for music. [Remark to Clifford Osmond.]

8 "You used to be in pictures. You used to be big." [William Holden in the role of Joe Gillis.] "I am big. It's the pictures that got small." [Gloria Swanson as Norma Desmond, in the 1950 film *Sunset Boulevard,* coscripted by a team of writers including Wilder.]

THORNTON WILDER (1897–1975). *American novelist and playwright*

1 Always look for a doctor who is hated by the best doctors.

2 Everybody's always talking about people breaking into houses, but there are more people in the world who want to break out of houses.

3 I rose by sheer military ability to the rank of corporal.

4 Ninety-nine percent of the people in the world are fools, and the rest of us are in great danger of contagion.

5 Success is paralyzing only to those who have never wished for anything else.

6 There comes a moment in everybody's life when he must decide whether he'll live among human beings or not—a fool among fools or a fool alone.

MICHAEL WILDING (1912–1979). *English actor*

You can pick out the actors by the glazed look that comes into their eyes when the conversation wanders away from themselves. [Attributed.]

JOHN WILKES (1725–1797). *English political leader*

"'Pon my honor, Wilkes, I don't know whether you'll die on the gallows or of the pox." [Earl of Sandwich] That must depend, my lord, upon whether I first embrace your lordship's principles or your lordship's mistresses. [Attributed.]

GEORGE F. WILL (1941–). *American journalist*

1 As advertising blather becomes the nation's normal idiom, language becomes printed noise.

2 Conservatives are pessimists, so when things go badly they have the pleasure of having their beliefs confirmed, and when things go well they enjoy the pleasant surprise.

3 Disparagement of television is second only to watching television as an American pastime.

4 Football combines the two worst features of American life. It is violence punctuated by committee meetings.

5 He believes everything he says at the moment he emphatically says it, and continues to believe it at full throttle right up to the moment he repudiates it. He has the weird sincerity of the intellectual sociopath, convinced that when he speaks, truth is an option but convenience is an imperative. [On Bill Clinton, 1999.]

6 Italy, anarchy tempered by bureaucracy.

7 Socialism is an expression of the disease for which it purports to be the cure. —See also Karl Kraus 3

8 The president's status varies directly with the Dow Jones Average.

9 The unpleasant sound emitting from Bush as he traipses from one conservative gathering to another is a thin, tinny "arf"—the sound of a lap dog. [On George Bush, 1986.]

10 The Washington style of apology is to say there were appearances of impropriety. [1991]

11 The worst feature of the 50s is that they were pregnant with the 60s.

12 Umpires should be natural Republicans—dead to human feelings. [On baseball umpires.]

ROBIN WILLIAMS (1952–). *American comedian and actor*

1 Do you think God gets stoned? I think so—look at the platypus!

2 I think Nancy does most of his talking; you'll notice that she never drinks water when Ronnie speaks.

3 I'm looking for Miss Right, or at least, Miss Right Now.
4 Shakespeare said, "Kill all the lawyers." There were no agents then.
5 Spring is Nature's way of saying, "Let's party!"
6 Why do they call it rush hour when nothing moves?

TED WILLIAMS (1918–). *American baseball player*
All I want out of life is that when I walk down the street, folks will say, "There goes the greatest hitter who ever lived."

TENNESSEE WILLIAMS (1911–1983). *American playwright*
1 It's good for a writer to think he's dying: he works harder.
2 Mendacity is a system that we live in. Liquor is one way out, an' death's the other.
3 There is a time for departure even when there's no certain place to go.
4 "They say nature hates a vacuum, Big Daddy." [Brick] "That's what they say, but sometimes I think that a vacuum is a hell of a lot better than some of the stuff that nature replaces it with." [Big Daddy, in the 1955 film *Cat on a Hot Tin Roof.*]
5 We have to distrust each other. It's our only defense against betrayal.
6 We're all of us sentenced to solitary confinement inside our own skins, for life!

GARRY WILLS (1934–). *American writer and academic*
1 Politics demands a great capacity for self-deception, which rescues the politician from hypocrisy.
2 Propaganda becomes at last more credible to its disseminators than to its targets. —See also Elbert Hubbard 34
3 Writing came easy—it would only get hard when I got better at it.

EARL WILSON (1907–1987). *American journalist*
1 Gossip is hearing something you like about someone you don't.
2 If you think nobody cares whether you're alive or not, try missing a couple of car payments.
3 Success is just a matter of luck. Ask any failure!

EDMUND WILSON (1895–1972). *American writer and literary critic*
1 Marxism is the opium of the intellectuals. —See also Karl Marx 5
2 No two people read the same book.
3 The cruelest thing that has happened to Lincoln since he was shot by Booth has been to fall into the hands of Carl Sandburg. [Referring to Sandburg's biography of Lincoln, 1926–1939.]
4 Uncle Win, picking pansies: "Y'know, if y'look at those long enough, they'll talk to you."

HAROLD WILSON (1916–). *British prime minister*
1 I have always said about Tony that he immatures with age. [On Tony Benn.]
2 I'm an optimist, but an optimist who carries a raincoat.
3 One man's wage rise is another man's price increase.
4 The practiced performances of latter-day politicians in the game of musical daggers: never be left holding the dagger when the music stops.

TOM WILSON (20th century). *American cartoonist*

1   A hug a day keeps the psychiatrist away.

2   About the only thing that happens to me on weekends is I get two days older. [Ziggy, Wilson's sad sack cartoon character.]

3   At the tone, the time will be later than you think. [Recorded message from the telephone time service.]

4   Boy, today's been one heck of a week!

5   Experience is what happens to you while you're waiting for something else to happen to you.

6   Funny, every time I make out my income tax, I find myself humming, "All of me, why not take all of me?"

7   How come when people are whispering, the only thing you can hear is your name?

8   How long have you been suffering these delusions of adequacy? [Psychiatrist to Ziggy, cartoon balloon.]

9   I have a feeling nothing's gonna happen to me today that I can handle.

10   "I have a problem, Doctor Schrink. I'm plagued by a terrible guilt complex. On the rare occasions when I don't have guilt feelings, I feel guilty for not feeling guilty. I can't stand it! Tell me doctor, how can I stop feeling guilty all the time?" [Ziggy] "The way to avoid a guilt complex is very simple, Ziggy. Don't ever do anything that you really enjoy!" [Psychiatrist, cartoon balloon.]

11   I like to smile at myself in the mirror 'cause I can always be sure I'll get a smile back!

12   I really should join an athletic club or something. If it wasn't for wrestling with my conscience, I'd get no exercise at all.

13   I remember when I dreamed of the day I'd be getting the pay I can't live on now.

14   I think I could enjoy the day more if it didn't start so early.

15   I tried to join Paranoids Anonymous, but no one would tell me where they were meeting.

16   I'm starting to get commercial breaks in my dreams. [Ziggy to psychiatrist, cartoon balloon.]

17   I've just got to stop putting things off, starting first thing tomorrow.

18   If I ever managed to "get it all together," I have a feeling I wouldn't know what to do with it.

19   If it wasn't for wrong numbers, I'd get no calls at all.

20   If people were put on this earth to help others, what are the others here for?

21   If they ever have a series about me on TV, it'd be a situation tragedy.

22   It's a typical case of depression. I'm giving you a prescription for some rose-colored glasses. [Psychiatrist to Ziggy, cartoon balloon.]

23   It's getting harder and harder to feel sorry for those less fortunate than myself.

24   It's not the big failures one minds so much. It's the constant pitter-patter of little defeats!

25 One comforting thing about not being anybody famous or important—you never have to worry about becoming a has-been.

26 Patience comes to those who wait.

27 So far my life's been a lot of on-the-job training. When do I get a shot at the real thing?

28 Sure the world's a mess now, but look at the bright side. Things will probably get worse! Then these will seem like the good old days!

29 The only thing that worries me about reincarnation is, how can I be sure I won't come back as myself?

30 The opportunities of life are limitless; unfortunately, so is my capacity for missing them.

31 The secret of living without frustration and worry is to avoid becoming personally involved in your own life.

32 There's no excuse for laziness, but I'm working on it.

33 Today is the tomorrow we worried about yesterday!

34 Waiting for the toast to pop up. It's probably the most exciting thing that will happen to me today.

35 WARNING! Excessive label-reading could be harmful to your peace of mind. [Sign in food market.]

36 We'll have you up and around in no time. Your insurance runs out Thursday! [Doctor to hospitalized patient, cartoon balloon.]

37 What this country needs is a credit card for charging things to experience!

38 When the going gets tough, the tough get going. And when the tough get going, the going gets tougher!

39 YIELD / but do not snivel! [Road sign.]

40 You can please some of the people some of the time, and all of the people some of the time, but some of the people you can't please none of the time. [Sage to Ziggy, cartoon balloon.]

WOODROW WILSON (1856–1924). *American president*

1 I have sometimes heard men say politics must have nothing to do with business, and I have often wished that business had nothing to do with politics.

2 If you want to make enemies, try to change something.

3 In public affairs, stupidity is more dangerous than knavery.

4 People will endure their tyrants for years, but they tear their deliverers to pieces if a millennium is not created immediately.

5 The office of president requires the constitution of an athlete, the patience of a mother, and the endurance of an early Christian.

6 The wisest thing to do with a fool is to encourage him to hire a hall and discourse to his fellow citizens. Nothing chills nonsense like exposure to the air.

7 When I give a man an office, I watch him carefully to see whether he is swelling or growing. The mischief of it is that when they swell they do not swell enough to burst.

WALTER WINCHELL (1897–1972). *American journalist*

1 A town that has to be seen to be disbelieved. [On Hollywood.]

2 Broadway is a street where people spend money they haven't earned to buy things they don't need to impress people they don't like.

3 Gossip is the art of saying nothing in a way that leaves practically nothing unsaid.

4 It's a sure sign of summer if the chair gets up when you do.

5 Nothing recedes like success. —See also Alexander Dumas 2

6 She's been on more laps than a napkin.

7 South Terrific! [On the 1949 musical *South Pacific*.]

8 They shoot too many pictures and not enough actors.

SHELLEY WINTERS (1922–). *American actress*

1 Every now and then when you're on the stage, you hear the best sound that a player can hear. It is a sound you can't get in movies or in television. It is the sound of a wonderful, deep silence that means you've hit them where they live.

2 He was able to do a very emotional scene with tears in his eyes and pinch my fanny at the same time. [On Frederic March.]

3 I did a picture in England one winter, and it was so cold I almost got married.

4 I think on-stage nudity is disgusting, shameful and damaging to all things American. But if I were twenty-two with a great body, it would be artistic, tasteful, patriotic and a progressive religious experience.

5 We had a lot in common: I loved him and he loved him.

LUDWIG WITTGENSTEIN (1889–1951). *Austrian-born British philosopher*

1 Piano playing, a dance of human fingers.

2 When I came home I expected a surprise and there was no surprise for me, so, of course, I was surprised.

3 Whereof one cannot speak thereon one must remain silent.

P. G. WODEHOUSE (1881–1975). *English novelist and humorist*

1 All the unhappy marriages come from the husbands having brains. What good are brains to a man? They only unsettle him.

2 He spoke with a certain what-is-it in his voice, and I could see that, if not actually disgruntled, he was far from being gruntled.

3 I spent the afternoon musing on Life. If you come to think of it, what a queer thing Life is! So unlike anything else, don't you know, if you see what I mean.

4 If I had to choose between him and a cockroach as a companion for a walking tour, the cockroach would have had it by a short head.

5 It has been my experience, sir, that no lady can ever forgive another lady for taking a really good cook away from her.

6 Roderick Spode? Big chap with a small mustache and the sort of eye that can open an oyster at sixty paces?

7 The least thing upset him on the links. He missed short putts because of the uproar of the butterflies in the adjoining meadows.

8 The lunches of fifty-seven years had caused his chest to slip down into the mezzanine floor.

9 The Right Hon. was a tubby little chap who looked as if he had been poured into his clothes and had forgotten to say "When!"

10 To my daughter Leonora without whose never-failing sympathy and encouragement this book would have been finished in half the time. [Dedication to *The Heart of a Goof*, 1926.]

11 Why don't you get a haircut? You look like a chrysanthemum.

THOMAS WOLFE (1900–1938). *American novelist*

"Where they got you stationed now, Luke?" said Harry Tugman peering up snoutily from a mug of coffee. "At the p-p-present time in Norfolk at the Navy base," Luke answered, "m-m-making the world safe for hypocrisy." [*Look Homeward, Angel*, 1929.]

VIRGINIA WOOLF (1882–1941). *English novelist*

1 I read the book of Job last night. I don't think God comes well out of it.

2 Never did I read such tosh. As for the first two chapters, we will let them pass, but the 3rd 4th 5th 6th—merely the scratching of pimples on the body of the boot boy at Claridges. [On James Joyce's *Ulysses,* 1922.]

3 Those comfortably padded lunatic asylums, which are known, euphemistically, as the stately homes of England. —See also Noel Coward 18

4 Women have served all these centuries as looking glasses possessing the magic and delicious power of reflecting the figure of man at twice its natural size.

ALEXANDER WOOLLCOTT (1887–1943). *American writer, drama critic, and humorist*

1 A broker is a man who runs your fortune into a shoestring.

2 All the things I really like to do are either immoral, illegal, or fattening.

3 I can't remember your name, but don't tell me.

4 I have no need of your God-damned sympathy. I only wish to be entertained by some of your grosser reminiscences. [Letter written a year before his death.]

5 The English have an extraordinary ability for flying into a great calm.

6 The worst sin of all is to do well that which shouldn't be done at all.

7 There is absolutely nothing wrong with Oscar Levant that a miracle couldn't fix.

8 To all things clergic / I am allergic.

HENRY WOTTON (1568–1639). *English poet and diplomat*

An ambassador is an honest man sent to lie abroad for the good of his country.

FRANK LLOYD WRIGHT (1867–1959). *American architect*

1 An expert is a man who has stopped thinking. Why should he think? He is an expert.

2 Early in life I had to choose between honest arrogance and hypocritical humility. I chose honest arrogance and have seen no occasion to change.

3 If you turned the country on its side, everything loose would fall into Southern California. [Attributed.]

4 New York: Prison towers and modern posters for soap and whisky. Pittsburgh: Abandon it.

5 The physician can bury his mistakes, but the architect can only advise his client to plant vines.

6 There are two kinds of architects in the world. There is every other architect, and there is me.

7 We should learn from the snail: it has devised a home that is both exquisite and functional. [Attributed.]

ED WYNN (1885–1965). *American comedian*

1 A comic says funny things; a comedian says things funny.

2 Success in life depends on two things: luck and pluck, luck in finding someone to pluck.

JONATHAN YARDLEY (1939–). *American literary critic*

1 Anyone foolish enough to buy it deserves the excruciating experience of reading it. [On Joe McGinniss's *The Last Brother: The Rise and Fall of Teddy Kennedy,* 1993.]

2 He was an endless delight to those of us who imagined ourselves to know what he was really saying. [On television broadcast journalist David Brinkley after his retirement in 1995.]

WILLIAM BUTLER YEATS (1865–1939). *Irish poet and editor*

1 All life weighed in the scales of my own life seems to me a preparation for something that never happens.

2 "How are you?" Not very well. I can only write prose today.

3 Wisdom is bodily decrepitude.

ANDREW YOUNG (1932–). *American clergyman and ambassador*

Nothing is illegal if a hundred businessmen decide to do it, and that's true anywhere in the world.

HENNY YOUNGMAN (1906–1998). *American comedian*

1 A doctor gave a guy six months to live, and he didn't pay his bill. So the doctor gave him another six months to live.

2 A man doesn't know what real happiness is until he's married. Then it's too late.

3 A man goes to a psychiatrist. The doctor says, "You're crazy." The man says, "I want a second opinion!" "O.K., you're ugly, too!"

4 Don't forget I was up early this morning. I was up at the crack of six, took a brisk walk to the window, was back in bed by 6:10. I stood under that cold shower for ten minutes. Tomorrow I'm going to turn the water on.

5 Eleven kids in our family. We were so poor we had to wear each other's clothes. It wasn't funny—I had ten sisters.

6 Gimme a table near a waiter. [On entering a restaurant.]

7 He's a real pain in the neck; of course, some people have a lower opinion of him.

8 He's frank and earnest with women. In Fresno he's Frank and in Chicago he's Ernest.

9 "How's your wife?" Compared to who?

10 I don't know what makes you so stupid, but it really works.

11 I haven't talked to my wife in three weeks. I didn't want to interrupt her.

12 I just made a killing in the stock market—I shot my broker.

13 I just solved the parking problem. I bought a parked car.

14 I miss my wife's cooking—as often as I can.

15 I once wanted to become an atheist, but I gave up—they have no holidays.

16 I read about the evils of drinking so I gave up reading.

17 I said to my wife, "Where do you want to go for our anniversary?" She said, "I want to go to somewhere I've never been before." I said, "Try the kitchen."

18 I was so ugly when I was born, the doctor slapped my mother.

19 I will never forget my school days. I was teacher's pet. She couldn't afford a dog.

20 I wish my brother-in-law would learn a trade, so we'd know what kind of work he was out of.

21 I'd like to say we're glad you're here. I'd like to say it.

22 I've been married for thirty-four years, and I'm still in love with the same woman. If my wife ever finds out, she'll kill me.

23 I've got two wonderful children, and two out of five isn't bad.

24 My father was never home; he was always away drinking booze. He saw a sign saying, "Drink Canada Dry." So he went up there.

25 My grandmother is over eighty and still doesn't need glasses. Drinks right out of the bottle.

26 My grandson, 22 years old, keeps complaining about headaches. I've told him 1,000 times, "Larry, when you get out of bed, it's feet first."

27 My wife is a light eater: as soon as it's light, she starts eating.

28 My wife is the sweetest, most tolerant, most beautiful woman in the world. This is a paid political announcement.

29 Some people ask the secret of our long marriage. We take time to go to a restaurant two times a week. A little candlelight, dinner, soft music, and dancing. She goes Tuesdays; I go Fridays.

30 Take my wife—please! [His signature line.]

31 The first part of our marriage was very happy. But then, on the way back from the ceremony . . .

32 There's no more crime in New York—there's nothing left to steal.

33 Want to drive somebody crazy? Send him a wire saying, "Ignore first wire."

34 When I was a kid, I had no watch. I used to tell the time by my violin. I'd practice in the middle of the night and the neighbors would yell, "Fine time to practice the violin, three o'clock in the morning!"

LIN YUTANG (1895–1976). *Chinese-born American writer*
Neckties strangle clear thinking.

ISRAEL ZANGWILL (1864–1926). *English novelist and playwright*

1 No man is a hero to his valet, or his relatives.

2 The way Bernard Shaw believes in himself is very refreshing in these atheistic days when so many believe in no God at all.

FRANK ZAPPA (1940–1993). *American rock musician*

1 Rock journalism is people who can't write interviewing people who can't talk for people who can't read.

2 Speed will turn you into your parents.

MORTIMER ZUCKERMAN (1937–). *American real estate investor, publisher, and nonpracticing lawyer*

Law practice is the exact opposite of sex: even when it's good, it's bad.

Category Index

Author's last name followed by entry number

Holmes 6
Johnson, S 76
Kirk
La Rochef 40
Little 2
Mencken 2
Montesquieu 1
Muggeridge 3
Nicolson 2
Peter 34
Shaw 56
Sitwell 1
Thomas, D 2
Updike 4
Voltaire 31
Boston
Allen, F 13
Bossidy
Coolidge 7
Boswell, James
Walpole 6
Botticelli
Ustinov 8
boxing
Louis
Schulberg 1
Boy George
Rivers 2
Boy Scouts
Lee, S
Braddock, Bessie
Churchill 67
bragging
Dean
Emerson 4
Hubbard, K
51
brain
Allen, W 43
Bierce 12
Dickinson 5
Frost 13
Malcolm X 3
Pope 1
Rosten 15
breakfast
Billings 54
brevity
Parker, D 2
Shakespeare 3
brides
Bierce 13
Brinkley, David
Yardley 2

Broadway
Cohan 2
Hayes 1
Winchell 2
brokers
Balzac 2
Wilde 125
Woollcott 1
Youngman 12
Bronx
Nash 18
brothels
Blake, W 5
brotherhood
Twain 111
brothers-in-law
Powell, A 1
Youngman 20
Browning, Robert
Wilde 62
Buchanan, Pat
Durst 9
Buck, Pearl
Porter, K 2
**Buckley, Jr,
William F**
Vidal 14
Buffalo, New York
Hubbard, E 37
bullying
Shaw 130
burdens
Schulz 14
Shaw 87
bureaucracy
Boren 4
Ford, G 2
Friedman 1, 2
Knoll 5
Lasch 1
McCarthy, M 2
Peter 8
Safire 4
Tuchman 1
Will 6
burning dinner
Piercy
Bush, George
Hightower 1
Leno 1
Perot 4
Quindlen
Richards 1
Will 9

Bush, George W
Durst 2
Ivins 2
Lebowitz 46
busibodies
Carroll, L 3
Emerson 44
Shaw 113
Ventura 1
Wilde 67, 100
business
Augustine 2
Coolidge 1
Dickens 4
Fields 5
Fry, S 4
Gates 1
Goldwyn 15
Harding 1
La Bruyère 1
Rogers 33
Veblen 3, 4
Wilson, W 1
businessmen
Puzo 2
Young
Byron, Lord
Byron 6–12
Macaulay 2
cabdrivers
Burns 7
Letterman 14
calamity
Bierce 14
Disraeli 12
Hayler
Twain 102
Calhoun, John C
Jackson, A 2
California
Allen, F 6
Anonymous
16
Capote 4
Didion 2
Sahl 4
Wright 3
calves
Allen, W 52
**Campbell, Mrs
Patrick**
Shaw 61
Canada
Thoreau 41

Ward, A 3
Youngman 24
canaries
Allen, G 4
candidates
Adams, F 8
Allen, G 2
Buchwald 2
Cahn 12
Hubbard, K 37
McCarthy, E 3
Perot 4
candor
Cahn 57
Lippmann 6
McLaughlin 6
cannibalism
Butler 20
Harburg 3
King, S 2
Mencken 45,
46
Schweitzer 2
Swift 12
canons
Bierce 15
Wellington 2
capitalism
Lincoln 43
Malcolm X 4
Marcuse
Shaw 88
Stoppard 12
**capitalism &
communism**
Galbraith 27
Mencken 83
**capitalism &
socialism**
Churchill 52,
55
Nixon 3
Spengler 3
Capone, Al
Hoover, H 3
Capote, Truman
Porter, K 1
Vidal 4
Carlyle, Thomas
Butler 16
Lowell, J 6
Carter, Jimmy
Carter 2, 3
Hope 4

McCarthy, E 2
Reagan, R 21,
  24
Carter, Rosalynn
Carter 5
Casablanca
Bogart, H 3, 4
Catch–22
Heller 1, 17, 18
**Catherine the
Great**
Attlee
Catholics
Amis 2
Orwell 22
cats
Krutch 1
Lichtenberg 13
Montaigne 15
celebrity
Allen, F 1
Boorstin 1, 3, 5
Chamfort 5
Davis, S 3
Disraeli 28
Eastwood 2
Kissinger 15
Mencken 3
Morrow
Newman 2
O'Rourke 19
Rich 2
celibacy
Johnson, S 50
Shaw 19
Socrates 4
cemetaries
Renard 1
censorship
Chesterton 24
Goodman, P 2
Hammett 2
Peter 1
Shaw 15
censure
Colton 16
Franklin 5
Swift 2
Washington 4
certainty
Forbes 8
Lara 6
Marquis 23
Maugham 18

Melbourne 2
Montagu, A 2
Montaigne 6
Mulleian
Russell 6, 18
Wilde 102
**Chamberlain,
Neville**
Bevan 5
Lloyd George 6
chance
France 1
Nietzsche 9
**Chandler,
Raymond**
Chandler 2
change
Angelou 1
Eisenh, D 7
Hellman 4
Hubbard, E 20
Irving 3
Mead 3
Mumford 4
Wilson, W 2
chaos
Levant 10
character
McLaughlin 4
Charing Cross
Pepys 2
charity
Hubbard, E 2
Nietzsche 4
Wilde 16
charlatans
Emerson 21
Charles I
Emerson 40
charm
Amiel
Barrie 5
Brown, J 1
Stevenson, A 1
chastity
Anonymous 17
Augustine 1
Billings 9
France 6
Huxley, A 1
Twain 99
cheating
Fields 2
Ventura 3

check enclosed
Parker, D 28
cheerfulness
Caine 1
Goodman, E 1
Pepys 2
Twain 20
chewing gum
Anonymous 108
Hubbard, E 38
Chicago
Quayle 2
chickens
Anouilh 5
childbirth
Allen, G 1
Mitchell, M 1
Mizner 15
Parker, D 4
Rivers 1, 6
children
Anonymous 131
Ayckbourn 1
Baldwin 2
Bennett, Al 14
Bombeck 6, 9,
  13, 16
Carney
Dangerfield 2
Ehrenreich 7
Fields 6, 8, 22,
  33
Forbes 3, 4
Goodman, E 3
Inge 8
Joubert 1
Keillor 6
Kingsolver 2
Lamb 6
Lebowitz 5, 6,
  11, 12, 20
Levenson 1
Lincoln 13
Parker, D 25
Peter 3
Roseanne 1
Schumpeter 2
Swift 12
Truman 8
Vidal 15
Youngman 5,
  23
Chopin, Frédéric
Ade 7

chorus girls
Allen, F 19
Marx, C
Bierce 16
Christianity
Butler 23
Byron 4
Chesterton 14
Nietzsche 14, 15
Shaw 18
Christmas
Bombeck 16
Fields 1
Keillor 2
church
Atkinson 1
Bruce 2
Keillor 13
Smith, Sy 11
Twain 21
**Churchill,
Randolph**
Waugh 8
**Churchill,
Winston**
Balfour 1
Beaverbrook 2
Bevan 1
Churchill 15, 22,
  24–29, 32, 44,
  53, 54, 62
Macmillan 5
Shaw 28
chutzpah
Levant 2
cigars
Adams, F 5
Marshall 3
circles
Stoppard 1
circumcision
Lloyd George
  11
cities
Kaufman, B 2
Snyder 2
Thoreau 3
Civil War
Mitchell, M 2
civilization
Gandhi 3
Garfield 2
Mencken 37
Miller, H 1

decision-making
Bierce 23
Cioran 26
Tuchman 3
Declaration of
Independence
Knoll 2
dedications
Adams, F 7
Twain 129
Wodehouse
10
defeat
Cioran 13
Shaw 136
Stevenson, A 2
defects
La Rochef 37
deference
Billings 11
defiance
Disraeli 32
White, E B 5
déjà vu
Berra 9
Delaney Club
Marx, G 19
delusion
Colton 6
Kerr, W 1
Szasz 2
Wagner 2
Whitehead 4
Wilson, T 8
demagogues
Kraus 7
Lewis, A 1
democracy
Bismarck 4
Blessington 1
Bukowski 7
Chesterton 4
Churchill 10
Coren
Eldridge 1
Hughes 3
Inge 2
Keller
King, F 1
Lowell, J 2
Mao
Mencken 27–29,
85, 94, 109
Peter 11

Russell 2, 4, 9,
25
Schumpeter 1
Shaw 25, 26,
134
Smith, Al 1
Tocqueville 1
White, E B 3
Wilde 20
Democrats
Baker, R 4
Greeley 1
O'Rourke 8
Rogers 18
Safire 11
Stevenson, A 7
denial
Mulroney
dentists
Allman
Perelman 1, 3
Wilde 56
depression
Wilson, T 22
depressions
Hoover, H 4
Reagan, R 21
Truman 15
Desborough, Lady
Asquith, M 5
desire
Proust 7
Swift 27
despair
Brodsky 4
Cioran 3
Edison 9
Hubbard, K 27
Wilde 84
desperation
Cioran 14
Thoreau 33
Thurber 11
despots
Blessington 1
Landor 2
Spencer 6
Tocqueville 2
Voltaire 34
destination
Berra 7
Peter 16
destiny
Bierce 24

details
Lincoln 39
devil
Defoe 5
Jung 3
Kraus 4
Mather
Dewey, Thomas E
Kennedy, J F 11
Taft
diaries
Bankhead 6
West, M 17
Wilde 48
Dickens, Charles
Bennett, Al 17
dictators
Branson
Bukowski 7
Churchill 11
Hancock 4
Mao
Thatcher 2
dictionaries
Anonymous 111
Johnson, S 19,
26, 48
dieting
Bombeck 5, 17
Lewis, J 3
Parton 1
difficulty
Churchill 39
digestion
Bierce 39
Butler 26
Hugo 4
dignity
Bennett, Ar 2
Diller, Phyllis
Hope 15
DiMaggio, Joe
Berra 2
Stengel 6
dinner parties
Maugham 3
diplomacy
Bierce 26
Chou En-lai
Durant 4
Frederick II 1
Galbraith 23
Goldberg 1
Herford 4

Napoleon 26
Pearson 1
Rogers 8, 32
Twain 108
diplomats
Cavour 1
de Gaulle 2
Kraus 2
Stalin 1
Stevenson, A
16
Stinnett
Ustinov 1, 3
Wotton
directors
Goldwyn 26
Penn, S
Wilder, B 3
dirt
Palmerston 2
dirty boots
Grant, U 8
disability
Humphrey 2
disaster
Waugh 3
West, R 5
discovery
Koestler 5
Morison
Morley, J 4
disease
Chesterfield 4
Darrow 7
Hazlitt 4
Johnson, S 55
Nicolson 1
Osler 1
Seneca 1
disenchantment
Sartre 4
disgruntled
Wodehouse 2
dismissal
Donne 1
Durocher 2
Stengel 5
Disraeli, Benjamin
Gladstone 3
distrust
Acheson 6
Longworth 5
Macmillan 2
Williams, Ten 5

fans
  Carson, Ja
  Davis, B 7
farming
  Sandburg 3, 4
  Warner, C 1
  White, E B 2
fashion
  Astor 3
  Bierce 33
  Greville 3
  Kruger 1
  Lauren
  Molière 2
  Morley, C 1
  Packard 1
  Santayana 2
  Shakespeare 26
  Shaw 34, 57
  Smith, L 4
  Thoreau 5
fast lane, the
  Hancock 17
Father McKenzie
  Lennon and
    McCartney 2
fathers
  Lardner 1
  Mumford 1
  Russell 32
  Shakespeare 15
  Twain 71, 143
  Wilde 26
  Youngman 24
faults
  Allen, W 60
  Anonymous 16,
    147, 150
  Eldridge 12
  Gandhi 2
  Hoffa 2
  Johnson, S 91
  La Rochef 7, 45
  Lynes 1
  Shenstone 2
  Smith, L 8
  Swift 34
  Talleyrand 6
  Thurber 16, 19
Faust
  Allen, W 4
fear
  Connolly 10
  Davis, E 1

Emerson 8
Hubbard, E 11
Schulz 9
Synge
fearlessness
  Cahn 16
fees
  Lincoln 46
feminism
  Loos
  O'Brien, E 2
  O'Rourke 6
  Rankin 1
  Thatcher 5
  West, R 2
Fields, W. C.
  Fields
    (generally)
  Rosten 14
  West, M 38
Fifties, the
  Will 11
fig tree
  Dickens 15
fighting
  Anonymous 110
  Dunne 8
  Fitzsimmons
  Harris 5
  Johnson, S 31
  Kafka 3
  Thurber 15
  Twain 126
  Voltaire 10
  Ward, A 2
films
  Anonymous
    88
  Baldwin 3
  Goldwyn 8, 16,
    22, 24, 30, 31,
    37
  Hitchcock 2
  Huxley, A 10
  Kael 6
  Liberace 1
  McLuhan 1
  Midler 2
  Rogers 30, 36
  Taylor, E 5
  Trillin 5
  Warner, H
  Wilder, B 5
  Winchell 8

financiers
  Pinero
first impulses
  Talleyrand 5
fish
  Broun 5
  Johnson, S 2
  Shakespeare 18
flattery
  Billings 11, 16,
    86
  Collins 1
  Colton 3, 6, 8
  Disraeli 9
  Eldridge 19
  Emerson 37
  France 2
  La Rochef 23,
    26
  Lincoln 23
  Mizner 5
  Shakespeare 37
  Shaw 141
  Sheen 1
  Sitwell 3
  Stevenson, A 8
  Wells, C 5
flaunting
  Brooks 1
  Forbes 11
fleas
  Jonson 2
  Twain 32
  Wagner 6
flies
  Nash 6
  Twain 89
flirts
  Casanova
  Talleyrand 9
  Wilde 88
flower in
buttonhole
  Thackeray 8
  Twain 141
flowers
  Bennett, Al 9
  Wilson, Ed 4
food
  Allen, W 53
  Anonymous 10
  Bombeck 9
  Bush, G 1
  Carroll, L 11

Child 1–3
Churchill 25
Dangerfield 8
Hancock 5
Johnson, S 5
Lebowitz 2, 4,
  9, 14, 24, 47
Leno 2
Meredith 3
Powell, A 2
Shaw 62
Taylor, E 3
Trillin 2
White, E B 5
Wilde 7
Wodehouse 8
food stamps
  Schroeder 1
fools
  Anonymous 1
  Billings 24, 51,
    79, 85, 95
  Butler 4
  Carnegie
  Eliot, G 5
  Esar 1
  Goldberg 2
  Hubbard, E 10
  Hubbard, K 1
  Inge 9
  Jackson, H 2
  La Rochef 30
  Mencken 8
  Mill 3
  Mizner 1
  Molière 1
  Morley, C 3
  Pearson 2
  Peter 55
  Pope 9, 13
  Rowland 2
  Sandburg 16
  Schopenh 17
  Shaw 37
  Shenstone 1
  Spencer 4
  Twain 13, 38, 81
  Voltaire 18, 25
  West, M 12
  Wilder, T 5, 6
  Wilson, W 6
  Youngman 7
fool's paradise
  Kaufman, G 8

generosity
  Mannes 2
  McLaughlin 18
genetics
  Knoll 6
genius
  Berenson 2
  Brown, R 5
  Bukowski 1
  Butler 6
  Edison 2
  Galbraith 5
  Herold 3
  Hubbard, E 13
  Levant 23
  Sheen 2
  Swift 33
  Valéry 6
  Wilde 28, 92
gentlemen
  Allen, F 2
  Anonymous 5
  Coward 1
  Herold 4
  Mencken 5
  O'Malley 1
  Russell 23
  Shaw 126, 143
  Smith, Sy 6
  West, R 1
  Wilde 1
genuineness
  Cahn 6
geology
  Emerson 36
George V
  Gandhi 1
  Milligan 4
Germany
  O'Rourke 18
Gershwin, George
  Levant 20
Gettysburg
Address
  Hurt
ghosts
  Johnson, S 11
Gibbon, Edward
  Gibbon 4, 11
  Guedalla 5
gifts
  Dangerfield 9
  Emerson 22
  Lamb 10

Parker, D 32
Rudner 1
Gingrich, Newt
  Thomas, H 2
girls
  Algren 1
  McGinley 2
Gladstone, William
Ewart
  Churchill 58
  Disraeli 4, 10,
    12, 20
  Russell 10
gluttony
  Billings 74
  De Vries 4
  Youngman 27
God
  Algren 1
  Allen, W 30, 31,
    53, 54
  Anonymous
    31–37, 112
  Anouilh 1
  Baring
  Barnes, P
  Boorstin 3
  Bruce 2
  Butler 3, 19
  Carlin 8
  Cervantes 1
  Churchill 24
  Cioran 12, 18
  Defoe 5
  Einstein 5, 6
  Fitzgerald, F 9
  France 1
  Harburg 2
  Heine 1
  Heller 6
  Hubbard, E 17
  Huxley, T 2
  Inge 4
  Koestler 3
  Lamott 1, 3
  Lec 6
  Lewis, C 3
  Mencken 15, 82
  Napoleon 25
  Nietzsche 6, 18
  North
  O'Malley 3
  Patchen 1
  Pope 18

Pryor 1
Renard 3
Russell 28
Safire 16
Sandburg 1
Shaw 17, 131,
  138
Smith, L 19
Stoppard 9
Szasz 3
Thoreau 7
Trudeau, G 2
Twain 84, 116
Updike 9
Voltaire 11, 20,
  33
Wagner 17
Walker 1
Whitehead 5
Wilde 49
Williams, R 1
Woolf 1
gold
  Billings 68
  Ovid 2
  Twain 109
  Walpole 2
golden rules
  Anonymous 115
  Billings 89
  Blake, W 2
  Dickens 4
  Hoffa 1
  Kissinger 8
  Lara 2
  Schulberg 2
  Shaw 27, 101
Goldwyn, Samuel
  Thurber 7
golf
  Hogan
  Lemmon
  Reagan, R 12
  Rogers 34
  Russell 32
  Wodehouse 7
Gone with the
Wind
  Cooper 1
good
  Billings 69
  Dunne 11
  La Rochef 46
  Lerner, A 3

Luce 6
Mencken 30
Orwell 17
Thurber 14
Twain 127
West, M 11, 40
Wilde 112
good & bad
  Allen, W 35
  Bagehot 6
  Brodsky 3
  Hubbard, E 14
  Madariaga 1
  West, M 41
  Whitman 6
  Wilde 54
good grief
  Schulz 3
good old days, the
  Wilson, T 28
Good Samaritan
  Thatcher 8
Gordian
  Gibbon 10
Gore, Al
  Durst 1
Gospels, the
  Whitehead 2
gossip
  Ade 6
  Caen 2
  Chamfort 9
  Hubbard, K 58
  Jong 5
  Kirk
  Kronenberger 1
  Longworth 4
  Peter 34
  Plato 2
  Rogers 10, 37
  Russell 22
  Sayers 1
  West, M 31
  Wilde 109, 110
  Wilson, Ea 1
  Winchell 3
government
  Berenson 3
  Buchwald 6
  Buckley 4
  Disraeli 2
  Dryden 6
  Emerson 16, 20,
    27

Jefferson 10
Johnson, S 37, 79
Jordan 1
Kennedy, J F 12
Mencken 13
Moynihan 2
Paine 3
Penn, W 1
Reagan, R 7–10
Reston 6
Rogers 31, 33, 41
Shaw 3, 98
Spencer 6
Stevenson, A 17
Voltaire 26
Wicker 2
Gracehoper
Joyce 5
graffiti
Bennett, Al 10
grammar
Ade 8
Safire 15
Grand Canyon
Marquis 19
grandchildren
Anonymous 40
Vidal 15
Youngman 26
grandparents
Hugo 3
Mumford 1
Sartre 6
Thatcher 10
Youngman 25
Grant, Cary
Grant, C 1
Hitchcock 4
Grant, Ulysses S
Grant, U 5
Lincoln 24
Twain 57
gratitude
Anonymous 38
Cervantes 2
Mitchell, M 4
gravity
Lavater 2
Gray, L Patrick
Ehrlichman
Gray, Thomas
Johnson, S 88

greatness
Boorstin 8
Forster 2
Franklin 3
Goodman, P 1
Herman 1
Levant 12
Mencken 87
Russell 31
Shaw 53
greed
Eldridge 4
Figes
McLaughlin 19
Trump 4
Greeley, Horace
Greeley 2
Green, Thomas
Jefferson
Houston
Greenspan, Alan
Mankoff 1
grief
Hubbard, K 24
Martial 1
Shakespeare 5
guests
Howells
Hubbard, K 25
Marx, G 8
O'Rourke 3
Shakespeare 34
guilt
Bombeck 1
Mead 5
Rivers 8
Wells, C 1
Wilson, T 10
Gulf War
Schroeder 4
gullibility
Anonymous 100
guns
Capone 4
habits
Cowper 2
Maugham 22
Proust 6
Twain 37, 90
Haig, Douglas
Beaverbrook 5
Liddell Hart 1
Lloyd George 4

hair
Herford 1
Malcolm X 3
Twain 145
Wodehouse 11
happiness
Bierce 40
Billings 48, 71, 94
Burns 2
Connolly 16
Ebner-Eschenb 3
Esar 6
Goldwyn 14
Hubbard, K 20
Levant 4
Marquis 7
Mencken 93
Mill 1
Nash 19
Nash 7
Russell 27
Schweitzer 1
Swift 5
Trevelyan 2
Wilde 86
Youngman 2
Happiness Is a Warm Puppy
Schulz 4
hard work
Wayne 2
Harding, Warren G
Harding 2, 3
Longworth 2
Mencken 40
hardware store
Hubbard, K 38
Harlow, Jean
Asquith, M 4
Harper & Brothers
Millay 1
Harriman, A. E.
Muir 1
Harriman, Averell
Beaverbrook 4
Harvard Law School
Trillin 1
Harvard University
Buckley 4

hate
Adams, H 5
Bierce 41
Cioran 17
Colton 10
Fields 16
Johnson, S 32
Smith, Sy 12
Sontag 1
Swift 11
headache
Didion 4
Emerson 11
Mencken 96
headlines
Levin 1
healing
Tomlin 1
health
Colton 12
Hancock 6
Schulz 10
heart attacks
Benchley 6
hearts
Fields 9
Pope 1
heaven
Caen 7
Dylan 1
Ford, He 3
Hubbard, E 16
Roosevelt, F 11
Shaw 58
Vidal 16
heaven & hell
Barrie 4
Billings 82
Twain 41
Warhol 1
heels
Ace, J 4
Hegel, Georg
Hegel 1, 2
Schopenh 10
heiresses
Dryden 1
helicopters
Johnson, L 16
hell
Frost 9
Horacek
Huxley, A 6
Phillips 1

Russell 30
Sartre 2
Shaw 7
Sheridan, P
Sherman 1
Hellinger, Mark
Fields 17
Hellman, Lillian
McCarthy, M 3
helping others
Baer 3
Lamott 1
Levant 3
Napoleon 21
Thoreau 17
Wilson, T 20
Hemingway,
Ernest
Fitzgerald, F 3
Lewis, W 2
Nabokov 2
Vidal 24
Henry, Patrick
Jones, M 2
Hepburn,
Katharine
Parker, D 20
Tracy 1
heretics
Gibbon 5
Whitehead 12
Herodotus
Kennedy, J F
19
heroism
Buckley 3
Dunne 19
Fitzgerald, F 11
Kennedy, J F 5
Mencken 81
Milligan 2
Nathan 5
Puzo 5
Rogers 17, 43
Stoppard 12
Zangwill 1
West, M 12
Peter 18, 19, 32
Hierocles
Johnson, S 25
highbrows
Matthews
hindsight
Wilder, B 2

hippies
Reagan, R 1
Hirschhorn
Museum
Huxtable 3
historians
Acton 1
Anonymous
113
Bierce 42
Butler 7
Churchill 21
Guedalla 3
Kennedy, J F 19
Mencken 41
history
Allen, W 40
Chesterton 9
Cioran 7
Eban 2
Eldridge 22
Emerson 28
Ford, He 4
Fuentes
Hancock 20
Hegel 3
Joyce 3
Kennedy, Ja 2
Liddell Hart 2, 3
Mailer 3
Marx, K 3
Morison
Orwell 6
Pascal 4
Peter 14
Powell, E
Saki 8
Sandburg 13
Taylor, A 1, 2
Twain 8
Voltaire 1
Walpole 1
Weil
Wells, H G 2
Hitler, Adolf
Churchill 32
hobbies
Lebowitz 3
hold me closer
Marx, G 4
holidays
Shaw 7, 122
holiness
Hubbard, E 28

Hollywood
Allen, F 12
Chandler 2
Geffen
Hopper
Jong 9
Levant 19
Mizner 16
Monroe 3
Parker, D 6
Winchell 1
home
Carlin 1
Frost 10
Hubbard, E 16
Hubbard, K 38
Miller, A
Shaw 44
Homer
Huxley, A 4
Shaw 151
homosexuality
Campbell 1
Crisp 1
Freud 12
Ginsberg 1
Jong 2
honesty
Billings 57
Bruce 8
Coward 9
Fitzgerald, F 4
Hubbard, K 50
Lewis, 1
Marquis 8
Shakespeare 21,
32, 36
Socrates 3
Twain 34, 44
honor
Emerson 29
Jonson 1, 2
Marx, G 20
Mencken 84
Twain 72
Hooker, Joseph
Lincoln 42
Hoover, J Edgar
Acheson 6
Bruce 6
Caen 6
Johnson, L 17
hope
Kerr, J 3

hopeless passion
Thackeray 9
Hopper, Hedda
Ustinov 5
horse sense
Fields 13
horses
Cooper 2
Grant, U 4
Leacock 6
Lincoln 18
Salinger 8
Sandburg 17
Simpson
hospitals
Wilson, T 36
hotels
Lebowitz 18
Twain 77
House Beautiful,
The
Parker, D 26
House of
Commons
Disraeli 24
House of Lords
Benn 3
House Un-
American Activ
Comm
Bogart, H 2
housework
Bombeck 2
Crisp 12
Diller 2, 5
Esar 3
Kingsolver 1
Kruger 4
Rivers 7
human nature
Talleyrand 2
Twain 46
humbug
Disraeli 2
Thackeray 2
Hume, Paul
Truman 9
humility
Barrie 7
Billings 75
Burton, Ro 2
Greville 2
Holmes 3
La Rochef 5

Ferlinghetti 2
Hoffer 14
Lennon and
  McCartney 5
Quayle 5
Smith, L 2
minorities
  Holmes, Jr 3
  Smith, Sy 9
miracles
  Ben-Gurion
  Johnson, L 10
  Paine 4
  Weizmann 2
  Woollcott 7
mirrors
  Cocteau 1
  Osborne 3
  Sandburg 16
  Wilson, T 11
  Woolf 4
misanthropy
  Hoffer 7
  Morrison 1
mischief
  Bulwer-Lytton 3
misers
  Billings 74
misery
  Jong 7
  Schopenh 6
  Shakespeare 19
  Shaw 112
misfortune
  Anonymous 57
  Billings 43
  La Rochef 8, 15
  Lowell, J 8
  Pope 10
  Wilde 63, 80
  Wilson, T 4
misogyny
  Allen, F 2
  Ayckbourn 4
  Coward 2
  Fields 18, 37
  Freud 17
  Mencken 5
  Meredith 2
  Ventura 2
missing a lot
  Marx, G 2,
missionaries
  Harburg 3

mistakes
  Bankhead 5
  Bierce 68
  Billings 78
  Connolly 6
  Hubbard, E 40
  La Guardia 2
  Orwell 24
  Peter 14
  Taylor, A 2
  Tucker, J 6
  Twain 3
  Wright 5
mistresses
  Beaverbrook 1
  Moore 2
  Wilkes
mobs
  Cioran 25
  Dickens 8
moderation
  Koestler 6
  Anonymous 7
  Kissinger 6
  Maugham 5
  Morgan, Robt 1
  Paine 2
**modern
inconveniences**
  Twain 4
modern times
  Butler 33
  Emerson 26
  Harvey 2
  Kronenberger
    3
  Lichtenberg 9
  Mailer 8
  Pepys 1
  Vidal 12
modesty
  Agate 2
  Anonymous
    84
  Beerbohm 2
  Bennett, Al 1
  Dali 1
  Galbraith 13
  Herford 7
  Howe 1
  Renard 2
  Reverdy
  Sitwell 2
  Twain 55

molehills
  Allen, F 3
  Peter 46
Mondale, Walter
  Reagan, R 27
money
  Agassiz
  Agate 3
  Algren 3
  Allen, W 39
  Anonymous
    119, 142, 146
  Baker, R 9
  Baldwin 4
  Baring
  Benny 3
  Billings 44, 45,
    46, 72, 87
  Bogart, H 1
  Brenan 7
  Buffett
  Butler 14
  Byron 16
  Chesterton 21
  Dali 3
  Dirksen
  Dostoyevsky 2
  Dylan 10
  Ehrenreich 4
  Emerson 13
  Fitzgerald, F 8
  Forbes 5
  Galbraith 16
  Getty 3
  Giraudoux 2
  Grant, C 5
  Greenspan 4
  Hamilton, W 1,
    5
  Heine 6
  Hightower 3
  Holmes 9
  Hope 11
  Howe 10
  Hubbard, K 41,
    56
  Johnson, S 86
  La Rochef 11
  Lapham 2
  Lewis, J 4
  Maugham 13
  McLaughlin 14
  Milligan 3
  Mizner 9

Moyers 2
Murchison
Nash 17
Parker, D 6
Pepys 3
Perot 1
Runyon 3
Safian
Sandburg 8
Shaw 64, 97
Skelton 1
Thatcher 8
Tolstoy 1
Twain 33, 42,
  134
Unruh
Updike 6
Veblen 1
Voltaire 38
Warhol 3
Whitehorn 3
Whitman 10
Wilde 130
monogamy
  Anonymous 13
monopolies
  Rees 1
Monroe, Marilyn
  Berra 2
Montagu, Mrs.
  Johnson, S 52
**Montgomery,
Bernard Law**
  Churchill 40
monuments
  Cioran 4
  Lec 7
moon
  Armstrong, N
  Baker, R 12
moral indignation
  De Sica
  Eldridge 5
  Wells, H G 6
morality
  Alcott
  Bierce 59
  Brecht 1
  Butler 20
  Feiffer 5
  Hamilton, A 1
  Johnson, S 14
  Jong 10
  Macaulay 8

Connolly 3
Dick 2
Fields 32
Ginsberg 2
Hancock 19
Kaufman, B 6
Keillor 1
Lennon 3
Stoppard 5
Tomlin 4
Vidal 18
Wagner 7, 9
reason
Chamfort 11
Chesterfield 14
Halifax 6
Hamilton, A 2
Hubbard, K 28
Montagu, A 1
Russell 15
Swift 17
Voltaire 22, 25
Wilde 15, 61
reason & passion
Connolly 13
Ovid 1
rebels
Bierce 73
Russell 13
reform
Dunne 2
Hazlitt 2
Johnson, S 51
Shaw 42
Twain 90
reformers
Billings 67
Dunne 5, 13
Eliot, G 7
Hubbard, E 35
Peter 44
Schopenh 13
Smith, L 1
Thoreau 8
regrets
Allen, W 17
Barrymore, J 1
Jackson, A 2
James, H 1
Johnson, S 43
Levant 13
Thoreau 9, 18
reincarnation
Allen, W 29

Carville 2
Miller, H 4
Warhol 6
Wilson, T 29
rejection
Lardner 3
relationships
Allen, W 2
Auden 1
Burns 1
Chamfort 15
Fisher 1
Kerr, J 5
relatives
Ade 1
Hubbard, K 7,
44
Kingsmill 2
Lamb 1
Sondheim
Thackeray 5
Wilde 7, 44
Zangwill 1
relativity
Einstein 11, 19
reliability
Doyle 1
religion
Bierce 45, 51,
74
Billings 61
Byron 6, 11
Chesterton 18
Colton 5
Disraeli 26
Edison 5
Emerson 30, 41
France 8
Freud 16
Gibbon 9
Hazlitt 6
Hope 2
Hubbard, K 46
Huxley, A 13
Inge 7
Lamb 6
Luce 3
Marx, K 5
Melbourne 3
Melville 2
Mencken 42,
48, 107, 111
Morley, J 1
Muggeridge 5

Napoleon 17
Nietzsche 1
Pascal 6
Rogers 14, 49
Shaw 46, 120
Sontag 4
Stendhal 1
Swift 31, 32
Ventura 1
Voltaire 5, 32,
38
Wilde 27
Halifax 5
remarriage
Johnson, S 47
Rembrandt
Hunt
remedies
Hubbard, K 31
Luther
remorse
Ade 5
Mencken 69
repartee
Broun 4
Chesterton 12
**repartee:
examples**
Churchill 4, 65,
67
Clay
Coolidge 11
Coward 20
Disraeli 20
Fields 29
Grant, C 2
Smith, Al 3
Talleyrand 11
Thurber 7
Toscanini 5
Tracy 1
West, M 15
Whistler 1
Wilde 28
repentance
Billings 32, 49
Eldridge 7
Hazlitt 10
repression
Shaw 11
Republicans
Cuomo 1
O'Rourke 8, 13
Quayle 4

Reagan, R 13
Rogers 29
Stevenson, A 7
Truman 4
Will 12
Roosevelt, F 12
Safire 6, 11
reputation
Billings 35, 88
Dewar 2
Ford, He 7
Howe 8
Keynes 4
McLaughlin 18
Mencken 90
Mitchell, M 5
Montaigne 1
Paar 2
Shaw 35
Veblen 1
West, M 23
Wilde 74, 125
research
Braun 1
resignations
Marx, G 19
respect
Dangerfield 3
de Gaulle 7
Hubbard, K 12
Johnson, S 90
Mencken 73
respectability
Hubbard, E 29
Morley, C 5
Shaw 73, 102
Stendhal 3
Twain 134
Volkart 5
Ward, A 11
Whitman 13
Wilde 112, 114
responsibility
O'Rourke 10
Shaw 66
Truman 23
restaurants
Berra 11
Youngman 6,
29
Revelations
Wilde 89
revolution
Abbey 1